THE NEW YORK
M · E · T · S

TWENTY-FIVE YEARS
OF BASEBALL MAGIC

CEWZAN GRAYSON

THE NEW YORK
M · E · T · S

TWENTY-FIVE YEARS
OF BASEBALL MAGIC

Jack Lang and Peter Simon

World Series Edition

HENRY HOLT AND COMPANY

NEW YORK

For Victoria, Randolph, and Brian, my all-star team; and for Wynne, who somehow managed us all.

—JACK LANG

For Peter Dean, my uncle, who hooked me on baseball at a tender and impressionable age at Ebbets Field, and with whom I have shared countless hours of quality Met time since; and to Ronni Simon, who has unflinchingly endured Met obsession and even showed genuine interest here and there.

—PETER SIMON

The authors would like to acknowledge *The Sports Encyclopedia of Baseball*, by David Neft and Richard Cohen, St. Martins Press, Inc., New York, for the use of the yearly summary statistics.

Published by Henry Holt and Company, Inc., 521 Fifth Avenue, New York, New York 10175.

Distributed in Canada by Fitzhenry & Whiteside Limited, 195 Allstate Parkway, Markham, Ontario L3R 4T8.

Produced by Rapid Transcript, a division of March Tenth, Inc. Designed by Stanley S. Drate/Folio Graphics Co., Inc.

Library of Congress Cataloging in Publication Data
Lang, Jack Frederick, 1921–
    The New York Mets : 25 years of baseball magic.
    1. New York Mets (Baseball team)—History.
I. Simon, Peter, 1947–   . II. Title.
GV875.N45L36   1986   796.357'64'097471   86–353
ISBN Hardbound: 0-8050-0467-X
ISBN Paperback: 0-8050-0466-1

First published in May 1986 by Henry Holt and Company, Inc. Revised and updated edition published in March 1987.

Printed in the United States of America

10 9 8 7 6 5 4 3 2 1

ISBN 0-8050-0467-X HARDBOUND

ISBN 0-8050-0466-1 PAPERBACK

◆ CONTENTS ◆

ACKNOWLEDGMENTS / 7

1 IT WAS ALL O'MALLEY'S FAULT / 11

2 LOSERS FROM THE START / 19

3 "TELL THEM I'M BEING EMBALMED" / 27

4 CASEY TELLS IT LIKE IT IS / 35

5 NEW BALLPARK, SAME OLD TEAM / 41

6 THE STENGEL ERA ENDS IN A MEN'S ROOM / 49

7 "THE FRANCHISE" / 57

8 HODGES COMES HOME / 65

9 THE YOUNG ARMS DEVELOP / 73

10 DIVISIONAL PLAY IS A BLESSING / 79

11 THE BEGINNING OF A MIRACLE / 87

12 THE METS STUN THE ORIOLES—AND THE WORLD / 93

13 HODGES CALLS THE SHOTS / 105

14 THE STRIKE, THE HEART ATTACK, THE NEW MANAGER / 117

15 "YOU GOTTA BELIEVE!" / 125

16 "IT'S OVER, YOGI, IT'S OVER" / 141

17 THE MIDNIGHT MASSACRE / 149

18 THE LADIES TRY TO RUN A BALL CLUB / 161

19 DOUBLEDAY TO THE RESCUE / 175

20 DR. K AND THE NEW METS / 195

21 DAVEY IS DETERMINED TO DOMINATE / 217

22 YOU GOTTA HAVE HEART / 229

INDEX / 249

◆ ACKNOWLEDGMENTS ◆

The authors wish to acknowledge, with special thanks, the many people who assisted in the preparation of this book: Dennis D'Agostino, Red Foley, Jay Horwitz, Bob Rosen, and Seymour Siwoff for their help with statistical information; Joseph Durso, Steve Marcus, and Arthur Richman for their help in researching specific events; Nancy Kiernan and Victoria Lang for typing the manuscript; Randolph Lang for his work as courier; *Daily News* photo librarian Eugene Ferrara for his time and special attention rifling through the archives; Louis Requena, who helped cut through the pecking order in the photo booth and also contributed his work; Danny Farrell of the *Daily News*, who helped greatly along the way. In addition, special thanks to Michael Brennan, Paul Leo, Mel Damski, and Michael Bamberger. Our editor, Jack Macrae, rates special praise for his immediate enthusiasm for the project, as does Sandra Choron, our agent, who believed in the project from the start and nurtured it along.

THE NEW YORK
M · E · T · S

TWENTY-FIVE YEARS
OF BASEBALL MAGIC

For the record, the official Mets team photograph for 1962, taken at the Polo Grounds in June.

1

◆ IT WAS ALL ◆
◆ O'MALLEY'S ◆
◆ FAULT ◆

Late in the afternoon of April 10, 1962, a group of ballplayers entered an elevator on one of the upper floors of the Chase Park Plaza Hotel in St. Louis. Halfway down to the lobby, the elevator became stuck between floors. When it was finally freed and descended, the ballplayers boarded a team bus to Busch Stadium, home of the St. Louis Cardinals. Upon arrival at the ballpark, the players were informed that their game was rained out.

Thus did the New York Mets begin their first season in the National League. It was an inauspicious start, and the team went on to establish records as the worst team in the history of baseball.

Comedians who previously were assured of a laugh any time they mentioned Brooklyn suddenly switched references to the Mets. Almost at once the Mets became the symbol of ineptness. No team before or since ever lost 120 games in one season. Many of the records for futility established in their initial year remain in the baseball record books to this day.

The 1962 Mets may have been laughable, but they also were lovable. Fans—particularly the young fans of New York dubbed "the New Breed" by sportswriter Dick Young—took them to their hearts. The fact that a man approaching his seventy-second birthday was their leader was of no small importance. The fans could identify with Casey Stengel. Casey displayed a youthful enthusiasm that belied his years, and he spoke the truth, which the fans appreciated. When the Mets were awful, he said so. When they won or did something special, he referred to them as "the amazin' Mets." Soon headlines of New York's tabloids referred to them simply as the "Amazin's."

Within weeks love affairs developed between the team and fans in cities far from New York. In Houston—where the rival Colt 45s were also in their infant season—a Mets fan club was formed that came out en masse when Casey Stengel brought his traveling show to town. In Milwaukee, where many New York–New Jersey–Connecticut students attended Marquette University, the bleachers included large groups of beer-drinking collegians expressing their adoration of the Mets. The Mets soon became the people's team.

It was an easy team to love. All that was required was patience. Clearly, the fans didn't expect much. One victory a week, Casey's hijinks, and some laughs seemed to be enough. Rooting for that first Mets team was like watching a baby learning to walk. There were a lot of flops between steps, a string of losses punctuated by the occasional victory. But the 1962 Mets were no kids. Most were graybeards in the game—players who had long since enjoyed their peak years and were fending off retirement in the safe haven of an expansion team.

Nonetheless the irrepressible Stengel had the future in mind; his never-ending sales pitch appealed to "the youth of America" to join the Mets. This was three years before the first free-agent draft. Young ballplayers fresh out of high school were free to sign with any club of their choosing, enabling hot prospects like Ed Kranepool and Rusty Staub to command big bonuses when they signed with the Mets and Colt 45s, respectively.

Casey tried every inducement imaginable to attract young talent to the club. Little did he imagine that seven years later, a young Mets team led by Gil Hodges—an original Met—would startle the baseball world by taking the National League Eastern Division crown, win the first playoffs ever, and then, after dropping the first game, sweep to four straight wins over the heavily favored Baltimore Orioles in the 1969 World Series.

In that miracle year of 1969, the Mets were truly amazing. But that first year, the one in which the team won only 40 games and lost 120, was just as unforgettable.

The frustrations began long before a game was played. The players offered to the New York and Houston clubs in the October 1961 expansion draft by the eight established clubs were enough to discourage both new clubs from making their required selections. In fact, the United Press reported on the eve of the expansion draft that once Paul Richards, general manager of the Houston club, saw a list of the available players, he threatened to boycott the draft completely.

Richards' threat was an idle one, as there was no way the Mets and Colt 45s could enter the league other than by selecting players from the pool provided by the eight existing clubs. It turned out to be a cheap way to buy a franchise. Years later, obtaining a major league club through expansion or purchase would cost many millions of dollars. But aside from their initial $50,000 induction fee, the cost of the Mets to their original owners in 1961 was the $1.8 million they paid for the drafted players.

Ironically, they got all that and more back from the Rheingold Brewery in New York even before they had a team.

Rheingold, a beer brewed in Brooklyn, with sales largely in the metropolitan New York area, was quick to seize upon the anticipated popularity of National League baseball returning to New York. The brewery negotiated a deal with the Mets for exclusive radio and television rights to all their games and paid a whopping $6 million for the first five years. Rheingold also agreed to purchase several thousand dollars' worth of tickets each season.

Not that money was in short supply. The largest single stockholder was Joan Whitney Payson, one of the country's richest women. Mrs. Payson, who had almost unlimited wealth of her own, was also married to Charles Shipman Payson, a multi-millionaire, who, unfortunately, as later events would reveal, had no real interest in the Mets or in baseball.

Joan Whitney Payson was an heir to the Whitney fortunes, along with her brother, John Hay Whitney. Together they owned the successful Greentree racing stable and John Hay Whitney, or Jock as he was known in racing circles, was ambassador to Great Britain. He also was publisher of the (now defunct) *New York Herald Tribune*.

Mrs. Payson was a longtime baseball fan of the New York Giants. She was a regular at the Polo Grounds and owned a box close to the Giants dugout. She genuinely enjoyed baseball and once told a friend and fellow fan that she would "love to own a piece of the Giants." She eventually did get hold of one share and was permitted, for sentimental reasons, to hold on to it even after she became principal owner of the Mets.

Mrs. Payson never intended to own a major league club, but she was in the right place at the right time and had the required resources when the New York Mets were created.

The 1957 season was the saddest of all in New York sports history. For a couple of years there had been rumblings by both the New York Giants and the Brooklyn Dodgers that they had to have better ballparks in better parts of town or they would consider shifting to other cities.

At first no one in any authority took them seriously. The Giants were an institution uptown at the Polo Grounds, even if their attendance was sinking below that of teams in smaller cities around the league. The Giants had won pennants in 1951 and 1954, but they were not drawing fans to their ancient ballpark on the edge of Harlem.

The Dodgers, the National League's most successful team of the postwar era, with pennants in 1941, 1947, 1949, 1952, 1953, 1955, and 1956, were drawing well at Ebbets Field. Yet Dodgers owner Walter F. O'Malley warned that he could not compete with other cities with their larger stadiums.

Both the Giants and the Dodgers asked the city for new ballparks. Ironically, no real or serious effort was made to build a stadium for the Giants. New York Mayor Robert Wagner and Parks Commissioner Robert Moses did offer the Dodgers a new municipal stadium in Flushing on the 1939 World's Fair site,

By 1969, the Mets had at last become amazing.
DAILY NEWS

but O'Malley held out for a ballpark in the borough of Brooklyn at Flatbush and Atlantic avenues—the end of the Long Island Railroad line. The city considered it an inappropriate site and those who knew the shrewd O'Malley well knew that he was of the same opinion.

When it was obvious neither team would get a stadium where it wanted one, both the Giants and Dodgers prepared to move. The Dodgers were ready to head west to Los Angeles, but O'Malley needed another team on the West Coast to make it worthwhile for teams from the East and Midwest to make the long flight to California. Horace Stoneham, principal owner of the Giants, originally planned to move his club to Minneapolis, where a new stadium was being built. O'Malley convinced him there was more gold in the hills of San Francisco.

On August 19, 1957, the Giants' board of directors voted approval for Stoneham to move the team to San Francisco. The lone dissenting vote was cast by one M. Donald Grant, a minority stockholder. Grant would later emerge as the single most influential figure with the Mets. It was Grant, the "friend and fellow fan," who had obtained one share of the Giants for Mrs. Payson. When she became the principal owner of the Mets, Grant became her confidant, her adviser, and chairman of the board of the Metropolitan Baseball Club, Inc.

O'Malley continued to string along the politicians and Dodgers fans until October 8, 1957. In the middle of the World Series between the New York Yankees and Milwaukee Braves, O'Malley sent an aide, Arthur E. Patterson, to post a brief notice on the Series press headquarters bulletin board officially announcing the move to Los Angeles. No press conference, no formal announcement, just a terse notice on a bulletin board. For the first time in the twentieth century, there would be no National League baseball in New York or Brooklyn. In 1958 the city and the fans from New York and nearby New Jersey and Connecticut had only the New York Yankees.

If Mayor Robert Wagner had dawdled while the Dodgers were making their moving threats—perhaps because he knew there was no way of stopping O'Malley—the mayor did not waste much time seeking a replacement once the two teams were gone. In October 1958 he appointed a committee to get New York back into the National League. New York City was desperate to get a National League team again. Any team.

The committee appointed by Mayor Wagner consisted of former Postmaster General James A. Farley, a devoted baseball fan; Bernard Gimbel, the famed New York merchant, whose only association with baseball was his daughter, who had married Hall of Famer Hank Greenberg; Clint Blume, a real estate executive; and William A. Shea, a prominent New York lawyer and sportsman who years later would be profiled in *New York* magazine as one of the city's most influential "power brokers."

As is usual with all committees, there was one person who did most of the work. In Mayor Wagner's committee it was Bill Shea, who had once owned the Long Island Indians in the by-then-defunct American Football League.

A hard-working, energetic man who had been active in the city's Democratic party, Shea had been born and raised in Brooklyn. An early Dodgers fan, he served as a young lawyer in the offices of the Brooklyn Trust Company with a fellow law clerk and friend named Walter F. O'Malley.

Although not the chairman of Wagner's committee, Shea was the workhorse. He immediately contacted existing clubs in Pittsburgh, Cincinnati, and Philadelphia in an effort to induce one to move to New York. Pittsburgh and Cincinnati both showed interest but later backed down.

It did not take Shea long to realize that kidnapping an existing franchise—as New York was accused of attempting—was not the route to follow. But he did not foresee any immediate expansion plans by the National League, either,

METS' COACHES, 1962–1986

Berra, Yogi	1965–71
Burgess, Tom	1977
Cottier, Chuck	1979–81
Dusan, Gene	1983
Frey, Jim	1982–83
Gibson, Bob	1981
Haddix, Harvey	1966–67
Harder, Mel	1964
Harrelson, Bud	1982–
Heffner, Don	1964–65
Hemus, Solly	1962–63
Herzog, Whitey	1966
Hornsby, Rogers	1962
Hoscheit, Vern	1984–
Howard, Frank	1982–84
Johnson, Deron	1981
Kress, Red	1962
Lavagetto, Cookie	1962–63
Maxvill, Dal	1978
Mays, Willie	1974–79
McCullough, Clyde	1963
McMillan, Roy	1973–76
Monbouquette, Bill	1982–83
Murphy, John	1967
Parker, Salty	1967
Pavlick, Greg	1985–
Pignatano, Joe	1968–81
Robinson, Bill	1984–
Robinson, Sheriff	1964–67, 1972
Ruffing, Red	1962
Sisler, Dick	1979–80
Sommers, Denny	1977–78
Spahn, Warren*	1965
Staub, Rusty*	1982
Stottlemyre, Mel	1984–
Valentine, Bobby	1983–
Walker, Rube	1968–81
Westrum, Wes	1964–65
White, Ernie	1963
Yost, Eddie	1968–75

*Player-Coach

From left: Mets President George Weiss, National League President Warren Giles, Commissioner Ford Frick, Mets owner Joan Payson, and Mets Chairman M. Donald Grant at the official christening on May 8, 1961

AP

METS' YEAR-BY-YEAR HOME ATTENDANCE

1962	922,530	1975	1,730,566
1963	1,080,108	1976	1,468,754
1964	1,732,597	1977	1,066,825
1965	1,768,389	1978	1,007,328
1966	1,932,693	1979	788,905
1967	1,565,492	1980	1,178,659
1968	1,781,657	1981	701,910
1969	2,175,373	1982	1,320,055
1970	2,697,479	1983	1,103,808
1971	2,266,680	1984	1,829,482
1972	2,134,185	1985	2,751,437
1973	1,912,390	1986	2,762,417
1974	1,722,209		

even though the league had discussed such plans both formally and informally in the recent past. Shea and the city got the message that the league had cooled on expansion when Warren C. Giles, president of the National League, was quoted as saying, "Who needs New York?"

In the post–World War II era, professional baseball had blossomed around the country with as many as fifty-eight minor leagues at one point. But with the advent of television, the minors began to shrivel. Even so, television whetted the appetites of several burgeoning cities around the country. Whereas cities like Atlanta, Houston, Buffalo, Denver, and Toronto had been willing to settle for minor league ball in the past, they now wanted the real thing—major league baseball. Because the existing American and National Leagues were not about to expand, the only solution seemed to be the creation of a third major league. Who better to spearhead that movement than Shea? Surely any league to be successful would need a team in New York.

Enter the Continental League, led by Shea and the most recognized baseball genius of modern times, Branch Rickey.

During World War II, George V. McLaughlin, president of the Brooklyn Trust Company, had lured Rickey away from St. Louis, where he had built the Cardinals into champions or perennial contenders. He duplicated that success in Brooklyn with the Dodgers where he also broke baseball's color line by signing Jackie Robinson. At the end of the 1950 season, Rickey sold his Brooklyn stock to O'Malley at a tremendous profit and moved on to Pittsburgh to rebuild the Pirates. It took Rickey a few years longer than expected, but he planted the seeds for the great Pirates teams that would flourish after his retirement.

If Shea was going to form a third league, he needed sound baseball advice, and there was no better adviser available anywhere than Branch Rickey. Together, Shea and Rickey formed a partnership to create the Continental League. In announcing formation of the league at a press conference in the downstairs room at Toots Shor's restaurant in New York City, both Shea and Rickey stressed their hope that the Continental League would be accepted "under the umbrella of organized baseball."

It was a vain hope, but the existing leagues watched with interest. Astute baseball men realized that plans for the Continental League provided the groundwork for expansion of the two major leagues. Eventually, their reasoning went, if the pressure for expansion won out, the existing major leagues could absorb the strong cities from the Continental League.

By the summer of 1960, with the Continental League experiencing major difficulties but hoping to get off the ground the following year, it became apparent some agreement with the majors would have to be reached. On a hot August afternoon at the Conrad Hilton Hotel in Chicago, following hours of meetings, the American and National leagues surprised the baseball world by agreeing to accept four Continental League teams for expansion within the major leagues, provided the upstart league disbanded itself. A deal was struck, and representatives of the four cities—New York, Houston, Minneapolis, and Denver—went home anticipating major league baseball in 1961, or in 1962 at the latest.

The New York group backing the Continental League franchise was largely brought together by Dwight F. "Pete" Davis, a wealthy Long Island sportsman whose family had originated the Davis Cup in tennis. It was Davis to whom Shea went when he sought to form the New York franchise. Both were Long Island Gold Coast residents, and Shea was confident that Davis, with his social background among Long Island's sporting elite, would come up with the right people to finance the franchise. Davis brought Mrs. Payson into the picture, and she in turn designated M. Donald Grant as her representative.

Another member of the original group was Mrs. Dorothy J. Killiam, a wealthy Canadian sportswoman and rabid Brooklyn Dodgers fan. Mrs. Killiam attended the World Series in New York whenever it was played there, arriving from Canada in her own private railroad car.

Davis, Mrs. Payson, and Mrs. Killiam each owned 30 percent of the Continental League franchise. Other, lesser shareholders were G. Herbert Walker, a prominent stockbroker, and William Simpson. When it became evident that Mrs. Killiam wanted to run the club, her partners bought her out. Later, Davis would sell out, too, and eventually Mrs. Payson owned 80 percent of the stock, with Grant and Walker holding the majority of the remaining 20 percent.

Shortly after the 1960 World Series, the National League met again in Chicago and awarded expansion franchises to the Continental League representatives from New York and Houston. Despite their August promises, the American League ignored the Continental representatives from Denver and Minneapolis and instead awarded franchises to other partnerships from Washington and Los Angeles, neither of which had been in the Shea-Rickey group. The American League decided to expand in time for the 1961 season; the Nationals agreed to wait until 1962.

With the October 17 decision New York once again had a National League franchise. Now all it needed was a team.

As co-founder of the Continental League, Branch Rickey brought in Charles Hurth to run the New York entry. Hurth was a veteran minor league baseball man from New Orleans. But the Mets felt a stronger, major league figure was needed. M. Donald Grant, who switched from president of the Mets to chairman of the board, led the search. He did not have to look long or far. The New York Yankees, with whom they would now share the city, soon provided the Mets with their man.

On October 17, 1960, the Yankees shocked the baseball world by announcing the "retirement" of Casey Stengel, the manager who had led them to ten

METS' ALL-TIME HOME RUN LIST

No.	Player	HR
1	Dave Kingman	154
2	Ed Kranepool	118
3	John Milner	94
4	Cleon Jones	93
5	George Foster	99
6	Tommie Agee	82
7	Darryl Strawberry	108
8	Rusty Staub	75
9	Ron Swoboda	69
10	Lee Mazzilli	61
11	Jim Hickman	60
12	Wayne Garrett	55
13	Frank Thomas	52
14	John Stearns	46
15	Donn Clendenon	45
16	Art Shamsky	42
17	Joel Youngblood	38
18	Charley Smith	36
19	Jerry Grote	35
	Steve Henderson	35
21	Keith Hernandez	47
22	Gary Carter	56
23	Ken Boswell	31
	Mookie Wilson	40
25	Hubie Brooks	28
	Joe Christopher	28

Branch Rickey (left), who created the ill-fated Continental League from which the Mets were born, studies an architect's model of Shea Stadium along with Mayor Robert Wagner and Bill Shea.
DAILY NEWS/HAL MATHEWSON

world championships in a dozen seasons. The Yankees called a press conference to announce Casey's "retirement," but the seventy-year-old manager made it plain the decision was not his.

"The Associated Press says you didn't retire, that you were fired," a reporter shouted to Stengel at the press conference.

"What does the United Press say?" he shouted back, drawing a laugh from the huge audience.

From the beginning, Stengel set the record straight.

"My services are no longer required," he said as Yankee officials turned red-faced.

But that was only Act One. Within a fortnight, on November 2, the Yankees called another press conference to announce the "retirement" of George M. Weiss, their veteran general manager and the man generally credited with putting together the great Yankee teams of the 1950s. Weiss was sixty-six, and the Yankees said they had adopted a retirement age of sixty-five. Weiss was to be paid for the next five years to serve in an advisory capacity with the Yankees. He also agreed not to become general manager of another major league team.

Weiss's name immediately surfaced in the newspapers as a possibility to head the Mets. Originally, Grant wanted Rickey to operate the club, but Rickey insisted on a free hand plus several millions of dollars to develop talent. Mrs. Payson, who had purchased Pete Davis's stock, which he sold upon learning that Grant, not he, would be calling the shots, was reluctant to give Rickey an open checkbook.

On March 14, 1961, Weiss was given the opportunity to build a new ball club. To satisfy the clause in his Yankee contract, he was named president rather than general manager of the Mets. Though the Yankees seethed, they were still obligated to pay him $35,000 a year for five years while Weiss did his best to lure fans away from Yankee Stadium.

The historic press conference announcing the hiring of Weiss was not even held in New York. Since most of the major sports columnists were in Miami, Florida, for the Patterson-Johansson fight, the decision was made to announce the appointment there, the day after Floyd Patterson knocked out Ingemar Johansson to become heavyweight champion of the world.

Weiss's immediate concern was where the Mets would play in 1962 when they entered the National League. The Yankees quickly ruled out any possibility of sharing Yankee Stadium in the Bronx.

An almost immediate setback was a vote by the New York State Assembly vetoing plans to build a municipal stadium for the club in the Flushing Meadow site proposed by Parks Commissioner Robert Moses. Weiss, while employed by the Yankees, had opposed the city's request for state funds to help out the fledgling Mets. The Albany veto came one day after Weiss officially joined the Mets. It was a blow, but not an irreversible one.

Politicians and businessmen, led by New York City's Mayor Wagner, Bill Shea, Robert Moses, and others, went to work. The State Assembly in Albany reconsidered and on March 16 took a second vote. This time they approved the new stadium.

By now, virtually everything the New York National League team did won back-page headlines in New York City's tabloids. Even their selection of a nickname became big news.

Mrs. Payson invited newspapermen to a cocktail party in her Manhattan apartment, where the sportswriters would narrow down the proposed list of nicknames to ten, after which the public would be asked to vote. The "finalists" in the nickname contest were: Continentals, Skyliners, Mets, Jets, Meadowlarks, Burros, Skyscrapers, Rebels, NYBs, and Avengers.

More than 1000 letters were received, and Mets emerged as the winning

THE YOUNGEST METS

	Birth Date	Age at 1st Game
Ed Kranepool	1944	17 yrs, 10 mths
Jim Bethke	1946	18 yrs, 5 mths
Jerry Hinsley	1945	19 yrs, 9 days
Kevin Collins	1946	19 yrs, 28 days
Dwight Gooden	1964	19 yrs, 4 mths
Nolan Ryan	1947	19 yrs, 7 mths
Greg Goossen	1945	19 yrs, 8 mths
Tim Foli	1950	19 yrs, 9 mths
Jose Oquendo	1963	19 yrs, 9 mths

Casey Stengel and newly appointed coach Cookie Lavagetto
hope to sweep their way through
the National League in 1962.
DAILY NEWS/JIM MOONEY

entry. The name became official on May 8, 1961. Skyliners was a close second.
Mrs. Payson herself preferred Meadowlarks. The announcement was something of an anticlimax. For months headline writers at the city newspapers had
been referring to the franchise as Mets, after the official name of the
corporation, the Metropolitan Baseball Club, Inc. For the record, the first
baseball writer to refer to the team as Mets, long before the nickname was
officially adopted, was veteran Dan Daniel of the *New York World Telegram*.

Once the bill was passed to proceed with construction of the municipal
stadium in Flushing Meadow, Weiss began the chore of finding a temporary
home for his new team. With nothing else available in New York City, Weiss
settled for the old, sadly-in-need-of-repair Polo Grounds. Home of the Giants
for half a century, the stadium had not been used for baseball since the 1957
season.

To get the Polo Grounds back in shape, Weiss found the ideal man in James
K. "Big Jim" Thomson. Thomson had been stadium manager of both Ebbets
Field and Yankee Stadium and was a no-nonsense boss who knew how to work
with construction gangs, ballpark personnel, and especially the unions. If there
was one thing he knew, it was how to manage a ballpark—in particular, how to
cut through red tape and get things done.

Thomson resigned from the Yankees during the 1961 season. He had less
than ten months to get the run-down Polo Grounds ready for the 1962
National League season.

Weiss, meanwhile, set about building his baseball organization. He retained
Hurth and Wid Matthews from the Continental League organization. Lou
Niss, a former Brooklyn newspaper editor who had been the Continental
League's publicity man, became the team's traveling secretary, while Tom
Meany, a veteran New York baseball writer and author, was named the club's
publicity director in October 1961.

During the summer of 1961, while Roger Maris and Mickey Mantle were
challenging Ruth's home run record for the Yankees, Weiss was assembling a
scouting staff. He went for such famous names as Rogers Hornsby, later to
become a Mets batting coach; Babe Herman; Johnny Murphy; and Gil
McDougald. Murphy would soon move into the front office as Weiss's right-
hand man and seven years later, in 1968, would become general manager.

Murphy, who was one of the great relief pitchers for the Yankees, had been with the Boston Red Sox for nearly two decades. His original title with the Mets was scouting supervisor of the New York–New England area. By 1962 he was the number 2 man in the organization behind Weiss.

Weiss still had no players and no manager. It would be October before the players were selected from a pool to be created by the eight existing National League clubs.

From the very beginning, when Weiss was hired, rumors of Casey Stengel's return to New York were rampant. Stengel was Weiss's man. He was popular with the press in New York. Certainly, with his more than fifty years experience in the game, he would be the ideal manager for a new ball club, even at age seventy.

Throughout the summer of 1961 Weiss tried to talk Stengel out of his enforced retirement. In July Weiss flew out to the All-Star Game in San Francisco to confer with Stengel. No official announcement followed.

Finally, in late September, at Weiss's suggestion, Mrs. Payson herself telephoned Casey in California. Stengel could not say no to the gracious lady. On September 29, 1961, the Mets made it official. Casey Stengel would be the first manager of the still playerless team.

T he Mets were losers even before they played their first game. The coin flip to decide which club would go first in the National League's expansion draft was won by the Houston Colt 45s.

The historic selection session was held in Cincinnati on Tuesday, October 10, 1961, the day following the conclusion of the New York Yankees–Cincinnati Reds World Series. Cincinnati was at the time the official headquarters of the National League.

The eight existing National League clubs created a pool of players for the two new teams. Each club put up fifteen names. Seven had to be players on their twenty-five-man active roster as of August 31, and the remaining eight were to come from their farm systems. New York and Houston each would be permitted to select sixteen players from the first pool at a price of $75,000 each. At the conclusion of that draft, each club could then select two more players from a second pool for $50,000 each. The final round of the draft would be from the "premium" players list. Each "premium pick" would cost $125,000, and each club would be permitted four picks.

Following Houston's selection of shortstop Ed Bressoud of the San Francisco Giants as first pick, the Mets dipped into the pool and came up with catcher Hobie Landrith, also from the Giants. Weiss, explaining the choice of the thirty-one-year-old journeyman receiver, said: "In building a ball club you have to start with a catcher and go from there." Stengel, who chatted with reporters following the selections, put it more succinctly: "You gotta have a catcher or you're going to have a lot of passed balls."

Ironically, after drafting Landrith first, he also was one of the first players the Mets traded in 1962. On May 9, after only twenty-three games behind the plate, Landrith was sent to the Baltimore Orioles in exchange for a player who would become synonymous with the Mets and their early ineptness. That player was first baseman Marv Throneberry, known forever in Mets lore as Marvelous Marv, a nickname he never quite understood. Today Throneberry is a member of the popular Miller Lite Beer commercials cast.

With each club making alternate selections, the Mets eventually wound up with twenty-two players—sixteen from the regular pool, two from the $50,000 pool, and four $125,000 premium picks. For $1.8 million, the Mets had themselves the nucleus of a major league ball club—one that would set an all-time major league record by losing 120 games.

The twenty-two original Mets, who have become the subject of trivia quizzes ever since, were:

- $125,000 "premium" picks—pitchers Jay Hook and Bob Miller; infielder Don Zimmer; outfielder Lee Walls
- $75,000 picks—pitchers Craig Anderson, Roger Craig, Ray Daviault, and Al Jackson; catchers Chris Cannizzaro, Clarence Coleman, and Hobie Landrith; infielders Ed Bouchee, Elio Chacon, Sammy Drake, Gil Hodges, and Felix Mantilla; outfielders Gus Bell, Joe Christopher, John DeMerit, and Bobby Gene Smith
- $50,000 picks—pitcher Sherman Jones; outfielder Jim Hickman

While these were the original players selected by the Mets, the first player to sign a New York contract was infielder Ted Lepcio. That event occurred on October 25, 1961. Lepcio, a free agent, had originally signed as a free agent with the Boston Red Sox as a bonus baby ten years earlier, when Johnny Murphy ran the Boston farm system. If Lepcio was the first player signed to a Mets contract, he also was the last to be released in spring training. Lepcio was cut the day the Mets prepared to head north.

Walls, one of the players drafted as a premium pick, never played for the Mets. Two months after his selection, Weiss sent Walls and a check for

$100,000 to the Los Angeles Dodgers in exchange for second baseman Charlie Neal.

Weiss's plan in selecting players differed from that of the Houston club. New York fans were starved for National League baseball, but the Mets needed names to attract the customers back to the ballpark. It was with that thought in mind that he blended his selections—some old familiar faces along with some new and, it was hoped, promising young players.

"The fans remember players like Gil Hodges, Don Zimmer, Roger Craig, and Gus Bell," Weiss explained to reporters covering the draft. "We have to give them some people they know."

Houston, on the other hand, was getting major league baseball for the first time. Paul Richards did not have the same problem Weiss did in New York. Houstonians would accept almost any team as long as it had major league brand approval. Richards selected younger, unproven players.

Among the players selected by the Mets, Hodges was thirty-three, with a chronic knee condition; Craig was thirty and only two years beyond a broken shoulder; and Bell was thirty-three.

With money to spend and several holes to fill on his roster, Weiss began calling on old friends and offering cash in exchange for ballplayers. It was a new and uncomfortable role for the former master dealer of the Yankees. In his Bronx days Weiss was accustomed to clubs coming to him begging for help. Now the shoe was on the other foot, and Weiss seemed humiliated by it all. But he bit his tongue and kept his checkbook open.

Within twenty-four hours of the draft, Johnny Antonelli, a one-time Polo Grounds favorite with the Giants, was purchased from Milwaukee. From the same club that same day, Weiss also acquired left-hander Ken MacKenzie, a former Yale University star.

By the end of the first week following the draft, Weiss also purchased first baseman Jim Marshall from San Francisco as well as former Brooklyn Dodgers favorite Billy Loes. Bob "Butterball" Botz and outfielder Neil Chrisley were also obtained from Milwaukee.

Many of the deals turned out to be just paper transactions that cost the Mets money. Antonelli refused to report, deciding instead to retire; but the Braves kept the money Weiss sent them in exchange for Antonelli's contract.

Loes, a native New Yorker and ex-Dodger considered a strange character by his peers, indicated he would join the club by his appearance, along with Stengel, on the Mets' float in the Macy's Thanksgiving Day parade. But he later changed his mind and retired before spring training.

Chrisley and Botz never made it out of spring training. Neither did Aubrey Gatewood or Howie Nunn, others Weiss acquired in his desperate pursuit of talent.

Six weeks following the draft, Weiss made the most significant deal of all for the fledgling club. For $125,000 and a "player to be named later," Weiss obtained slugger Frank Thomas from the Milwaukee Braves. Thomas wound up as the most productive hitter the Mets had in their first year. The thirty-four home runs he hit and the ninety-four runs he batted in while playing the first year in the Polo Grounds remained club records for almost two decades.

On December 8, 1961, an aging but still able Richie Ashburn was purchased from the Chicago Cubs for a reported $100,000. Ashburn, thirty-two, went on to become the first .300 hitter in Mets history, batting .308 his only season in New York. He then retired to the broadcasting booth to announce games for the Philadelphia Phillies, the club he began with and where he had his greatest years.

By the end of 1961, Weiss had put together not only a ball club but an organization as well. Ground for the new stadium in Flushing had been broken

Mets owner Joan Payson visits with a few of her newly acquired players during spring training. The Mets are (from left): Don Zimmer, Casey Stengel, Frank Thomas, and Gus Bell.

on October 28, around the same time Weiss was making front office appointments.

Lou Niss outlasted all of Weiss's appointments, remaining the traveling secretary until he was forced into retirement at the end of the 1979 season. Niss knew more about the behind-the-scenes activities of the Mets than anyone in the club's employ. Fortunately for many, he never wrote the book he kept threatening to write. His proposed title was considered a classic by the sportswriters who traveled regularly with the team. "The title of my book," Niss regularly joked, "will be *The Club That Didn't Cost a Nickel and Never Spent a Dime.*"

Weiss took great care in hiring his broadcasting team. Tom Gallery, a longtime head of NBC Sports, recommended Lindsey Nelson to Weiss. Nelson was known primarily as a football broadcaster. But he had worked for some time on baseball's "Game of the Day" radio broadcasts and was comfortably familiar with the sport. Hank Greenberg, a Hall of Famer and friend, recommended former home-run king Ralph Kiner as the color man. Kiner, who had one year of radio-TV experience in Chicago, was hired. Bob Murphy, out of Tulsa, Oklahoma, was the most experienced baseball broadcaster of the trio hired by Weiss. Murphy, a fan as well as a good reporter, had worked in broadcasting for nine years covering, first, Boston Red Sox, then Baltimore Orioles games.

Weiss also named another retired ex-Yankee, Gus Mauch, as the team's trainer, and when Yankee owner Dan Topping moved his team's training site from St. Petersburg to Fort Lauderdale, the new Mets chief quickly signed a long-term contract to bring the Mets to St. Petersburg.

But the longtime Yankee training site on Florida's West Coast provided some problems. The Soreno Hotel, where the Yankees had stayed for years, did not accept blacks as guests, and the Mets had a half dozen or so black players on their roster.

Niss came to the rescue. He located some native New Yorkers, owners of the Colonial Inn on St. Petersburg Beach, who were willing to accept the Mets players regardless of color. So the Colonial Inn, a Catskill-type resort hotel, became official winter headquarters of the New York Mets, even though Weiss continued to live in the Soreno Hotel.

Spring training 1962 was a ball, thanks to the presence of Casey Stengel. There was not much in the way of talent in the Mets training camp, and Stengel was quick to acknowledge that reality.

The reporters assigned to cover the Mets in their infant season were young but experienced. They had covered the Brooklyn Dodgers and New York Giants and were also aware that the talent was thin. "The Old Man," as Stengel was admiringly called, soon had the reporters writing about everything but the players' ineptitude. He regularly rambled on for hours and hours, telling anecdotes from his past, relating humorous yarns, and generally "selling" the Mets as a new and promising franchise that would bring joy to long-starved National League fans in New York.

Not that the writers covering the club were fooled or misled. They, too, were aware that fans back home were nourishing hope for their new team and wanted only good news. Why spoil it with bad news? The Mets had not yet lost their first game.

On one occasion, when it had become apparent that the Mets could use another pitcher or two, a young man named John Pappas showed up in camp and asked for a tryout. He lived in the borough of Queens, had read of the team's pitching shortage, and was certain he could make the club. Although he

Assorted Mets gather for photographers on the first day of spring training, 1962. Among the first of the pitchers and catchers to put on their uniforms are *(from left):* Jay Hook, catchers Hobie Landrith (the first Met acquired from the expansion draft), Chris Cannizzaro, and Joe Ginsberg (who wound up with only five official at-bats before departing).
UPI/BETTMAN NEWSPHOTO

In spring training, the projected Mets starting rotation as envisioned by Casey Stengel. From left: Roger Craig (who wound up losing twenty-four games), Jay Hook (who lost nineteen), Bob Miller, Craig Anderson (who went 3–17), and Al Jackson (who went 8–20).

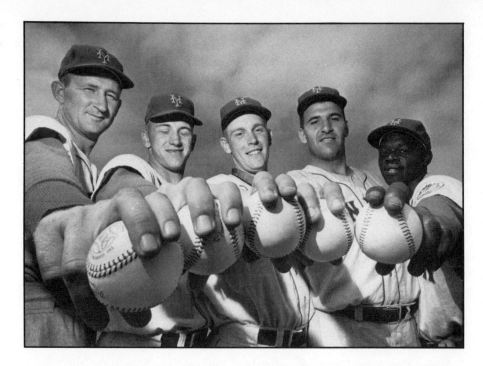

had no previous professional experience, he was, he said, in shape and ready for a tryout. He had worked himself into shape throwing a baseball against the wall under the Queensboro Bridge for two months.

The Mets wanted Pappas to go away, but reporters, sensing a story, urged Johnny Murphy to give him a tryout. Grudgingly, the tryout was arranged, but not at Huggins-Stengel Field, where the Mets trained and where reporters might be witness to the event. Murphy arranged for the tryout at an out-of-the-way high school field late one afternoon. He was happy to report later—so as to discourage other aspiring amateurs—that Pappas probably could not have made a high school team.

That was just one of the stories to come out of spring training 1962. There were enough "names" in camp to provide fodder for the reams of copy that reporters sent back north via Western Union every day.

To the Brooklyn "alumni association" in camp, Weiss had added Clem Labine, a longtime Dodgers bullpen favorite. Also on hand was catcher Myron "Joe" Ginsberg, a veteran of several American League teams.

In addition, several non-roster players from minor league clubs were brought in for tryouts. That group included people like Ray Apple, Jim Burnette, Ed Donnelly, Bruce Fitzpatrick, Dawes Hamilt, Marc Hoy, Evans Killeen, Bill Robinson, and Bill Whalen, the latter two without previous professional experience.

And then there was Roderick "Hot Rod" Kanehl.

Kanehl had played eight years in the minors as an infielder-outfielder. His contract was purchased from Nashville, where he had batted .304 in 1961.

Kanehl was picked up because he had once impressed Stengel in a Yankee camp by jumping over a fence in an attempt to catch a fly ball. Originally signed by the Yankees, Kanehl became an overnight success in the Mets camp. Not only was Stengel always praising him, but reporters reveled in writing about a player who got away from the Yankees and was making it with their new crosstown rivals.

The highlight of spring training 1962 came on Thursday, March 22. That was the day the Mets and Yankees faced each other for the first time. The Yankees, led by Ralph Houk, Casey's successor, played it like just another exhibition game, which, of course, it was. But Stengel, ever conscious of the headline possibilities and the ticket sales back in New York, treated it like a World Series game.

Stengel started his best player at every position, and his number 1 pitcher, Roger Craig, worked a full six innings and was followed to the mound by the number 2 pitcher, left-hander Al Jackson. The Yankees, who had a 10–1 exhibition record at the time, ho-hummed their way into the game. They were surprised to find it a contest. Trailing 3–2 in the ninth inning, they tied the score and threatened to send the game into extra innings.

The Mets were not to be outdone. In the bottom of the ninth, outfielder Joe Christopher tripled to left and scored the winning run on a pinch single by Richie Ashburn. Howie Nunn, who never pitched a regular season game for the Mets, became the winning pitcher by getting the last out in the top of the ninth.

Stengel reacted to the stunning 4–3 victory by remaining in the dugout for interviews. Long after the final out, with many of the 6,277 partisan fans waiting in the stands, Stengel took bows all the way to the clubhouse as the senior citizens of St. Petersburg cheered.

The Mets hosted a victory cocktail party at the Soreno Hotel after the game; in New York joyous National League fans jammed their favorite bars, including Toots Shor's, to celebrate victory over "the hated Yankees."

"It's like New Year's Eve in this joint," Shor told Stengel by telephone.

The *New York Daily News* considered it an important enough story to play on the front page. The *New York Times* made the Mets victory the lead sports story of the day.

Less than a week later, the Mets visited Fort Lauderdale, home of the Yankees, and lost, 3–2. Again Stengel started Roger Craig. But this time the Yankee victory was treated like just another exhibition game. After all, the Yankees were supposed to beat a team of discards like the Mets.

The spring of '62 was full of surprises.

Casey heads the welcoming parade up Broadway just before the Mets opened their first game at home.
DAILY NEWS

The fans showed up to witness the return of National League baseball to New York, on April 13, 1962.
LOUIS REQUENA

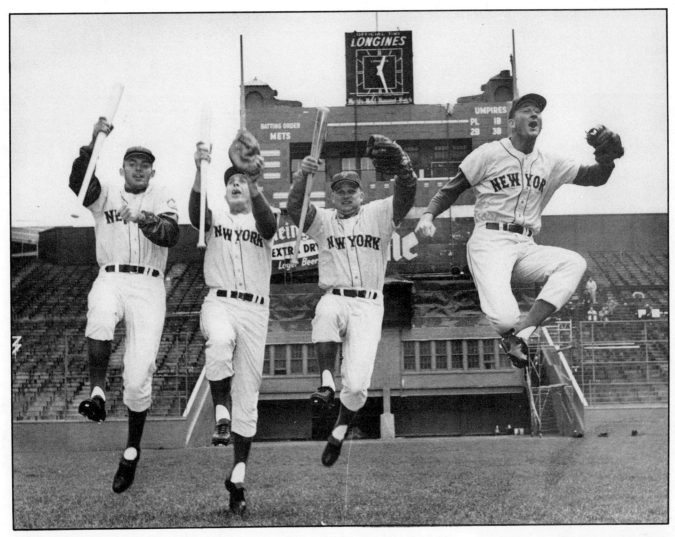

Evans Killeen, who had had a brief experience with the Kansas City A's before being sent back to the minors, pitched well in squad games and was slated for a real shot at making the club. The morning of the day he was supposed to pitch in his first exhibition, Killeen cut his thumb shaving. We never found out why he was shaving his thumb, one wag remarked. Killeen was never heard from again.

Dawes Hamilt, another player without experience, told one reporter he didn't think he'd get a good shot because he was Jewish.

Sherman "Roadblock" Jones, something of a braggart, made the club in spring training and was scheduled to start the second game of the season. On the club's flight from Florida, Jones burned himself with a matchbook. Fortunately only one game was played in St. Louis, and with a day off before the second game was to be played in New York, Jones had time to recover. He pitched in only eight games; he was 0–4 when he was sent down to Syracuse on May 9.

The Mets managed to post a 12–15 record in their first spring training ever, a record they would have difficulty matching in later years.

It was a team of battered veterans Weiss and Stengel had put together, even though a few of the older players claimed they were not yet tired from the wars.

They soon would be.

Pre-season enthusiasm runs rampant at the Polo Grounds on April 9, a day before they opened the season in St. Louis. From left: Frank Thomas, Gil Hodges, Don Zimmer, and Roger Craig. Little did they realize that they would wind up losing a record 120 games.
UPI/BETTMAN NEWSPHOTO

It wasn't until April 28 that the Mets finally won their first game at home. In the sixth inning, "Hot" Rod Kanehl, the Mets' celebrated utility man, pinch ran for Sammy Taylor and scored a go-ahead run on a wild pitch by Chris Short (who is covering the plate). The Mets wound up beating the Phillies, 8–6.

DAILY NEWS/PHIL GONZALEZ

The Mets played their first official game on the night of April 11, 1962, in St. Louis, behind Roger Craig, the starting pitcher. Experience was all they had going for them.

The infield consisted of first baseman Gil Hodges, second baseman Charlie Neal, shortstop Felix Mantilla, and third baseman Don Zimmer. In the outfield were Frank Thomas, Richie Ashburn, and Gus Bell. Craig, who entered the season with a 49–38 lifetime record, was on the mound, and Hobie Landrith was behind the plate.

After only three innings, the Mets trailed by a score of 5–2. Hodges hit the first home run in Mets history that night, and Neal also homered. Despite the homers, Larry Jackson, who would prove to be one of the Mets' all-time tormentors, coasted to an easy 11–4 St. Louis victory.

The Mets flew back to New York that night, and the following day they were accorded a heroes' welcome with a parade up lower Broadway and a reception on the steps of City Hall. They were officially greeted and welcomed to the city by Mayor Robert Wagner.

As fate would have it, the Mets opened their home season on Friday, April 13, at the ancient Polo Grounds on the banks of the Harlem River. There were flurries of snow and the temperature was in the forties, hardly the kind of weather in which to begin the home baseball season. Even the fans' enthusiasm was dampened by the weather. Only 12,000 attended.

Roadblock Jones pitched the first home game for the Mets and lost to the Pittsburgh Pirates 4–3. The age of the team was starting to show after only one game. Hodges missed the home opener because of a pulled leg muscle and an aching knee. He would not be able to return to the lineup on a regular basis for ten days.

Meanwhile, the Mets were losing games and winning fans. The Pirates swept the three-game weekend series before the Houston Colt 45s came to town and, with a 5–2 victory in eleven innings, extended the Mets' losing streak to five games.

It was in that short stretch at home that Mets fans—or "the New Breed," as they had been dubbed—began to sense the futility of the situation. Chants of "Let's go, Mets!" began to rock the Polo Grounds rafters. No matter how far behind the team might be, the fans let loose their soon familiar cheers. At times it was done derisively, but it was always done with infectious enthusiasm. One such chant was rewarded with a positive response in the bottom of the ninth inning in the game against Houston when Gus Bell hit a game-tying home run. But the Mets lost in the eleventh when Herb Moford delivered up a three-run home run to Don Buddin.

The losing continued. By the time the Mets won their first game, they had established a record for worst starts in major league history—they were 0–9, with Jones 0–3 after those nine games and Craig and Jackson both 0–2, while Bob Miller and Herb Moford were 0–1.

The only starter who had escaped a loss in that stretch was Jay Hook, an All-America collegian from Northwestern University who wrote articles on the aerodynamics of the curveball—something he could articulate clearly on paper but couldn't throw with authority when he took the mound.

Hook eventually earned his niche in history by becoming the first Mets pitcher to win a game. It happened the night of April 23 in Pittsburgh against the Pirates, who were on a ten-game winning streak. Hook was magnificent. He held the Pirates to five hits and walked only one batter, pitching a complete game and winning by a lopsided 9–1 score.

It was a historic victory, and even though the Mets were scheduled to fly by charter plane to Cincinnati immediately after the game, Stengel advised Niss to hold the plane until the baseball writers got all the material they needed to

3

◆ "TELL THEM ◆
◆ I'M BEING ◆
◆ EMBALMED" ◆

OPENING DAY LINEUP 1962

Ashburn, cf
Mantilla, ss
Neal, 2b
Thomas, lf
Bell, rf
Hodges, 1b
Zimmer, 3b
Landrith, c
Craig, p

THE METS' FIRST GAME EVER
(April 11, 1962)

New York

	AB	R	H	RBI
Ashburn, cf	5	1	1	0
Mantilla, ss	4	1	1	0
Neal, 2b	4	1	3	2
Thomas, lf	3	0	0	1
Bell, rf	3	0	1	0
Hodges, 1b	4	1	1	1
Zimmer, 3b	4	0	1	0
Landrith, c	4	0	0	0
Craig, p	1	0	0	0
Boucheeª	0	0	0	0
Moorhead, p	1	0	0	0
Moford, p	0	0	0	0
Labine, p	0	0	0	0
Marshallᵇ	0	0	0	0
Totals	33	4	8	4

St. Louis

	AB	R	H	RBI
Flood, cf	4	3	2	1
Javier, 2b	5	3	4	1
White, 1b	4	1	2	3
Musial, rf	3	1	3	2
Landrum, rf	1	0	0	0
Boyer, 3b	4	0	1	2
Minoso, lf	4	0	1	1
Oliver, c	4	1	2	0
Gotay, ss	4	1	0	0
Jackson, p	4	1	1	1
Totals	37	11	16	11

ª Walked for Craig in fourth. ᵇ Walked for Labine in ninth.

Pitching	IP	H	R	ER	BB	SO
Jackson (W, 1–0)	9	8	4	4	4	2
Craig (L, 0–1)	3	8	5	5	0	1
Moorhead	3	6	5	2	1	1
Moford	1	1	0	0	0	0
Labine	1	1	1	0	0	0

2B—Musial, Mantilla, Boyer, Oliver (2). HR—Hodges, Neal. SB—Flood (2), Javier. SF—Thomas, Flood, White. E—Mantilla, Neal, Boyer. PO-A—New York 24–11, St. Louis 27–10. DP—Jackson, Javier and White; Gotay, Javier and White. LOB—New York 7, St. Louis 5. Balk—Craig. U—Gorman, Jackowski, Sudol, Forman. Time—2:53. Attendance—16,147.

write their stories. "They may not get this opportunity very often," the wise old manager suggested to his traveling secretary.

Winning did not become a habit, and the Mets dropped the next three games following Hook's surprising Pittsburgh victory. Then, on April 28 and 29, for the first time in their young history, the Mets won two in a row. Craig pitched three innings of shutout relief in an 8–6 win over Philadelphia, and the next day Al Jackson hurled the first shutout in club history by scattering eight Philadelphia hits for an 8–0 win. The Mets were now 3–12.

Each of these milestones was recorded with great enthusiasm by the youthful press corps covering the Mets. George Weiss did not comprehend the manner in which the press covered the club. Shy, secretive, and for the most part embarrassed by his team's showing, he did not fully understand the press hype that followed each milestone, good or bad.

Realizing the potential of being in on the club's birth, I began collecting statistics and anecdotes during that first year. Unfortunately, most of them were on the negative side. It was easy to uncover records for futility that the Mets had equaled or surpassed. Soon I was branded "a negative reporter" by Weiss's forces. Other writers delighted in picking up on these "negative" statistics, which I happily shared. But I was frowned upon by the club brass.

Once, as another negative record was being approached, I sought out *The Little Red Book of Baseball*—the official baseball record book—in the Polo Grounds press box. Publicity director Tom Meany and promotions director Julius Adler tried to hide the book from me, so I telephoned the Elias Sports Bureau, publishers of the book, and Seymour Siwoff, who owned the bureau, provided me with the information I sought.

Stengel was never a part of the combine that sought to deprive the writers of information. On the contrary, he spoke freely of possible deals and trade rumors and was available at all hours of the day and night. Especially the nights. If you needed him, Stengel could usually be found at the hotel bar where he held court. Niss was usually at his side.

On the weekend of May 18–20 in Milwaukee, the Mets achieved new heights. A week earlier in New York, on May 12, the Mets won a doubleheader for the first time with Craig Anderson, a reliever, becoming the first Mets pitcher to win two games in one day.

In Milwaukee on Friday night, May 18, the Mets lost to Warren Spahn. But they came back to squeeze out a 6–5 win on Saturday afternoon and the next day won another doubleheader from the Braves by scores of 7–6 and 9–6 with Ken MacKenzie winning in relief and Al Jackson as a starter.

At this point in their history, the Mets had won twelve games in their first thirty-one; five of the victories had been at the expense of the Milwaukee Braves, a team that had sold them many of their players.

The bus ride to the airport after the doubleheader win was a particularly joyful one. Upon arrival, Niss was advised by United Airlines sports representative Jim Henderson that the plane for their chartered flight to Houston had developed engine trouble. A new plane was being flown in from Denver. Meanwhile, the Mets were to be guests of United at a cocktail party in a private room. The party lasted until midnight, when the replacement plane finally arrived. Most of the Mets were glad to board it so they could get some sleep. Not Stengel.

In his usual front row seat, the Old Man continued his nonstop talking as coaches Cookie Lavagetto, Solly Hemus, Red Kress, and Red Ruffing took turns sitting alongside him. When each man's time was up, he'd change seats with the next coach and return to his own seat to try to sleep.

Around 4 A.M., the pilot informed Niss that the Houston airport was closed because of fog. The plane would have to land in Dallas and wait for the fog to clear before continuing on to Houston. When the plane touched down in Dallas, Stengel told Niss to "wake up the writers and tell them I'm buying breakfast."

When the plane finally took off again for Houston and landed, followed by a long ride to the hotel, it was close to 8 A.M. It was the club's first visit to Houston, and the hotel in which the Mets were staying had been recommended by the Houston ball club because of its proximity to the Colts' ballpark. It was known simply as the Hi-Way House and the description fit. As the bellman deposited my bags in the room, he smirked and said, "If there is anything you want—and I mean anything—just give me a call."

By the time the Mets checked into the hotel, the seventy-one-year-old Stengel had been up a full twenty-four hours without rest. He had managed the team to two victories and continued to talk most of the rest of the time. Always eager to talk to newspapermen, Stengel knew that in every town the Mets visited for the first time, sports columnists would be out early in the morning for interviews. But by now even Casey was wearing down. As Niss handed him his hotel room key, the Old Man turned to him and said, "If any of the writers come looking for me, tell them I'm being embalmed." The remark became a classic in Stengel lore.

That was how life was with Stengel that first year. The more the Mets failed, the more laughs he provided.

Frank Thomas, the slugger purchased from Milwaukee, found the Polo Grounds, with its short foul lines, a perfect park for the right-handed pull hitter that he was. There were times Stengel thought he was overdoing it in trying to pull the ball.

On the left field fence, a clothing company advertised that the player hitting the sign most often would win a boat. Stengel tired of Thomas pulling every pitch and admonished him for it one day.

"If you want to own a boat, join the Navy," the Old Man told him.

Ironically, the boat was eventually won by Marv Throneberry, a left-handed batter, who drove many balls to the opposite field.

Players pose for photographers after the Mets' first home win ever—on April 29, 1962. From left: Rod Kanehl, Jim Hickman, Gil Hodges, Frank Thomas, and Charlie Neal.

DAILY NEWS/PHIL GONZALEZ

FIRST METS' VICTORY
(April 23, 1962)

New York

	AB	R	H	RBI
Mantilla, 3b	3	2	3	1
Chacon, ss	4	2	3	2
Bell, rf	3	0	1	1
B. Smith, rf	1	0	1	2
Thomas, lf	2	0	1	1
DeMerit, lf	1	0	0	0
Bouchee, 1b	2	0	0	0
Hodges, 1b	3	0	2	0
Neal, 2b	5	1	2	0
Hickman, cf	4	1	0	0
Cannizzaro, c	3	1	0	0
Hook, p	4	2	1	2
Totals	35	9	14	9

Pittsburgh

	AB	R	H	RBI
Virdon, cf	4	0	0	0
Groat, ss	4	0	1	0
Skinner, lf	4	0	1	1
Stuart, 1b	4	0	0	0
Clemente, rf	4	0	0	0
Burgess, c	1	0	0	0
McFarlane, c	2	0	0	0
Hoak, 3b	2	0	1	0
Mazeroski, 2b	3	0	0	0
Sturdivant, p	0	0	0	0
Olivo, p	1	0	1	0
Schofield[a]	1	1	1	0
Lamabe, p	0	0	0	0
Logan[b]	1	0	0	0
Haddix, p	0	0	0	1
Totals	31	1	5	1

[a]Singled for Olivo in sixth. [b]Grounded out for Lamabe in eighth.

Pitching	IP	H	R	ER	BB	SO
Sturdivant[X] (L, 1-1)	1	3	5	5	2	0
Olivo	5	7	2	1	1	1
Lamabe	2	3	2	2	1	3
Haddix	1	1	0	0	0	2
Hook (W, 1-0)	9	5	1	1	1	2

[X]Pitched to three batters in second.

DP—Chacon, Neal, and Bouchee; MacFarlane and Mazeroski. LOB—New York 7, Pittsburgh 4. E—Virdon, Groat, Stuart. PO-A—New York 27–10; Pittsburgh 27–9. 2B—Neal, Olivo, Mantilla, Thomas. 3B—B. Smith. S—Mantilla. SF—Bell, Thomas, Mantilla. WP—Sturdivant. U—Walsh, Conlan, Burkhart, Pelekoudas. Time—2:40. Attendance—16,176.

Don Zimmer, first in a long line of third basemen, played a brief but memorable role for the Mets in 1962, enduring a hitless streak of 0–34 and winding up with only four hits in fifty-two official at-bats.

Mets first baseman "Marvelous" Marv Throneberry—the all-time favorite butt of jokes—is seen here in a classic pose, trying his best but ultimately unable to field a bad throw. Throneberry, who wound up batting .244 with sixteen home runs, could never understand why he was affectionately ridiculed by players and fans alike. In this shot, Cardinals pitcher Bob Gibson reaches safety on the errant throw (the third such throw of the inning) in a game that the Cards eventually won 15–1 on July 8.

Telling Stengel stories was a favorite pastime of ballplayers and sportswriters. Joe Pignatano, one of a half dozen catchers employed by the Mets in their first season, was himself a part of at least two tales.

Pignatano was purchased from the Giants on July 13. Since the Giants were in Philadelphia at the time, Piggy took the train to New York at noon and arrived at the Polo Grounds around 3 P.M. for a night game. After being outfitted with a uniform by equipment manager Herb Norman, Pignatano went out and sat on the dugout bench. Shortly thereafter he was joined by Stengel and the two sat and chatted for more than an hour.

About five o'clock, when I arrived at the ballpark, I extended greetings to Pignatano, an old friend from the days when I'd covered the Dodgers and he was breaking in with Brooklyn. Then I turned to Stengel, who had been chatting for over an hour with Piggy, and asked him who was catching that night.

"I'll catch that new kid we just got from the Giants if he ever gets here," Stengel replied.

Pignatano spent most of his time with the Mets in the bullpen, where he also learned about life with Stengel.

"The Old Man called up one day on the bullpen phone and told me to get 'Nelson' warmed up," Pignatano relates. "I didn't know what he was talking about. We didn't have anybody named Nelson. I told him that but he repeated he wanted 'Nelson' to warm up. So I just took a baseball and put it on the rubber and said to the guys in the bullpen, 'He wants Nelson.' Bob Miller got up immediately and grabbed the ball. 'He always calls me "Nelson," ' Miller said."

Miller was one of two Millers with the team that year. There was Bob Miller the right-hander and Bob Miller the left-hander. They simply were referred to as righty Bob Miller and lefty Bob Miller . . . or R. B. Miller and R. L. Miller. They also roomed together, which added to the confusion.

Righty Bob Miller was a starting pitcher who epitomized the Mets that first season. He pitched well but simply could not win a game. He continued to lose close games, and reporters gathered around him after each defeat to report his reactions.

On September 29, the next to the last day of the season, Miller was on the verge of entering the record books. He was 0–12, and only one other pitcher in baseball history had ever gone 0–13 in a season. But against the Chicago Cubs that afternoon, Miller won, 2–1, and finished with a 1–12 record. Instead of the half-dozen sportswriters who were usually on hand to crowd around Miller's locker and report his reactions, I was the only writer there on that final Saturday afternoon. Unfortunately, I was "covering" for four papers that day and didn't have time to visit the clubhouse, so what Miller had to say after finally winning a game was never recorded.

If Miller escaped the record book, the Mets did not. Some of 1962's highlights:

Following their doubleheader victory in Milwaukee May 20, the Mets proceeded to lose seventeen games in a row. Some of the losses in that streak were not to be believed.

Against the Giants in Candlestick Park, the Mets had a 5–4 lead entering the eighth inning. The losing streak was about to end at five. But Willie Mays hit a home run off Hook in the bottom of the eighth to tie it. And in the tenth, after Felix Mantilla homered to put the Mets ahead again, Mays came up in the bottom half and hit another homer with a man on to win it.

Two days later, Mays and Elio Chacon, Roger Craig, and Orlando Cepeda became involved in a brawl. The Mets lost the fight and also the game and next day flew home after losing two more.

The Mets had a chance to end the losing streak in the second game of the doubleheader. Jim Hickman's three-run home run gave them a 5–2 lead with two innings to go. But the Giants tied it and then won it on a passed ball.

As Stengel had said at the draft a year before, "You gotta have a catcher or you're gonna have a lot of passed balls." The Mets had a lot of catchers that first year—six in all—and a lot of passed balls, twenty-six in all.

One of the half dozen catchers was Harry Chiti, purchased from Cleveland on April 26, 1962, for "a player to be named later." After batting .195 in fifteen games, Chiti himself became the "player to be named later." He was sent to Jacksonville in payment for himself.

Losses exceeded victories by a 3–1 margin that first season; and while the Mets were not good, they were so inept they were lovable. One of the players the fans took a real shine to was Marv Throneberry. Marv had great minor league stats, but he never could put it together in the majors. In his first year with the Mets he batted only .244, but his sixteen home runs immediately established him as a favorite. Trouble was, the fans loved him more for his mistakes than they did for the little talent he showed.

Once when Throneberry hit a triple to drive in two runs, he was ruled out for failure to touch first base. The bow-legged Stengel came roaring out of the dugout to protest to the second base umpire. But his fury was tempered somewhat by first base coach Cookie Lavagetto.

"Don't argue too much, Case," Lavagetto cautioned as the Old Man passed him. "I think he missed second base, too."

Don Zimmer will forever be remembered by Mets fans as a player who almost went hitless in his Mets career. Zimmer was actually 3-for-12 after his first three games at third base. But he then went 0-for-34. He ended his skid with a double on May 4 and two days later was traded.

"They traded him while he was hot," one reporter said.

Weiss traded Zimmer to Cincinnati, then operated by Bill DeWitt. For many years, while running the St. Louis Browns, DeWitt had dealt with Weiss at the Yankees, and Weiss frequently unloaded inferior quality upon him. But now the tables were turned. DeWitt, with a competitive Cincinnati team, sent the Mets third baseman Cliff Cook in exchange for Zimmer. It wasn't until they got him that the Mets discovered Cook had a chronic back problem and had difficulty bending over to field ground balls.

Players continued to come and go throughout the 1962 season as Weiss picked up anyone who might be an improvement over what he already had. As a result, a total of seventeen pitchers and twenty-eight position players were employed.

Of the pitchers, Roger Craig was the biggest winner, with ten victories—one-quarter of the entire team total. But Craig also lost twenty-four. He had to win three of his last four decisions to achieve the ten victories. Al Jackson was another twenty-game loser, and Jay Hook came perilously close with nineteen. (Three twenty-game losers would have set a record.) Hook lost ten of his last eleven decisions.

Ken MacKenzie appeared in forty-two games in relief and was the only pitcher with a winning record. If people accused Stengel of being too old to manage, asserting that he fell asleep in the dugout during games or did not know what was going on around him, you could not prove it by MacKenzie.

One day when the left-hander was in a particularly ticklish relief situation, Stengel hobbled out to the mound to offer some advice. "Make out like you're pitching against Harvard," he suggested.

No matter how quickly the losses mounted, the Mets were loved. Fans took to them like parents to a newborn child. Their every achievement, no matter how minuscule, was cheered. Eventually the fans began to show their love in

METS' THIRD BASEMEN, 1962–1986 (80 TOTAL)

Almon, Bill	Johnson, Bob
Alomar, Sandy	Johnson, Howard
Ashford, Tucker	Jones, Ross
Aspromonte, Bob	Kanehl, Rod
Backman, Wally	Kingman, Dave
Bailor, Bob	Klaus, Bobby
Boswell, Ken	Knight, Ray
Boyer, Ken	Kolb, Gary
Bressoud, Ed	Linz, Phil
Brooks, Hubie	Maddox, Elliott
Buchek, Jerry	Mankowski, Phil
Burright, Larry	Mantilla, Felix
Carter, Gary	Martinez, Teo
Chacon, Elio	Mitchell, Kevin
Chapman, Kelvin	Moock, Joe
Charles, Ed	Moran, Al
Collins, Kevin	Moreno, Jose
Cook, Cliff	Napoleon, Dan
Cubbage, Mike	Neal, Charley
Drake, Sammy	Otis, Amos
Fernandez, Chico	Pfeil, Bobby
Ferrer, Sergio	Phillips, Mike
Flynn, Doug	Puig, Rich
Foli, Tim	Ramirez, Mario
Foster, Leo	Randle, Lenny
Foy, Joe	Reynolds, Tommie
Fregosi, Jim	Samuel, Amado
Gardenhire, Ron	Schreiber, Ted
Garrett, Wayne	Smith, Charley
Graham, Wayne	Staiger, Roy
Green, Pumpsie	Stearns, John
Grote, Jerry	Stephenson, John
Hebner, Richie	Tuefel, Tim
Heidemann, Jack	Thomas, Frank
Heise, Bob	Torre, Joe
Herrscher, Rick	Trevino, Alex
Hickman, Jim	Valentine, Bobby
Hiller, Chuck	Weis, Al
Hunt, Ron	Youngblood, Joel
Hurdle, Clint	Zimmer, Don

In May the Mets made a few moves to bolster their "attack." Wilmer "Vinegar Bend" Mizell *(left)* and first baseman Marv Throneberry *(center)* chat with coach Harry "Cookie" Lavagetto. Mizell (who wound up 0–2 with a 7.34 ERA) was obtained in a trade with the Pirates, and Throneberry was bought from the Baltimore Orioles to play first base for the injury-plagued Gil Hodges.

UPI/BETTMAN NEWSPHOTO

Dodgers luminaries Junior Gilliam and Sandy Koufax (number 32) try to prevent the Mets' Elio Chacon from going from first to third on a single.

DAILY NEWS

the only visible way they could—with banners. Messages painted on bedsheets began to appear throughout the Polo Grounds testifying to the devotion these fans had. They also testified to their sense of humor.

"To err is human, to forgive is a Mets fan," proclaimed one banner, as the Mets continued to fumble along. Another banner, in succinct expression of the sentiments of the fans, read: "Pray."

At first the Mets management objected to the banners and ejected fans who unfurled them in the stands from the park. Weiss's official position was that the banners barred the view of other fans. But the press was quick to criticize the club's reactions, defending the banners and the enthusiastic display by the fans. Eventually, Weiss capitulated and banner-bearing fans were permitted to

1962

NAME	G by POS	B	AGE	G	AB	R	H	2B	3B	HR	RBI	BB	SO	SB	BA	SA
NEW YORK 10th 40-120 .250 60.5	CASEY STENGEL															
TOTALS			30	161	5492	617	1318	166	40	139	573	616	991	59	.240	.361
Marv Throneberry	1B97			28	116	357	29	87	11	3	16	49	34	83	1	.244	.426
Charlie Neal	2B85, SS39, 3B12	R	31	136	508	59	132	14	9	11	58	56	90	2	.260	.388
Elio Chacon	SS110, 2B2, 3B1	R	25	118	368	49	87	10	3	2	27	76	64	12	.236	.296
Felix Mantilla	3B95, SS25, 2B14	R	27	141	466	54	128	17	4	11	59	37	51	3	.275	.399
Richie Ashburn	OF97, 2B2	L	35	135	389	60	119	7	3	7	28	81	39	12	.306	.393
Jim Hickman	OF124	R	25	140	392	54	96	18	2	13	46	47	96	4	.245	.401
Frank Thomas	OF126, 1B11, 3B10	R	33	156	571	69	152	23	3	34	94	48	95	2	.266	.496
Chris Cannizzaro	C56, OF1	R	24	59	133	9	32	2	1	0	9	19	26	1	.241	.271
Rod Kanehl	2B62, 3B30, OF20, 1B3, SS2	R	28	133	351	52	87	10	2	4	27	23	36	8	.248	.322
Joe Christopher	OF94	R	26	119	271	36	66	10	2	6	32	35	42	11	.244	.362
Gene Woodling	OF48	L	39	81	190	18	52	8	1	5	24	24	22	0	.274	.405
Sammy Taylor	C50	L	29	68	158	12	35	4	2	3	20	23	17	0	.222	.329
Choo Choo Coleman	C44	L	24	55	152	24	38	7	2	6	17	11	24	2	.250	.441
Gil Hodges	1B47	R	38	54	127	15	32	1	0	9	17	15	27	0	.252	.472
Ed Bouchee	1B19	L	29	50	87	7	14	2	0	3	10	18	17	0	.161	.287
Cliff Cook	3B16, OF10	R	25	40	112	12	26	6	1	2	9	4	34	1	.232	.357
Rick Herrscher	1B10, 3B6, OF4, SS3	R	25	35	50	5	11	3	0	1	6	5	11	0	.220	.340
Gus Bell	OF26	L	33	30	101	8	15	2	0	1	6	10	7	0	.149	.198
Joe Pignatano	C25	R	32	27	56	2	13	2	0	0	2	2	11	0	.232	.268
Sammy Drake	2B10, 3B6	B	27	25	52	2	10	0	0	0	1	7	12	0	.192	.192
Hobie Landrith	C21	L	32	23	45	6	13	3	0	1	7	8	3	0	.289	.422
Jim Marshall	1B5, OF1	L	30	17	32	6	11	1	0	3	4	3	6	0	.344	.656

Harry Chiti 29 R 8-41, John DeMerit 26 R 3-16, 1 Don Zimmer 31 R 4-52, 1 Bobby Gene Smith 28 R 3-22, Ed Kranepool 17 L 1-6, Joe Ginsberg 35 L 0-5

NAME	T	AGE	W	L	PCT	SV	G	GS	CG	IP	H	BB	SO	ShO	ERA
		27	40	120	.250	10	161	161	43	1430	1577	571	772	4	5.04
Roger Craig	R	31	10	24	.294	3	42	33	13	233	261	70	118	0	4.52
Jay Hook	R	25	8	19	.296	0	37	34	13	214	230	71	113	0	4.84
Al Jackson	L	26	8	20	.286	0	36	33	12	231	244	78	118	4	4.40
Ken MacKenzie	L	28	5	4	.556	1	42	1	0	80	87	34	51	0	4.95
Craig Anderson	R	24	3	17	.150	4	50	14	2	131	150	63	62	0	5.36
Bob Miller	R	26	2	2	.500	0	17	0	0	20	24	8	8	0	7.20
Galen Cisco	R	26	1	1	.500	0	4	2	1	19	15	11	13	0	3.32
Ray Daviault	R	28	1	5	.167	0	36	3	0	81	92	48	51	0	6.22
Willard Hunter	L	28	1	6	.143	0	27	6	1	63	67	34	40	0	5.57
Bob Miller	R	23	1	12	.077	0	33	21	1	144	146	62	91	0	4.88
Herb Moford	R	33	0	1	.000	0	7	0	0	15	21	1	5	0	7.20
Larry Foss	R	26	0	1	.000	0	5	1	0	12	17	7	3	0	4.50
Bob Moorhead	R	24	0	2	.000	0	38	7	0	105	118	42	63	0	4.54
Vinegar Bend Mizell	L	31	0	2	.000	0	17	2	0	38	48	25	15	0	7.34
Sherman Jones	R	27	0	4	.000	0	8	3	0	23	31	8	11	0	7.83
Dave Hillman	R	34	0	0	.000	1	13	1	0	16	21	8	8	0	6.19
Clem Labine	R	35	0	0	.000	0	3	0	0	4	5	1	2	0	11.25

roam the park expressing, on bedsheets, their love for this bumbling team. Banner Day has since become one of the club's major promotions.

The Mets were eliminated from the pennant race early. The exact date was August 7 in Los Angeles when their record fell to 29–82. Since they were no longer capable of playing even .500 ball on the 162-game schedule, they could no longer possibly win the pennant. That had been obvious from opening day, but the Mets were obligated to play out the schedule to prove it. In the first year of the 162-game schedule, the Mets set records for the fewest victories and most losses. The record stands to this day.

It could have been worse. One game on their schedule was rained out and another wound up in a tie—otherwise they might have lost 122 games.

Richie Ashburn, one of the more consistent players for the Mets in 1962 (he led the team with a .306 batting average), celebrates a big day at the Polo Grounds, where he went 3–4 with two home runs and three RBIs.
DAILY NEWS/WALTER KELLEHER

Little Al Jackson, who emerged in 1962 as an inconsistent but occasionally brilliant starter (four shutouts), pitches against the Reds on August 5. His final stats included an 8–20 record and 4.40 ERA, the best among the Mets' starting staff.
UPI/BETTMAN NEWSPHOTO

June 1963—one of the first banners to appear on the Mets scene. At first, banners were disapproved of by the Mets brass and attempts were made to ban them. But sportswriters and fans eventually convinced management otherwise, and banners became an institution at Mets games, at home *and* away.

asey Stengel put the entire picture into proper perspective on opening day of the 1963 season. After Ernie Broglio of the St. Louis Cardinals shut the Mets out on two hits—both of them by Larry Burright—Casey expressed his disappointment. "We're still frauds. We're cheating the public."

Weiss winced at his manager's candid appraisal. The president of the Mets had worked hard over the winter to try and improve the last-place club. He had purchased or traded for pitchers Tracy Stallard and Carlton Willey and infielders Chico Fernandez, Pumpsie Green, Burright, Tim Harkness, Ted Schreiber, Al Moran, and a kid named Ron Hunt. He brought up Larry Bearnarth and Ed Kranepool, who still had rookie status, and even brought back one of the all-time Brooklyn greats, Duke Snider.

But the improvement was hardly noticeable. The Mets opened the season by dropping their first eight games before beating Milwaukee, 5–4, on April 19. The winning hit was a double by Hunt, the rookie who had been purchased over the winter from Milwaukee. The winning pitcher was Ken MacKenzie, another former Milwaukee farmhand.

Joan Payson was so elated over the first victory that she sent a bouquet of roses to Hunt's wife, Jackie. On another occasion later in the season, she sent roses to Hunt himself, only then to be advised that one of the second baseman's many allergies was to roses.

Weiss had acquired Pumpsie Green from Boston, where he had become somewhat of a celebrity as the first black player to don a Red Sox uniform. Boston owner Tom Yawkey was one of the last to lift the color barrier; when he finally gave in it was Green, a seven-year minor league veteran, the Sox selected.

Under tremendous pressure, Green averaged .250 in four years with the Red Sox but only made headlines the day he and pitcher Gene Conley went AWOL. They got off the team bus in New York and said they were going to Israel. Why Israel was never explained. Both were missing for several days and were fined when they finally returned.

Green came to the Mets along with pitcher Tracy Stallard and shortstop Al Moran in exchange for Felix Mantilla, one of the original Mets. It was another one of Weiss's deals that did not work out. Although Green hit .278 playing third base, he was gone the next year.

Stallard, who had the dubious distinction of throwing the pitch that Roger Maris hit for his sixty-first home run in 1961, was 16–37 in his two years with the Mets, including a 10–20 record in 1964. He was a handsome, after-hours person who fit right into New York night life. He sublet the Manhattan apartment owned by actress Julie Newmar and settled in to enjoy the pleasures the Big Apple had to offer.

Al Moran, the third player in the deal with Green, was the Mets' regular shortstop in 1963 but a .193 average cost him his job, and after sixteen games in 1964 he was gone.

Of all the players Weiss purchased or traded for in those early years, Hunt was by far the best. In his rookie season with the Mets, Hunt batted .272 and was voted the team's most valuable player after leading the club in hitting, runs, base hits, and doubles. In the Rookie-of-the-Year vote conducted by the Baseball Writers Association of America at the conclusion of the season, the only player good enough to beat Hunt out for that award was a Cincinnati Reds rookie named Pete Rose.

Hunt's trademark, for which the fans loved him, was a dirty uniform. He was a scrapper who would do anything to win a game. His belly-flop slides into first and other bases soon became a passion with him, delighting the fans, who had little else to cheer about.

OPENING DAY LINEUP 1963

Burright, 2b
Coleman, c
Kranepool, rf
Snider, cf
Thomas, lf
Harkness, 1b
Neal, 3b
Moran, ss
Craig, p

And the 1963 season is officially under way with this pitch from Roger Craig to Curt Flood of the Cardinals on April 9 at the Polo Grounds. Craig went on to lose twenty-two games while winning only five but had a fairly respectable ERA of 3.78.
UPI/BETTMAN NEWSPHOTO

The most popular player acquisition in 1963 was bringing the Duke of Flatbush back to New York. In the first home game of the year on April 9, Snider knows he will be well received as he stands against the famous concrete Polo Grounds left field wall to thank his newly formed fan club. In 106 games, he batted .245 and hit fourteen home runs.
UPI/BETTMAN NEWSPHOTO

Hunt soon realized there were other ways to reach first base than with a walk or a hit. Getting hit with a pitch was just as good. In his rookie year, he was hit thirteen times. The only National League player hit more often was Frank Robinson, who at times was hit purposely and other times because he crowded the plate.

Getting hit by a pitcher seemed an obsession with Hunt, but he did not really turn it into an art until 1968, when he was with the Giants. That year he "took" twenty-five pitches in the arms, ribs, back, or legs. In 1971, when he was with Montreal, he established a modern major league record by being hit fifty times in one season.

Lou Niss, the team's traveling secretary, always had a problem with Hunt's family tickets when the team played in St. Louis, Ron's hometown.

"Not all members of his family spoke to each other," Niss recalled, "so I had to split them up. One part of the family sat on the first-base side of the field, the other on the third-base side. It was a little confusing trying to remember who spoke to whom."

Duke Snider joined the Mets at the end of spring training after sixteen years with the Dodgers. Weiss figured he would find the short fences at the Polo Grounds inviting. Snider did hit fourteen homers, but his .243 average was a sign that his career was at an end.

Weiss had also hoped Snider would help a promising young prospect like Ed Kranepool. Fresh out of James Monroe High School in the Bronx, where he had bettered Hall of Famer Hank Greenberg's home run record, Kranepool was the Mets' first bonus baby. He signed in the summer of 1962 for an $85,000 bonus and, after only forty-one games in the minors and a few games at the Polo Grounds late that year, he opened the 1963 season with the Mets. He was the bright hope for the future, especially with Gil Hodges requiring more and more rest because of an aching knee.

Snider was standing behind the batting cage at the Polo Grounds one day watching Kranepool try to battle his way out of a slump. In early July the kid was hitless in twenty-three consecutive plate appearances, during which time he failed to get a ball out of the infield. Snider, thinking he would offer the kid a tip, was shocked when Kranepool ungraciously rejected his advice.

"You ain't going so hot yourself," Kranepool snapped at the future Hall of Famer, who only recently had hit his 400th career home run.

Kranepool subsequently wound up at Buffalo but came back to stay in 1964 and put in eighteen years with the Mets before they finally released him at the end of the 1979 season. He had batted .261 in his career, including .300 and .323 in 1974 and 1975 respectively. He was one of the most popular Mets of all time, and popular especially with Mrs. Payson. She gave orders that he was never to be traded and, despite numerous attempts by her general managers to rescind that order, Kranepool never wore another major league uniform after 1964.

The Mets searched for any ray of hope that would signal an improved team in their second season. Carlton Willey, another ex-Brave, provided some sunlight by winning three of his first four decisions. But by the middle of June, the team had dragged him down with them, and Willey, a soft-spoken man from Maine, was below .500 with a 5–6 record. He finished the year at 9–14.

On May 22, while they were on the West Coast, the Mets lost one of their most popular players when Gil Hodges was released so he could accept an offer to manage the Washington Senators. Hodges had not been playing regularly; in fact, his chronic right knee pain had put him on the disabled list during his last two weeks with the team. Though his career as a player was over, a new one as a manager was starting—one that would have a strong influence on the Mets' turnabout half a dozen years later.

The day after the Mets released Hodges, Washington sold veteran outfielder Jimmy Piersall to the Mets. Weiss insisted there was no connection between the two transactions, although in the nation's capital, the Senators were telling their writers that Piersall had been sent to the Mets in exchange for Hodges.

Piersall, a colorful if eccentric character who had once had a mental breakdown, fit right in with the comical Mets. He had hit ninety-nine home runs in an American League career with Boston, Cleveland, and Washington and threatened to "do something different" when he hit number 100. He did. On June 23, against the Philadelphia Phillies at the Polo Grounds, Jimmy hit a solo home run off Dallas Green and circled the bases running backward.

"I really wanted to run the bases in the reverse order—third, second, and first," Piersall said later, "but the umpires told me I'd be out if I did, so I did the next best thing."

Stengel saw some humor in the Piersall show but, for the most part, he did not enjoy having the outspoken center fielder in the same dugout. Piersall had been critical of Stengel when both were in the American League, and Casey was not one to forget.

Piersall lasted only forty games with the Mets and was released on July 22 with a .194 average. But he had one last hurrah before his release.

It was in 1963 that the Mayor's Trophy Game between the Yankees and the Mets was inaugurated, all proceeds going for the promotion of sandlot baseball in New York City. It was also the first time the arch rivals met in the Big Apple.

On the night of June 20, before a crowd of 50,000—most of them boisterous, banner-bearing Mets fans who invaded Yankee Stadium—the two teams squared off. The Yankees, who had played a regular season game in the afternoon, treated the game as a routine exhibition. Not the Mets. Stengel used two of his best pitchers—Jay Hook and Carlton Willey—to beat the Yankees, 6–2. Again it was headlines the struggling Mets were after, and once again Casey knew how to get them. The Yankees could argue all they wanted that Ralph Houk had used a bunch of scrubs in the game. The final score was all the Mets fans cared about.

Clarence "Choo Choo" Coleman was one of the more colorful members of the original Mets. While his career stats never amounted to much (in 261 games he had eighty-five hits in 415 at-bats with nine home runs and twenty-six RBIs), his name caught the imagination of the fans, and in many ways, he symbolized the early futility of the Mets. He played as a second-string catcher in 1962, the regular catcher in 1963, made a brief reappearance in 1966, and then was finally let go. Ralph Kiner often referred to him as his toughest interviewee. His response to most questions, including the origin of his nickname, was usually, "Yeh, bub."

DAILY NEWS/PAUL DE MARIA

Homer was the official mascot of the Mets and had his own seat on a platform behind home plate. Originally sponsored and paid for by Rheingold, he later became the house pet of Al Moore, promotional director of the brewery. Homer was frequently shown during Rheingold commercials and was a big favorite of the fans.

LOUIS REQUENA

Casey Stengel offers some constructive criticism as he shows young Ed Kranepool (only eighteen) the proper batting stance. It was Stengel who insisted that the Krane remain with the Mets when almost everyone else thought he should be returned to the minors. Perhaps he should have—in starting seventy-five games he hit only .209 with two home runs and fifteen RBIs.

UPI/BETTMAN NEWSPHOTO

Piersall was one of the stars of that victory. He led off the game with a double and scored on a wild pitch. In the third, when the Mets scored five runs, Piersall again led off with a hit. The next day, flush with success, the Mets returned to the Polo Grounds, where they polished off the Phillies, 3–1, behind the strong pitching of Al Jackson. Shortly thereafter they entered into a fifteen-game losing streak; they then won three out of the next four games. But on July 28, in Houston, the Mets established a modern major league record by dropping their twenty-second consecutive road game. Losing streaks continued to be common—they had clearly established themselves as all-time losers in virtually every department. One certain loser was Roger Craig, the beleaguered "ace" of the pitching staff.

In spite of the fact that he pitched well and had an earned run average of 3.78, Craig lost twenty-two games and won only five. Of his twenty-two defeats, eighteen came in succession, tying a modern National League record. Roger won on April 29, when he beat Los Angeles, 4–2, for his second victory of the season. He did not win again until August 9. He tried everything. He even changed his uniform number from 38 to 13 in an attempt to change his luck.

Craig's eighteenth consecutive loss on August 4 also was his twentieth of the season. He thus became the first National League pitcher since Paul Derringer in 1933 and 1934 to lose twenty games in two consecutive seasons. He was also the first New York pitcher to lose twenty in consecutive seasons since Harry McIntyre had done so with Brooklyn a half century earlier in 1905 and 1906.

When Craig finally did stop his losing streak, in a game against the Chicago Cubs at the Polo Grounds, it was a grand slam home run by Jim Hickman in the bottom of the ninth inning that ended his nearly four months of misery.

Of Craig's twenty-two losses in 1963, five were by scores of 1–0. It was indicative of the support he got.

Craig was not alone as a loser. Five other pitchers lost ten or more. Not one of the starters had a winning record. Only Al Jackson, with thirteen, won as many as ten games.

One pitcher who certainly understood Roger Craig's feelings was Craig Anderson, a big right-handed reliever out of Lehigh University who was picked up in the expansion draft. After winning both games in relief in a May 12, 1962, doubleheader, Anderson failed to win another game for the next three seasons. He lost his last sixteen in 1962, two more in 1963, and one in 1964, to finish his Mets career in a nineteen-game losing streak.

The Mets' only improvement in their second season was eleven more victories. They led the majors again with 111 losses and were forty-eight games behind the Dodgers when they finished their season in Houston. Eleven days earlier they had played the last game ever at the Polo Grounds, by dropping a 5–1 decision to Philadelphia. It seemed fitting that the last pitcher to lose a game in the Polo Grounds was Craig Anderson.

On June 23 Jimmy Piersall, who had a brief but memorable stint with the Mets, hit his one hundredth career home run and, as promised, ran around the bases backward to the amazement of teammates and fans alike. Tim Harkness waits patiently at the plate.
DAILY NEWS

1963

NAME	G by POS	B	AGE	G	AB	R	H	2B	3B	HR	RBI	BB	SO	SB	BA	SA
NEW YORK 10th 51-111 .315 48 TOTALS		CASEY STENGEL	27	162	5336	501	1168	156	35	96	459	457	1078	41	.219	.315
Tim Harkness	1B106	L	25	123	375	35	79	12	3	10	41	36	79	4	.211	.339
Ron Hunt	2B142, 3B1	R	22	143	533	64	145	28	4	10	42	40	50	5	.272	.396
Al Moran	SS116, 3B1	R	24	119	331	26	64	5	2	1	23	36	60	3	.193	.230
Charlie Neal	3B66, SS8	R	32	72	253	26	57	12	1	3	18	27	49	1	.225	.316
Duke Snider	OF106	L	36	129	354	44	86	8	3	14	45	56	74	0	.243	.401
Jim Hickman	OF82, 3B59	R	26	146	494	53	113	21	6	17	51	44	120	0	.229	.399
Frank Thomas	OF96, 1B15, 3B1	R	34	126	420	34	109	9	1	15	60	33	48	0	.260	.393
Choo Choo Coleman	C91, OF1	L	25	106	247	22	44	0	0	3	9	24	49	5	.178	.215
Rod Kanehl	OF58, 3B13, 2B12, 1B3	R	29	109	191	26	46	6	0	1	9	5	26	6	.241	.288
Ed Kranepool	OF55, 1B20	L	18	86	273	22	57	12	2	2	14	18	50	4	.209	.289
Joe Christopher	OF45	R	27	64	149	19	33	5	1	1	8	13	21	1	.221	.289
Norm Sherry	C61	R	31	63	147	6	20	1	0	2	11	10	26	1	.136	.184
Chico Fernandez	SS45, 3B5, 2B3	R	31	58	145	12	29	6	0	1	9	9	30	3	.200	.262
Joe Hicks	OF41	L	30	56	159	16	36	6	1	5	22	7	31	0	.226	.371
Cliff Cook	OF21, 3B9, 1B5	R	26	50	106	9	15	2	1	2	8	12	37	0	.142	.236
Duke Carmel	OF21, 1B18	L	26	47	149	11	35	5	3	3	18	16	37	2	.235	.369
Jesse Gonder	C31	L	27	42	126	12	38	4	0	3	15	6	25	1	.302	.405
Larry Burright	SS19, 2B15, 3B1	R	25	41	100	9	22	2	1	0	3	8	25	1	.220	.260
Jimmy Piersall	OF38	R	33	40	124	13	24	4	1	1	10	10	14	1	.194	.266
Ted Schreiber	3B17, SS9, 2B3	R	24	39	50	1	8	0	0	0	2	4	14	0	.160	.160
Sammy Taylor	C13	L	30	22	35	3	9	0	1	0	6	5	7	0	.257	.314
Dick Smith	OF10, 1B2	R	24	20	42	4	10	0	1	0	3	5	10	3	.238	.286
Pumpsie Green	3B16	B	29	17	54	8	15	1	2	1	5	12	13	0	.278	.426
Chris Cannizzaro	C15	R	25	16	33	4	8	1	0	0	4	1	8	0	.242	.273

Marv Throneberry 29 L 2-14, 1 Gil Hodges 39 R 5-22, Cleon Jones 20 R 2-15

NAME	T	AGE	W	L	PCT	SV	G	GS	CG	IP	H	BB	SO	ShO	ERA
		27	51	111	.315	12	162	162	42	1427	1452	529	806	5	4.12
Al Jackson	L	27	13	17	.433	1	37	34	11	227	237	84	142	0	3.96
Carl Willey	R	32	9	14	.391	0	30	28	7	183	149	69	101	4	3.10
Galen Cisco	R	27	7	15	.318	0	51	17	1	156	165	64	81	0	4.33
Tracy Stallard	R	25	6	17	.261	1	39	23	5	155	156	77	110	0	4.70
Roger Craig	R	32	5	22	.185	2	46	31	14	236	249	58	108	0	3.78
Jay Hook	R	26	4	14	.222	1	41	20	3	153	168	53	89	0	5.47
Ken MacKenzie	L	29	3	1	.750	3	34	0	0	58	63	12	41	0	4.97
Larry Bearnarth	R	21	3	8	.273	4	58	2	0	126	127	47	48	0	3.43
Grover Powell	L	22	1	1	.500	0	20	4	1	50	37	32	39	1	2.70
Craig Anderson	R	25	0	2	.000	0	3	2	0	9	17	3	6	0	9.00
Don Rowe	L	27	0	0	.000	0	26	1	0	55	59	21	27	0	4.25
Ed Bauta	R	28	0	0	.000	0	9	0	0	19	22	9	13	0	5.21
Steve Dillon	L	20	0	0	.000	0	1	0	0	2	3	0	1	0	9.00

**After losing eighteen straight games (tying an all-time record)
luckless Roger Craig decides to wear number 13 on the back of his
uniform to see if it might change things. Casey Stengel is support-
ive of the move, as nothing has worked up to now.**

If the Mets were not much better in 1964, at least they would lose in pleasant surroundings. It was the dawn of a new era in New York baseball. The municipal stadium that Walter O'Malley had rejected and Horace Stoneham was never offered opened on April 17 with 48,736 paying customers plus several thousand politicians and guests of the Mets.

At the behest of Mayor Robert F. Wagner, the Board of Estimate named the stadium "William A. Shea Stadium," a reward for the popular attorney who had worked so hard to bring National League baseball back to New York. It had cost $20 million and was financed through the issuance of New York City bonds. The stadium was designed by the architectural firm of Praeger-Kavanaugh-Waterbury and was an all-purpose stadium that would seat 55,300 for baseball and 60,000 for the New York Jets football team, who would occupy it at the conclusion of the baseball season. The Mets were the principal tenants, a fact that gnawed at the Jets in later years. By the terms of their lease, the Jets were unable to use the stadium while the Mets were still playing baseball. In 1969 and 1973, when the Mets were engaged in the World Series, the Jets found themselves orphans of the road.

The winter weather in New York plus the usual union problems in the building trades slowed progress of the stadium's construction. When the Mets and Pittsburgh Pirates arrived at the park to play in the official opener the morning of April 17, sod was still being put in place in the right field area. Two hours before game time, workmen were erecting portions of the plywood outfield fence and painting it while Guy Lombardo's band played on the field.

Hope springs eternal in the hearts of baseball fans, a cliché Mets fans were forced to embrace from the start. The fans were especially hopeful that new surroundings would finally bring out the best in the club, which had already lost 231 of the 322 games played the first two years.

The major acquisitions over the winter were George Altman, Jack Fisher, Bill Wakefield, Bob Taylor, and Amado Samuel, not exactly the material around which to build a championship team.

Altman was an outfielder who had hit .274 for St. Louis in 1963 but did not figure in the Cardinals' future plans. The Mets traded Roger Craig to St. Louis to get both Altman and Wakefield. Fisher was obtained from the Giants for $30,000 in a supplemental draft after the Mets and Colt 45s complained about the quality of players offered them in the original draft.

Taylor was another conditional purchase from the Milwaukee Braves, who were getting rich unloading their excess players on the desperate Weiss. Originally signed by the Braves for a whopping $150,000 bonus in 1956, he was a catcher-outfielder who had showed some promise in Triple-A ball but never in the majors. Samuel and Adrian Garrett were two more Milwaukee farmhands Weiss grabbed up just for the sake of adding some new faces.

Of the players added, only Fisher made a significant contribution. Altman left after one season to play in Japan. Wakefield won three, lost five, and was gone the next year, although he did relieve in what was then a club record of sixty-two games. Taylor hung on a few years but barely hit his weight. Samuel, an infielder, was gone by July.

Fisher became a regular starter and won ten games, but he quickly fell into step with other Mets pitchers by losing seventeen. The next year he lost twenty-four. Despite his losing ways, Fisher was a workhorse. He pitched 200 or more innings four straight years. His best year was 1966, when he won eleven and lost only fourteen.

There was a festive air at Shea Stadium that first season, some of it generated by the World's Fair in progress across from the ballpark in Flushing Meadow. That in itself was an attraction, but with the Mets in a new ballpark

5

• NEW •
• BALLPARK, •
• SAME OLD •
• TEAM •

OPENING DAY LINEUP 1964

D. Smith, 1b
Samuel, 2b
Hunt, 3b
Thomas, lf
Hickman, cf
B. Taylor, c
Christopher, rf
Moran, ss
Jackson, p

adjacent to the Fair, Flushing became a mecca for tourists. After drawing 922,530 and 1,080,108 in their first two years at the Polo Grounds, attendance at Shea Stadium the first season soared to 1,732,597. Only the Los Angeles Dodgers, with a far better ball club, outdrew the Mets among the twenty major league ball clubs.

Opening day was no different for the Mets in one respect. They were losers again. After opening on the road with two losses to the Phillies, the Mets came home to entertain the Pirates. But the Pirates, playing behind Bob Friend, proved to be rude guests.

Fisher started the first game ever at Shea Stadium, pitching surprisingly well for seven innings. In the seventh, he was relieved by Ed Bauta, a late addition to the 1963 pitching staff. Bauta wound up the loser in the ninth inning when Bill Mazeroski drove in the winning run in a 4–3 Pirates victory.

Now the Mets were 0–3. How long would they go before winning their first game of the season.

In the second game at Shea, Pittsburgh won again. This time the score was 9–5, and some pundits suggested that the Mets, 0–9 and 0–8 at the outset of their first two season respectively, were going to make it 0–7 in their third year.

But little Al Jackson, who eventually wound up with an 11–16 record, put an end to the losing streak, not only beating the Pirates but shutting them out as well, 6–0.

That victory did not reverse the overall trend. The Mets went on to lose eight straight and did not win again until it was Jackson again on the mound, pitching a brilliant two-hit shutout that beat Cincinnati's Jim Maloney, 3–0. It was only May 2 and already the Mets were 3–11.

It was obvious, from that start, that the Mets were not very strong, despite the glowing reports that had come out of spring training.

In those easygoing Florida days, Stengel had nothing but raves for a rawboned slugger named Ron Swoboda, fresh off the University of Maryland campus.

"He hits baseballs over buildings," Stengel glowed after one particularly long exhibition home run.

Swoboda (now a broadcaster in Arizona) never lived up to expectations. His best year with the Mets was 1967, when he batted .281 with thirteen homers; three disappointing seasons followed before he was traded to Montreal on March 31, 1971—only hours before a spring training game against St. Louis.

Swoboda was always a character. He annoyed some of the older members of the Mets by wearing love beads with tie-dyed blue jeans and a T-shirt to the ballpark and played his part right to the end. After announcing the trade that sent him to Montreal and brought shy outfielder Don Hahn to the Mets, the club announced that Swoboda would speak to the writers in the press room underneath the first base stands. When the writers had all assembled, Swoboda suddenly burst into the room wearing a Captain Marvel T-shirt and shouting "Shazam!" He said he was sorry to be leaving New York, because he owned a home on Long Island, but he was happy to be going to a club that wanted him. Three months later he was back in New York. The Expos traded him to the Yankees on June 25.

At the opening ceremony at Shea Stadium, Bill Shea pours water taken from the Gowanus Canal with his right hand and the Harlem River with his left. Shea Stadium was thus inaugurated on April 17, 1964.

DAILY NEWS/BILL MEURER

After two years in the Polo Grounds, 48,736 Mets fans jumped for joy at the sparkling newness of Shea. With its parking lots, unobstructed seats, and updated press facilities (to say nothing of the dugout and clubhouse, which were no longer located in center field), everyone seemed pleased with the new facility. Through the years, Shea has proven to be a better park for pitchers than hitters. Batters complain of poor visibility and swirling winds (especially at night), and the ball doesn't carry as well as at other National League parks.

DAILY NEWS

Stengel was also high on Bob Schmidt, a left-handed pitcher from Long Island, who had won seventeen games the year before for Jamestown and was drafted out of the Detroit organization. (Stengel's enthusiasm was short-lived. Schmidt didn't make it out of spring training.) Cliff Cook was returning to try third base again after back surgery. Steve Dillon was the subject of several stories, mainly because he had a huge nose, was left-handed, and looked like the great Warren Spahn. He was from the Bronx in New York and had been drafted away from the rival Yankees. There also were promising graduates of the Mets' own farm system, notably an outfielder named Cleon Jones and Dick Selma, a pitcher.

The big thrower in camp, of course, was Willey. His nine victories the previous year, plus an impressive 3.10 earned run average, led Mets followers to believe that at last they had a winning pitcher. But early in spring training, Willey was hit in the jaw by a line drive off the bat of Detroit's Gates Brown. Forced to live on a liquid diet with his jaws wired, Willey lost considerable weight as well as his strength. When he finally did pitch again in June, he was not the same pitcher.

On July 26, with his record 0–2, Willey "felt something give" in his right elbow as he served up a home run pitch to Joe Torre. After resting ten days,

METS' YEARLY PITCHING LEADERS

Year	Wins	Losses
1962	Graig, 10–24	Craig, 10–24
1963	Jackson, 13–17	Craig, 5–22
1964	Jackson, 11–16	Stallard, 10–20
1965	Fisher, 8–24	Fisher, 8–24
	Jackson, 8–20	
1966	Fisher, 11–14	Fisher, 11–14
	Ribant, 11–9	
	B. Shaw, 11–10	
1967	Seaver, 16–13	Fisher, 9–18
1968	Koosman, 19–12	Cardwell, 7–13
1969	Seaver, 25–7	Gentry, 13–12
1970	Seaver, 18–12	McAndrew, 10–14
1971	Seaver, 20–10	Ryan, 10–14
1972	Seaver, 21–12	Koosman, 11–12
		Seaver, 21–12
1973	Seaver, 19–10	Matlack, 14–16
1974	Koosman, 15–11	Matlack, 13–15
1975	Seaver, 29–9	Koosman, 14–13
		Tate, 5–13
1976	Koosman, 21–10	Lolich, 8–13
1977	Espinosa, 10–13	Koosman, 8–20
1978	Espinosa, 11–15	Espinosa, 11–15
		Koosman, 3–15
1979	Swan, 14–13	Falcone, 6–14
1980	Bomback, 10–8	Burris, 7–13
1981	Allen, 7–6	Zachry, 7–14
	Zachry, 7–14	
1982	Swan, 11–7	Scott, 7–13
1983	Orosco, 13–7	Torrez, 10–17
1984	Gooden, 17–9	Terrell, 11–12
1985	Gooden, 29–4	Fernandez, 9–9
1986	Ojeda, 18–5	McDowell, 14–9

Carlton came back to throw his last baseball of the season on August 14. He suffered an acute tear of the right elbow. (Willey tried again in 1965, appearing in thirteen games. On May 12, 1965, he was sent to the minors, never to be heard from again.)

There was one humorous incident in 1964's spring training that I recall with delight. It happened during the opening weekend series of exhibition games the Mets played with the Mexico City Reds in Mexico City March 6, 7, and 8.

Stengel and the club were being treated royally by their hosts. On the morning of their final game, the Mets had to pack early and send their luggage ahead. Following the game, upon arrival at the airport, Casey's wife, Edna Stengel, discovered, to the consternation of all, that she had packed her passport in her luggage. When Mexican officials refused to permit her through customs, Casey concurred with their decision.

"If she ain't got no passport she can't go," he said, apparently quite willing to leave his bride of forty-nine years in a foreign country without a passport.

United States embassy officials finally succeeded in persuading the Mexican government to allow Mrs. Stengel to board the Mets' plane.

Despite their usual and normal marital tiffs, Casey and Edna were a loving couple who traveled the world over several times. Casey was always the center of attention and Edna accepted that. He got along with virtually everyone; bartenders and newspapermen in particular doted on him.

Stengel's ability to work with anyone is typified by the many coaching changes he accepted in his three and a half years with the Mets. Weiss, for the most part, picked the coaches. Casey went along with his suggestions.

For the 1962 season, Solly Hemus, Cookie Lavagetto, Rogers Hornsby, Red Kress, and Red Ruffing served as coaches. By 1963, Kress and Hornsby were gone, and Ernie White and Clyde McCullough were added. Hemus, Lavagetto, McCullough, and White were replaced after the 1963 season by Wes Westrum, Don Heffner, Mel Harder, and Sheriff Robinson.

The Westrum-Lavagetto switch had a unique twist. Lavagetto, a longtime Brooklyn favorite and one-time Washington manager, longed to be closer to his Oakland, California, home and expressed that desire to both Stengel and Weiss. It was general knowledge that Lavagetto would leave at the end of the season, perhaps to serve as a West Coast scout for the Mets.

On the eve of the 1963 All-Star game in Cleveland, Stengel and I had closed the press headquarters bar and were on our way back to our hotel around 1 A.M. As we stepped out of a cab, Stengel, out of the corner of his eye, spotted a red neon sign about a block and a half away that simply said "BAR."

1964

NAME	G by POS	B	AGE	G	AB	R	H	2B	3B	HR	RBI	BB	SO	SB	BA	SA
NEW YORK 10th 53-109 .327 40	CASEY STENGEL															
TOTALS			27	163	5566	569	1372	195	31	103	527	353	932	36	.246	.348
Ed Kranepool	1B104, OF6	L	19	119	420	47	108	19	4	10	45	32	50	0	.257	.393
Ron Hunt	2B109, 3B12	R	23	127	475	59	144	19	6	6	42	29	30	6	.303	.406
Roy McMillan	SS111	R	33	113	379	30	80	8	2	1	25	14	16	3	.211	.251
Charley Smith	3B85, SS36, OF13	R	26	127	443	44	106	12	0	20	58	19	101	2	.239	.402
Joe Christopher	OF145	R	28	154	543	78	163	26	8	16	76	48	92	6	.300	.466
Jim Hickman	OF113, 3B1	R	27	139	409	48	105	14	1	11	57	36	90	0	.257	.377
George Altman	OF109	L	31	124	422	48	97	14	1	9	47	18	70	4	.230	.332
Jesse Gonder	C97	L	28	131	341	28	92	11	1	7	35	29	65	0	.270	.370
Rod Kanehl	2B34, OF25, 3B19, 1B2	R	30	98	254	25	59	7	1	1	11	7	18	3	.232	.280
Hawk Taylor	C45, OF16	R	25	92	225	20	54	8	0	4	23	8	33	1	.240	.329
Larry Elliott	OF63	L	26	80	224	27	51	8	0	9	22	28	55	1	.228	.384
Frank Thomas	OF31, 1B19, 3B2	R	35	60	197	19	50	6	1	3	19	10	29	1	.254	.340
Chris Cannizzaro	C53	R	26	60	164	11	51	10	0	0	10	14	28	0	.311	.372
Bobby Klaus	3B28, 2B25, SS5	R	26	56	209	25	51	8	3	2	11	25	30	3	.244	.340
Amado Samuel	SS34, 3B17, 2B3	R	25	53	142	7	33	7	0	0	5	4	24	0	.232	.282
Dick Smith	1B18, OF13	R	25	46	94	14	21	6	1	0	3	1	29	6	.223	.309
Tim Harkness	1B32	L	26	39	117	11	33	2	1	2	13	9	18	1	.282	.368
Johnny Stephenson	3B14, OF8	L	23	37	57	2	9	0	1	1	2	4	18	0	.158	.211
Wayne Graham	3B11	R	27	20	33	1	3	1	0	0	0	0	5	0	.091	.121
Al Moran	SS15, 3B1	R	25	16	22	2	5	0	0	0	4	2	2	0	.227	.227
Larry Burright	2B3	R	26	3	7	0	0	0	0	0	0	0	0	0	.000	.000

NAME	T	AGE	W	L	PCT	SV	G	GS	CG	IP	H	BB	SO	ShO	ERA
		26	53	109	.327	15	163	163	40	1439	1511	466	717	10	4.25
Al Jackson	L	28	11	16	.407	1	40	31	11	213	229	60	112	3	4.27
Jack Fisher	R	25	10	17	.370	0	40	34	8	228	256	56	115	1	4.22
Tracy Stallard	R	26	10	20	.333	0	36	34	11	226	213	73	118	2	3.78
Galen Cisco	R	28	6	19	.240	0	36	25	5	192	182	54	78	2	3.61
Larry Bearnarth	R	22	5	5	.500	3	44	1	0	78	79	38	31	0	4.15
Willard Hunter	L	30	3	3	.500	5	41	0	0	49	54	9	22	0	4.41
Bill Wakefield	R	23	3	5	.375	2	62	4	0	120	103	61	61	0	3.60
Frank Lary	R	34	2	3	.400	1	13	8	3	57	62	14	27	1	4.58
Ron Locke	L	22	1	2	.333	0	25	3	0	41	46	22	17	0	3.51
Tom Parsons	R	24	1	2	.333	0	4	2	1	19	20	6	10	0	4.26
Dennis Ribant	R	22	1	5	.167	1	14	7	1	58	65	9	35	1	5.12
Gary Kroll	R	22	0	1	.000	0	8	2	0	22	19	15	24	0	4.09
Craig Anderson	R	26	0	1	.000	0	4	1	0	13	21	3	5	0	5.54
Jay Hook	R	27	0	1	.000	0	3	2	0	10	17	7	5	0	9.00
Carl Willey	R	33	0	2	.000	0	14	3	0	30	37	8	14	0	3.60
Jerry Hinsley	R	20	0	2	.000	0	9	2	0	15	21	7	11	0	8.40
Ed Bauta	R	29	0	2	.000	1	8	0	0	10	17	3	9	0	5.40
Darrell Sutherland	R	22	0	3	.000	0	10	4	0	27	32	12	9	0	7.67
Tom Sturdivant	R	34	0	0	.000	1	16	0	0	29	34	7	18	0	5.90
Steve Dillon	L	21	0	0	.000	0	3	4	2	3	4	2	1	0	9.00

"There's one still open—let's go," Stengel said as he handed the cabbie a five-dollar bill and started for the bar.

The two of us continued to talk baseball in the little neighborhood-type bar, a couple of blocks off Lake Erie. Seated down at the opposite end of the long bar was Westrum, then a San Francisco Giants coach.

Familiar with Westrum from his days as a New York Giants catcher, I walked down to his end of the bar and said hello. Then I invited him to join Stengel and me at the other end. Bashful and reluctant at first, Westrum finally acquiesced, and soon he and Stengel were deep in baseball conversation. I left them a little after 2 A.M., and Westrum told me the next day that they had remained until closing.

That winter, Stengel, Weiss, and Giants owner Horace Stoneham arranged a swap. Lavagetto became a coach for the Giants and Westrum joined the Mets as a coach. Stengel revealed in later conversations that, although he knew Westrum as a fine defensive catcher from his old Giants days in New York, he was unaware of Westrum's keen baseball knowledge until that night in the Cleveland bar. A year later, when Casey broke his hip in a fall, Westrum was the coach he handpicked to fill in for and eventually replace him as manager.

As the 1964 season progressed, it was again obvious the Mets were destined for another cellar finish. They settled into tenth place for good on April 23, when Tracy Stallard lost a 5–1 decision to Dick Ellsworth of the Chicago Cubs. They never got out of the basement again. At the All-Star break in July, after being shut out, 5–0, by the Dodgers' Sandy Koufax, they were twenty-seven games out of first place.

In connection with the opening of Shea Stadium and as an added attraction to the World's Fair, the Mets hosted the All-Star game in 1964. The only Met to appear in the game was Ron Hunt, who had been voted to the starting lineup as the second baseman. A crowd of 50,844 attended the gala event played on a warm, sunny afternoon. Hunt kept the Mets fans happy with a single in one of his three trips to bat. And Johnny Callison of the Phillies made the day a complete success for the National League with a three-run home run in the bottom of the ninth off Dick Radatz, to give the senior circuit a come-from-behind 7–4 victory. That game tied the All-Star series at seventeen victories for each league and was the beginning of the National League's dominance in the midsummer classic.

Shea Stadium was the scene of two other memorable events in its infant season.

First, there was the incredible doubleheader that lasted nearly ten hours, played on May 31, the official celebration of Memorial Day. Three weeks later, on June 21, Father's Day, Jim Bunning of Philadelphia pitched a perfect game. It was the second time in their first three years that the Mets were victims of a no-hitter.

The May 31 marathon doubleheader was the longest doubleheader in major league history. The first game of the Sunday twin bill, which the San Francisco Giants won, 5–3, in a routine nine innings, started at 1:08 P.M. The second game, which took twenty-three innings to complete, ended at 11:25 P.M. The official playing time for the two games was nine hours and fifty-two minutes. There were 57,037 fans on hand at the start of the doubleheader. Barely 15,000 were left when the final out was recorded thirty-five minutes before midnight. The Giants also won that game, 8–6.

Several noteworthy events took place in the Memorial Day doubleheader.

The Giants and Mets played thirty-two innings of baseball, a one-day major league record. Twenty-two dozen baseballs were used. The Harry M. Stevens concessionaires ran out of hot dogs. Roy McMillan, playing shortstop for the Mets, speared a line drive in the fourteenth inning and turned it into a triple play. Bobby Bolin, the Giants' beanpole pitcher, blew a 6–1 lead in the sixth inning that sent the game into extra innings.

NEW YORK METS AT CHICAGO CUBS
(May 26, 1964)

New York

	AB	R	H	RBI
D. Smith, 1b	6	3	5	2
Hunt, 2b	5	2	4	1
Thomas, lf	5	3	2	1
Stephenson, lf	0	0	0	0
Hickman, cf	5	3	3	3
Christopher, rf	5	2	1	2
C. Smith, 3b	6	2	3	5
McMillan, ss	5	1	2	1
Samuel, ss	1	0	0	0
Cannizzaro, c	5	2	2	1
Fisher, p	6	1	1	1
Totals	49	19	23	17

Chicago

	AB	R	H	RBI
Stewart, 2b	4	0	0	0
Brock, rf	4	0	0	0
Williams, lf	4	0	1	0
Santo, 3b	4	0	1	0
Banks, 1b	3	1	1	0
Rodgers, ss	3	0	0	0
Ranew, c	3	0	0	0
Cowan, cf	3	0	1	1
Buhl, p	0	0	0	0
Schurr, p	0	0	0	0
Burton[a]	0	0	0	0
Slaughter, p	0	0	0	0
Amalfitano[b]	1	0	0	0
Hobbie, p	0	0	0	0
Spring, p	0	0	0	0
Burke[c]	1	0	0	0
Elston, p	0	0	0	0
Totals	30	1	4	1

[a]Walked for Schurr in third, [b]Lined out for Slaughter in fifth, [c]Flied out for Spring in eighth.

Pitching	IP	H	R	ER	BB	SO
Fisher (W, 2–4)	9	4	1	1	1	3
Buhl (L, 4–2)	.1	5	4	4	1	1
Schurr	2.2	3	3	2	0	3
Slaughter	2	6	2	2	0	1
Hobbie	1	4	4	4	1	1
Spring	2	0	0	0	0	0
Elston	1	5	6	6	1	1

2B—Cannizzaro 2, Thomas, Williams, D. Smith. 3B—Christopher, D. Smith. HR—C. Smith. SB—D. Smith. E—Rodgers. PO-A—New York 27-11, Chicago 27-10. DP—McMillan, Hunt, D. Smith; Rodgers, Stewart, Banks. LOB—New York 8, Chicago 3. HP—Hobbie (Cannizzaro); Elston (Christopher). BK—Spring. PB—Ranew. U—Conlan, Harvey, Venzon, Weyer. Time—2:49. Attendance—2,503.

On June 21, Jim Bunning of the Phillies pitched the only perfect game against the Mets (one of six no-hitters the club has suffered). Mets batter John Stephenson struck out on this pitch to complete the pitching masterpiece.
DAILY NEWS

Gaylord Perry, who entered the game in the thirteenth inning and pitched ten innings of shutout ball for the Giants, later admitted it was in this game that he first experimented with a spitball, an illegal pitch that was part of his repertoire for nineteen years.

Willie Mays, the premier center fielder of his time, shifted in extra innings from his outfield spot to shortstop and back to center field.

The Giants used five pitchers with Perry gaining the victory. Galen Cisco, the sixth pitcher employed by Stengel, worked a full nine innings in relief and became the loser in the twenty-third inning. Del Crandall's two-run ground-rule double proved to be the winning hit.

Ed Kranepool, who had been called up from Buffalo to report in time for the Sunday doubleheader, had actually played a Saturday night doubleheader for the minor league club and remained up all night in order to get to Shea Stadium. He then played all thirty-two innings of the Mets' doubleheader against the Giants.

The long day's journey into night created havoc with Sunday night television ratings in New York. If some fans were not already watching the game on their TV sets, hourly news bulletins advised viewers that the game was still in progress. Many immediately switched to WOR-TV, the New York channel carrying the game.

A popular network TV show of that era was "What's My Line?," hosted by John Daly. When Daly came on the air at 10:30 P.M. he made reference to the fact that backstage he had been watching "the most fantastic baseball game I have ever seen." He then told his nationwide audience of the game in progress at Shea Stadium. Immediately, thousands of viewers in the New York tri-state area switched from "What's My Line?" to the Mets game. Network officials later acknowledged that Daly's remarks had lowered the ratings for his own show.

The Bunning perfect game came in the first game of the Father's Day doubleheader and was witnessed by his wife, Mary, and daughter Barbara, the eldest of seven Bunning children. Six years earlier, Bunning had pitched a no-hitter for Detroit against Boston in Boston's Fenway Park. That was the first no-hitter the Red Sox had suffered at home in thirty-two years. In their first year at Shea the Mets were already victims of a no-hitter.

Bunning retired all twenty-seven Mets he faced, striking out pinch hitter Johnny Stephenson to end the game. It was only the eighth perfect game in baseball history and the first in the National League in eighty-four years.

The Mets employed twenty pitchers during the 1964 season. Not one of them had a winning record. The best of the twenty was Al Jackson, who won his eleventh game in a classic duel with the peerless Bob Gibson on October 2 in St. Louis.

The Cardinals were attempting to overtake the staggering Phillies and Cincinnati Reds on the final weekend of the season. But in a Friday night game that opened a weekend series, Jackson outpitched Gibson 1–0, with a five-hit gem.

The Mets put a further crimp in the Cards' pennant plans the next day with a seventeen-hit attack that produced a 15–5 victory. Tom Parsons pitched one-run ball for five and one-third innings, his only win of the year.

But on the final day of the season, trying for a sweep that would possibly eliminate the Cardinals, the Mets lost, 11–5. They managed to knock out Curt Simmons, but Gibson came on in relief to hold them and give St. Louis the National League championship.

On September 29, the day the Mets embarked on their final road trip of the season, Weiss announced that the seventy-four-year-old Stengel would return as manager for another season. There had been a strong anti-Stengel movement for some months. Critics of the Old Man argued that his age was a detriment to a club stressing a youthful movement. Howard Cosell, then a young WABC announcer and never without a large tape recorder strung over his shoulder, was active in the movement. Cosell did a pregame radio show with ex-Dodgers pitcher Ralph Branca and was openly critical of Stengel's strategy.

Alvin Dark and Leo Durocher were two of many named as logical successors to Stengel. Nonetheless Weiss overcame internal and external opposition and succeeded in bringing Stengel back for a fourth year in 1965.

The humor of the fans in response to the 1964 Mets was established early in the season. At the tail end of a fifteen-game road trip in May 1964—a trip in which they won only four games and lost eleven—the Mets went into Chicago and erupted for an incredible nineteen runs in a twenty-three-hit attack against Cubs pitchers that produced a 19–1 victory. Radio and TV broadcasts in New York carried the startling news that the Mets had scored nineteen runs. But one Connecticut fan, catching only the final words of the bulletin, was in a quandary. He called the *Waterbury Republican* to check:

"I just heard that the Mets scored nineteen runs today. Is that right?" he asked the sports department.

"That's right, nineteen runs," he was assured.

"Did they win?" the fan inquired.

JIM BUNNING'S PERFECT GAME VS. METS (July 21, 1964)

Philadelphia

	AB	R	H	RBI
Briggs, cf	4	1	0	0
Herrnstein, 1b	4	0	0	0
Callison, rf	4	1	2	1
Allen, 3b	3	0	1	1
Covington, lf	2	0	0	0
Wine[a], ss	1	1	0	0
T. Taylor, 2b	3	2	1	0
Rojas, ss, lf	3	0	1	0
Triandos, c	4	1	2	2
Bunning, p	4	0	1	2
Totals	32	6	8	6

New York

	AB	R	H	RBI
Hickman, cf	3	0	0	0
Hunt, 2b	3	0	0	0
Kranepool, 1b	3	0	0	0
Christopher, rf	3	0	0	0
Gonder, c	3	0	0	0
R. Taylor, lf	3	0	0	0
C. Smith, ss	3	0	0	0
Samuel, 3b	2	0	0	0
Altman[c]	1	0	0	0
Stallard, p	1	0	0	0
Kanehl[b]	1	0	0	0
Sturdivant, p	0	0	0	0
Stephenson[d]	1	0	0	0
Totals	27	0	0	0

[a]Ran for Covington in sixth. [b]Grounded out for Wakefield in sixth. [c]Struck out for Samuel in ninth. [d]Struck out for Sturdivant in ninth.

Pitching	IP	H	R	ER	W	SO
Bunning (W, 7–2)	9	0	0	0	0	10
Stallard (L, 4–3)	5⅔	7	6	6	4	3
Wakefield	⅓	0	0	0	0	0
Sturdivant	3	1	0	0	0	3

PO-A—Philadelphia 27–7, New York 27–8. LOB—Philadelphia 6, New York 0. 2B—Triandos, Bunning. HR—Callison (10). SH—Herrnstein, Rojas. WP—Stallard. U—Sudol, Pryor, Secory, Burkhart. Time—2:29. Attendance—32,026.

In 1965, after three disastrous seasons, it is time for the Mets to get serious. Before the opening day game at Shea, Casey gives the Mets' starting lineup a pep talk. From left: Billy Cowan (CF), Roy McMillan (SS), Johnny Lewis (RF), Ed Kranepool (1B), Joe Christopher (RF), Charlie Smith (3B), Bobby Klaus (2B), Chris Cannizzaro (C), and Al Jackson (P).

As the Mets entered their fourth season in the National League there were many changes within the organization, and more would follow. Vaughan "Bing" Devine, who had put together the St. Louis team that defeated the Yankees in the 1964 World Series, was brought in as assistant to George Weiss. Devine had resigned from the Cardinals the previous August when he lost the confidence of St. Louis owner Gussie Busch.

Two New York favorites were added to the Mets cast. Eddie Stanky, long a favorite with Brooklyn Dodgers and New York Giants fans and a former manager of the Cardinals, was hired as director of player development. Many sensed that Stanky was waiting in the wings to replace Stengel.

In an even more popular move, the Mets announced on November 17, 1964, that Yogi Berra had been hired to serve as one of Stengel's coaches. Berra had led the Yankees to the pennant in 1964, but the Yankees' general manager, Ralph Houk, and owner Dan Topping were disenchanted with him and gave Berra his walking papers the day after the Series ended. They offered him a token job as a super scout.

On the same day, in St. Louis, Johnny Keane retired after managing the Cardinals to the world's championship. Within the week, the Yankees announced that Keane had been hired to replace Berra. The season was over, but baseball continued to make big headlines.

Berra accepted the Mets' offer in November after mulling over the Yankees' offer. His wife, Carmen, incensed over the treatment he had received from the Yankees, urged Yogi to reject them and join the up-and-coming Mets.

With both Berra and Stanky under contract, the Mets did not lack for potential successors to the seventy-four-year-old Stengel. But when the job did become available, neither one of them was chosen. Westrum was Stengel's handpicked successor, and he became interim manager in July 1965.

When Berra was hired, it was announced he would be a nonplaying coach. One week later, when the Mets purchased forty-three-year-old Warren Spahn from Milwaukee, they gleefully announced that the veteran left-hander would serve as both pitcher and pitching coach. Spahn had won 356 games for the Braves in Boston and Milwaukee but was only 6–13 in 1964. Nevertheless, the Mets felt he had something left.

And the Mets had their fourth pitching coach in four years.

For the first time, in the spring of 1965, there was some hope for the future. For a change, some talented young prospects appeared on the roster, players who in later years would help turn things around at Shea.

One of the young pitchers was Frank "Tug" McGraw, whom Spahn immediately took under his wing. Another promising youngster was Dennis Ribant, obtained from Milwaukee the previous summer in exchange for Frank Lary just two months after the Mets had purchased Lary from the very same club.

Outfielder Cleon Jones, fresh from a .278 season in Buffalo, where he hit sixteen homers, looked solid. Also back for another look was slugger Swoboda, who had hit eighteen home runs in the minors the previous summer. Outfielder Johnny Lewis, obtained from St. Louis for Tracy Stallard, was another strong prospect. In these three the Mets felt they had the makings of a fine young outfield.

They opened the season on a too-familiar note. Al Jackson lost a 6–1 decision to Don Drysdale and the Dodgers at Shea Stadium. In the third game of the season the Mets went ten innings and nipped the Houston club, 5–4, with eighteen-year-old rookie Jim Bethke the winning pitcher in relief. The youth of America theme that Stengel had been ballyhooing for four years was finally bearing fruit. Bethke won one more game in relief a month later, but

6

♦ THE ♦
♦ STENGEL ♦
♦ ERA ♦
♦ ENDS IN A ♦
♦ MEN'S ♦
♦ ROOM ♦

OPENING DAY LINEUP 1965

Cowan, cf
McMillan, ss
Lewis, rf
Kranepool, 1b
Christopher, lf
C. Smith, 3b
Klaus, 2b
Cannizzaro, c
Jackson, p

By 1965 the fans no longer applauded when their lovable Mets looked ridiculous in the field. In this particular comedy of errors, Roy McMillan collides with Chuck Hiller on a pop fly on July 6 as the ball lands safely for a double.

was back in the minors in June, in the Marines in September, never to appear in another game with the Mets. He departed with a perfect 2–0 record.

The first game the Mets won that year was on a home run by Bobby Klaus, a light-hitting second baseman who was filling in for the injured Ron Hunt. Hunt had hurt his right hand playing handball during the winter.

Another early season home run came off the bat of pinch hitter Ron Swoboda in the second game. It was his first major league hit in his second major league at bat. By July 5, Swoboda had fifteen homers and was the new hero of Shea Stadium. He hit only four more in the second half of the season, but his total of nineteen was a record for a Mets rookie. As the club happily pointed out, Swoboda's nineteen homers exceeded the freshman totals of such well-established stars as Mickey Mantle, Roger Maris, and Stan Musial. However, in his nine years in the majors, Swoboda never again hit nineteen in a single season. His next-best year was 1967, when he hit thirteen.

The Mets flirted with a .500 record for a couple of weeks and were 6–7 as late as April 25. They then settled into the same old losing ways, and by the end of April they were again in tenth place. By the middle of June they had lost twice as many games as they had won.

Victories were few and far between, and trips to the West Coast were usually a disaster. The first one in April, however, provided the Mets and their fans with some season highlights.

On April 20, in his second start as a Met, Spahn proved he could still go the route when he bested Claude Osteen of the Dodgers, 3–2, in a tight duel in Dodger Stadium. Spahn had to survive a two-run ninth inning rally; when he got the final out he leaped in the air with joy.

After losing the remaining two games in Los Angeles, the Mets moved up to San Francisco, where they took three out of four from the Giants in an amazing weekend series. The opener on Friday night, April 23, resulted in one of the greatest comebacks in Mets history to that point.

Trailing, 8–2, in the eighth and with Gaylord Perry in apparent control, the

METS' YEAR-BY-YEAR RECORD

Year	W–L	Pct	Pos	GB–A	Manager
1962	40–120	.250	10	60½	Stengel
1963	51–111	.315	10	48½	Stengel
1964	53–109	.327	10	40	Stengel
1965	50–112	.309	10	47	Stengel, Westrum
1966	66–95	.410	9	28½	Westrum
1967	61–101	.377	10	40½	Westrum, Parker
1968	73–89	.451	9	24	Hodges
1969	100–62	.617	1-East	+8	Hodges
1970	83–79	.512	3-East	6	Hodges
1971	83–79	.512	3-East (T)	14	Hodges
1972	83–73	.532	3-East	13½	Berra
1973	82–79	.509	1-East	+1½	Berra
1974	71–91	.438	5-East	17	Berra
1975	82–80	.506	3-East(T)	10½	Berra, McMillan
1976	86–76	.531	3-East	15	Frazier
1977	64–98	.395	6-East	37	Frazier, Torre
1978	66–96	.407	6-East	24	Torre
1979	63–99	.389	6-East	35	Torre
1980	67–95	.414	5-East	24	Torre
1981	41–62	.398	5-East	18½	Torre
1982	65–97	.401	6-East	27	Bamberger
1983	68–94	.420	6-East	22	Bamberger, Howard
1984	90–72	.556	2-East	6½	Johnson
1985	98–64	.605	2-East	3	Johnson
1986	108–54	.667	1-East	+21½	Johnson

Mets narrowed the deficit to 8–4. In the ninth, Ron Swoboda and Jesse Gonder led off with home runs, and suddenly it was 8–6. With some help from a shoddy San Francisco defense, the Mets eventually tied the score. The game continued on into the eleventh inning, when the Mets won it, 9–8, without a base hit. Joe Christopher walked, stole second, went to third on the catcher's throwing error, and scored on Charley Smith's sacrifice fly.

The following day the Mets again staged a comeback, with three runs in the ninth for a 7–6 victory. The winning runs were delivered by Danny Napoleon, a rookie outfielder from Trenton, New Jersey, who had had only one year of minor league experience before joining the Mets. Napoleon slammed a bases-loaded pinch triple to win the game. In the boisterous Mets clubhouse after the game, Stengel could be heard yelling "Vive la France!"

Napoleon was about as French as Stengel, but the name was enough of a connection for Casey. The Old Man always seemed to have a grip on any situation and the quip to fit it.

A young player named Greg Goossen, age twenty, joined the Mets that spring. He was a big, strong catcher who looked like a ballplayer, but Stengel needed only to see him a few times to realize looks are not enough to make a ballplayer. When visiting columnists came into the Mets camp, Casey raved about the young talent on hand. Goossen, of course, had to be included in this assessment.

"And we have this fine young catcher named Goossen who is only twenty years old, who in ten years has a chance . . ." Stengel stopped. For a split second he was stumped. Then he continued in classic Stengelese, ". . . in ten years he has a chance to be thirty."

The Mets completed their big weekend in San Francisco on May 25 by splitting a doubleheader, winning the second game, 4–3. Swoboda was the slugging hero with a double and a home run; Spahn again went nine innings.

At the age of forty-four, "Spahnie" really couldn't cut it anymore for the Mets. Although he showed flashes of his former skill with five complete games, he ended the season with a 4–12 record and a 4.36 ERA.

UPI/BETTMAN NEWSPHOTO

Mets manager for three and a half years, Casey Stengel finally calls it quits on September 2, when management officially retired his uniform number (37).
DAILY NEWS/TOM GALLAGHER

Two days later the Mets made headlines in the New York tabloids when they activated Yogi Berra. It was two years since Berra had last been active as a player with the Yankees, but heeding the pleas of Weiss and Stengel, he reluctantly agreed to return behind the plate.

Berra's debut as a Mets player was as a pinch hitter in Cincinnati on May 1. His first appearance behind the plate was at Shea Stadium on May 4 against Philadelphia. The fans welcomed him warmly, and Yogi responded with two singles in three trips and scored the decisive run in a 2–1 Al Jackson victory.

A week later, on May 11, after explaining to Stengel that he no longer felt comfortable at the plate, Yogi was removed from the active list. He had gone to the plate nine times, delivered two hits, and retired with a .222 batting average. Six years later he was elected to the Baseball Hall of Fame.

On May 10, 1965, Casey, wearing baseball spikes, slipped on a concrete walk outside the dressing room at West Point and fractured his wrist. The Mets were in West Point to play an annual exhibition game, which New York major league clubs had been doing for years. Stengel's critics seized upon the accident as another opportunity to point out that at his age, seventy-four, he was too frail to be managing.

The following night, playing against St. Louis, the Mets suffered an even more damaging blow. Hunt, their scrappy second baseman, dislocated his left shoulder in a collision with Phil Gagliano. He was sidelined for three months. The day after the accident, Weiss purchased Chuck Hiller from San Francisco, where he was batting .143. Hiller's fielding had earned him the nickname of "Iron Hands." He fit right in with the Mets.

The Mets just could not avoid the unusual or the bizarre. They had already been the victims of no-hit games twice in their first three years. In their fourth they were again no-hitted, this time for ten innings. Nevertheless they managed to win the game in the eleventh, and Jim Maloney of the Cincinnati Reds, who had stopped them cold for ten, was the loser. Maloney struck out eighteen batters but lost when Johnny Lewis homered over the center field fence in the eleventh.

That 1–0 victory was the Mets' only win in a sixteen-game stretch.

One month after they had been no-hitted for ten innings by Maloney, the Mets came the closest ever to having a no-hit game of their own. On July 21 in Pittsburgh, little Alvin Jackson, who had won only four games while losing a dozen, held the Pirates hitless for seven and one-third innings before Willie Stargell singled to end the spell. It was the longest stretch any Mets pitcher had held another team hitless. Jackson wound up with a two-hitter and the Mets with a 1–0 victory.

The Mets had gala plans for the weekend of July 24–25. Not only would they stage their annual Oldtimers' Day, at which former stars of the game were invited back for an afternoon of nostalgia, but they also would celebrate Stengel's upcoming seventy-fifth birthday. Because the Mets would be on the road on Stengel's actual birthday date, July 30, the party was to be held as part of the Oldtimers' Day celebration. Promotion director Arthur Richman and public relations director Harold Weissman put together a stunning show.

The party was set for Sunday, July 25; the night before, a party welcoming the "Oldtimers" was held at Toots Shor's restaurant in Manhattan. It was a gala evening. At the end of the festivities, Stengel was persuaded by club comptroller Joseph DeGregorio to spend the night at his home in Beechhurst so he would be near the ballpark the next morning.

Stengel never made it to the ballpark the next day. To this day the real story has never emerged. But somehow—either on a fall he took in the men's room at Toots Shor's or later getting in or out of DeGregorio's car—Stengel fractured his hip. He wound up in the hospital. He had managed his last game and left with a Mets career record of 175–404. But if he did not win many games, Casey did draw headlines and fans for the club, and the owners prospered as a result of his humor and 'round-the-clock campaigning on the Mets' behalf.

Newly acquired second baseman Chuck Hiller (taking over for injured Ron Hunt) signs Casey's cast while Yogi Berra helps out. Hiller had a so-so year with a .238 batting average and twenty-one RBIs.
DAILY NEWS/CHARLES HOFF

1965

NAME	G by POS	B	AGE	G	AB	R	H	2B	3B	HR	RBI	BB	SO	SB	BA	SA
NEW YORK 10th 50-112 .309 47					CASEY STENGEL 31-64 .326			WES WESTRUM 19-48 .284								
TOTALS			27	164	5441	495	1202	203	27	107	460	392	1129	28	.221	.327
Ed Kranepool	1B147	L	20	153	525	44	133	24	4	10	53	39	71	1	.253	.371
Chuck Hiller	2B80, OF4, 3B2	L	30	100	286	24	68	11	1	5	21	14	24	1	.238	.336
Roy McMillan	SS153	R	34	157	528	44	128	19	2	1	42	24	60	1	.242	.292
Charley Smith	3B131, SS6, 2B1	R	27	135	499	49	122	20	3	16	62	17	123	2	.244	.393
Johnny Lewis	OF142	L	25	148	477	64	117	15	3	15	45	59	117	4	.245	.384
Jim Hickman	OF91, 1B30, 3B14	R	28	141	369	32	87	18	0	15	40	27	76	3	.236	.407
Ron Swoboda	OF112	R	21	135	399	52	91	15	3	19	50	33	102	2	.228	.424
Chris Cannizzaro	C112	R	27	114	251	17	46	8	2	0	7	28	60	0	.183	.231
Joe Christopher	OF112	R	29	148	437	38	109	18	3	5	40	35	82	4	.249	.339
Bobby Klaus	2B72, SS28, 3B25	R	27	119	288	30	55	12	0	2	12	45	49	1	.191	.253
Billy Cowan	OF61, 2B2, SS1	R	26	82	156	16	28	8	2	3	9	4	45	3	.179	.314
Danny Napoleon	OF15, 3B7	R	23	68	97	5	14	1	1	0	7	8	23	0	.144	.175
Johnny Stephenson	C47, OF2	L	24	62	121	9	26	5	0	4	15	8	19	0	.215	.355
Ron Hunt	2B46, 3B6	R	24	57	196	21	47	12	1	1	10	14	19	2	.240	.327
Jesse Gonder	C31	L	29	53	105	6	25	4	0	4	9	11	20	0	.238	.390
Gary Kolb	OF29, 1B1, 3B1	L	25	40	90	8	15	2	0	1	7	3	28	3	.167	.222
Cleon Jones	OF23	R	22	30	74	2	11	1	0	1	9	2	23	1	.149	.203
Hawk Taylor	C15, 1B1	R	26	25	46	5	7	0	0	4	10	1	8	0	.152	.413
Jimmie Schaffer	C21	R	29	24	37	0	5	2	0	0	1	1	15	0	.135	.189
Bud Harrelson	SS18	R	21	19	37	3	4	1	1	0	2	2	11	0	.108	.189
Greg Goossen	C8	R	19	11	31	2	9	0	0	1	2	1	5	0	.290	.387
Kevin Collins	3B7, SS3	L	18	11	23	3	4	1	0	0	0	1	9	0	.174	.217
Yogi Berra	C2	L	40	4	9	1	2	0	0	0	0	0	3	0	.222	.222

NAME	T	AGE	W	L	PCT	SV	G	GS	CG	IP	H	BB	SO	ShO	ERA
		26	50	112	.309	14	164	164	29	1455	1462	498	776	11	4.06
Al Jackson	L	29	8	20	.286	1	37	31	7	205	217	61	120	3	4.35
Jack Fisher	R	26	8	24	.250	1	43	36	10	254	252	68	116	0	3.93
Gary Kroll	R	23	6	6	.500	1	32	11	1	87	83	41	62	0	4.45
Galen Cisco	R	29	4	8	.333	0	35	17	1	112	119	51	58	1	4.50
Warren Spahn	L	44	4	12	.250	0	20	19	5	126	140	35	56	0	4.36
Darrell Sutherland	R	23	3	1	.750	0	18	2	0	48	33	17	16	0	2.81
Larry Bearnarth	R	23	3	5	.375	1	40	3	0	61	75	28	16	0	4.57
Jim Bethke	R	18	2	0	1.000	0	25	0	0	40	41	22	19	0	4.28
Dick Selma	R	21	2	1	.667	0	4	4	1	27	22	9	26	1	3.67
Gordie Richardson	L	25	2	2	.500	2	35	0	0	52	41	16	43	0	3.81
Tug McGraw	L	20	2	7	.222	1	37	9	2	98	88	48	57	0	3.31
Dave Eilers	R	28	1	1	.500	2	11	0	0	18	20	4	9	0	4.00
Carl Willey	R	34	1	2	.333	0	13	3	1	28	30	15	13	0	4.18
Dennis Ribant	R	23	1	3	.250	3	19	1	0	35	29	6	13	0	3.86
Frank Lary	R	35	1	3	.250	1	14	7	0	57	48	16	23	0	3.00
Larry Miller	L	28	1	4	.200	0	28	5	0	57	66	25	36	0	5.05
Tom Parsons	R	25	1	10	.091	1	35	11	1	91	108	17	58	1	4.65
Bob Moorhead	R	27	0	1	.000	0	9	0	0	14	16	5	5	0	4.50
Rob Gardner	L	20	0	2	.000	0	5	4	0	28	23	7	19	0	3.21
Dennis Musgraves	R	21	0	0	.000	0	5	1	0	16	11	7	11	0	0.56

Yogi Berra comes out of retirement for a brief fling with the Mets. Shown here striking out against the Braves in May, his career stats with the Mets didn't compare favorably to those he compiled with the Yankees. In the two games that he started, he batted nine times, had two hits, and struck out three times.
UPI/BETTMAN NEWSPHOTO

Ron Hunt was off to a good season but was hurt badly in a collision with Phil Gagliano of St. Louis on May 11 as he attempted to field a batted ball. This photo, taken on May 17, shows Hunt recovering from a shoulder separation, still tracking the Mets' progress on the radio.
DAILY NEWS/TOM BAFFER

From his hospital bed Casey selected Westrum over Berra to run the club. Westrum had no managerial experience; Berra had those years with the Yankees. Even during Stengel's Yankee years he frequently referred to Yogi as "my assistant manager." Still, as Casey had promised, Westrum got the nod to fill in on an interim basis. Stengel fully expected to return to the dugout when his hip mended.

It became obvious in the weeks that followed that Stengel would not be back. On August 30, five weeks after his fall, Stengel made it official. He was retiring for good, and this time the decision was his.

"I got this limp," he said of his fractured hip, "and if I can't walk out there to take the pitcher out, I can't manage."

On the afternoon of September 2, Stengel appeared at Shea Stadium for the final time. His uniform, number 37, was retired in pregame ceremonies. After a luncheon in the Diamond Club, Stengel watched the first five innings of a game with Houston from a box on the press level. Then he hobbled out of the park, his active baseball career at an end fifty-five years after it had started in Kankakee, Illinois.

Under Westrum for the remainder of the season, the Mets won nineteen and lost forty-eight. They won only seven games in September. On the next to the last day of the season, they played twenty-seven innings against Philadelphia and were scoreless—after losing the opener of a twin bill, 1–0, they played an eighteen-inning scoreless tie in the nightcap.

One historical New York triumph that should not be overlooked came on the night of August 26, 1965, at Shea Stadium when, in a David-and-Goliath match, Tug McGraw, just eight days shy of his twenty-first birthday, out-pitched the great Sandy Koufax.

Koufax was one of those overwhelmingly talented pitchers who, along with Juan Marichal, Larry Jackson, Don Drysdale, and Bob Friend, delighted in beating up on the Mets. Koufax had whipped the Mets thirteen times in succession when he went against McGraw, who up to then had only one win in his brief major league career. Seven and two-thirds innings of outstanding pitching allowed Tug to be the giant killer. He became the first Mets pitcher to beat Koufax (5–2).

During the early years, great attention was paid to certain particular accomplishments, as opposed to major feats, such as winning the pennant. One such victory came the day the Mets first beat Sandy Koufax, who was then the best pitcher in baseball. On August 28 at Shea, Tug McGraw picked up the victory and is congratulated by teammates Joe Christopher *(left)* and Ron Swoboda *(right),* who hit back-to-back home runs in the 5–2 victory.
UPI/BETTMAN NEWSPHOTO

Though McGraw thought he had the world by the tail after that win, he didn't win another game that year, dropping his last five decisions before entering the Marine Corps on September 23.

Tug had signed with the Mets because his older brother, Hank, whom he idolized, had signed with them earlier for a $15,000 bonus. Hank was a catching prospect who never made it. The Mets first saw Tug soon after Roy Partee came to scout Hank. Tug signed for $7,000 and immediately used the money to buy a new car.

"I was originally an outfielder, but one day they had no one else to pitch so I pitched," Tug recalled. "That was in my junior year in high school. I had a nice, slow curve and I could get it over, and that was what the scouts liked about me."

In his later years, McGraw threw hard and also developed a screwball that enabled him to strike out right-handed hitters.

The club's record at the 1965 season's end was 50–112. That was three more losses than they had suffered the previous year. There were almost no signs of progress—Jack Fisher lost twenty-four games and Jackson lost twenty. No pitcher on the team won more than eight games.

After four full seasons the Mets had lost 452 games, entitling them to a solid hold on last place in each of those years.

Ken Boyer, the former all-star with the Cardinals, played 130 games at third base for the Mets and batted .266 and led the team in RBIs with sixty-one. In this shot, Boyer, also known for his fielding, makes a spectacular bare-handed catch on the railing against his former teammates at Shea on August 7.

The Stengel era was over but Weiss refused to retire. Exercising an option clause in his contract, Weiss insisted on remaining as president for another year. He had operated baseball clubs for a half century and it was not easy for him to quit. This only made the situation embarrassing for Devine, who had come over from St. Louis expecting to replace Weiss at the start of the 1966 season. Instead, Der Bingle, as he was known to the baseball press, had to remain in the wings as Weiss's assistant.

Under Westrum in 1966, the Mets showed their first signs of improvement, slight though it was. They won a club high of 66 games and, for the first time in their brief history, did not lose 100. They even beat out the long-established Chicago Cubs and finished in ninth place.

Westrum was not a popular choice to manage the club. Some members of the board of directors felt they needed a bigger name. But Weiss backed Wes, so the quiet, self-effacing man remained. All things considered, Westrum did a fine job that year.

Westrum was not a learned man, and he was frequently guilty of malapropisms that the press delighted in reporting.

One evening Casey Stengel had been regaling the boys in the press room for more than an hour with humorous stories. Westrum just sat and listened, enjoying the anecdotes along with everyone else. When Casey finally departed, Westrum sat shaking his head.

"Boy, when they made him they threw away the molding," Westrum remarked of Stengel.

In the first exhibition game of the 1966 season, Westrum's first full year at the helm, the Mets and Cardinals battled back and forth before the Mets finally won in extra innings.

"Whew! That was a real cliffdweller!" Westrum exclaimed to reporters as they trooped into his office.

Nineteen sixty-six was a year in which the Mets began to bring along some of the young players they had developed in their farm system or obtained in trades. One who benefited greatly from Westrum's guidance was Jerry Grote, a young catcher previously obtained from the Houston club in exchange for Tom Parsons and "cash." It later turned out that pitcher Gary Kroll was also part of the deal. (Weiss would never admit it because that made it appear he was giving up two players for one, but Houston officials readily admitted the deal was Grote for Parsons and Kroll.) Parsons, incidentally, was the last pitcher ever to start a game managed by Stengel. Parsons lasted only five innings in the July 24, 1965, game and was the losing pitcher.

Even though Weiss was unwilling to admit to the two-for-one swap with Houston, it eventually proved to be one of his best deals. Grote became an outstanding defensive catcher for the Mets for a dozen years. Not only was he a workhorse, but pitchers like Tom Seaver and Jerry Koosman praised him as "the best catcher" they ever worked with. Grote was the number 1 catcher almost his entire career with the Mets and caught for the two pennant teams in 1969 and 1973. Jerry had an irritating personality, but no one denied he could catch. Of all the players who appeared in a Mets uniform, no one had a more chameleonlike personality. He was a handsome Texan out of San Antonio who could charm you one moment and have you wanting to choke him the next. His teammates, whether they liked him or not, got along with him on his terms. It was only because he was such a tremendous defensive catcher, with a macho approach to the game, that he earned their respect in the clubhouse.

Grote intimidated the young pitchers on the staff, and they feared his trips to the mound. He would come out and chew them up and down whenever he didn't like what they threw or the way they were throwing. Only Seaver and Koosman refused to be intimidated.

Young Tom Seaver, in his rookie season, looks deflated after suffering a difficult loss on June 24 against the Phillies, 6–5, on a three-run homer by Richie Allen in the late innings. However, Seaver rebounded nicely with a season record of 16–13, 170 strikeouts, 2 shutouts, and a tidy 2.76 ERA.
DAILY NEWS/DANNY FARRELL

OPENING DAY LINEUP 1966

Jones, rf
Hunt, 2b
Boyer, 3b
Stuart, 1b
Hickman, cf
Swoboda, lf
Grote, c
McMillan, ss
Fisher, p

Grote learned early that Seaver in particular would not tolerate his bullying tactics. Grote had already established himself as the regular catcher in early 1966. Seaver was a rookie in 1967. In one early game that season, Grote called for a pitch and Seaver shook him off. Grote put his fingers down for the same pitch again, and again Seaver shook him off. Grote stormed to the mound demanding to know why Seaver would not throw the pitch he was calling for.

"Because I'm the pitcher and I'm going to be responsible for what happens after I throw it," Seaver admonished him. "I'll throw the pitch I want to throw."

Grote turned tail and retreated to his position behind the plate. He had met his match. Seaver never again had trouble with him. In later years, Tom praised Grote as the best defensive catcher he had ever worked with. But they worked together on Tom's terms, not Jerry's.

Grote's life was never easy. His first two marriages ended in divorce. Later he put almost all his money into the cattle business only to watch it disappear without a trace. In 1985 he managed two teams in the Detroit Tigers farm system; he was released at the end of the season because the Tigers did not care for the way he handled their young players.

Westrum's strategy in spring training 1966 was to convince the Mets they really were better. His theme all spring was motivation. Along this line, he posted signs throughout the clubhouse—in the shower room, and on the bulletin boards. "If you think you can, you can," the signs read. How much Westrum really believed that became evident to the writers in the annual spring training pool.

Every year, since 1962, I had conducted a spring training pool based on the team's exhibition record. Writers, broadcasters, club officials, and the manager and coaches put up $1 each and made their predictions. The pool was worth about $40. It was a fun thing.

After weeks of posting his "You can if you think you can" signs, Westrum made his prediction on the eve of the first exhibition game. He picked the team to play .500 ball—fourteen wins and fourteen losses. In other words, to break even. Mediocrity.

So much for motivation.

Westrum did have some new players to work with his first year. Veteran third baseman Ken Boyer had been obtained from St. Louis and shortstop Ed Bressoud from Boston. Four years earlier, Bressoud had been Houston's first pick in the original expansion draft. Another veteran, pitcher Jack Hamilton, was obtained from Detroit in a cash deal. Hamilton, a jovial fellow, admitted he threw the spitball. He was the pitcher who accidentally ended the career of Boston Red Sox star Tony Conigliaro when one of his pitches sailed in and hit Conigliaro in the head.

There were two incidents in spring training that year you will not find in any record book but which are part of the Mets' zany history. One involved Westrum, the other a pitcher named Dave Eilers.

Eilers had been obtained on waivers from Milwaukee late in the 1965 season. He had won one and lost one with the Mets and was trying to retain a spot on the roster. In an exhibition game in Clearwater against the Phillies in March, Eilers appeared in relief in the middle innings. It is the custom in spring training for pitchers to run in the outfield after they finish pitching. So when Eilers left at the end of the seventh, pitching coach Harvey Haddix—the fifth pitching coach in six years—told Eilers to "run in the outfield until the game's over." Haddix presumed it would be over in two innings.

But the Mets and Phillies played an extra-innings game that day that lasted fifteen innings. In the bottom of the fifteenth—dutifully obeying his coach's orders—a nearly exhausted Eilers was still running in the outfield. Eilers' protruding ears had already earned him the nickname "Dumbo" from his teammates. The incident in Clearwater gave new meaning to the nickname.

The incident concerning Westrum also involved public relations director Harold Weissman, his wife, Helen, and their French poodle, "Scoops." The Weissmans, childless, treated the poodle like a member of the family.

Around the swimming pool at the Colonial Inn one afternoon, another dog barked and snapped at Scoops. Helen Weissman feared her "baby" had been bitten, or at least scratched. She called for a local veterinarian to pay a house call to examine Scoops.

That same day, Westrum, who suffered from gout, was felled by an attack in his big toe and went right from practice to bed.

Some time later, the veterinarian called by Helen Weissman arrived at the Colonial Inn, picked up a house phone in the lobby, and asked for "Weissman's room." The switchboard operator, thinking he had said "Westrum's room," connected him with the Mets' new manager.

When Westrum answered the phone he heard a "doctor" at the other end inquiring "What's wrong with your dog?"

"Oh, Doc, my dogs are really killing me. Come right up," Westrum said.

It wasn't until the veterinarian got to Westrum's room that he realized he was being asked to examine the manager's gout-swollen toe rather than the Weissmans' poodle.

The Mets lost only the opener at the start of the 1966 season and then won two in a row. But after flirting with seventh and eighth place for a month and playing close to .500 ball, they settled into ninth place on May 25th and never got any higher. Nor any lower, either. For the first time in their history, the Mets were free of tenth place.

There was a blend of youth and age that season, and there were some encouraging signs. Cleon Jones established himself in the outfield and batted .274. Ed Kranepool hit sixteen home runs to lead the club. The aging Ken Boyer batted .266, hit fourteen homers, and led the club with sixty-one RBIs.

The biggest improvement was in the pitching. For the first time in five years, no one lost twenty games. Jack Fisher was the big loser, with fourteen. But Fisher, Dennis Ribant, and Bob Shaw, a June acquisition for cash from San Francisco, each won eleven games. Shaw actually posted a winning 11–10 record, a new plateau for a Mets starter.

By the time the 1967 season rolled around, Weiss had finally been retired and replaced by Devine. That Bing's tenure would be only temporary was obvious from the start. He didn't even bother to move his family to New York. He lived at the New York Hilton and commuted to St. Louis on weekends.

But in the one year he was at the switch, Bing rarely let a day go by without making some move. As a result, in 1967 the Mets used a record twenty-seven pitchers and twenty-seven position players. Two decades later, the fifty-four players employed by the Mets that one year under Devine was still a National League record.

There was, however, among the twenty-seven pitchers employed that season, one who would soon turn the franchise around. He came to the Mets out of a hat; no magician ever pulled out a bigger prize.

George Thomas Seaver was his name. In later years he would become

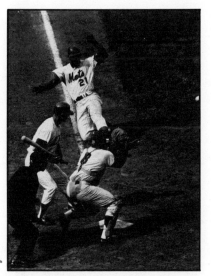

The brightest aspect of the 1966 season was the emergence of Cleon Jones, a hot prospect up from the Mets organization. In this shot, taken on June 5, the daring Jones tries to steal home against the Dodgers but is tagged out by John Roseboro as Roy McMillan steps out of the way.
DAILY NEWS/FRANK HURLEY

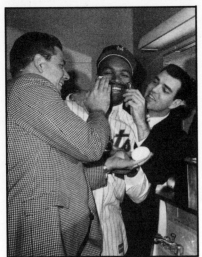

By way of welcoming him to the Mets, pitcher Jack Fisher (*left*) and first baseman Ed Kranepool try to shave off Tommy Davis's newly acquired moustache at the Shea Stadium locker room on December 15, 1966. Davis came to the Mets from L.A., where he'd won a few batting titles, in exchange for the very popular Ron Hunt.

UPI/BETTMAN NEWSPHOTO

known as "Tom Terrific" and "the Franchise." He was the first pitcher in the club's infant years to give promise of brighter days ahead.

Seaver was out of Fresno, California, and had attended the University of Southern California after serving briefly in the Marine Corps. The Dodgers had drafted him, but he preferred to remain in college. In January 1966, after selecting him in the special phase of the free agent draft, the Milwaukee/Atlanta Braves signed Seaver to a $50,000 bonus contract. The contract later was voided because it violated the college rule. According to the whistle-blowers—believed to be the Dodgers—Seaver's college team had already begun its season. In reality, what USC had done was play an exhibition game or two with a Marine Corps team. But the complaining team carried enough weight for Baseball Commissioner William D. Eckert—in the first year of his brief reign—to declare Seaver a free agent.

Actually, Eckert had little choice. Seaver's father, a prosperous California businessman and former member of golfing's Walker Cup team, had threatened to sue major league baseball if his son was denied the start of his professional career. Having signed a professional contract, Seaver was no longer eligible for college ball. And under the decision voiding his Braves contract, he would be unable to sign with another club for six months. The elder Seaver argued that his son had to be one or the other—a collegian or a professional starting on his career.

So Commissioner Eckert held a special drawing. He sent telegrams to all clubs advising them that Seaver was up for grabs to anyone willing to match the Braves' $50,000 bonus. Only three clubs responded—the Mets, Philadelphia, and Cleveland. On Sunday, April 3, Commissioner Eckert stuck his hand in the hat of Joe Reichler, his assistant, and pulled out the paper with the Mets' name on it. That afternoon, scout Nelson Burbrink signed Seaver, and the following season Tom joined the Mets; he was the number 2 starter on the staff right from the start.

At the end of the year, Seaver's 16–13 record was the best ever by a Mets pitcher. Tom's talent was immediately recognized around the league, and it came as no surprise when the Baseball Writers Association of America voted him National League Rookie of the Year.

Other young players also gave the promise of better days ahead. On the pitching staff were the talented new hurlers Jerry Koosman and Tug McGraw; in the infield, Bud Harrelson emerged as the shortstop of the future with some brilliant fielding plus a .254 batting average.

But although the young talent from the Mets farm system began to surface,

1966

NAME	G by POS	B	AGE	G	AB	R	H	2B	3B	HR	RBI	BB	SO	SB	BA	SA
NEW YORK 9th 66-95 .410 28.5	WES WESTRUM															
TOTALS			28	161	5371	587	1286	187	35	98	534	446	992	55	.239	.342
Ed Kranepool	1B132, OF11	L	21	146	464	51	118	15	2	16	57	41	66	1	.254	.399
Ron Hunt	2B123, SS1, 3B1	R	25	132	479	63	138	19	2	3	33	41	34	8	.288	.355
Ed Bressoud	SS94, 3B32, 1B9, 2B7	R	34	133	405	48	91	15	5	10	49	47	107	2	.225	.360
Ken Boyer	3B130, 1B2	R	35	136	496	62	132	28	2	14	61	30	64	4	.266	.415
Al Luplow	OF101	L	27	111	334	31	84	9	1	7	31	38	46	2	.251	.347
Cleon Jones	OF129	R	23	139	495	74	136	16	4	8	57	30	62	16	.275	.372
Ron Swoboda	OF97	R	22	112	342	34	76	9	4	8	50	31	76	4	.222	.342
Jerry Grote	C115, 3B2	R	23	120	317	26	75	12	2	3	31	40	81	4	.237	.315
Chuck Hiller	2B45, 3B14, OF9	L	31	108	254	25	71	8	2	2	14	15	22	0	.280	.350
Billy Murphy	OF57	R	22	84	135	15	31	4	1	3	13	7	34	1	.230	.341
Roy McMillan	SS71	R	35	76	220	24	47	9	1	1	12	20	25	1	.214	.277
Larry Elliot	OF54	L	28	65	199	24	49	14	2	5	32	17	46	0	.246	.412
Johnny Lewis	OF49	L	24	65	166	21	32	6	1	5	20	21	43	2	.193	.331
Johnny Stephenson	C52, OF1	L	25	63	143	17	28	1	1	1	11	8	28	0	.196	.238
Jim Hickman	OF45, 1B17	R	29	58	160	15	38	7	0	4	16	13	34	2	.238	.356
Hawk Taylor	C29, 1B13	R	27	53	109	5	19	2	0	3	12	3	19	0	.174	.275
Bud Harrelson	SS29	B	22	33	99	20	22	2	4	0	4	13	23	7	.222	.323
Dick Stuart	1B23	R	33	31	87	7	19	0	0	4	13	9	26	0	.218	.356
Greg Goossen	C11	R	20	13	32	1	6	2	0	1	5	1	11	0	.188	.344
Danny Napoleon	OF10	R	24	12	33	2	7	2	0	0	0	1	10	0	.212	.273
Shaun Fitzmaurice	OF5	R	23	9	13	2	2	0	0	0	0	2	6	1	.154	.154

Choo Choo Coleman 28 L 3-16, Lou Klimchock 26 L 0-5

NAME	T	AGE	W	L	PCT	SV	G	GS	CG	IP	H	BB	SO	ShO	ERA
		26	66	95	.410	22	161	161	37	1427	1497	521	773	9	4.17
Dennis Ribant	R	24	11	9	.550	3	39	26	10	188	184	40	84	1	3.21
Bob Shaw	R	33	11	10	.524	0	26	25	7	168	171	42	104	2	3.91
Jack Fisher	R	27	11	14	.440	0	38	33	10	230	229	54	127	2	3.68
Jack Hamilton	R	27	6	13	.316	13	57	13	3	149	138	88	93	1	3.93
Bob Friend	R	35	5	8	.385	1	22	12	2	86	101	16	30	1	4.40
Dick Selma	R	22	4	6	.400	1	30	7	0	81	84	39	58	0	4.22
Rob Gardner	L	21	4	8	.333	1	41	17	3	134	147	64	74	0	5.10
Bill Hepler	L	20	3	3	.500	0	37	3	0	69	71	51	25	0	3.52
Jerry Arrigo	L	25	3	3	.500	0	17	5	0	43	47	16	28	0	3.77
Darrell Sutherland	R	24	2	0	1.000	1	31	0	0	44	60	25	23	0	4.91
Larry Bearnarth	R	24	2	3	.400	0	29	1	0	55	59	20	27	0	4.42
Tug McGraw	L	21	2	9	.182	0	15	12	1	62	72	25	34	0	5.37
Dave Eilers	R	29	1	1	.500	0	23	0	0	35	39	7	14	0	4.63
Dick Rusteck	L	24	1	2	.333	0	8	3	1	24	24	8	9	1	3.00
Ralph Terry	R	30	0	1	.000	1	11	1	0	25	27	11	14	0	4.68
Nolan Ryan	R	19	0	1	.000	0	2	1	0	3	5	3	6	0	15.00
Gordie Richardson	L	26	0	2	.000	1	15	1	0	19	24	6	15	0	9.00
Larry Miller	L	29	0	2	.000	0	4	1	0	8	9	4	7	0	7.88
Dallas Green	R	31	0	0	.000	0	4	0	0	5	6	2	1	0	5.40

the team's record did not improve. In fact, the Mets of 1967—Westrum's second year—were not as good as they were in 1966. The 1967 team won only 61 and retreated by losing 101. The team also fell back to tenth place.

Seaver was the only starter able to win. Dennis Ribant, the ace of the 1966 staff, had been traded the previous winter by Devine in one of his first "major" deals. It turned out to be a fiasco.

On December 6, 1966, three weeks after he replaced Weiss, Devine sent Ribant and minor leaguer Gary Kolb to Pittsburgh for veteran pitcher Don Cardwell and a highly touted young center fielder named Don Bosch. In the press conference announcing the deal, Devine offered affidavits from other baseball people suggesting Bosch's defensive play would make people forget the great Willie Mays. The Bosch buildup went on all winter and all spring. The kid was likened to every great center fielder who had ever lived by baseball people who saw him in the minors. Bosch's arrival in spring training was eagerly anticipated, not only by Westrum, who had played with Mays and never seen Bosch play, but by the baseball writers, who could not wait to write about this potential superstar.

Bosch was late arriving at camp, which only created more interest when he did arrive. It was explained that Bosch had been forced to quit winter ball because of an illness and that he had gone home to rest before reporting to the Mets.

The morning Bosch finally did arrive, he was immediately surrounded by the large New York press corps. To a young player used to one-man minor league coverage, a dozen New York scribes gathering around your locker can be frightening.

As it turned out, Bosch was a very frightened young man. But it wasn't the baseball writers who frightened him. Bosch, it soon became apparent, was nervous by nature—sensitive and a worrier. He was only twenty-four, but he already had premature gray hair and ulcers. And now, after all the winter buildup and comparisons to Mays and another great center fielder, Curt Flood, Bosch was definitely on the hot seat. He was under the microscope with every play he made.

Westrum stood off to the side and surveyed the scene as reporters flocked around Bosch's locker. He looked at the five-foot eight-inch 160-pounder and shook his head.

"My God, they sent me a midget," he remarked. "He doesn't even look like a ballplayer."

If Bosch had been a take-charge, defensive whiz in the minors, he was far from that in the majors. The Mets learned that in an early exhibition game. Center fielders are, by nature of their position, supposed to catch any ball they can get to. But on one drive to right center, which he could easily have caught, Bosch yelled to the right fielder, "You take it."

Once the season opened, Bosch was a total flop. He was a switch hitter who could not hit from either side of the plate, although he did get the Mets' first base hit of the 1967 season off Bob Veale of Pittsburgh at Shea Stadium on April 11. He also was the first Met to hit a home run right-handed and left-handed, but everything was downhill after that. By June Bosch was no longer with the club. He was sent to Jacksonville to get his act together. It did not help. In the forty-four games he appeared with the Mets, Bosch hit a minuscule .140. In fifty games the following season, the little center fielder hit .171, and in October 1968 he was unloaded to Montreal for cash. He was one of the all-time Mets disappointments.

A week before the ill-fated Bosch trade, on November 29, 1966, after five seasons in which he failed to hit above .257, Jim Hickman was traded along with Ron Hunt to the Dodgers in what at that time was considered a big deal.

Casey gives some advice to his successor, Wes Westrum, in spring training.
DAILY NEWS/BOB OLNEY

BEST CAREER HOME RUNS AGAINST THE METS

Willie Stargell	59
Willie McCovey	48
Henry Aaron	45
Mike Schmidt	43
Willie Mays	38
Billy Williams	34
Dick Allen	33
Tony Perez	30
Joe Torre	30
Jim Wynn	28
Lee May	28

In exchange the Mets were getting Tommy Davis, a Brooklyn boy who had been the National League batting champion in 1962 and 1963. Of course, if he had still had those early-day skills, Davis never would have been traded by the Dodgers.

Davis, besides being an outstanding hitter, had boasted great speed. But on May 1, 1965, he'd fractured his ankle sliding and his skills were diminished forever after. Even with a bad ankle that limited his running, Davis came back to hit .313 in 1966. But the Dodgers would never have traded him if they had felt he could return to his early form. He couldn't. In one season with the Mets, Davis hit .302 with sixteen home runs, but his speed was gone. Inadvertently, Davis did help the Mets win their first pennant. He was the principal figure for the Chicago White Sox in the deal that brought Tommie Agee and Al Weis to the Mets. Davis, Jack Fisher, pitcher Billy Wynne, and minor league catcher Dick Booker were the players the White Sox received in exchange.

James Lucius Hickman was a soft-spoken, slow-talking outfielder from Henning, Tennessee, signed originally by the Cardinals and drafted by the Mets out of the 1961 expansion pool. He was the last player they selected and turned out to be one of the best

Jim was not easily motivated. He once confessed he would be just as happy working in the cotton mills back in Henning. "But the lint keeps getting in my nostrils," he complained.

Jim had talent but was reluctant to push himself to the limit. On September 3, 1965, he hit three home runs off Ray Sadecki of St. Louis, the first Met ever to accomplish that feat. When informed after the game that only a handful of players ever hit four in a game, Hickman replied dryly, "I wish someone had told me. I'd have tried for another."

Casey Stengel and Wes Westrum, who managed Hickman, were driven to distraction by his failure to swing at pitches. It is not recorded officially, but it is generally conceded that Jim Hickman took more third strikes with his bat on his shoulder than any other Met in the period he played for the New York team.

◆　◆　◆

Day in and day out Devine sought to make deals that would improve the club. Players were coming and going in a steady stream. Some did not last long

1967

NAME	G by POS	B	AGE	G	AB	R	H	2B	3B	HR	RBI	BB	SO	SB	BA	SA
NEW YORK 10th 61-101 .377 40.5		WES WESTRUM 57-94 .377			SALTY PARKER 4-7 .364											
TOTALS			27	162	5417	498	1288	178	23	83	461	362	981	58	.238	.325
Ed Kranepool	1B139	L	22	141	469	37	126	17	1	10	54	37	51	0	.269	.373
Jerry Buchek	2B95, 3B17, SS9	R	25	124	411	35	97	11	2	14	41	26	101	3	.236	.375
Bud Harrelson	SS149	B	23	151	540	59	137	16	4	1	28	48	64	12	.254	.304
Ed Charles	3B89	R	32	101	323	32	77	13	2	3	31	24	58	4	.238	.319
Ron Swoboda	OF108, 1B20	R	23	134	449	47	126	17	3	13	53	41	96	3	.281	.419
Cleon Jones	OF115	R	24	129	411	46	101	10	5	5	30	19	57	12	.246	.331
Tommy Davis	OF149, 1B1	R	28	154	577	72	174	32	0	16	73	31	71	9	.302	.440
Jerry Grote	C119	R	24	120	344	25	67	8	0	4	23	14	65	2	.195	.253
Tommie Reynolds	OF72, 3B5, C1	B	25	101	136	16	28	1	0	2	9	11	26	1	.206	.257
Bob Johnson	2B39, 1B23, SS14, 3B1	R	31	90	230	26	80	8	3	5	27	12	29	1	.348	.474
Larry Stahl	OF43	L	26	71	155	9	37	5	0	1	18	8	25	2	.239	.290
John Sullivan	C57	R	26	65	147	4	32	5	0	0	6	6	26	0	.218	.252
Ken Boyer	3B44, 1B8	R	36	56	166	17	39	7	2	3	13	26	22	2	.235	.355
Don Bosch	OF39	B	24	44	93	7	13	0	1	0	2	5	24	3	.140	.161
Al Luplow	OF33	L	28	41	112	11	23	1	0	3	9	8	19	0	.205	.295
Greg Goossen	C23	R	21	37	69	2	11	1	0	0	3	4	26	0	.159	.174
Chuck Hiller	2B14	L	32	25	54	0	5	3	0	0	3	2	11	0	.093	.148
Phil Linz	2B11, SS8, 3B1, OF1	R	28	24	58	8	12	2	0	1	4	4	10	0	.207	.241
Amos Otis	OF16, 3B1	R	20	19	59	6	13	2	0	1	5	1	13	0	.220	.254
Bob Heise	2B12, SS3, 3B2	R	20	16	62	7	20	4	0	3	3	1	6	0	.323	.387
Joe Moock	3B12	L	23	13	40	2	9	2	0	0	5	0	7	0	.225	.275
Hawk Taylor	C12	R	28	13	37	3	9	3	0	0	4	2	8	0	.243	.324
Ken Boswell	2B6, 3B4	L	21	11	40	2	9	3	0	1	4	1	5	0	.225	.375

Johnny Lewis 27 L 4-34, 1 Sandy Alomar 23 B 0-22, Bart Shirley 27 R 0-12, Kevin Collins 20 L 1-10, Ralph Terry 31 R 0-0, Jerry Hinsley 23 R 0-0, Al Schmelz 23 R 0-0

NAME	T	AGE	W	L	PCT	SV	G	GS	CG	IP	H	BB	SO	ShO	ERA
		27	61	101	.377	19	162	162	36	1434	1369	536	893	10	3.73
Tom Seaver	R	22	16	13	.552	0	35	34	18	251	224	78	170	2	2.76
Jack Fisher	R	28	9	18	.333	0	39	30	7	220	251	64	117	1	4.70
Don Cardwell	R	31	5	9	.357	0	26	16	3	118	112	39	71	3	3.58
Don Shaw	L	23	4	5	.444	3	40	0	0	51	40	23	44	0	3.00
Ron Taylor	R	29	4	6	.400	8	50	0	0	73	60	23	46	0	2.34
Hal Reniff	R	28	3	3	.500	4	29	0	0	43	42	23	21	0	3.35
Bob Hendley	L	28	3	3	.500	0	15	13	2	71	65	28	36	0	3.42
Cal Koonce	R	26	3	3	.500	0	11	6	2	45	45	7	24	1	2.80
Bob Shaw	R	34	3	9	.250	0	23	13	3	99	105	28	49	1	4.27
Jack Hamilton	R	28	2	0	1.000	1	17	1	0	31	24	16	22	0	3.77
Les Rohr	L	21	2	1	.667	0	3	3	0	17	13	9	15	0	2.12
Dick Selma	R	23	2	4	.333	2	38	4	0	81	71	36	52	0	2.78
Dennis Bennett	L	27	1	1	.500	0	8	6	0	26	37	7	14	0	5.19
Chuck Estrada	R	29	1	2	.333	0	9	2	0	22	28	17	15	0	9.41
Bill Graham	R	30	1	2	.333	0	5	3	1	27	20	11	14	0	2.67
Danny Frisella	R	21	1	6	.143	0	14	11	0	74	68	33	51	0	3.41
Bill Denehy	R	21	1	7	.125	0	15	8	0	54	51	29	35	0	4.67
Nick Willhite	L	26	0	1	.000	0	4	1	1	8	9	5	9	0	9.00
Jerry Koosman	L	24	0	2	.000	0	9	3	0	22	22	19	11	0	6.14
Jack Lamabe	R	30	0	3	.000	1	16	2	0	32	24	8	23	0	3.94
Tug McGraw	L	22	0	3	.000	0	4	4	0	17	13	13	18	0	7.94
Joe Grzenda	L	30	0	0	.000	0	11	0	0	17	14	8	9	0	2.12
Bill Connors	R	25	0	0	.000	0	6	1	0	13	8	5	13	0	6.23
Billy Wynne	R	23	0	0	.000	0	9	1	0	9	12	2	4	0	3.00

enough for fans even to get to know them. Nick Willhite, a pitcher, was obtained in a deal for Jack Hamilton from California on June 10. Two weeks later he was gone. He had appeared in only four games.

Others had even less exposure. Les Rohr, a big bonus prize, appeared in just three games. Al Schmelz pitched in two. Bill Wynne was in half a dozen. Wayne Graham was one of the many third basemen the Mets used. He appeared in five games.

One of the players Devine obtained that hectic year was Ed Charles, supposedly a washed-up third baseman who came by way of Kansas City. Charles, thirty-four, joined the Mets in early May and remained for three years. He was an integral member of the 1969 World Championship team, sharing third base duties with Wayne Garrett and Bobby Pfeil.

By August, with the team back in tenth place, Westrum worried about his future. A smart baseball man, he knew he was not particularly popular with his bosses upstairs, and he found it difficult to accept the team's poor play on the field. A brutally frank man, he often sat with reporters after a game and discussed the situations that had been played out on the field. When something was particularly bad, he was quick to say, "Oh, my God, wasn't that awful!"

Westrum also suffered from Yogi Berra's presence as one of the coaches he'd inherited. Berra was a soon-to-be-elected Hall of Famer. Yogi was as recognizable as Stengel. Westrum was just another face in the crowd. And he seethed inside over this lack of recognition.

On Saturday afternoon, July 29, the Mets played a rare day game in Los Angeles because they were scheduled for an even rarer doubleheader the following afternoon. Following the game, I was seated at the Hilton Hotel lobby bar along with Westrum and Berra, discussing another tough loss. A patron in the bar recognized Berra and approached him and asked for an autograph "for my son." (Baseball personalities quickly learn that autographs are always for a "son" or "grandson" or "nephew" who is "the world's greatest baseball fan.") Berra, who was seated alongside Westrum, obliged by signing a piece of paper. Then the gentleman inquired of him, "Is the guy next to you anybody?"

It was this kind of indignity and lack of recognition that gnawed at Westrum. One year earlier he had suffered similar embarrassment when Whitey Herzog served as one of the Mets coaches. Herzog was an outgoing personality, a flamboyant third base coach who earned the respect of the fans, the players, and the baseball writers for his willingness to gamble in sending runners home. Writers who found Westrum a dull interview after a game could always go to Herzog, who would have something bright and quotable to offer.

Westrum soon recognized Herzog as a potential threat to replace him. By 1967, Herzog was moved up to the front office as a "special assignment" scout. Herzog later became director of player development and is considered by most baseball men to be the man responsible for putting together the Mets' great farm system.

Herzog, who managed the St. Louis Cardinals to National League championships in 1982 and 1985, might still be in the Mets organization but for being passed over for manager by M. Donald Grant in 1972. Shortly thereafter he voluntarily left the Mets.

By late 1967, Westrum and the fans were getting restless. The Mets were no longer cute. It had been fun early on to root for the inept Marv Throneberry and perennial losers like Roger Craig and Jack Fisher, to dream of Swoboda hitting sixty home runs. But the losing had gone on too long. This was, after all, the Mets' fifth year, and in five years there had been no noticeable improvement.

Westrum waited for the front office to announce he would be retained for the 1968 season. It was not uncommon for a manager to be rehired for another year with only a few weeks left in the schedule. When the Mets failed to give him that reassurance, Westrum walked into Shea Stadium on September 21 and tendered his resignation. With eleven games remaining, Coach Salty Parker was appointed interim manager to handle the club on the final trip to the West Coast. Parker had no more success than his friend Westrum. Under Parker, the Mets won four and lost seven.

Preparations were made to find a permanent successor to Westrum.

When Weiss ran the Mets, he alone made the major decisions. But upon Weiss's retirement, M. Donald Grant began to throw his weight around. Grant had always been the power behind Mrs. Payson, the principal owner, but his influence was not felt strongly until Weiss was out of the picture. Devine, who was happy to have the job, went along with almost everything Grant decreed. That included the naming of the next manager. If Devine had any candidates of his own, they never surfaced. That was because Grant made it known whom he wanted and told Devine to work out the details.

Gil Hodges was Grant's one and only choice, and it was Hodges who led the Mets out of the wilderness and managed them to an incredible World Series win over the heavily favored Baltimore Orioles in 1969. Grant soon discovered that Hodges was not someone he could order around. Winning a World Series made Hodges that much tougher for Grant to handle. Some years later he admitted that he was "afraid" to make certain suggestions to his manager.

Hodges was the perfect choice to manage the Mets. There were the sentimental ties to New York which made him a standout candidate. A Brooklyn Dodgers star of great magnitude on the 1950s teams, he was an Indiana boy who had married a Brooklyn girl, Joan Lombardi, and remained in Brooklyn the year round, both when the Dodgers still were in Brooklyn and long after they had moved to Los Angeles.

One obstacle stood in the way of the Mets' bringing Hodges back to New York to manage. He was under a long-term contract to the Washington Senators—the second team of Senators, born out of American League expansion in 1961. (The original Senators had moved to Minneapolis that year to become the Minnesota Twins.) The Senators were quite happy with the job Hodges had done for them. In his four-plus years at the helm, Hodges had moved the Senators from tenth to a tie for sixth place. He had served his apprenticeship and proved himself among his peers as a sound baseball manager.

When the Washington club at first balked at letting Hodges return to New York, Grant could not understand their posture. The Mets' board chairman acted as if his team had merely "loaned" Hodges to Washington for four years and was entitled to recall him any time they so desired.

Negotiations continued for several weeks before the problem was resolved. Johnny Murphy, a former New York Yankees relief ace and a longtime baseball official, was assistant general manager of the Mets. The Washington general manager was George Selkirk, a former Yankee outfielder and one-time roommate of Murphy. Grant dispatched Murphy to Washington to resolve the problem.

It may never have been settled but for one thing. Hodges was anxious to return to New York. He would abide by the terms of his Washington contract if necessary, but he made it clear that he yearned to return to New York and his family. Managing the Mets would provide him that opportunity.

Details finally were worked out. The Mets would send Washington cash in excess of $100,000—believed to be $150,000—plus pitcher Bill Denehy in exchange for the right to negotiate with Hodges.

Hodges was easy to deal with, especially when the Mets offered him the security of a three-year contract at a salary of $60,000 annually. It was more money than he had ever made as a player.

Because word of Hodges' rejoining the Mets was no longer a secret, the club did not wait long to make the announcement official. On the morning of October 11 in Boston, just hours before the sixth game of the World Series between Boston and St. Louis was to commence, the Mets announced Hodges as their new manager.

8

♦ HODGES ♦

♦ COMES ♦

♦ HOME ♦

OPENING DAY LINEUP 1967

Bosch, cf
Jones, rf
Boyer, 3b
Davis, lf
Swoboda, 1b
Buchek, 2b
Grote, c
Harrelson, ss
Cardwell, p

On December 15, 1968, right after Gil Hodges was named the new manager for the Mets, he relaxed with his drum set at his bowling alley in Brooklyn.

Yogi Berra, rejected a second time as possible manager, was retained as a coach with Hodges' full agreement. But Gil brought with him from Washington his other coaches—pitching coach Rube Walker, third base coach Eddie Yost, and bullpen coach Joe Pignatano. It was a homecoming for all. Besides Hodges, who played and lived in Brooklyn, Walker had been a second-string catcher for the Dodgers. Yost, who spent most of his career in Washington and Detroit, was a New York native from Ozone Park, Long Island. Pignatano, also from Brooklyn, had played briefly with the Dodgers, A's, Giants, and the Mets.

That in itself was a refreshing change—a manager with coaches of his own choosing. Previous managers Stengel and Westrum had been obliged to accept the coaches the front office handed them. Even though Berra was a holdover from the previous regime, Hodges welcomed him. Yogi was no threat and Yogi knew the National League, having served in it for three years as a coach. Hodges and the handpicked aides he brought with him from Washington had only been away from the league for a short time.

On December 5, another major change was made. This time Devine resigned to return to his native St. Louis, where the repentant Cardinals had realized their mistake and brought Bing back as general manager. To succeed Devine, the Mets selected Johnny Murphy, who probably deserved the job in the first place. Murphy was a fastidious individual, a stickler for details, a fine evaluator of talent, and exuded class. He had been in the Mets organization from the first year, knew the players as well as anyone, and had the respect of other baseball professionals. His biggest plus, perhaps, was his willingness to dispute Grant on baseball matters. Grant, a fan, thought he knew baseball as well as the baseball men he hired. He sat in on front office strategy sessions and did not hesitate to express his views. Those views did not always match those of the professionals he hired, but few people were willing to argue with him.

One who did was Whitey Herzog. Whitey snickered at some of Grant's appraisals of players and was not opposed to arguing with the chairman of the board when he disagreed with him. More than once Herzog told Grant he didn't know a hill of beans about baseball. That outspokenness contributed to Herzog's eventually leaving the Mets in 1973 to manage the Texas Rangers.

Devine's departure for St. Louis was considered a blessing in disguise by those who knew Hodges best. If there was one motto Hodges preached, it was stability. When he decided on his twenty-five-man squad in spring training, those were the twenty-five men with whom he would sink or swim during the season. A former Marine platoon leader, Hodges believed in knowing the people with whom he was going and who might have his future in their hands. Hodges could not have tolerated the constant shuffling of personnel that went on during Devine's one year as general manager.

In Hodges' first year as manager, the Mets used only fourteen pitchers and a total of thirty-four players—twenty less than Westrum had handed to him by Devine the previous year. Of course, the quality of Hodges' players was an improvement.

In his first few months as manager, Gil urged the acquisition of certain American League players he knew. One was J. C. Martin, a left-handed hitting catcher who came from the Chicago White Sox in payment for Ken Boyer, who had been dealt to the Sox in late July.

On November 8, 1967, the Mets sent pinch hitting specialist Bob W. Johnson to the Cincinnati Reds for Art Shamsky. Shamsky could play the outfield as well as first base and was the left-handed bat that Gil Hodges wanted on the bench. Although hitting only .238 his first year with the Mets, Shamsky was a key player in the 1969 pennant drive. He batted .300 and hit fourteen home runs. After hitting eleven homers and batting .293 in 1970,

Shamsky tailed off to .185 in 1971 and went to St. Louis in an eight-player deal on October 18.

The deal helped the Mets win another pennant. One of the players obtained was right-handed pitcher Harry Parker, who won eight and lost four for the 1973 champions. Also obtained in the deal was Jim Beauchamp, a useful pinch hitter on the 1973 champs. A shoulder injury incurred years before in the minors finally ended Beauchamp's career in 1973.

But the big deal Hodges had been pushing for came through on December 15, 1967. Desperate for a center fielder and a reserve shortstop who could fill in for Bud Harrelson when he went off to serve his military duty, the Mets obtained outfielder Tommie Agee and infielder Al Weis.

American League Rookie of the Year with the Chicago White Sox in 1966, when he hit twenty-two homers, stole forty-four bases, and knocked in eighty-six runs, Agee had slumped from .273 to .234 and hit only fourteen home runs in 1967. He was ripe to be traded, and Hodges saw in Tommie a player who could fill a huge hole in his outfield. If there was one thing the Mets lacked in their early years—besides a third baseman—it was a center fielder. Now, at last, they had one.

Spring training 1968 was unlike any of the first six under Stengel and Westrum. The lack of talent was obvious in the early years, and frivolity prevailed with Stengel in charge. The Old Man knew you could not mask a loser. Westrum attempted to bring some order to the camp in 1966 with his motivational approach, but that lasted only until people realized that the motivation was being wasted on washed-up veterans or talent-short youngsters.

Under Hodges, it was strictly business. More than one observer likened it to a Marine boot camp, with Hodges the drill sergeant. The one difference was that, unlike Marine drill instructors, Hodges did not yell his commands. He was the quintessential quiet man. An imposing figure, six feet two inches with 210 pounds spread evenly about his huge frame, he had hands about twice the size of most people's. Nevertheless, in his career as an active player he had assumed the role of peacemaker in fights. Obviously, his experiences as a Marine in the South Pacific had left a lasting impression on him.

I recall an afternoon in Louisville, where the Mets were playing a night exhibition, and a group of us including Hodges went to a local movie house to see a picture about Marines in the South Pacific that featured considerable killing. I was seated alongside Hodges in the darkened theater, and every time another Marine or enemy soldier was shot, I could hear him silently mutter "Amen."

Hodges was not given to emotional displays. He held in his anger and his frustration. Whatever he had to say to a player, he said in private. He never, to my knowledge, "chewed out" a player in front of the other players. But woe unto anyone who was called into Gil's office for a reprimand. It may not have been loud but it was thorough, and a player thus summoned would know that he had been chastised.

On the other hand, Hodges had great patience. If a player was willing to work on his faults—and no one dared not—Hodges or his aides would spend hours helping him. Gil was a stickler for details, for doing things the right way. He stressed fundamentals like no one before him. He had played on great Dodgers teams where fundamentals had been stressed by Branch Rickey, and he had learned early that the only way to do anything was to do it right. Some of Hodges' early drills in the Mets camp that first spring became a bore for the players involved. Hodges was planting the seeds that would later bear fruit. Basic baseball, Hodges knew, can often see you through—especially if the talent is a little short.

Although he was all business on the field, Hodges had another side. He enjoyed toying with and teasing the press corps in the rap sessions that followed each workout. He particularly enjoyed putting some young reporter on the spot, but then would just as quickly ease him off it to avoid further embarrassment. Playing games with the press seemed almost an obsession with Hodges.

I'll never forget the time in the spring of 1969 when he was asked for a prediction on how many games the Mets might win. Hodges replied: "Eighty-five, a minimum of eighty-five."

In *The Sporting News*, baseball's national weekly, I wrote that week: "Eighty-five? Did the man really say 85? That's four games over .500—a pace the Mets have never reached—and not more than ten games away from the pennant."

In his book, *The Game of Baseball*, Hodges relates that incident.

"I couldn't resist the urge to have a little fun with Jack, and I mentioned to him that his story was inaccurate. He looked at me like he was just waiting for me to deny that I'd said eighty-five games, but I just said, 'Eighty-five games isn't four games over .500. It's eight games over .500. If we win eighty-five, we'll lose seventy-seven. That's eight games.' "

I looked at him, realized he was in one of his teasing moods, and just said to him, "That's worse."

Hodges loved mind games and riddles. One of his favorite riddles concerned a man accused of murder who showed up in court with his twin brother, admitted the crime, and threw himself on the mercy of the court.

"He was immediately released," Hodges would say. "Why?"

After his audience pondered that for a while without a solution, Hodges supplied the answer.

"The man and his brother were Siamese twins," he explained with a grin. "The court couldn't put the guilty man away without putting the innocent man away as well."

Hodges also was meticulous when it came to dress codes. He insisted his players at all times be perfectly groomed on the field. He would not accept sloppiness. Players frequently enjoy running around with their caps off, especially in the spring. Whenever Hodges saw a player do so he would leave a note on the player's locker room stool. If it happened again, a fine would follow.

Hodges usually communicated in that manner when he fined a player. On the player's stool would be a note that read, "You owe me $25" for whatever the offense might be. Only rarely did he mention fines in front of the entire team.

Pignatano, Gil's closest friend and regarded by members of the press corps as "a soldier in the Hodges family," relates this story.

"Gil once was standing across the street from our hotel when he saw four players getting into a cab about ten minutes before curfew. He waited around about a half hour and the players did not return. The next day in the clubhouse Gil made a little speech and said he knew about some players breaking curfew and he was giving them an opportunity to save money. By the end of the day, he said, he expected checks on his desk for $50 from each of them, and that would be the end of it. But he also said if he didn't get $50 from each, he would hold another meeting the next day and he would name names. The fine also would be double.

"It not only worked"—Piggy giggled—"Gil got more than he expected. When workout was over that day, there were seven checks on his desk, each for $50."

Hodges, incidentally, saved all money collected in fines during the season and at the end of the year donated the money to some worthy charity.

Besides the all-business camp that Hodges operated in the spring of 1968,

METS' RECORD IN ONE-RUN GAMES

Year	W	L
1962	18	39
1963	21	29
1964	17	30
1965	20	32
1966	25	24
1967	25	29
1968	26	37
1969	41	23
1970	24	27
1971	31	27
1972	33	15
1973	31	32
1974	17	36
1975	23	29
1976	30	30
1977	13	22
1978	27	35
1979	24	35
1980	26	34
1981	14	12
1982	23	31
1983	28	29
1984	29	20
1985	33	31
1986	29	20
Totals	628	748

Nolan Ryan, with his blistering heater, impresses Mets coaches (*from left*) Wes Stock, Rube Walker, Eddie Yost, and Yogi Berra in spring training. Ryan wound up with a record of 6–9 with a 3.09 ERA and 133 strikeouts in 134 innings.
DAILY NEWS

the Mets had something else in their favor. Their farm system finally was delivering the long-awaited young talent necessary to build a winner.

Besides Seaver, McGraw, and Koosman, the young pitchers in camp that spring included Nolan Ryan, Jim McAndrew, Dan Frisella, Dick Selma, and Steve Renko.

A promising young receiver also on hand was Steve Chilcott, who had been the Mets' number 1 draft pick in June 1966. The Mets had bypassed Reggie Jackson to draft Chilcott. Rumors were afloat that the front office had nixed Jackson's selection because of his color and the fact that his girlfriend was a white woman. The Mets vehemently denied the charge and insisted that Chilcott was drafted because they desperately needed a catcher for the future and Chilcott was the best catching prospect in the country. Besides, they said,

Newly acquired Tommie Agee (in a deal for Tommy Davis) takes a cut in a spring training game against the Red Sox. Although he disappointed everyone with a meager .217 batting average and only five home runs, he rebounded with a sterling 1969 campaign.
DAILY NEWS

METS' TRIPLE PLAYS

May 30, 1962 vs. Los Angeles at Polo Grounds
(second game)
Chacon (ss)—Mantilla (2b)—Hodges (1b)
BATTER: Willie Davis

May 31, 1964 vs. San Francisco at Shea
(second game)
McMillan (ss)—Kranepool (1b)
BATTER: Orlando Cepeda

April 15, 1965 vs. Houston at Shea
Lewis (rf)—Cannizzaro (c)—McMillan (ss)
BATTER: Jimmy Wynn

September 28, 1966 vs. Chicago at Shea
Bressoud (3b)—Hiller (2b)—Hickman (1b)
BATTER: Joe Amalfitano

August 3, 1982 at Chicago
Bailor (ss)—Backman (2b)—Kingman (1b)
BATTER: Larry Bowa

September 29, 1982 vs. Chicago at Shea
Giles (2b)—Staub (1b)
BATTER: Keith Moreland

Casey Stengel had personally scouted the boy and recommended him. Chilcott never made the Mets' season lineup (nor did Steve Renko).

Harrelson was back again at shortstop, with Al Weis as a backup. Ken Boswell was emerging as a good-hitting, average-fielding second baseman, and Ed Kranepool, despite his childish ways and negative approach, had established himself as the first baseman. Only third base was open and Ed Charles, approaching his thirty-fifth birthday, won the job after being brought to camp as an invited player. Charles, who had hit only .238 in 1967, was sent back to the minors. But he regained his job in the final days of spring training.

With Agee set in center and Cleon Jones in left, the Mets had an adequate outfield. Ron Swoboda and Art Shamsky would platoon in right. The pitching staff, headed by Seaver, seemed the best ever. Ryan was the hardest-throwing pitcher in the minors, and Hodges thought he could make it in the big leagues despite obvious control problems. Koosman, who had been on the verge of being released a few years earlier, was retained at the urging of Walker, the pitching coach. Koosman had had a mediocre 11–10 record at Jacksonville in 1966, but he threw hard and he was a left-hander and the Mets needed a left-hander.

Koosman was good copy for the writers covering the club. He was a big, good-natured farmboy from Appleton, Minnesota, and loved putting people on. He managed to convince some that he had stayed in shape during the long, snowbound winter months by "throwing to my brother, Orville, in the barn."

There were, however, two stories about Koosman that were true. One was the manner in which the Mets had obtained him. John Luchese, an usher who had worked for the Mets at the Polo Grounds and Shea Stadium, had a son in the Army who caught Koosman at Fort Bliss, Texas. Young Luchese had written his dad about this hard-throwing left-hander and suggested the Mets sign him. Red Murff, a scout, was instructed to take a look at Koosman. Murff was so impressed he signed Koosman shortly after his discharge.

An ex-soldier in the mid-'60s, Koosman was a free spirit who did not always abide by the curfew rules. He was almost released at Auburn, New York, where he pitched for the Mets farm team in 1966. The next year he was about to be cut again when Joe McDonald, the assistant farm director, requested he be retained—at least until his first payday. McDonald had wired Koosman some money after Jerry's car broke down en route to spring training and figured he would not be able to get the money back until Koosman received his paycheck.

Twice on the verge of being cut, Koosman went on to become the best left-handed pitcher in the Mets' young history.

After almost a month of training, the Mets opened the 1968 exhibition schedule on March 9 against the St. Louis Cardinals at Al Lang Field. On the very first pitch in the very first inning, Bob Gibson of the Cardinals hit Tommie Agee in the head.

Welcome to the National League, Mr. Agee.

Fortunately, Agee was wearing a helmet. But he did suffer a concussion and was sidelined for several days.

The fact that the Mets had a new leader and new talent was not reflected in their spring record. They won only nine games, the fewest in their history, and lost eighteen, the most ever. Hodges remained calm. It was only the beginning. His long hours of work and instruction would pay off, he was certain. He then predicted seventy victories—four more than Westrum's 1966 Mets achieved.

The Mets left Florida on April 3 and headed west. They were opening the season in San Francisco on April 9 and were scheduled for exhibitions in Phoenix, Anaheim, and Palm Springs. After the Phoenix game they learned of the assassination of Dr. Martin Luther King in Memphis on April 4. They played the next night in Anaheim but merely went through the motions over the weekend in Palm Springs, unsure of how properly to observe the passing of the great civil rights leader.

The season was scheduled to open April 9. The Mets players voted not to play, in observance of the funeral of Dr. King. Commissioner Eckert, in New York, finally left it up to the individual clubs. The Giants wanted to play but the Mets would not. So the 1968 season did not open until April 10.

The Mets had lost every opening day for six straight years. It was one "negative" statistic that remained constant. With Seaver pitching an outstanding game, the Mets took a 4–2 lead into the ninth inning. The losing streak was about to be broken in Hodges' first game at the helm. Then, suddenly, it appeared that things had not changed all that much since he left the team in 1963.

Willie Mays opened the ninth with a single off the glove of Ed Charles. Willie McCovey popped out, and the Mets were two outs from their first opening day victory ever.

A passed ball moved Mays to second, and J. C. Martin took a foul ball off his finger and he suffered a fracture. It would be a month before he could catch again.

When Jim Ray Hart singled up the middle, Mays raced home and it was 4–3. Frisella was brought in to face Nate Oliver, and he immediately surrendered a single.

Jesus Alou was the next batter. Hodges visited the mound and advised Frisella on how to pitch to Alou. Hodges was hardly back to the bench when Alou doubled. Hart scored and so did Oliver as Harrelson's relay from the outfield sailed past Grote at the plate.

It later developed that Frisella had ignored Hodges' orders to throw his sinker, instead throwing a curve that Alou laced to left field.

One thing was certain. The Mets were still winless on opening day.

The next night they were a .500 ball club when Koosman, in his first start, pitched a brilliant four-hitter to beat Bill Singer and the Dodgers, 4–0.

From Los Angeles, the Mets moved on to Houston. It was there that Nolan Ryan won his first major league game, pitching six and two-thirds innings of three-hit ball and striking out eight. In that Easter Sunday game, Ryan, in an amazing performance, struck out seven of the first ten batters he faced. He eventually left with a blister on his finger, a problem he would endure throughout most of his Mets career.

Dan Frisella atoned for his opening day performance by completing Ryan's shutout, and the Mets won, 4–0.

But the following day the Houston club scheduled the game for a 7:30 P.M. start. The Mets, who had started spring training in mid-February, were heading for home at the end of the game after two months on the road. Their departure from Houston was delayed.

Seaver and Don Wilson, two of the hardest throwers in the game at the time, started against each other. At the end of nine innings, it was a 0–0 tie. Wilson left for a pinch hitter. After ten innings it was still a scoreless tie and Seaver departed.

By midnight, when the two teams had played a total of twenty-three innings, it still was a 0–0 game.

In the twenty-fourth inning, at approximately 1:30 A.M., Norm Miller of Houston led off with a single off Les Rohr. Nearly seven hours earlier, Rohr had thrown batting practice for the Mets. When Jimmy Wynn attempted to bunt, Rohr committed a balk and Miller was waved to second. Hodges ordered an intentional pass to Wynn. Both runners advanced a base when Rusty Staub grounded out and John Bateman was given the second intentional pass of the inning.

Bob Aspromonte followed with what should have been a cinch double play ball. But the ball took a funny bounce, went right past Al Weis, and Miller raced home with the winning run. The Astros won, 1–0, in twenty-four innings after six hours and six minutes of sheer futility on the part of the Mets.

"I blew it," was Weis's honest admission after the game. "Not so," said Johnny Murphy, who had suffered through the entire game.

"The infield in the Astrodome is bad enough," Murphy complained. (The Astrodome had not yet turned to Astro-turf and still featured a natural if pitiful playing field.) "If they drag the infield after five innings, why don't they do it after every five. That ball would not have taken the bounce it did if the infield had been dragged."

That winter, Murphy pushed for and succeeded in getting approval of legislation that major league infields must be manicured by the grounds keepers after every five innings. On infields with natural grass and dirt surfaces, as at Shea Stadium, it is still called the "Murphy Drag" when grounds keepers smooth out the infield dirt.

As if losing in twenty-four innings and playing over six hours wasn't tough enough to take on getaway day, the Mets ran into one more problem. When they landed at LaGuardia airport around 6 A.M., one of the players' garment bags became caught in the conveyor belt that moved personal luggage from the plane to the terminal. Everyone had to wait an extra hour until the bag was freed and all luggage was moved by hand to the terminal. It was a fitting end to the club's longest spring training in history following the night of their toughest and longest defeat.

n opening day at Shea, April 17, 1968, a star was born. If ever a young man confirmed a pitching coach's faith, Jerry Koosman did that when he shut out the San Francisco Giants, 3–0, with a seven-hit, ten-strikeout masterpiece. It was the first win in a home opener for the Mets in their seven-year existence.

Koosman had shown terrific stuff in shutting out the Los Angeles Dodgers six days earlier, but he struck out only three in that game. It was the ten-strikeout performance before a standing-room-only crowd of 52,079 at Shea that convinced one and all that at last the Mets had two solid starting pitchers in Seaver and Koosman.

No Met had ever pitched consecutive shutouts until Koosman came along. It did not take long for National League batters to realize that Koosman was for real. His first twenty-one innings of the season were scoreless, tying a club record, and by July he had established a Mets record with six shutouts. A seventh shutout in September tied the all-time National League record for rookie pitchers, first set by Irving M. Young of the Boston Braves in 1905 and matched six years later by the great Grover Cleveland Alexander. No National League rookie had matched it until Koosman. The left-hander might have established a new record if he had gotten more support from his teammates. On August 9, in a seventeen-inning game the Mets played with the Giants at Shea Stadium, Koosman pitched scoreless ball for the first twelve, but the Mets could not score for him.

The Mets had Koosman to thank for keeping them halfway respectable the first few weeks of the 1968 season. In their first fifteen games, they won only six, and Koosman won four of those six. When Jerry finally did lose for the first time to the Chicago Cubs, it was a tough 3–2 defeat. But his four straight victories had tied another club record. Clearly, Koosman was going to be a big pitcher for the Mets. By the end of June, the personable farm boy from Minnesota was 11–2 and headed for the first twenty-win season in club history. His popularity matched that of Seaver and there was no jealousy on Tom's part. In fact, the "Tom and Jerry Show" was a clubhouse highlight after winning games. They joked and kidded one another and got along famously.

It was not easy for Seaver to find much humor in his start. While Koosman kept winning, Seaver kept losing, but through no fault of his own. The Mets simply stopped scoring when Tom started. Or when they did score, it was hardly enough. In his first seven starts, the Mets supported Seaver with only twelve runs, and his record was 1–3. By early June, Seaver had pitched into extra innings four times in thirteen starts and won only once. By the end of May he was saddled with a 2–5 record.

Then things took a turn for the better. On June 5, he pitched into the eighth inning to gain credit for a 4–2 win over Chicago. Five days later he outpitched Don Sutton of the Los Angeles Dodgers to win a 1–0 duel in Dodger Stadium. Seaver followed with victories in his next three decisions, and suddenly he was on a five-game winning streak. His final two victories, closing out the month of June, were shutouts of the Cincinnati Reds and Houston Astros, tying the back-to-back shutout record Koosman had established earlier in the year. Seaver also set a club record with twenty-two consecutive scoreless innings.

It was around this time that I first referred to him in a story as "Tom Terrific," a nickname that has stuck with him.

By the end of June, the Mets were as high as seventh place in the standings. In addition to Seaver and Koosman, the young, hard-throwing Ryan was making his presence known. After striking out forty-four batters in his first five starts, covering a total of thirty-five innings, Ryan established a club record on May 14 when he fanned fourteen Cincinnati Reds in a 3–2 win. His

OPENING DAY LINEUP 1968

Harrelson, ss
Boswell, 2b
Agee, cf
Swoboda, rf
Kranepool, 1b
Shamsky, lf
Martin, c
Charles, 3b
Seaver, p

Cleon Jones slides in safely after a wild pitch on June 16 against the Giants. Jones led the team with a .297 average and stole twenty-three bases and was second to Ed Charles with fifteen home runs.

record at that point was 4–2, and he was being compared with Bob Feller, Sandy Koufax, Bob Gibson, and other hard throwers.

Unfortunately, as good as he was, Ryan had a problem. In almost every start he developed a blister on the middle finger of his pitching hand. Trainer Gus Mauch, a veteran of many seasons, remembered that pickle brine had a tendency to toughen skin. So one day Mauch stopped in a delicatessen near the Bronx Concourse Hotel where he and his wife, Mary, maintained an apartment. Mauch purchased a couple of kosher pickles and asked for some extra brine.

Mauch instructed Ryan to dip his finger in the pickle brine between starts, hoping it would toughen the skin. For a while, the brine appeared to have a positive effect. When reporters questioned Mauch about the details of the miracle brine that enabled Ryan to keep throwing sans blisters, the trainer obliged with the type of brine and used the name of the delicatessen where he purchased it. The very next day, the Bronx delicatessen had a sign in its window—"Nolan Ryan buys his pickle brine here."

Mauch's remedy was short-lived. Even though Lou Napoli, the bartender in the press room and a former prize fighter, also supplied brine to help toughen the skin on Ryan's finger, on July 30 the pitcher developed blisters severe enough for him to be placed on the disabled list. Ryan went on two weeks of Army duty ten days later and never won another game that season. But in his twenty-one games, which included 134 innings, Ryan struck out 133 batters. Only Seaver and Koosman struck out more, and both worked the full season.

There were others on the pitching staff who were starting besides Seaver, Koosman, and Ryan. Don Cardwell, a veteran who had come over in the Bosch deal and won five games in 1967, was off to a miserable start. He was 1–8 by the middle of June. Al Jackson, who was back for a second tour, ended June with a 1–3 record. Cal Koonce, a veteran who admitted throwing the spitball, was used exclusively in relief and was 0–3 at the midway point. But Dick Selma, a former teammate of Seaver's at Fresno High, suddenly turned into a winner. He had been 2–4 as a rookie in 1967 but was 7–1 by June 21. Almost overnight, the Mets had a respectable set of starters with Seaver, Koosman, and Selma.

On July 21, needing an extra starter for a doubleheader in St. Louis, the Mets dipped into their farm system and brought up Jim McAndrew, a right-hander from Lost Nation, Iowa. McAndrew was virtually a sacrificial lamb. They started him against Bob Gibson. Despite a strong effort, McAndrew lost, 2–0, and was rewarded with a trip back to Jacksonville. A week later, when Ryan went on the disabled list with blisters, McAndrew was recalled.

The Mets' pitching rotation took on a new dimension in 1968 with the addition of Nolan Ryan (*left*), who along with Tom Seaver (*right*) and Jerry Koosman produced an awesome threesome who came of age during the championship year of 1969.

DAILY NEWS

1968

NAME	G by POS	B	AGE	G	AB	R	H	2B	3B	HR	RBI	BB	SO	SB	BA	SA
NEW YORK	9th 73-89 .451 24		GIL HODGES													
TOTALS			26	163	5503	473	1252	178	30	81	434	379	1203	72	.228	.315
Ed Kranepool	1B113, OF2	L	23	127	373	29	86	13	1	3	20	19	39	0	.231	.295
Ken Boswell	2B69	L	22	75	284	37	74	7	2	4	11	16	27	7	.261	.342
Bud Harrelson	SS106	B	24	111	402	38	88	7	3	0	14	29	68	4	.219	.251
Ed Charles	3B106, 1B2	R	33	117	369	41	102	11	1	15	53	28	57	5	.276	.434
Ron Swoboda	OF125	R	24	132	450	46	109	14	6	11	59	52	113	8	.242	.373
Tommie Agee	OF127	R	25	132	368	30	80	12	3	5	17	15	103	13	.217	.307
Cleon Jones	OF139	R	25	147	509	63	151	29	4	14	55	31	98	23	.297	.452
Jerry Grote	C115	R	25	124	404	29	114	18	0	3	31	44	81	1	.282	.349
Art Shamsky	OF82, 1B17	L	26	116	345	30	82	14	4	12	48	21	58	1	.238	.406
Al Weis	SS59, 2B29, 3B2	B	30	90	274	15	47	6	0	1	14	21	63	3	.172	.204
Phil Linz	2B71	R	29	78	258	19	54	7	0	0	17	10	41	1	.209	.236
J. C. Martin	C53, 1B14	L	31	78	244	20	55	9	2	3	31	21	31	0	.225	.316
Jerry Buchek	3B37, 2B12, OF9	R	26	73	192	8	35	4	0	1	11	10	53	1	.182	.219
Kevin Collins	3B40, 2B6, SS1	L	21	58	154	12	31	5	2	1	13	7	37	0	.201	.279
Larry Stahl	OF47, 1B9	L	27	53	183	15	43	7	2	3	10	21	38	3	.235	.344
Don Bosch	OF33	B	25	50	111	14	19	1	0	3	7	9	33	0	.171	.261
Greg Goossen	1B30, C2	R	22	38	106	4	22	7	0	0	6	10	21	0	.208	.274
Mike Jorgensen	1B4	L	19	8	14	0	2	1	0	0	0	0	4	0	.143	.214
Bob Heise	SS6, 2B1	R	21	6	23	3	5	0	0	0	1	1	1	0	.217	.217
Duffy Dyer	C1	R	22	1	3	0	1	0	0	0	0	1	1	0	.333	.333

NAME	T	AGE	W	L	PCT	SV	G	GS	CG	IP	H	BB	SO	ShO	ERA
		27	73	89	.451	32	163	163	45	1483	1250	430	1014	25	2.72
Jerry Koosman	L	25	19	12	.613	0	35	34	17	264	221	69	178	7	2.08
Tom Seaver	R	23	16	12	.571	1	36	35	14	278	224	48	205	5	2.20
Dick Selma	R	24	9	10	.474	0	33	23	4	170	148	54	117	3	2.75
Don Cardwell	R	32	7	13	.350	1	29	25	5	180	156	50	82	1	2.95
Cal Koonce	R	27	6	4	.600	11	55	2	0	97	80	32	50	0	2.41
Nolan Ryan	R	21	6	9	.400	0	21	18	3	134	93	75	133	0	3.09
Jim McAndrew	R	24	4	7	.364	0	12	12	2	79	66	17	46	1	2.28
Al Jackson	L	32	3	7	.300	3	25	9	0	93	88	17	59	0	3.68
Danny Frisella	R	22	4	4	.333	2	19	4	0	51	53	17	47	0	3.88
Ron Taylor	R	30	1	5	.167	13	58	0	0	77	64	18	49	0	2.69
Billy Connors	R	26	0	1	.000	0	9	0	0	14	21	7	8	0	9.00
Les Rohr	L	22	0	2	.000	0	2	1	0	6	9	7	5	0	4.50
Bill Short	L	30	0	3	.000	1	34	0	0	30	24	14	24	0	4.80
Don Shaw	L	24	0	0	.000	0	7	0	0	12	3	5	11	0	0.75

Jerry Koosman shows his form in pitching a shutout against the Giants in the Shea opener on April 17, beating the Giants 3–0 and ending a seven-year opening-day jinx. Koosman shut out the Dodgers on the second day of the season and thus became the first pitcher to record two successive shutouts.

It is the custom of all ball clubs to seat the wives and family of ballplayers together in one section, usually the screened-in area behind home plate so that the players' children are not endangered by foul balls. In the course of a game, wives chatter back and forth, gossiping as wives will. Although most of the gossip is innocent enough, there are certain incidents involving players on the road that players do not want their wives to hear. For some reason gossip of the latter sort began to spread, and most of it appeared to emanate from conversations with Mrs. McAndrew. His teammates concluded that Jim must have been carrying home stories that were best kept among the boys and tagged him with the nickname "Moms" by way of voicing their conclusion.

McAndrew quickly ran his record to 0–5. And after winning a brilliant 1–0 from Steve Carlton on August 26, McAndrew lost his next start to Carlton, 2–0, in a return match. It was the fifth shutout loss in seven starts for McAndrew, a record that still stands.

Scoring runs was a problem for the Mets. Agee, who had been brought in to supply power and speed to the offense, did neither. At the end of half of the season, the center fielder had three home runs, three stolen bases, and only ten runs batted in. His average was .174. Agee had gotten off to a record start for futility when he went hitless for thirty-four at-bats between April 15 and May 1. Even a three-game benching did not help. Not since Don Zimmer in 1962 had any Met gone hitless in thirty-four consecutive trips to the plate. When Agee finally broke out of his slump with a single off the Phillies' Larry Jackson on May 1, he received a standing ovation from 11,450 fans.

But Agee was not alone in his futility. None of the Mets hit for average, with the exception of Cleon Jones and Jerry Grote. Jones began to develop as one of the league's better hitters, with a .297 average; Grote had his best year, with a .282 mark.

What the Mets lacked, besides a .300 hitter, was someone who could drive in runs. Swoboda, who batted only .242 and did not play every day, eventually led the club with fifty-nine RBIs. Ed Charles, who was not even on the roster in spring training, led the club in home runs, with fifteen. When the final league statistics were in that season, the Mets were last in team batting, with a .228 average, and next to last in runs scored, with 473.

But if they were down at the bottom of the pack offensively, they were virtually at the top in pitching. The Mets staff allowed fewer runs than any other pitching staff in the league, just 499, and the team earned run average was 2.72—fourth best in the league among ten teams.

So good was the pitching that the Mets staff turned in twenty-five shutouts, eight of them combined shutouts in which Nolan Ryan was the starter. Koosman, with seven, tied the rookie record. Seaver had another five, and Selma three. Only the National League champion St. Louis Cardinals had more, with thirty—and Bob Gibson accounted for thirteen of those.

Even the defense was better under Hodges' constant prodding for perfection. Gil stressed total concentration on routine plays, assuming that once his players learned to do the simple things right, the more spectacular plays would follow. He was right. The Mets made only 133 errors and had the fourth best fielding average in the league. The number of errors was in marked contrast to the 210 committed in 1962 by the original Mets.

The Mets clearly were coming of age and starting to gain respect around the rest of the league. With two starters like Seaver and Koosman, a strong-armed catcher like Grote, and a budding .300 hitter in Jones, the Mets were no longer the laughing stock of the league. At All-Star time, Grote was selected by other National League players to be the starting catcher, and Seaver and Koosman were named to the pitching staff. It was the first time the Mets had more than one player on the All-Star team.

Grote caught the first five innings of the game in the Houston Astrodome that year, and Seaver and Koosman contributed strong relief to the National League's 1–0 victory. Seaver pitched two scoreless innings and struck out five of the American League's best. Koosman ended the game by striking out Carl Yastrzemski, the only batter he faced.

On September 13, with Koosman pitching a 2–0 shutout against Pittsburgh, the Mets achieved new heights. That victory was their sixty-seventh of the year, surpassing the previous high of sixty-six achieved under Westrum in 1966.

Now the Mets were only three victories away from the seventy Hodges had predicted possible back in the spring. Another week would pass before those three became a reality.

McAndrew achieved number 68 with a 3–2 win over Chicago. There was reason for great rejoicing, especially by McAndrew. The three runs were the most support the Mets had provided him in his first ten major league starts.

Three days later, on September 20, the Mets achieved Hodges' goal. Seaver won the first game of a doubleheader in Philadelphia, 3–2, and after Don Cardwell gave up four runs in the first inning in the second game, the Mets rallied for a 5–4 victory. Because victories number 69 and 70 came on the same day, the exhilaration in the Mets clubhouse that night was akin to a New Year's Eve celebration. The next night McAndrew beat Rick Wise, 5–2, and the Mets had exceeded Hodges' prediction of seventy wins.

Four days later, in Atlanta, on the final road stop of the year, Hodges, who had in his first year removed all comedy from Mets baseball and turned the team into serious performers, was felled by a heart attack.

It was a pleasant September evening and Hodges, as he often did, pitched batting practice before the game. He regarded it as an exercise that helped keep him in shape. He had been hampered by a cold for several days and felt weak in the first inning of the game against the Braves. When he told his pitching coach, Rube Walker, that he was going back to the clubhouse to lie down, Walker immediately sensed something was wrong. It was not like Hodges to leave the dugout during a game.

Back in the clubhouse, Hodges stretched out on the trainer's table and complained of chest pains. Gus Mauch, the trainer, immediately called for a doctor, who advised that Hodges be taken to the Henry Grady Hospital, less than a mile from Atlanta Stadium. There, after tests, it was confirmed that Hodges had suffered a heart attack.

Upstairs in the press box, none of the writers were even aware that Hodges had left the bench, much less the ballpark—or that he had suffered a heart attack. It was not until the writers entered the clubhouse for their postgame interviews that the manager's absence was noted.

At first the coaches and club publicist Harold Weissman were evasive in answering questions as to Hodges' whereabouts. But a clubhouse attendant inadvertently let out that Hodges had left in an ambulance an hour earlier.

The secrecy that followed would have delighted the Kremlin. Hodges' coaches—especially Pignatano—were absolutely silent. They were determined that any suggestion that "their man" had suffered a heart attack would not leak out. When the press found out anyway, Pignatano pleaded for our silence.

"It will kill Joan if she hears it or reads it," he warned.

Joan Hodges had been called in Brooklyn to be told that her husband had taken ill, but she was not advised of the seriousness of his illness. It was too late for her to catch a plane out of New York. She would not be able to get to Atlanta and her husband's bedside until the next morning. Meanwhile, the Mets staff was resolute that she must not hear radio or television reports or read newspaper stories of Gil's attack.

For the next few hours, there was considerable bickering between the press corps and the coaches and club officials over the seriousness of Hodges' attack.

Ron Swoboda hits one of his eleven home runs during the '68 season against the Dodgers on April 21 at Shea. Cleon Jones (number 7) and Ed Kranepool offer congratulations (long before "high fives" became the vogue) as umpire Lee Weyer mills in the background.
DAILY NEWS

Gil Hodges and general manager Johnny Murphy check out the possibilities in the dugout at Shea during July. This is one of the last photos ever taken of Murphy, who died of a heart attack on January 14, 1970. Hodges had a heart attack in Atlanta in August 1968 but recovered.
LOUIS REQUENA

CY YOUNG AWARD WINNERS

Year	Player
1969	Tom Seaver
1973	Tom Seaver
1975	Tom Seaver
1985	Dwight Gooden

Though every attempt possible was made to suppress the news, the story was too big to go unreported. When calls to Henry Grady Hospital revealed that Hodges was in the intensive care unit, reporters quickly informed their home offices. The stories were filed.

The man who had managed the Mets to the greatest season in their history would not be able to finish out his first season.

Only one question remained: Would he ever manage again? The question went unanswered for months.

Doctors described Hodges' heart attack as "mild." Even so, they would not permit him to be moved to New York, so the manager of the Mets remained in Henry Grady Hospital for one month, with his wife constantly at his side. When Hodges was finally well enough to leave the hospital, he visited his Brooklyn home briefly and then went to St. Petersburg, Florida, the Mets' spring training base, for another month of rest and recuperation.

Through it all, reporters covering the Mets on a regular basis were advised that Hodges would not accept phone calls nor could he be interviewed. However, the Mets, especially Grant, had always considered the *New York Daily News* their "unofficial house paper." Reporters from other papers were constantly annoyed that stories appeared in the *Daily News* before they appeared anywhere else. While no one denied that the *News'* Dick Young was a most resourceful reporter, it seemed likely that at times stories were leaked to Young and others at the *Daily News*.

These suspicions were more or less confirmed in November, when the *Daily News* ran four pages of "exclusive" photos of Gil and Joan Hodges relaxing in Florida and walking the beaches along the Gulf of Mexico. Complaints that other papers should have been given equal access fell on deaf ears.

With their manager in an Atlanta hospital, the Mets finished the season by exceeding even Gil's expectations. After losing the night their skipper was stricken, the Mets came back to win the next night, when Seaver shut out the Braves, 3–0 on a three-hitter. It was Tom's sixteenth win of the season, matching his rookie total, and the seventy-second win of the season for the Mets.

Returning home for a final weekend, the Mets lost to the Phillies, 3–2, in eleven innings, but Koosman came back the next night to win, 3–1, and the Mets had seventy-three wins under their belts. They had finished ninth but were only eight games away from becoming a .500 club. Mets fans were ecstatic. For Koosman, it was his nineteenth victory of the season, but it was not enough to earn him the Rookie-of-the-Year Award Seaver had obtained with sixteen victories the previous season. Koosman had stiffer competition in the person of Johnny Bench, a young catcher who broke in that season with Cincinnati. In the voting results announced in November, Bench beat Koosman out for the award by one point.

Hodges' first season as manager was an overwhelming success. The club had shown vast improvement in every department but hitting and had won a record number of games. The only question unanswered was whether Hodges would be able to return to the dugout in 1969.

As time passed, Hodges' condition improved. Whatever worries the Mets might have had about seeking a replacement eventually evaporated. Hodges was given a clean bill of health by his doctors. He had given up smoking three packs of cigarettes a day, which was his habit prior to his heart attack, and followed a rigid diet. Few people outside of his family and closest friends saw Hodges that winter, but the Mets were assured by the doctors and by Gil himself that his health was good enough for him to return to the dugout in 1969. How well he would hold up under the strain of managing a team and the travel involved with a ball club remained to be seen. But Hodges was eager to return and the Mets, with fingers crossed, welcomed him back.

The Mets were guaranteed a higher finish in 1969 before the first ball was thrown. That assurance came during the All-Star break in Houston in July 1968. Four months earlier, on April 19, the National League had agreed, with some reluctance, to expand to twelve teams. One month later, on May 27, franchises were granted to groups representing San Diego and Montreal. But, unlike the American League, the National League did not immediately agree to divisional play. It was possible, under the original National League expansion plan, for teams to finish eleventh and twelfth.

Finally, in Houston, on the eve of the All-Star game, National League owners consented to divisional play—six teams in each division, which, of course, meant no team could finish lower than sixth. For the Mets and Astros, accustomed to finishing ninth and tenth, this was a happy thought.

The next decision was in which division to place the teams. Simple geography dictated that the St. Louis Cardinals had to be in the Western Division. But the Cardinals, citing a long rivalry with Chicago, insisted on being in the same division as the Cubs. Since divisional play meant an unbalanced schedule, the Cardinals would not give up lucrative home dates with the Cubs.

Mets chairman N. Donald Grant argued the same point. He was against divisional play because it deprived the Mets of big dates with the Giants and Dodgers—the two most popular draws in New York. It was impossible to put Los Angeles and San Francisco in the same division with the Mets, but it was possible to put Chicago and St. Louis in the same division. With that decided, Atlanta and Cincinnati, two teams east of both St. Louis and Chicago, were placed in the Western Division. Not smart, just conciliatory.

It also was agreed that the divisional leaders would meet at the end of the season in a best-of-five playoff series to determine the National League champions. That was a blessing for the Mets, given their strong, young pitching. In a short series, pitching almost always dominates.

By the time spring training arrived for the 1969 season, there were other changes. Eckert had been relieved of his duties as commissioner at the major league meetings in San Francisco the previous December. He was replaced in February, on an interim basis, by Bowie K. Kuhn, a lawyer for the National League. Kuhn was given a one-year contract calling for a $100,000 salary.

Kuhn found himself dealing with an inherited problem within weeks after taking over. The Major League Players Association, upset that contributions to their pension fund and other fringe benefits were not being met, urged all players not to sign 1969 contracts until agreement was reached.

The spring of 1969 began with a strike of sorts. Players traveled to their spring training sites but did not report to camp. In St. Petersburg, Tom Seaver organized an informal camp for Mets players in a little park at the south end of St. Petersburg Beach. It was voluntary and informal, and it consisted basically of pitchers and catchers who reported early. The drills were short, there was considerable joking with the press, and the daily sessions lasted little more than an hour. But a camaraderie developed among the players that was to serve the young team well in the coming season.

On February 25, the dispute between the players' union and the owners was resolved. Kuhn, working behind the scenes, had helped bring about a settlement. Not all owners were happy with the agreement. For one thing, the players got almost everything they were asking for, and just in time, apparently, as there were indications the players' solidarity might have cracked if agreement had not been reached before spring training. Yet it was clear when Kuhn and union head Marvin Miller reached their agreement that the Players Association had taken on new strength.

There was only one problem as far as the players were concerned. Pitchers,

OPENING DAY LINEUP 1969

Agee, cf
Gaspar, rf
Boswell, 2b
Jones, lf
Charles, 3b
Kranepool, 1b
Grote, c
Harrelson, ss
Seaver, p

The Mets display their starting lineup for 1969 the day before the opening day game at Shea. From left: Tommie Agee (CF), Rod Gaspar (RF), Ken Boswell (2B), Cleon Jones (LF), Ed Charles (3B), Ed Kranepool (1B), Jerry Grote (C), Bud Harrelson (SS), and Tom Seaver (P).

who usually need three to four weeks to limber up, had their conditioning programs cut in half. Exhibition games were scheduled for the first week in March, less than ten days after the settlement.

In part because of Seaver's informal training camp, the Mets had a surprisingly good spring in their second year under Hodges. They won fourteen out of twenty-four, but they were still nagged by the previous year's problems. Murphy had been unable to swing a major deal for the RBI man they needed. On March 17, in West Palm Beach, the Mets came close.

The Mets decided that Joe Torre, a Brooklyn-born catcher who belonged to the Atlanta Braves, would be the answer to their long-ball problems. Torre had hit an average of twenty homers a year for the Braves in Milwaukee and had twice driven in 100 runs. However, Torre and Braves general manager Paul Richards were having their difficulties, and Richards was looking to trade him.

The Mets played an exhibition game with the Braves in West Palm Beach on St. Patrick's Day. They had every hope of taking Torre with them when they left town. Unfortunately, Richards demanded two Mets players in exchange—the hard-throwing Ryan and Amos Otis, a promising prospect. The Mets rejected the deal. They would give up Ryan but not Otis. Otis—"Famous Amos," as he would later be dubbed by the New York press—had batted .286 with Jacksonville, where he hit fifteen homers and drove in seventy runs. Three years earlier Amos had been drafted out of the Boston Red Sox organization as a shortstop, but he had been converted to a center fielder by the Mets.

So the Mets opened the season without a power hitter. Hodges tried one experiment in spring training that failed. He attempted to convert Otis into the third baseman the Mets so desperately needed. Otis was not enamored of the idea. He was a sensitive individual who feared failure at the new position, especially in front of the big crowds in New York City. After an unhappy spring and a .151 batting average in forty-eight games as a third baseman–outfielder, Otis was optioned to the Tidewater farm on June 15. Six months later he was traded to Kansas in one of the worst deals the Mets ever made.

When Otis flopped in the third base trial, Ed Charles, soon to be thirty-six, inherited the job. He shared the bag with Wayne Garrett, an infielder the Mets had plucked out of the December draft for $25,000. It was the best $25,000 the Mets ever spent. Garrett remained a solid performer with the Mets for eight years. Donna Garrett, his tall, beautiful wife, drew almost as much attention daily as Wayne did. She became a "leader" among the wives and frequently traveled with the team.

There was no indication of what the season would hold when the Mets opened the 1969 campaign with another loss. The fledgling Montreal Expos were their guests opening day at Shea Stadium, and the Expos wound up winning their first major league game, 11–10. Don Shaw, one of the players the Mets lost to the Expos in the expansion draft, was the winning pitcher for Montreal. And the Mets, in their ninth year in the National League, still were without an opening day victory.

But the next day they won, 4–2, when Tug McGraw relieved for six and one-third innings and held the Expos to one run. But the absence of a full spring training began to show. McGraw developed a sore left arm in the game and did not pitch again for two weeks.

Having introduced Seaver, Koosman, and McAndrew to the National League in the two previous years, the Mets introduced another strong thrower in 1969 when Gary Gentry made his debut; his appearance gave the Mets one of the toughest pitching staffs in the league. Gentry's first major league start was a 9–5 win over the Expos in which he allowed only two runs.

The Mets went into a tailspin following that game and lost four in a row before Gentry pitched again and beat the Phillies, 6–3.

Koosman, who had some arm problems in spring training, lost his first two starts, to St. Louis and Pittsburgh respectively. He shut out the Pirates, 2–0, in his third start, but on April 29, pitching against Montreal, he had to leave the game in the fifth inning. He was then sent home for examination and evaluation by Dr. Peter LaMotte, the team physician. Dr. LaMotte diagnosed Koosman's ailment as a shoulder strain, and Jerry was advised to rest for a full week. When Koosman did attempt to pitch again, the pain persisted. It was May 24—almost one month—before he was ready to start again, this time against Houston. The rest had obviously helped. Koosman pitched three-hit ball for seven innings and gave up only two runs—but lost because the Mets scored only one.

Four days later, against the San Diego Padres at Shea Stadium, Koosman demonstrated that his recovery was complete. He pitched ten shutout innings and struck out fifteen. Fourteen of the strikeouts came in the first nine innings, to tie the club record set a year earlier by Ryan.

Further evidence of Koosman's recovery came in his next five starts. He won four of them and allowed only one run in his loss June 13 to the Dodgers. When he shut out the Cardinals, 1–0, on June 22, for his second consecutive blanking and third of the season, Koosman had pitched twenty-three consecutive scoreless innings, a new club record.

While Koosman was off to a 5–4 start in the won-lost column and Seaver was winning ten of his first thirteen decisions, the Mets also were getting good pitching from McAndrew, Ryan, and Gentry. Yet they remained in the lower echelon of the National League's Eastern Division right up to the end of May. On May 30 they were in fourth place, nine games off the pace.

On June 2nd, when he defeated the Dodgers, 2–1, at Shea Stadium, Koosman pitched the Mets to a .500 record—23–23. The following night it was Seaver, fittingly enough, who turned the Mets into "contenders." All along, Hodges had preached that the Mets could not be considered contenders until they reached .500. Then it was up to them to move beyond the level of mediocrity, which Seaver did with a 5–2 win over the Dodgers. One month earlier, on May 21, Seaver had pitched the Mets to .500 for the first time in history, but they had been unable to maintain that pace. Now he had pitched them beyond .500. Could they finally get it right?

Wayne Garrett, the "Huckleberry Finn" of the Mets, gets ready to take a few swings during batting practice. He was drafted as a utility infielder for only $25,000. He broke in in 1969 and played a platoon role at third for most of his days with the team. Although his lifetime average was only .230, he showed surprising power in the two seasons he played regularly. DAILY NEWS/GENE KAPPOCK

They did. The following night, June 4, an unheralded left-hander named Jack DiLauro, recently brought up from Tidewater and making his first start for the Mets, shut out the Dodgers on two hits for nine innings. The Mets eventually won the game, 1–0, in fifteen innings when Garrett singled and the winning run scored on a Willie Davis error.

That victory came in the middle of an eleven-game winning streak, the longest in Mets annals to that point. While they were winning, the Mets were also advancing into second place, and the rest of the league was beginning to take notice. Then, on the morning of June 15, the trading deadline, Murphy pulled off the deal of the decade for the Mets. He presented Hodges with first baseman Donn Clendenon, the power hitter and RBI man the Mets were lacking in the middle of their lineup. At long last, the Mets had some offense to match that fine young pitching.

Clendenon, thirty-three, had been selected off the Pittsburgh roster by Montreal in the October 1968 expansion draft. When he advised the Expos on January 22, 1969, that he had no desire to play in Montreal, he was traded to Houston along with Jesus Alou in exchange for Rusty Staub.

After first indicating to Houston officials that he would report, Clendenon had second thoughts. He announced his "retirement," saying he was going to work for the Scripto Pen Company. The Astros wanted the deal voided, but the Expos claimed they had dealt in good faith. Besides, they were happy with Staub, and Staub had no desire to return to Houston.

It was left to Commissioner Kuhn to resolve the problem. On April 8, the Montreal club sent pitchers Jack Billingham and Skip Guinn to Houston in place of Clendenon. If the Houston club was less than thrilled with the arrangement, they had no choice but to accept it. Kuhn had so ruled, and in the first few months of his office the commissioner acted decisively.

The plot thickened a few weeks later when Clendenon decided to "un-retire" and join Montreal. The Expos, of course, had offered him more money.

After just thirty-eight games and with Clendenon hitting .240, the Expos traded the big first baseman to the Mets for third baseman Kevin Collins, and minor league pitchers Steve Renko, Jay Carden, and Dave Colon.

Murphy was ecstatic over the deal. It was his first big one as the Mets' general manager, and he gave up virtually nothing to get Clendenon. The deal immediately paid off. In his first sixteen games, Clendenon drove in either the lead run or the winning run and the Mets continued to win.

They remained in second place for a month but didn't get close enough to the first place Cubs to be considered a threat until early July, when the Cubs visited Shea Stadium. For the first time in their history, the Mets had a "crucial" series. They had narrowed the deficit between themselves and the Cubs to five games by knocking off the Cardinals and Pirates, winning five in a row.

On the afternoon of July 8, the Cubs came to town and 32,278 fans showed up to watch the Mets do battle with Leo Durocher's first place team. On an earlier visit to Chicago in May, the Mets and Cubs had taken to throwing baseballs at each other. Tom Seaver had flattened Cubs third baseman Ron Santo with a pitch and, when Seaver appeared at the plate in the third, Bill Hands hit Seaver in the back with a pitch. Seaver retaliated in the inning's bottom half by hitting Hands in the stomach with one of his pitches. The umpires intervened to prevent a riot.

There was bad blood between the two teams from the start, and now first place was at stake. It was Koosman's turn to pitch, and the left-hander was equal to the occasion. Jerry gave up three runs, two of them on solo homers by Ernie Banks and ex-Met Jim Hickman. Koosman was losing by a 3–1 score going into the last of the ninth when the Mets got the break they were waiting for. Cubs center fielder Don Young got a bad break on a short fly by Ken

Ed Charles, who had fifteen home runs for the season, is congratulated by Jerry Grote (number 15) and Bud Harrelson (number 3) on May 4 after hitting a two-run homer against Chicago. He drove in five runs in a 7–3 victory.
DAILY NEWS/FRANK HURLEY

Boswell. The ball fell in for a double. Clendenon came off the bench as a pinch hitter and slammed a towering drive to the left center wall. Young got a glove on it but then dropped the ball as he banged into the fence, allowing Boswell to reach third. Clendenon, representing the tying run, was on second. Cleon Jones, who had been leading the league in hitting with a .360 average, immediately tied the score with a double to left, and a few moments later Kranepool lined an outside pitch from Ferguson Jenkins to left. Jones scurried home with the winning run.

With three runs in the ninth inning, the Mets had let the Cubs know their challenge was for real. The Cubs also discovered that Don Young was no center fielder.

Seaver started the next night, and the New York City Fire Department, whose responsibility it is to prevent overcrowding at public events, looked the other way as the Mets jammed better than 58,000 into the horseshoe-shaped stadium. It was the largest crowd ever to watch the Mets at home. Millions more watched on TV in New York and Chicago. Little did anyone realize that a baseball masterpiece was about to unfold.

Tom Terrific turned in a classic performance—in his mind it was the best game he ever pitched in the majors. He still refers to it as the "game I'll never forget."

What Seaver did that night was to retire every batter he faced for eight innings. Twenty-four Cubs in succession came to the plate and went back to the dugout with their bats in their hands. With one out in the ninth, Seaver's

Ken Boswell was hit in the elbow by a pitch thrown by left-hander George Stone of Atlanta, and Cleon Jones banged his first grand slam home run right afterward as the Mets beat Atlanta and Phil Niekro 6–3 on May 14 at Shea. Jones led the Mets in many offensive categories in 1969 with an incredible .340 batting average and a .482 slugging percentage. Boswell wasn't too shabby at .279, either.

dream of a perfect game ended when Jimmy Qualls, playing center field in place of Don Young, lined a clean single to left center.

Disappointed but still in command, Seaver retired the next two batters for a one-hit, 4–0 shutout that included eleven strikeouts. It also moved the Mets to within three games of first place.

On the following afternoon the Cubs knocked Gentry out of the box with a five-run fifth inning and won easily, 6–2, with Hands pitching a three-hitter for Chicago. After the game, Cubs manager Leo Durocher was asked if "those were the real Cubs."

"No, those were the real Mets," the Lip barked.

One week later in Chicago, the two adversaries squared off again. This time the Cubs drew first blood as Hands outdueled Seaver to win, 1–0. Billy Williams singled home Don Kessinger with the only run of the game.

Gentry was the next day's pitcher in Wrigley Field, and he atoned for the setback of the previous week by outpitching former Met Dick Selma, 5–4. The Mets had given up Selma to Montreal in the expansion draft and did not consider it any great loss. Selma had arrived in camp one spring to have trainer Gus Mauch discover a large scar on the back of his right shoulder. It was only then that Selma revealed he had undergone shoulder surgery a month before spring training without bothering to advise the club or seek permission.

In Gentry's win over Selma, the most stunning blow of the day was struck by Al Weis, the light-hitting shortstop filling in for Harrelson, who was serving time with his Army unit. Weis broke a 1–1 tie in the fourth inning with a three-run home run over the left field fence—his first home run of the season. Another home run by Boswell provided the winning margin, as the Mets reduced Chicago's lead to four and one-half games.

The final game of the series matched ex-Cub Don Cardwell against Ferguson Jenkins, Chicago's perennial twenty-game winner. The Mets jumped on Jenkins for four runs in the first inning. Tommie Agee homered for two more runs in the second, and Cardwell was coasting. But he could not hold the lead. First Jim McAndrew and then Cal Koonce took turns trying to protect it. Then, with the Cubs trailing by only one run, Weis—of all people—hit his second home run in two days. Art Shamsky's two-run homer in the eighth iced it, and the Mets won, 9–5, to move to within three and one-half games of first place.

Once again they suffered a letdown after the big series. They split four games against the Expos in Montreal and went home to do the same against Cincinnati. After having taken four out of six from the Cubs in successive series, they were still four and one-half games behind Chicago.

Then the Houston Astros came to town. It was a humiliating experience for at least one Met.

On the afternoon of July 30, the Mets entertained the Astros in a make-up doubleheader. The Astros entertained themselves by annihilating the Mets, 16–3 and 11–5. It was in that doubleheader that the Mets learned, if they did not already know it, that Hodges would tolerate nothing less than a 100 percent effort at all times.

In the first game, which Koosman started, the Astros scored eleven runs in the ninth inning when both Denis Menke and Jimmy Wynn hit grand slam home runs. In the second inning of the second game, which Gentry started, Houston brightened the scoreboard lights with ten runs.

It was in that ten-run inning that Hodges noted a lackadaisical effort by Jones in pursuit of an extra base hit to left field. Emerging from the dugout and walking in slow, deliberate steps, the manager started out onto the field. Everyone expected him to stop at the mound and change pitchers. But Hodges walked past the mound, past the shortstop, and on out to left field. There he confronted Jones, inquired of his physical condition, then did a complete turnabout and walked just as slowly back to the dugout. Behind Hodges by a few steps, walking just as slowly and with head hung low, Jones followed.

Later there was a concocted story that Jones had suffered a pulled leg muscle. The Mets players knew otherwise. Hodges was annoyed at the lack of effort Jones displayed and had yanked him. No other manager had ever walked to the outfield so deliberately to remove a player.

Jones, despite the fact that he was the club's leading hitter, did not play the next day, and the Mets lost, 2–0, as the Astros' Tom Griffin outpitched Seaver. The Mets were now six games behind the Cubs. In the next few weeks the Cubs soared in the Chicago sunshine while the Mets began to fade.

For the next two weeks the Mets played .500 ball, winning seven and losing seven. Three of the losses were to the very same Astros who had torn them apart in New York. In a disastrous series in the Houston Astrodome, McAndrew, Koosman, and Gentry lost by scores of 3–0, 8–7, and 8–2, respectively. Following the final defeat in Houston on August 13, which dropped them into third place, the Mets were nine and one-half games out of first place. It was as far from the top as they had been all year, and whatever illusions they might have had about catching the Cubs began to disappear. It had been fun while it lasted, but the team wasn't ready for a trip to the summit.

Or so everyone thought.

Ron Swoboda, a.k.a. Saboda by Casey Stengel, leaps in vain for a home run at Shea on August 10.
DAILY NEWS/FRANK HURLEY

he Mets had two days off to ponder their fate following the blowout in Houston. Returning home, they had an off-day, followed by a rained-out game, which resulted in a make-up doubleheader on Saturday, August 16. When Seaver and Ron Taylor combined for a 1–0 win in the first game and McAndrew and McGraw won the second game, 2–1, it was the start of an incredible stretch that would see the Mets win thirty-eight of their last forty-nine games, survive a brief losing streak in which they actually gained ground, and end up becoming the first expansion team to win a championship of any kind. They also became the first team to win three titles in one year.

With the introduction of divisional play, the Mets were able to win the National League Eastern Division title; the National League pennant, following a playoff with the Western Division champions; and, finally, the World Series.

This was on the heels of a ninth place finish the previous year. Not even the Miracle Boston Braves of 1914 matched the accomplishments of the Amazing Mets.

With the doubleheader victory on August 16, the Mets began a home stand in which they won nine out of ten games from the three West Coast clubs. Then on August 17 they swept the Padres in another doubleheader by identical 3–2 scores, with Koosman and Cardwell the winners. Duffy Dyer, who had spent a good part of the season in the minors, won Koosman's game with a three-run home run.

On August 19, the Giants came to town, and the Mets registered one of their finest victories of the season when Tommie Agee hit a home run off Juan Marichal with one out in the fourteenth inning for the only run of the game. Gentry pitched the first ten innings and McGraw the last four for the shutout.

It was in that fourteen-inning, 1–0 classic that cynics began to suspect divine intercession. In the thirteenth inning Hodges made a surprise defensive move. He took his shortstop, Bob Pfeil, and placed him in the left field corner of the outfield. Left fielder Jones was moved to left center, the center fielder to right center, and the right fielder played the right field corner. A four-man outfield was not an everyday occurrence, but everyone with any smattering of baseball knowledge knew what Hodges had in mind. He was not going to let Giants slugger Willie McCovey get an extra base hit. If he poked a single through the vacant shortstop hole, fine. The Mets were willing to give the feared power hitter a single.

Sure enough, Hodges' strategy paid off. McCovey sent a screaming drive to left center that Jones caught by leaping high against the fence. He was playing almost in a direct line with McCovey's screamer. Had Cleon been playing his normal left field position, there was little chance he could have made the catch.

As if that win was not enough to fire up Mets fans—and believe me, it did!—McAndrew came back the next day to blank the Giants, 6–0, with a two-hitter. In successive games the young Mets pitcher had held the Giants—one of the powers of the West—scoreless.

Unfortunately, the Mets could not sweep the series. Seaver, who had been experiencing stiffness in his pitching shoulder, gave up six runs in seven innings. The Mets battled back to tie the score, but Ron Taylor picked up the loss in the eleventh when Agee misjudged a routine fly ball.

The Dodgers came to town next, and when the Mets swept them in three games, the nine and a half game deficit of eleven days earlier had been reduced to five. The Mets were back in the race.

Although the Mets enjoyed going west to play in California, they rarely had much success there. A combination of jet lag and time changes worked against the top performance required when battling the Dodgers and Giants, perennial championship contenders. Now that San Diego was included on the West Coast itinerary, they provided the Mets with a soft touch, at least in the Padres' infancy. The Mets kept their streak going when Seaver, McAndrew, and Koosman all pitched complete games with 8–4, 3–0, and 4–1 victories over the Padres. McAndrew, stymied by his team's inability to score during his rookie year, resolved that dilemma this time by holding the opposition scoreless. Shutting out the Padres on August 26, "Moms" tied the club record of twenty-three consecutive scoreless innings.

Moving up to San Francisco, the Mets continued to whittle away at the Chicago lead. After Marichal shut out the Mets and Gentry, 5–0, in the first of four games, the Mets came back to beat Gaylor Perry in ten innings the next day, 3–2, with McGraw holding off the late inning Giant threats. The first game of the Sunday doubleheader gave Seaver his fourth straight win and nineteenth victory of the season. In blanking the Giants, 8–0, Seaver struck out eleven to prove he was over his shoulder injury. The Giants came back to win the second game of the doubleheader, 3–2, when Ron Taylor forced in the winning run with a bases-loaded walk in the eleventh.

Los Angeles was the next and last stop on the trip, and it was not a good one. The Dodgers won two of the three games. Koosman was raked for five runs in the first inning to lose the Labor Day opener, 10–6. Gentry won the second game, 5–4, despite the fact he almost blew a 5–1 lead in the ninth. McGraw got the final out by striking out Willie Davis, the hottest hitter in the league at the time.

Davis, who had already hit in thirty consecutive games for a Dodgers record, gained his revenge the next night—with some help from Hodges. Davis was hitless in the game when he came to bat in the ninth with the score tied and a man on second. With first base open, Hodges could have ordered the hot hitter walked intentionally, and no one would have blamed him—except 45,000 Dodgers fans. Hodges let Davis keep his streak alive, and the center fielder responded with a double off DiLauro to give Los Angeles a 5–4 win. That loss dropped the Mets five games behind with twenty-nine games to play. It was not an insurmountable obstacle, but the Cubs were playing so well it was difficult to imagine the Mets catching up to them.

Returning home to the friendly confines of Shea Stadium, the Mets got a break when they learned that Pittsburgh had whipped the Cubs in an afternoon game at Wrigley Field. Seaver was on the mound for the Mets in the first game of a twi-night doubleheader, and 40,450 fans were on hand to see Tom Terrific become the first twenty-game winner in Mets history. He did not disappoint them. With a neat five-hitter, Seaver trimmed the Phils, 5–1, and moved the Mets back to within four games of first place. McAndrew lost the second game, 4–2, on an unearned run, and the Mets were four and a half out.

Cardwell's experience under fire would benefit the Mets in the stretch. The thirty-three-year-old veteran came back the next afternoon to combine with McGraw for a 6–0 shutout of the Phillies. Fans hung around the ballpark after the game to see the final score from Chicago posted, and when it showed a 13–4 Cubs loss, the New Breed was in seventh heaven. The following day, with Ryan taking over for Gentry in a 3–3 tie and pitching scoreless ball the last three innings, the Mets rallied against Bill Champion and trounced the Phillies, 9–3. In Chicago, meanwhile, the Pirates were blowing a lead but then tied the score and won in the eleventh inning on a Willie Stargell home run.

Now the Mets were only two and a half games out of first place, and the Cubs were coming to Shea Stadium for two consecutive nights. New York was all worked up over the pennant race, and Hodges' young Mets were taking it in stride. After all, they had Koosman and Seaver going for them. And in what baseball writers love to refer to as "the all-important loss column," the Mets were only one down. (Why it is referred to as "the all-important loss column" is simple: If you have played a game and lost it, you cannot erase that loss; but if you have not played a game, there is still an opportunity to win it. A loss is a loss is a loss. Only a game not yet played can become a victory.)

The Mets had only one serious problem going into the crucial two-game series with the Cubs. Jones, the league's leading hitter with a .348 average, had a rib cage injury and a pulled leg muscle. He had been out for a week and was not ready for the first game against the Cubs. Hodges had been platooning Art Shamsky and Swoboda in right field, but he now had to use Shamsky, a left-handed batter, in left field against Chicago pitcher Bill Hands.

If the Cubs were looking to renew the beanball battle staged earlier in Chicago, they had come to the wrong stadium.

After Koosman retired the Cubs in order in the first inning, Hands took the mound for the Cubs and immediately fired his first pitch perilously close to Agee's head. Agee hit the dirt, got back up on his feet, and glared at the Chicago pitcher. Hands then retired Agee, Garrett, and Clendenon in order. Since Cubs captain Ron Santo was first up in the second inning, he knew what to expect. So did everyone else in the park. Santo, who did a heel-kicking jig in the outfield after every Cubs victory at home, had also been critical of the Mets, promising baseball writers they would collapse in the stretch.

Koosman replied to the message Hands had delivered to Agee by drilling a fastball into Santo's right elbow on his very first pitch. Unlike the experience in Chicago, where the dugouts emptied and players were ready to brawl, this time no one stirred. Koosman had sent Santo and the Cubs a message: Don't fool with our hitters unless you want the same in exchange.

Hands's knockdown pitch in the first inning was meant to intimidate Agee. It didn't. In his second time at bat in the third inning, Tommie hit a two-run home run. After the Cubs tied the score in the sixth inning on singles by Don Kessinger, Glenn Beckert, and Billy Williams plus a sacrifice fly by Santo, the Mets pushed across the winning run in the inning's bottom half on a double by Agee and a single by Garrett.

In the biggest series of their young lives the Mets had beaten the Cubs, 3–2, in the first game, with Koosman pitching a seven-hitter and striking out thirteen. Now they were only a game and a half out and tied in the all-important loss column.

With Seaver on the mound against Ferguson Jenkins the next night, the Mets jumped off to a lead in the first inning on a two-run double by Ken Boswell. Cleon Jones, back in the lineup, opened the third inning with a single. After the Cubs botched an infield run-down play, Clendenon whacked an opposite-field home run over the right field fence and it was 4–0. Shamsky hit another solo homer in the fifth, and Seaver breezed home a 7–1 winner with a five-hitter. It was his twenty-first victory of the season.

The Mets had conquered the Cubs once again, but still they were not in first place. They were one up in the loss column but one behind in the win column. Though thoroughly beaten in a series they had to win, the Cubs left town still in first place by a half game. They had lost six of their last eight games with the Mets and suddenly began to realize that the pennant they thought was theirs in July was now in jeopardy.

The two-game Chicago sweep made believers out of the Mets. In just a month they moved from being nine and a half games out to only a half game from first place. The Impossible Dream was just around the corner.

One day after the Cubs left town, the Mets moved into first place for the first time, initially by a percentage point, then by a half game. They did it by sweeping a doubleheader from Montreal.

The Mets fell behind the Expos in the opener on September 10 but were handed the tying run when Montreal pitcher Mike Wegener balked. The game went into extra innings; after eleven Wegener had fanned fifteen Mets. But in

METS CLINCH NATIONAL LEAGUE EAST CROWN (September 24, 1969)

St. Louis

	AB	R	H	RBI
Brock, lf	4	0	2	0
Flood, cf	1	0	0	0
Davalillo, cf	3	0	1	0
Pinson, cf	4	0	0	0
Torre, 1b	4	0	0	0
McCarver, c	3	0	0	0
Shannon, 3b	3	0	1	0
Javier, 2b	3	0	0	0
Maxvill, ss	1	0	0	0
White, ph	0	0	0	0
DaVanon, ss	0	0	0	0
Carlton, p	0	0	0	0
Giusti, p	1	0	0	0
Hague, ph	1	0	0	0
Campisi, p	0	0	0	0
Simmons, ph	1	0	0	0
Grant, p	0	0	0	0
Totals	29	0	4	0

New York

	AB	R	H	RBI
Harrelson, ss	3	1	1	0
Agee, cf	3	1	0	0
Jones, lf	4	0	0	0
Clendenon, 1b	3	2	2	4
Swoboda, rf	3	1	0	0
Charles, 3b	4	1	1	2
Grote, c	4	0	2	0
Weis, 2b	4	0	0	0
Gentry, p	4	0	0	0
Totals	32	6	7	6

Pitching	IP	H	R	ER	W	SO
Carlton (L, 17–11)	⅓	3	5	5	2	1
Giusti	4⅔	2	1	1	2	2
Campisi	2	1	0	0	0	3
Grant	1	1	0	0	0	1
Gentry (W, 12–12)	9	4	0	0	2	5

E—DaVanon. DP—New York 2. LOB—St. Louis 4, New York 6. 2B—Grote. HR—Clendenon 2 (15), Charles (3). Time—2:02. Attendance—54,928.

the twelfth Jones singled with two out, and Rod Gaspar, a part-time outfielder, drew a walk that pushed Cleon into scoring position, whereupon Boswell singled home, giving the Mets a 3–2 win and moving them into first by one one-hundredth of a percentage point. Fans in the stand went wild when "We're Number One" flashed on the big scoreboard in right field.

The Mets had Ryan going for them in the second game of the doubleheader. Ryan had not won as a starter in over a month and had been used sparingly because of the recurrent blisters. This night he was the fireballer that everyone has come to know. Ryan pitched a three-hitter. He struck out eleven and went nine innings for only the second time in the season as the Mets romped to a 7–1 victory.

Shortly after ten o'clock, while Ryan was in the process of mowing down the Expos, the scoreboard flashed the news the Mets fans had been awaiting—the Cubs had lost in Philadelphia by a 6–2 score. Win or lose in the second game, the Mets would be in first place when they went to bed that night. At approximately 11:20 they completed their sweep of the Expos. Now the Amazin's had a solid one-game lead over the Cubs.

Applications for World Series tickets swamped the Mets office the next day.

The following afternoon, still in a state of euphoria from their ascent to first place, the Mets completed a sweep of the Expos when Gentry pitched a six-hit shutout and the team rolled to a 4–0 victory. It was the Mets' eighty-fifth victory of the season—exactly the number Hodges had told me in April the Mets were capable of winning. And there were still twenty games remaining on the schedule.

Gentry's victory was followed that night by another Chicago defeat, which put the Mets two full games in front. It was a particularly bitter defeat for the Cubs, inasmuch as the winning run scored when Selma, the one-time Met, tried to pick a runner off at third base and threw past Santo, who was not anticipating the pick-off. Selma and Santo had been the cheerleaders of the Cubs during the summer months when Chicago was riding high. Selma would work up the bleacher bums in left field with a cheerleading act before the games, and Santo's heel-kicking jig became a ritual after every victory.

Big as Gentry's victory was, the Mets also suffered a loss when Jones strained a muscle in his rib cage again and was forced to leave the game after only two trips to the plate. It would be two weeks before the Mets' leading hitter could return to the lineup.

The September 11 loss was the eighth in a row for the Cubs. It also was the seventh straight win for the Mets. With eight victories in nine home games and a two-game lead, the Mets began a road trip to Pittsburgh, St. Louis, and Montreal. It was a ten-day period in which the Mets could do no wrong. If ever there was reason to believe they were a team of destiny, those ten days confirmed it.

The Mets began by playing a twi-night doubleheader in Pittsburgh on September 12. Koosman pitched the first game, allowed only three hits, and won, 1–0, by driving in the game's only run. It was Koosman's first and only RBI of the season.

What would Cardwell do for an encore in the second game? Cardwell was a good-hitting pitcher. He proved it by duplicating Koosman's first-game hero-ics, driving in the only run in another 1–0 victory.

Thus the Mets won two games by identical 1–0 scores, and in each game the pitcher drove in the only run. Not overlooked by their opponents was the fact that the Mets got two more excellent pitching performances against one of the best-hitting teams in baseball.

The win streak continued the following day with Seaver beating Luke Walker, 5–2. It was his twenty-second win of the season and sixth in a row. Ron Swoboda provided him with the winning runs, hitting the first grand slam

home run of his career in the eighth inning to snap a 1–1 tie. The Cubs, meanwhile, had ended their losing streak against the Cardinals in St. Louis, but they continued to lose ground. Swoboda's slam had boosted the Mets into a three and one-half game lead.

Even when their win streak was snapped at ten by Steve Blass and the Pirates on September 14, the Mets did not lose ground, because in St. Louis Bob Gibson outpitched the Cubs' Ken Holtzman, and Lou Brock homered in the tenth inning to give St. Louis a 2–1 win.

From Pittsburgh the Mets traveled to St. Louis, where they scored what Stengel would classify as another "amazing" victory. On the night of September 15, the Cardinals' Steve Carlton turned in what at that time was the greatest single strikeout performance in major league history. He struck out nineteen batters. And he lost, 4–3.

All four Mets runs were driven in by Swoboda, who hit a two-run homer in the fourth inning and another two-run homer in the eighth inning. Both times Carlton tried to throw a fastball past the free-swinging Swoboda, and both times Ron connected for a home run. He had hit three home runs in three games and won two of them for the Mets.

The Cubs also lost to Montreal, 8–2, and the Mets were four and one-half games in front with only fifteen games remaining on their schedule. The Mets got a further break when the game of September 16 was rained out. Because the Mets were not scheduled again in St. Louis and because the Cardinals were playing in New York the next week, the rained-out game was transferred to Shea Stadium. That gave the Mets the home field advantage.

Pitching remained the Mets' strong suit when they traveled up to Montreal and got two more shutout performances, this time from Koosman and Seaver. On successive nights they blanked the Expos, 5–0 and 2–0, and when the Cubs lost another game the Mets grabbed a five-game lead.

The champagne was being iced for celebration of the divisional championship when the Mets arrived home September 19 for a weekend series with Pittsburgh. The party was put on hold when the Pirates turned spoilsports and won both ends of a twin-night doubleheader. Nearly 52,000 fans went home disappointed when Ryan lost the first game, 8–2, and McAndrew dropped the second one, 8–0. However, the Cubs also lost, so the Mets dropped only a half game of their lead.

What happened the next day was not to be believed. The Mets actually were held hitless, and still they did not lose ground in the pennant race. Bob Moose of Pittsburgh turned in the no-hitter, and the Mets lost, 4–0. Their lead remained intact when Chicago also lost. The Mets had dropped three in a row for the first time since late July and lost only one game in the standings.

Their winning ways returned the next afternoon when the Mets swept a doubleheader from the Pirates, 5–3 and 6–1, behind Koosman and Cardwell, the same two pitchers who had pitched 1–0 victories in Pittsburgh the previous week. This time they had some support.

St. Louis came to Shea on Monday night, September 22, to play the rained-out game of the previous week. Seaver, with another brilliant effort, beat the Cardinals, 3–1, allowing only four hits.

It took eleven innings the next night, but the Mets moved to within one win of the division title when they beat the great Bob Gibson, 3–2. The Cubs lost earlier in the day.

On September 24, the Mets locked it up with Gentry outpitching Carlton and Clendenon hitting a three-run home run and Charles a two-run home run for a 6–0 victory. Not even a Chicago victory in the afternoon could deny the Mets their miracle championship. Ironically, two players not even on the roster in spring training—Clendenon and Charles—were the heroes on the fateful night.

It was ironic that the final two outs of the game should be registered by Joe Torre, the slugger the Mets had failed to obtain in spring training. Torre, who later became manager of the Mets, bounced into a double play at 9:07 P.M., and the Mets officially became National League Eastern Division champions when Clendenon snuggled the relay throw from Weis in his big mitt.

In the stands, 56,000 fans were delirious. Thousands of young fans raced onto the field, tearing up pieces of turf as souvenirs. In the boisterous Mets clubhouse, everyone, including sportswriters, was either doused with champagne or thrown into the showers fully clothed.

"I really didn't think we'd come as far as we have as fast as we have," said Hodges. "But now that we're here, I see no reason to stop. I just hope I don't spoil things for the future by getting so far ahead of schedule. My master plan really was to move up a few notches at a time."

After years of frustration and depression, Mets fans finally have something to go wild about as their team wins the Eastern Division on September 24, 1969.
DAILY NEWS/JOHN DUPREY

12

• THE METS •

• STUN •

• THE •

• ORIOLES—•

• AND THE •

• WORLD •

As the Mets prepared for the first scheduled playoff in major league history, they were the hottest team in baseball. Nine and one-half games back on August 13, they overtook the Cubs on September 10, winning thirty-eight of their last forty-nine games. They had accomplished this minor miracle with outstanding pitching and indifferent hitting. Only twice in their last forty-nine games did they score as many as eight runs in a single game.

Seaver and Koosman were simply fantastic in the stretch. Seaver won ten in a row from August 9 until the end of the season, had an overall 25–7 record and a 2.21 earned run average. While Seaver was winning ten in a row, Koosman was winning eight out of nine. Cardwell, who was 3–9 in late July, won five straight while the Mets were overtaking the Cubs. Gentry, a rookie, contributed thirteen victories. McAndrew, despite a losing 6–7 record, won three key games in mid-season. The Mets staff, overall, turned in a league-leading twenty-eight shutouts—more than one-quarter of the victory total.

What the Mets had to go with their strong young starting staff was an equally effective bullpen. Of the 100 games won, 35 were saved by McGraw, Taylor, and Koonce. Taylor, the right-handed reliever, had a 9–4 record and thirteen saves. McGraw was the left-hander Hodges called on in emergencies. Tug responded with a 9–3 record and twelve saves. Koonce was invaluable in the middle innings and occasionally came through in the final innings. The right-hander compiled a 6–3 record and earned seven saves.

Jones did not win the batting championship despite an effort on Hodges' part late in the season to help him. Hodges used Cleon in the lead-off spot the last week to give him an extra at-bat in each game. But Jones finished in third place with .340—Pete Rose led the league with .348, and Roberto Clemente batted .345. Cleon's .340 in 1969 remains the highest single season batting average for any Met.

Agee rebounded from .217 in 1968 to bat .271 in 1969. He also led the club with twenty-six home runs and 76 RBIs.

Although he had disdained platooning, Hodges did a remarkable job of juggling the talent he had to get the most out of four players at two positions. Clendenon did not hit for average after he was acquired from Montreal, but he did give the Mets a right-handed first baseman to share the duties with the left-handed-hitting Kranepool. Between them they hit twenty-three home runs and knocked in eighty-six runs, a respectable production for any manager. Even more productive was the right field tandem of Ron Swoboda and Art Shamsky. Swoboda, the right-handed hitter, batted only .235 but was highly productive with fifty-two runs batted in. The left-handed Shamsky hit .300 and drove in forty-seven runs. Between them, the Mets right fielders hit twenty-three homers and drove in ninety-nine runs.

It was fortunate that the Mets did not have another home game to play after clinching the Eastern Division against the Cardinals. Shea Stadium would have been unplayable for the next few days. Fans had ripped up so much sod that it took stadium boss Jim Thomson and head grounds keeper John McCarthy and his crew several days to get the field back in shape.

The Mets did not stop winning after the clincher. They went on to Philadelphia, where they swept a three-game series, giving their still undecided playoff opponents something to think about by holding the Phillies scoreless in all three games.

Koosman pitched a four-hit, 5–0 shutout; Seaver allowed only three hits in a 1–0 win that was his twenty-fifth of the year; and Gentry, Ryan, and Taylor combined for a 2–0 win in the finale. The Mets pitching staff had four consecutive shutouts behind them as they traveled to Chicago for the final series of the season.

Fans run amuck after the Mets beat Atlanta on October 6, capturing the National League Pennant.
DAILY NEWS

Cub fans, anticipating weeks earlier this might be the deciding series of the season, had purchased tickets long in advance, so Wrigley Field was packed even though the Cubs had since been eliminated from contention. The unruly Bleacher Bums, as some Chicago fans had become known, refused to accept the mathematics that said the race was over. They paraded through the stands and across the top of the Mets dugout, carrying banners and proclaiming, "We're Number One!" The Mets responded by stretching their winning streak to ten games, with a twelve-inning, 6–5 victory. It wasn't until the final day of the season that the Mets finally lost one. It was their sixty-second defeat of the season. But they had won an even hundred—fifteen more than Hodges had predicted in the spring—and finished eight full games ahead of the devastated Cubs.

The Atlanta Braves, who were almost as hot as the Mets down the stretch, took a little longer to clinch the Western Division title. Atlanta won seventeen of their final twenty, including ten in a row at the end. Phil Niekro pitched the clincher to beat the Cincinnati Reds, 3–2, on September 30 for the tenth straight win.

During the regular season, the Mets won ten out of twelve from the Braves, and they were favored to win the playoffs. Hardly anyone expected them to win the way they did. The Mets simply swept the Braves aside three straight and did it with a devastating attack rather than airtight pitching. In the three games the Mets scored twenty-seven runs on thirty-seven hits and walloped six home runs.

In the opener in Atlanta on October 4, Seaver opposed Niekro. Neither was able to finish. Seaver, who allowed eight hits and five runs and left the game trailing by a run after seven innings, picked up the victory when the Mets jumped on Niekro for five runs in the eighth and an eventual 9–5 victory.

Niekro could blame his defeat on poor support. After a Garrett double and a Jones single tied the score in the eighth and took Seaver off the hook, Shamsky delivered his third single of the game, sending Cleon to second. When Boswell's bunt attempt was aborted and Jones was caught off second base, Atlanta catcher Bob Didier committed an unpardonable sin. He threw behind the runner; Cleon took off for third and slid in safely.

Boswell followed with a bouncer to the mound and the Braves went for a double play. Jones, who had held at third on the double play attempt, scored the go-ahead run when first baseman Orlando Cepeda took Kranepool's grounder and threw wildly to the plate for an error.

One out later, the Braves walked light-hitting Bud Harrelson intentionally. It was a sign for Hodges to look around on his bench for someone to hit for Seaver. He selected J. C. Martin, and the part-time catcher, who had hit a mere .209 during the regular season, responded with a single to center on the first pitch. Two runs scored on the hit, and another came around when Tony Gonzalez let the ball get by him for an error. The Mets magic was still working.

Game Two started out to be a cakewalk for the Mets. Koosman was handed an 8–0 lead after only four innings as the Mets pounded Atlanta starter Ron Reed for one run in the first and three more in the second. They added two more in each of the third and fourth innings off Paul Doyle and Milt Pappas. With Koosman on the mound, an 8–0 lead seemed insurmountable.

But after scoring one run in the fourth, the Braves ripped Koosman for five runs in the fifth. Three of the Atlanta runs came on a home run by Hank

The Mets' four-man rotation that took the team to the top in 1969. From left: Tom Seaver, Jerry Koosman, Gary Gentry, and Nolan Ryan. Three out of those four pitchers were still active in 1985 and contributed to their respective clubs. Gary Gentry was later traded to Texas and finished his career in 1976. Seaver went from the Mets in 1977 to the Reds, back to the Mets, to the White Sox, and in 1986 to the Red Sox. Koosman left the Mets in 1978 for the Twins, later went to the Phillies, and was finally released in 1985. Ryan went to the Angels in 1971 and later to the Astros.
DAILY NEWS/BILL MEURER

Aaron, who hit one in each of the three playoff games. Clete Boyer singled home two more and Koosman was replaced by Taylor. The right-handed reliever got the final out of the inning and pitched a scoreless sixth before giving way to McGraw, who blanked the Braves the final three.

There were three home runs by the Mets in that game, the first two by Agee and Boswell. In the seventh, Jones hit the third one, but only after almost decapitating his close friend Agee. The center fielder was on third when he suddenly decided to try and steal home. But no one told Jones, who was at the plate. As the Braves pitcher went into his windup, Agee streaked for home; the ball approached the plate, and Jones swung. What followed was a vicious foul that barely missed skulling Agee. It was a frightening incident for both, but Jones calmed down enough to hit a home run over the left field fence and a shaken Agee trotted home.

Shea Stadium was jammed with 53,195 fanatics when the third game was played in New York on October 6. Tickets for the playoffs were harder to obtain than seats for *Rosencrantz and Guildenstern Are Dead*, the hottest Broadway show of the day.

Gentry was the Mets pitcher, while Pat Jarvis started for Atlanta. It was do-or-die for the Braves. They'd had trouble with the Mets all season, and now they would have to beat them three in a row in the Mets' home park to emerge the champions. There was some hope when Aaron tagged Gentry for a long, two-run home run in the first inning.

In the third inning, Gonzalez singled and Aaron doubled. When Rico Carty hit a long drive to left that was barely foul, Hodges wasted no time. He went to his bullpen and brought in Ryan. It was too early in the game for Hodges to go to McGraw or Taylor, the short relievers, and Hodges knew that Carty was a free swinger. So, with a 1–2 count on Rico, Ryan entered the game and fired a fastball Carty never saw for strike three. After walking Cepeda intentionally, Ryan struck out Clete Boyer and got Didier on an easy fly.

After Agee homered in the third, Boswell hit a two-run home run in the fourth to give the Mets a 3–2 lead. But Ryan was tagged for a two-run home run by Cepeda in the fifth and the Braves were ahead again, 4–3. It was a nail-biter.

In the bottom of the fifth, Ryan, who had hit .114 during the season, opened with a single, and one out later Garrett—the very same Garrett who had been drafted out of the Braves farm system for $25,000 ten months earlier—lined a home run into the right field bullpen. Garrett had hit only one home run all season and batted .218 as a utility man.

The Mets went on to add another run in the fifth and still another in the sixth, and with Ryan pitching shutout ball the final four innings, the Mets wound up with a 7–4 victory. They had polished off the Braves three in a row and almost made it look easy. In one year they had risen from ninth place to become champions of the National League, all of this only seven years after they had entered the record books as the worst team in baseball history with only 40 victories and 120 defeats.

Throughout the playoffs, M. Donald Grant sat in a box alongside the Mets dugout pounding his fist into a glove. The glove belonged to Bobby Pfeil, a young utility infielder who had been declared ineligible for post-season play because of roster limits.

"Bobby can't be in the playoffs, but I'm wearing his glove to make him feel a part of it," said Grant gratuitously.

"I can't believe I'm even here," said Pfeil, who watched the playoffs from the stands and later celebrated with his teammates in the clubhouse. "I was in St. Petersburg with the Tidewater club when the Mets opened the season. Now I'm here and we're the National League champions. This is unreal. After seven years in the minors, I'm on a major league club—a championship club. It'll take a few days for this to sink in."

The Mets clubhouse was in pandemonium. The Braves clubhouse was a morgue.

"They beat the hell out of us," said a stunned Luman Harris, the manager of the Braves.

"The Mets really are amazing," said home run champ Hank Aaron.

Paul Richards, the Atlanta general manager, had another suggestion.

"They ought to send the Mets to Viet Nam. They'd end the war in three days."

As underdogs—young underdogs—the Mets were the toast of the country. A bunch of players made a sing-along record, the entire team was treated to a party by New York Governor Nelson Rockefeller at his Fifth Avenue apartment, and offers to endorse products at fat fees were coming in every day. Tom Seaver arranged to co-author a book and comedian Phil Foster, a rabid baseball fan, planned a Las Vegas act in which a dozen players would sing, dance in a chorus line, and tell jokes.

But first the Mets had a date to play the Baltimore Orioles, champions of the American League, in the World Series.

Despite all their heroics in winning everything in the National League, the Mets went into their first World Series as decided underdogs. The Baltimore team they would play had just overwhelmed the Minnesota Twins in three straight to take the American League pennant. They were a veteran team with considerable experience in post-season play, and they regarded the Mets as upstarts.

"Bring on Ron Gaspar!" shouted Frank Robinson of the Orioles, blurring the distinction between Ron Swoboda and Rod Gaspar—Robinson gave the impression he didn't know one from the other. In the eyes of the Orioles, the Mets were a bunch of virtual unknowns, while the Orioles' own lineup was studded with established stars—Frank Robinson himself, Brooks Robinson, Boog Powell, Paul Blair, and Don Buford, plus starting pitchers Jim Palmer, Dave McNally, and Mike Cuellar. The three pitchers combined had won fifty-nine games during the season.

Nothing happened in the first game to change anyone's opinion that the Orioles would probably sweep the Mets as easily as they had the Minnesota Twins.

Seaver, who had won twenty-five games during the regular season, saw his first pitch of the game rocked for a home run by Buford. Swoboda went back to the right field fence and made a futile leap for the ball. Whatever chance he might have had of catching the ball was eliminated when he timed his leap improperly. He was coming down as the ball sailed over his head.

Cuellar was virtually unhittable. For the first six innings he held the Mets scoreless. Meanwhile, the Orioles were adding three more runs to their lead in the fourth inning. Seaver retired the first two batters in the inning, but before he could get the third one, Elrod Hendricks singled, Davey Johnson walked, Mark Belanger singled, Cuellar singled, and Buford doubled.

The Mets' lone run of the game came in the seventh when Clendenon singled, Swoboda walked, and Grote singled to load the bases. A sacrifice fly by Weis scored one run; Brooks Robinson saved another for the Orioles when he came in to scoop up Rod Gaspar's slow roller and threw him out on a close play for the third out of the inning. The Mets did get two runners to base in the ninth and had Shamsky up with two out. A home run would have tied the score. But Shamsky grounded out and the cocky Orioles trotted off the field. Three more wins and they would be world champions.

The situation in the second game was a little different. Koosman was the dominant pitcher this time. For six innings, the Orioles could not get a hit off the left-hander. Koosman, who had thrown six shutouts and part of two more during the regular season, nursed a 1–0 lead provided by Clendenon's fourth inning home run off McNally.

Met pitcher Jerry Koosman (right) examines the bandaged wrist of teammate J. C. Martin before the fifth game of the World Series. Martin was hit by the thrown ball in game four as he was running to first on the sacrifice bunt. In the scramble, the Orioles allowed Rod Gaspar to score the winning run from second base.

UPI/BETTMAN NEWSPHOTO

Davey Johnson, now manager of the Mets, is out trying to steal second on October 15 as Bud Harrelson reaches for a throw from Grote. Umpire Lee Weyer gets ready to make the call.

DAILY NEWS/DANNY FARRELL

Blair opened the seventh with a single, stole second, and came home with the tying run on a single by Brooks Robinson.

It remained a 1–1 game until the ninth when, with two out, Ed Charles bounced a single through the left side. Hodges flashed the hit-and-run sign to Grote, and the little catcher drove a hit past the shortstop. Charles was able to make it to third. Now it was Weis's turn to play the role of World Series hero, and the slender infielder came through with a single to left that brought Charles home. The Mets had a 2–1 lead and Koosman, who had thrown a two-hitter to this point, needed only three outs for the Mets to even the Series.

The first two outs came easy, but the Mets sweated out the third. With two out and Frank Robinson the batter, Hodges used his four-man outfield strategy, and millions of fans watching the Sunday game on television saw it for the first time. The strategy was to prevent Robinson, a power hitter, from

Manager Gil Hodges (left) rushes to congratulate J. C. Martin on his game-winning bunt after the 2–1 Mets victory over the Orioles. In the center is Donn Clendenon, who hit a homer in the second inning.

UPI/BETTMANN NEWSPHOTO

getting an extra-base hit that would put him in scoring position with the tying run. The plan came to naught when Koosman walked Robinson on a 3–2 pitch. Then he also walked Powell, and the Orioles got the tying run to second without a base hit. That brought right-hander Brooks Robinson to the plate. Brooks already had one of the two hits off Koosman, and Hodges was taking no chances. He signaled to the bullpen for Taylor.

Taylor's control was not much better than the tiring Koosman's. He quickly fell behind in the count, 3–1, but Robinson obliged by bouncing to Charles at third. But this was no routine play. Charles first started for third to tag the bag and force Frank Robinson but suddenly realized he could not beat the runner so hurried a throw to first. It was in the dirt, but Clendenon, an experienced first baseman, dug it out for the final out. The fact that Brooks Robinson did not run all that well averted an infield hit and a bases-loaded situation.

The jubilant Mets had their first World Series victory, and now they were going home to friendly Shea Stadium for the next three games. No matter what happened there, they could not be swept in four games by the Orioles as the oracles had predicted. And what happened at Shea in the next three games was just a repeat of the mysterious and miraculous events that had followed the Mets the final two months of the season.

With the familiar "Let's go, Mets!" chants rocking Shea Stadium, the Mets shocked the Orioles with a 5–0 win as Gentry and Ryan combined for a four-hitter. Palmer lasted only six innings for Baltimore and gave up four of the five runs, three of them in the first two innings.

Agee opened the offensive game for the Mets with a home run over the center field fence. The 56,335 fans were beside themselves. And when the Mets added two more runs in the second for a 3–0 lead, the stadium literally rocked from the foot-stomping that accompanied each Baltimore out. Gentry himself accounted for the two runs in the second when he doubled over Blair's head in right center after Grote had walked and Harrelson singled—all with two out.

In the fourth inning the Orioles began to think they were fighting a force other than the Mets. Frank Robinson singled with one out and took third on another single by Powell. After Gentry fanned Brooks Robinson, Hendricks sent a screamer to left center that had "double" and "two runs" written all over it. But Agee, a superb center fielder, timed the ball perfectly and caught it as he crashed into the left center field fence. Catching it was one thing, holding on to the ball after the crash was something else—the white of the ball showed through the webbing of Agee's glove.

All the Orioles were on their feet on the dugout steps, suddenly realizing all those things they had read about the Miracle Mets might be true. Three innings later they were sure.

Gentry, who had allowed only three hits and two walks up to the seventh, suddenly lost all control and walked Belanger, Dave May, and Buford in succession to load the bases with two outs. That was all for Gentry; Hodges waved Ryan in from the bullpen.

Bringing in a pitcher with Ryan's control problems in a bases-loaded situation in the World Series was a courageous move on Hodges' part. But he had done it before, and virtually every move the manager made had worked for two months. Why not now?

Ryan quickly got two strikes over on Blair, and the center fielder was in a hole. But seconds later, Mets fans were treated to another miracle. Blair hit a long drive, this one to the warning track in right center. Agee, again taking off at the crack of the bat, kept running to his left and back toward the fence. Just as the ball was about to hit the edge of the dirt on the warning track, Agee dove through the air, skidded along the ground, and came to a stop with the ball nestled safely in his glove. A miracle catch.

Agee later said he thought he might have caught the ball without a dive but that the wind had become a factor. "The wind dropped the ball right down, and I had to hit the dirt."

"If the ball had fallen safely, I might have had an inside-the-park home run," commented Blair sadly. "I was at second base when he caught it."

The Orioles, retreating from the dugout steps once again, shook their heads in disbelief.

The Mets, who were taking all these heroics in stride because they were by now used to them, padded their lead when Grote doubled home another run in the sixth and Kranepool homered over the right center fence in the eighth. Kranepool, of all the Mets, particularly savored the joy of those victorious afternoons. He had been with the club the longest and had played on Mets teams that were accustomed to losing 100 games a year.

Gaspar, the unknown, was in right field for defense in the ninth inning of the third game and caught the first two flies for outs. Then another few moments of optimism for the Orioles. Belanger got on base with a walk, Clay Dalrymple with an infield hit, and Buford walked to load the bases. Hodges did not weaken. He stayed with Ryan, and the big right-hander threw a called third strike past Paul Blair to end the game and give the Mets the lead in the Series.

Stranger-than-fiction occurrences continued in the fourth game. Seaver, who had lost the first game, was back for another try. When Seaver arrived at the ballpark, he faced a controversial situation that would have unnerved most athletes. Citizens opposed to the war in Viet Nam had declared it Moratorium Day, and outside Shea Stadium they were passing out mimeographed sheets announcing that Seaver had urged the United States to get out of Viet Nam. Apparently he had considered taking out an ad in the *New York Times* to express his opposition to the United States' involvement in the war. He decided against the ad, but that day the *Times* carried his picture on the front

Many people associated with the Mets still consider this catch by Ron Swoboda the most dramatic and spectacular in their history. Coming in the fourth game of the World Series, this slicing liner to the right by Brooks Robinson was just barely within Swoboda's reach. He decided to go for it, and in doing so, prevented an additional run from scoring (although Frank Robinson, already on third, tagged up and scored). The Mets won the game, 2–1.
DAILY NEWS/FRANK HURLEY

page and mentioned not only that he was pitching but also his opposition to the war.

Seaver refused to comment on the papers being handed out outside the park. He said he would have a statement to make after the game regarding his feelings on the war. But in the flush of another victory that moved the Mets to within one game of winning the World Series, Seaver's comments on Viet Nam went unrecorded.

Seaver pitched a dandy game. Thanks to offense and defense provided by Clendenon, he took a 1–0 lead into the ninth inning. Clendenon had homered off Cuellar on a 3–2 pitch for a 1–0 lead in the second and helped preserve it with a couple of outstanding fielding plays.

In the ninth, with one out, Frank Robinson and Boog Powell singled to put runners on first and third. Brooks Robinson followed with a slicing, opposite-field liner to right center that Swoboda should have played safely on one bounce and conceded the run. Instead, Swoboda dove through the air, landed on his face, and came up with the ball for the second out. Frank Robinson, who couldn't believe what he was witnessing, scored after the catch with the tying run. Swoboda followed by misjudging Hendricks' fly ball but adjusted in time to make a running catch for the third out.

Seaver, still pitching, repulsed a Baltimore threat in the top of the tenth inning. In the bottom half, the Orioles knew they were snakebit when once again the Mets scored the winning run on a strange play.

Grote opened the Mets tenth with a fly to shallow left field. It was a catchable ball, but Buford, the left fielder, getting a late start, could not reach it. Neither could Belanger, the shortstop, who was backing up for it, nor Blair, who raced in from center field. What should have been an easy out became a double.

Gaspar was sent in to run for Grote, and Weis was handed an intentional walk. J. C. Martin was sent up to pinch hit for Seaver. Orioles coach Billy Hunter, running the club in the absence of manager Earl Weaver, who had been ejected in the third inning for protesting too vigorously the calls behind the plate, called on Pete Richert, a left-hander, to relieve Bob Hall.

Martin followed with the sacrifice attempt the Orioles were anticipating, but when Richert fielded the ball and threw to first, his throw hit Martin on the wrist, ricocheted past first into right field, and Gaspar raced home from second base with the run that made the Mets 2–1 winners and gave them a commanding 3–1 lead in the Series.

Richert and the Orioles argued long after the game that Martin was not outside the foul line when running to first, as he should have been to avoid being hit by the ball. Some photographs showed the runner in fair territory, suggesting he should have been declared out. Umpire Shag Crawford said it was a judgment call, and in his judgment Martin's foot had touched the right field foul line. Sure, said the Orioles. What else would you expect a National League umpire to say?

Koosman and McNally were the starting pitchers again in the fifth game, but this time Koosman was not as overpowering as he had been in the second game. Belanger singled to open the second inning, and then, with everyone in the ballpark expecting McNally to bunt, the Orioles pitcher instead swung away and drove Koosman's first pitch into the left field bullpen. Two outs later Frank Robinson also homered, and suddenly Mets fans were beginning to worry that the age of miracles was over.

At that point, the Orioles had four hits off Koosman. However, they got only one more the remainder of the game, as Koosman went all the way to pitch the Mets to a 5–3 victory and the unexpected World Series triumph.

Plate umpire Lou DiMuro, an American Leaguer, replaced Crawford as the

center of controversy in this one. In the sixth inning when it appeared a Koosman pitch had hit Frank Robinson on the thigh, DiMuro ruled that it had hit Robinson's bat first. The Orioles lost the long argument that followed. In the bottom of the same inning, McNally hit Cleon Jones on the foot with a pitch. When DiMuro refused to accept the fact that the ball had hit the Mets slugger in the foot, Hodges emerged from the Mets dugout carrying a baseball with a smudge on it. Hodges said it was the same ball that had hit Cleon and that the smudge was shoe polish, which should be proof enough. DiMuro agreed and reversed himself, sending Jones to first base.

Weaver could not believe that DiMuro, an umpire from his own league, could rule one way on Robinson and then reverse himself on Jones because Hodges had produced a baseball with a smudge on it. DiMuro told Weaver to sit down and shut up.

Clendenon followed with a line drive off the auxiliary scoreboard in left field for his third home run in three games. The Orioles' lead was cut to 3–2.

Weis, the hero of the big Chicago series with his two home runs, looked like a Babe Ruth again when he hit the second pitch McNally threw him in the sixth for a home run over the 371-foot marker in left center for the game-tying run. It was the only home run he hit at Shea Stadium all season!

Jones opened the eighth inning with a double off the fence in left center off reliever Ed Watt and scored the tie-breaking run when Swoboda doubled down the left field line as Buford made a backhanded pickup of the ball. One out later, first baseman Boog Powell muffed a low line drive by Grote for an error. When Powell recovered and threw to first, Watt couldn't handle the ball and dropped it for another error. Swoboda, who never stopped running, scored all the way from second. The Mets were ahead, 5–3, and only three outs away from the summit.

Koosman kept the adventure alive when he walked Frank Robinson to open the ninth. Powell, a slugger capable of tying the game with one swing, was an easy out for Koosman, who got him to bounce to second baseman Weis. But the Mets failed to get the double play, settling instead for the force at second. Brooks Robinson, also capable of hitting a home run, lifted a fly ball to Swoboda in right, and now only one out stood between the Mets and the world championship.

It came at exactly 3:17 P.M., when Davey Johnson lofted a routine fly ball to

Jones. The left fielder knelt on one knee after making the catch. It was almost as if he was genuflecting and thanking the gods for the miracles they had bestowed.

"It was like an avalanche. There was no way we were going to be able to stop this team," said Baltimore Orioles general manager Frank Cashen as he made the obligatory visit to the Mets clubhouse to congratulate the conquering heroes.

Three months after Neil Armstrong was the first man to step on the moon, the Mets were baseball champions of the universe. The Impossible Dream had been realized.

After watching Agee and Swoboda rob his team of base hits on successive days, Baltimore manager Earl Weaver was asked if the Mets were in fact "a team of destiny." "No," he replied tartly, "I believe they are a team with some fine defensive outfielders."

Responding to questions about his daredevil catch, Swoboda explained, "It's really not a gamble. You either try to catch it or watch it roll to the fence. You say to yourself, 'Let's go and get it,' and that's what I did."

Stengel, who was there at the start before anyone dreamed of a Mets World Series, reveled in the joy of the hour.

"This club doesn't make many mistakes now, you can see they believe in each other, and the coaches all live in New York and you can get them on the phone," Stengel rambled. "So I'm very proud of these fellas, which did such a splendid job, and if they keep improving like this, they can keep going to Christmas. The Mets are amazing."

As Davey Johnson's fly ball to left field is caught by Cleon Jones, Jerry Koosman jumps on Jerry Grote and Donn Clendenon runs toward Ed Charles (number 5) to shake hands and share the precious moment of final victory.
DAILY NEWS/PAUL DE MARIA

Tom Seaver and Gary Gentry survey the damage to Shea's playing surface following the World Series final victory.
LOUIS REQUENA

Pandemonium erupted. Players rushed to get off the field before the fans ripped the uniforms off their backs. Everything that wasn't nailed down was grabbed for souvenirs. Jones and Agee didn't even bother to try for the dugout. Instead they raced for the bullpen gate in right center to get off the field and continued on to the clubhouse in the runway under the stands.

The celebration in the Mets clubhouse made Times Square on New Year's Eve look tame indeed. Case upon case of champagne was brought in for the celebration. Several of the players were only a few years above the legal drinking age, but who was drinking? Most of the bubbly was being squirted into people's faces or being poured over the heads of unsuspecting victims.

"I never saw anything like this," said Yogi Berra, who had been in more than a dozen Yankee pennant celebrations.

1969

NAME	G by POS	B	AGE	G	AB	R	H	2B	3B	HR	RBI	BB	SO	SB	BA	SA
NEW YORK 1st 100-62 .617				**GIL HODGES**												
TOTALS			27	162	5427	632	1311	184	41	109	598	527	1089	66	.242	.351
Ed Kranepool	1B106, OF2	L	24	112	353	36	84	9	2	11	49	37	32	3	.238	.368
Ken Boswell	2B96	L	23	102	362	48	101	14	7	3	32	36	47	7	.279	.381
Bud Harrelson	SS119	B	25	123	395	42	98	11	6	0	24	54	54	1	.248	.306
Wayne Garrett	3B72, 2B47, SS9	L	21	124	400	38	87	11	3	1	39	40	75	4	.218	.268
Ron Swoboda	OF97	R	25	109	327	38	77	10	2	9	52	43	90	1	.235	.361
Tommie Agee	OF146	R	26	149	565	97	153	23	4	26	76	59	137	12	.271	.464
Cleon Jones	OF122, 1B15	R	26	137	483	92	164	25	4	12	75	64	60	16	.340	.482
Jerry Grote	C112	R	26	113	365	38	92	12	3	6	40	32	59	2	.252	.351
Rod Gaspar	OF91	B	23	118	215	26	49	6	1	1	14	25	19	7	.228	.279
Al Weis	SS52, 2B43, 3B1	R	31	103	247	20	53	9	2	2	23	15	51	3	.215	.291
Art Shamsky	OF78, 1B9	L	27	100	303	42	91	9	3	14	47	36	32	1	.300	.488
Donn Clendenon	1B58, OF1	R	33	72	202	31	51	5	0	12	37	19	62	3	.252	.455
J. C. Martin	C48, 1B2	L	32	66	177	12	37	5	1	4	21	12	32	0	.209	.316
Bobby Pfeil	3B49, 2B11, OF2	R	25	62	211	20	49	9	0	0	10	7	27	0	.232	.275
Ed Charles	3B52	R	34	61	169	21	35	8	1	3	18	18	31	4	.207	.320
Amos Otis	OF35, 3B3	R	22	48	93	6	14	3	1	0	4	6	27	1	.151	.204
Duffy Dyer	C19	R	23	29	74	5	19	3	1	3	12	4	22	0	.257	.446

Kevin Collins 22 L 6-40, Jim Gosger 26 L 2-15, Bob Heise 22 R 3-10

NAME	T	AGE	W	L	PCT	SV	G	GS	CG	IP	H	BB	SO	ShO	ERA
		26	100	62	.617	35	162	162	51	1468	1217	517	1012	28	2.99
Tom Seaver	R	24	25	7	.781	0	36	35	18	273	202	82	208	5	2.21
Jerry Koosman	L	26	17	9	.654	0	32	32	16	241	187	68	180	6	2.28
Gary Gentry	R	22	13	12	.520	0	35	35	6	234	192	81	154	3	3.42
Tug McGraw	L	24	9	3	.750	12	42	4	1	100	89	47	92	0	2.25
Ron Taylor	R	31	9	4	.692	13	59	0	0	76	61	24	42	0	2.72
Don Cardwell	R	33	8	10	.444	0	30	21	4	152	145	47	60	0	3.02
Cal Koonce	R	28	6	3	.667	7	40	0	0	83	85	42	48	0	4.99
Nolan Ryan	R	22	6	3	.667	1	25	10	2	89	60	53	92	0	3.54
Jim McAndrew	R	25	6	7	.462	0	27	21	4	135	112	44	90	2	3.47
Jack DiLauro	L	26	1	4	.200	1	23	4	0	64	50	18	27	0	2.39
Danny Frisella	R	23	0	0	.000	0	3	0	0	5	8	3	5	0	7.20
Jesse Hudson	L	20	0	0	.000	0	1	0	0	2	2	2	3	0	4.50
Al Jackson	L	33	0	0	.000	0	9	0	0	11	18	4	10	0	10.64
Bob Johnson	R	26	0	0	.000	1	2	0	0	2	1	1	1	0	0.00
Les Rohr	L	23	0	0	.000	0	1	0	0	1	5	1	0	0	27.00

T he parties continued long after the World Series ended. A ticker tape parade up Broadway, the kind Charles Lindbergh received after his solo flight to Paris, was accorded the Mets the Monday following the marvelous triumph. It was the third such parade up lower Broadway that year and the biggest. In January the New York Jets had been saluted for their Super Bowl victory over the Baltimore Colts. In August, Neil Armstrong and the Apollo II astronauts were honored. But the turnout for the Mets was greater than the previous two.

A reception at City Hall followed, and the Mets presented the City of New York with the pitching rubber from Shea Stadium, signed by Seaver, Koosman, and Gentry, the three pitchers credited with the four World Series triumphs. The Mets then were driven to a public gathering in Bryant Park on 42nd Street, where another huge lunchtime crowd had gathered to cheer them. Following a luncheon at the plush Four Seasons restaurant, the Mets were taken by bus back to Flushing, where that night they attended the Jets' 1969 home opener against the Houston Oilers.

Grant and Murphy had decided a few days after the final Series victory to offer Hodges a new contract. They decided on three years at $70,000 a year. Hodges readily accepted, and the Mets spent the rest of the off-season attending banquets and dinners and accepting awards and all the other glory that goes with becoming world champions. They also pocketed $18,338 apiece as the winners' share of the World Series pool. For some, it was more than they had made during the season. The seven Mets who starred in comedian Phil Foster's Las Vegas night club act later each picked up another $10,000 for two weeks of fun.

For people like Murphy, it was back to business shortly after the partying ceased. The Mets had won, but still they were far from being a complete team. They needed a third baseman with experience—Charles had been released at the end of October. Five weeks later the Mets concluded the deal they believed to be the answer to their infield weakness. In a deal with Kansas City, with Hodges' urging, the Mets obtained Joe Foy in exchange for pitcher Bob Johnson and outfielder Amos Otis. It developed into one of the worst deals the club ever made, and it certainly did not fill the hole at third base.

Foy, Bronx-born, had played four years in the American League with Boston and Kansas City. Hodges knew, or should have known through the grapevine, that Joe was having personal difficulties. That became obvious once the 1970 season started. He missed seventy-two games with the Mets, batted a disappointing .236, and was released outright to the Tidewater farm club in October. In later years, Foy returned to the Bronx, where he became a counselor in a drug rehabilitation program.

That was Johnny Murphy's last major deal. He did not live long enough to see how badly it turned out. On December 30, 1969, he suffered a heart attack at his Bronxville home. He was taken to a local hospital where two weeks later, on January 14, 1970, he died of a second massive heart attack. The Mets were stunned. Not only had they lost their top front office baseball executive, but they had no immediate replacement—at least no one who could debate baseball decisions with Grant and win.

Herzog would have been an ideal choice to move up from his position as director of player development—no one knew the organization better than Whitey. But Herzog was too strong-minded and too opinionated for Grant's tastes. He had frequently told the Mets' chairman of the board in organizational meetings that he should let his baseball men make the baseball decisions. This rankled Grant, who fancied himself a much better evaluator of talent than his more experienced personnel.

Murphy's successor, selected five days after the popular general manager's death, was Bob Scheffing, a big, easygoing former catcher, manager, broadcas-

13

♦ HODGES ♦
♦ CALLS ♦
♦ THE SHOTS ♦

OPENING DAY LINEUP 1970

Agee, cf
Harrelson, ss
Foy, 3b
Jones, lf
Shamsky, 1b
Swoboda, rf
Garrett, 2b
Grote, c
Seaver, p

ter, and scout lured to New York by Grant. Scheffing was well liked by baseball people, made a good impression in manner and dress, and certainly knew baseball, but he didn't seem to want the general manager's job.

Scheffing and his wife, Mary, were living in Scottsdale, Arizona. Scheffing's salary as a Mets special assignment scout was more than adequate; the arrangement left him at home to play golf and be with Mary, which was all he needed. The last thing the Scheffings wanted to do was move to New York. Spurred on by Grant's urging and the promise of a luxury apartment overlooking Little Neck Bay near Shea Stadium, Scheffing finally accepted.

In hiring Scheffing, Grant gained a more powerful voice on matters affecting the players, because Scheffing rarely opposed Grant. Hodges became the single strong voice to oppose Grant in the higher echelons of the Mets organization. Grant made this clear to me when he expressed his fear of Gil one night after an incident involving Seaver.

Seaver was sitting on the bench one night when a bat flew out of the hands of the hitter and struck Seaver directly. Television cameras captured the incident, so fans at home as well as in the stadium watched in horror as Tom left the dugout in pain, accompanied by trainer Tom McKenna. The obvious question: How badly was Seaver hurt?

Harold Weissman, the public relations director, would not call the dugout or clubhouse to ascertain the extent of Seaver's injury—would not because he could not.

The 1969 World Champions
DAILY NEWS/GENE KAPPOCK

New York is covered with ticker tape on October 20 following the Mets' World Series victory. At the center, Gil Hodges and his wife, Joan, atop a limo, are mobbed by fans.
DAILY NEWS/FRANK HURLEY

"Gil has a rule," Weissman explained to reporters. "We can't call down. He'll call us."

Hodges had no conception of press deadlines or the news value of such stories and was in no hurry to call the press box. On radio and television, meanwhile, Lindsey Nelson, Bob Murphy, and Ralph Kiner could only tell their vast audience that there was no news yet on how seriously Seaver might have been injured by the flying bat. They were as much in the dark as we all were.

Finally, after the game, it was explained that Seaver was okay. Miraculously, he was only shaken up by the flying bat, which had narrowly missed his head. (It caught him in the chest.)

The next night as I parked in the special lot in front of Shea Stadium reserved for newspapermen, I encountered Grant, who had just arrived in his chauffeured limousine. I tried to explain to him the needless anxiety caused by the informational time lag we had encountered the night before. I explained Gil's rule, as detailed by Weissman.

"It seems everyone is afraid of Gil," I said to Grant. "Can't you do something about it."

"I'm afraid of him, too," Grant said, smiling.

Grant then got very upset when I reminded him we were not talking about just another player, but about Seaver.

On December 16, 1969, Tom Seaver was announced winner of the Sports Illustrated Sportsman of the Year Award and accepted the trophy. At the ceremony, General Manager John Murphy said that if Tom ever wanted to be adopted, he and his wife, Bette, would be happy to do the honors. Around this time, Seaver became known in the press box as "the Franchise." He was the Mets' most valuable chattel, the one player who was able to lead them out of the wilderness and the player they could least afford to lose. His 1969 numbers spoke for themselves: 25–7, 2.21 ERA, 5 shutouts, 208 strikeouts in 273 innings.

DAILY NEWS

"He's 'the Franchise,' " I pointed out.

Grant lost his cool.

"Don't you call Seaver the franchise," he bellowed. "Mrs. Payson and I are the franchise."

With that, he turned and strode into the stadium. I followed, trying to explain that we were dealing in semantics, that the writers referred to Seaver as the Franchise only because his coming had turned things around for the team. After all, he was the best pitcher in the National League.

Grant kept shouting back at me, "Mrs. Payson and I are the franchise!"

Hodges' Law remained in force, and whenever a player was hurt or removed from a game for some unusual reason, the press, radio, and TV corps had to wait until the manager or one of his aides decided it was time to tell us what had happened.

On April 7, 1970, the Mets began their defense of the National League championship by winning an opening day game for the first time; the victory was against the Pirates in Pittsburgh. It took eleven innings before Clendenon broke a 3–3 tie with a two-run pinch single. Seaver pitched well for eight, and Taylor was superb in relief for the win. Another monkey had slid off the Mets' backs. After nine years, they had finally won an opener.

There were no miracles in 1970. The team that could do nothing wrong the last two months of 1969 was suddenly back on a treadmill fighting to play .500 ball. Koosman suffered from tendonitis of the left elbow. He pitched ineffectively during the first month and a half, winning only two of his first nine starts before he was sidelined for three weeks in June.

Seaver was Seaver. He won his first six starts, including a performance on April 22 against San Diego at Shea Stadium that ranks as one of the finest pitching jobs of all time. Four days earlier, Ryan had pitched a classic one-hitter against the Phillies, setting a club record with fifteen strikeouts. It was an ephemeral record. Tom Terrific struck out a record nineteen batters in the Padres game, including the last ten in a row. No one had ever fanned nineteen batters in a day game, and no one had ever struck out the last ten in succession.

In the game, which he won, 2–1, Seaver allowed only two hits. Unfortunately one of them was a second inning home run by Al Ferrara. In addition to striking out the last ten, Seaver retired the last sixteen batters he faced. Besides Ferrara's homer, the only other Padre to get a base hit was Dave Campbell in the third, who singled off Foy's glove at third.

"Everybody congratulated me when I got number sixteen in the eighth," Seaver recalled after his record-tying performance, "but I just told them, 'Let's get me some more runs.' All I could think of was that Carlton struck out nineteen of us and still lost."

1970

NAME	G by POS	B	AGE	G	AB	R	H	2B	3B	HR	RBI	BB	SO	SB	BA	SA
NEW YORK 3rd 83-79 .512 8	GIL HODGES															
TOTALS			27	162	5443	695	1358	211	42	120	640	684	1062	118	.249	.370
Donn Clendenon	1B100	R	34	121	396	65	114	18	3	22	97	39	91	4	.288	.515
Ken Boswell	2B101	L	24	105	351	32	89	13	2	5	44	41	32	5	.254	.345
Bud Harrelson	SS156	B	26	157	564	72	137	18	8	1	42	95	74	23	.243	.309
Joe Foy	3B97	R	27	99	322	39	76	12	0	6	37	68	58	22	.236	.329
Ron Swoboda	OF100	R	26	115	245	29	57	8	2	9	40	40	72	2	.233	.392
Tommie Agee	OF150	R	27	153	636	107	182	30	7	24	75	55	156	31	.286	.469
Cleon Jones	OF130	R	27	134	506	71	140	25	8	10	63	57	87	12	.277	.417
Jerry Grote	C125	R	27	126	415	38	106	14	1	2	34	36	39	2	.255	.308
Art Shamsky	OF58, 1B56	L	28	122	403	48	118	19	2	11	49	49	33	1	.293	.432
Wayne Garrett	3B70, 2B45, SS1	L	22	114	366	74	93	17	4	12	45	81	60	5	.254	.421
Dave Marshall	OF43	L	27	92	189	21	46	10	1	6	29	17	43	4	.243	.402
Mike Jorgenson	1B50, OF10	L	21	76	87	15	17	3	1	3	4	10	23	2	.195	.322
Al Weis	2B44, SS15	R	32	75	121	20	25	7	1	1	11	7	21	1	.207	.306
Ken Singleton	OF51	B	23	69	198	22	52	8	0	5	26	30	48	1	.263	.379
Duffy Dyer	C57	R	24	59	148	8	31	1	0	2	12	21	32	1	.209	.257
Ed Kranepool	1B8	L	25	43	47	2	8	0	0	0	3	5	2	0	.170	.170

Tim Foli 19 R 4-11, Rod Gaspar 24 B 0-14, Ted Martinez 22 R 1-16, Leroy Stanton 24 R 1-4

NAME	T	AGE	W	L	PCT	SV	G	GS	CG	IP	H	BB	SO	ShO	ERA
		26	83	79	.512	32	162	162	47	1460	1260	575	1064	10	3.45
Tom Seaver	R	25	18	12	.600	0	37	36	19	291	230	83	283	2	2.81
Jerry Koosman	L	27	12	7	.632	0	30	29	5	212	189	71	118	1	3.14
Jim McAndrew	R	26	10	14	.417	2	32	27	9	184	166	38	111	3	3.57
Gary Gentry	R	23	9	9	.500	1	32	29	5	188	155	86	134	2	3.69
Danny Frisella	R	24	8	3	.727	1	30	1	0	66	49	34	54	0	3.00
Ray Sadecki	L	29	8	4	.667	0	28	19	4	139	134	52	89	0	3.88
Nolan Ryan	R	23	7	11	.389	1	27	19	5	132	86	97	125	2	3.41
Ron Taylor	R	32	5	4	.556	13	57	0	0	66	65	16	28	0	3.95
Tug McGraw	L	25	4	6	.400	10	57	0	0	91	77	49	81	0	3.26
Ron Herbel	R	32	2	2	.500	1	12	0	0	13	14	2	8	0	1.38
Dean Chance	R	29	0	1	.000	1	3	0	0	3	2	0	0	0	13.50
Don Cardwell	R	34	0	2	.000	0	16	1	0	25	31	6	8	0	6.48
Rich Folkers	L	23	0	2	.000	2	16	1	0	29	36	25	15	0	6.52
Cal Koonce	R	29	0	2	.000	0	13	0	0	22	25	14	10	0	3.27

Seaver threw 136 pitches in the game, 65 of which were recorded on the pitching chart as fastball strikes. In all he threw 81 fastballs. In the last couple of innings, when he was striking out every player who came to the plate against him, he threw nothing but high fastballs.

Seaver was the only pitcher that year to get off to a winning start, but then even he found it tough going. Following his 6–0 start, Tom lost five of his next six decisions. On June 4 he was at 7–5 in the won-lost column. In his next start on June 9, Seaver three-hit the Houston Astros for a tight 2–1 win that was to begin an eight-game winning streak. On August 10 he improved his record to 17–6 and seemed a cinch to win twenty again, but then his pitching turned sour. He lost seven of his next eight decisions and finished the season with a disappointing 18–13 performance.

Disappointment was the name of the game for most of the year. In addition to the Foy fiasco—there were times Hodges would not even play him—Jones's average slumped from .340 to .277. Kranepool's abysmal .118 start resulted in a move back to the minors in June and the making of a bitter young man. Charles had been released before the season started, so most of the third base work fell to Wayne Garrett.

Several of the Mets batters lived up to expectations. Clendenon, in this his first full year and playing more often than he had in the championship season, batted a solid .288, with twenty-two homers and ninety-seven runs batted in. Garrett raised his average from .218 to .254 and hit a dozen home runs—three more than he had delivered in four minor league seasons. Even Agee, despite a 1-for-25 slump at the start of the season, batted a robust .286, with twenty-four homers. He also struck out 156 times and made thirteen outfield errors. From mid-April until mid-June, Agee compiled a twenty-game hitting streak that seemed to embarrass him. After he had hit in the first nine games of the streak, he was benched for three days by Hodges. In most batting streaks, a player will hit well over .300; Agee's mark was .268—in his streak!

It was that kind of year for Agee. In late May he suffered from indigestion and chest pains and missed several games. A week later he hit into three double plays in one game. Then he hit .364 in June and set a new club record with eleven home runs in one month. He hit for the cycle (homer, triple, double, single) in a July 6 game and also compiled a nineteen-game hitting streak. But throughout the last half of the season, the center fielder was troubled by a twisted left knee that inhibited his running. He set a club record with his twenty-fourth stolen base on August 4 but stole only eight in the next two months.

For the most part, it was the pitching that let the Mets down in 1970. They won seventeen fewer games than in their championship season and finished in third place in the National League's Eastern Division, six games behind Pittsburgh.

Cardwell was sold to Atlanta in July. Gentry had shoulder trouble in his sophomore season and won only nine games. Koosman, who had won nineteen and seventeen respectively in his first two seasons, was plagued by a sore elbow all season and won only twelve. McAndrew won ten games, four more than the previous year. He also doubled his losses to fourteen. And Ryan, who was hustling back and forth from military obligations in Texas, was also a loser, with a 6–11 record. Nolan did not win a single game after August 4. Taylor and McGraw saved twenty-three games, but they also lost ten and were not given as many opportunities for wins as they had been granted the previous year.

The Mets had their best period from June 12 to July 9. They won twenty of twenty-seven and took over first place with that streak. But on July 11 they dropped to second place after losing to Montreal, and they didn't see the top

On April 14, opening day at Shea, Joan Payson, in her proudest moment, hoists the World Championship flag up the center field pole.
DAILY NEWS/PAUL DE MARIA

again until briefly on September 9–10, when they were tied for the lead with Pittsburgh. Seventeen days later, before 50,469 Pittsburgh fans, the Mets were eliminated from the pennant race when Dock Ellis beat McAndrew in a 2–1 duel. The Mets headed home for a final four-game series with the Cubs. That series had been deemed important a few weeks earlier but now meant nothing for either team.

◆   ◆   ◆

It was up to Scheffing to patch up the Mets in the off-season. The Mets were confident it would not require all that much to see them bounce back—a player here or there but no major surgery on the roster. If the pitching staff bounced back, so would the team, the management reasoned. And they were bringing up Jon Matlack, who had won a dozen games for Tidewater. The best left-hander in the Mets farm system, he was expected to fit right in as a regular starter.

The only deal of any consequence Scheffing engineered during the off-season brought in handsome, Brooklyn-born Bob Aspromonte. Ten years earlier, Aspromonte had been one of Houston's premium picks in the expansion draft. He had played in the majors for both Houston and Atlanta and had batted .255 for nine seasons, but he had never revealed any power. At thirty-two, the Mets figured he would prove a serviceable third baseman for the next few years.

There were other new faces that year, all products of the farm system. Tim Foli was a promising shortstop, Mike Jorgensen a first baseman-outfielder, and Ken Singleton a switch-hitting outfielder. Whether or not they were ready for the Mets, Foli and Singleton were ready to test a long-standing unwritten major league rule by becoming interracial roommates. Both had played together in the minors. Lou Niss, the Mets' traveling secretary, was impressed when the two players—Foli, white, and Singleton, black—came to him and suggested the arrangement. Niss checked it out with Hodges and the arrangement was approved.

Right field was opened up for Singleton to take over full-time on March 31 when Swoboda, one of the heroes of the Miracle of '69, was traded to Montreal for Don Hahn, an outfielder of little note.

Sure enough, the pitching staff showed signs of their 1969 energy when Seaver, Koosman, and Ryan all got off to winning starts. The Mets even won the opening day game in the cold and snow at Shea Stadium, beating Montreal, 4–2. The game lasted only five innings; it probably should not even have started, considering the weather. When it began to snow heavily and the temperature dropped below 32, there was no way the game could resume.

Two days later when the weather cleared, ex-Met Steve Renko outpitched Gentry for a 6–2 Montreal victory, and the Mets dropped into a second place tie. For the next two months they were up and down, in and out of first place, holding it for an eighteen-day stretch in May but dropping back as far as third by Memorial Day.

On June 9, Seaver raised his record to 8–2 with a 4–2 victory over San Diego. Two days later Tug McGraw lost in extra innings, 3–2, to San Francisco, and the Mets dropped out of first place once and for all. They remained in second place until the middle of July but were only seven games (47–40) above .500 and struggling. The first week in June, with his record at 3–4, Koosman took cortisone shots for his ailing elbow. He came back ten days later to pitch poorly in relief, and then five days later he lost in Pittsburgh when Willie Stargell hit a two-run home run.

The Mets' hopes were lifted briefly when the gutsy Koosman went nine innings and beat Montreal, 2–1, on a three-hitter on June 26. However, he failed to strike out a single batter in the game, a sure sign the fastball was

OPENING DAY LINEUP 1971

Agee, cf
Harrelson, ss
Jones, lf
Shamsky, rf
Clendenon, 1b
Boswell, 2b
Aspromonte, 3b
Grote, c
Seaver, p

missing. After two more losing starts, Koosman was placed on the disabled list July 7. Besides tendonitis of the elbow, he also had a rib cage injury and experienced difficulty breathing. He did not pitch again for a month and ended the season with a disappointing 6–11 record.

Matlack, the left-hander the Mets had expected to make the staff, failed to survive spring training. He was called up twice from Tidewater during the season and appeared in seven games. He finished 0–4. Only Seaver and Gentry held up their share of the load. Seaver won twenty games once again; Gentry won a dozen, a record just one game above .500.

Seaver continued to pitch magnificently. In August he established a club record by pitching thirty-one consecutive scoreless innings. On September 26, in an almost perfect game against Pittsburgh, Tom Terrific retired eighteen batters in succession, pitching a one-hitter. It was his third one-hit game in as many seasons. In it he struck out ten Pirates, one of thirteen games in the season in which he fanned ten or more batters; he fanned a total of 289 batters in 1971 to break his own National League record for most strikeouts by a right-handed pitcher. Seaver won the league earned run title with a sensational 1.76, the best ERA record of his career through 1985.

On July 9, Tom Seaver hits his first major league home run and is congratulated by Bud Harrelson. Seaver went on to pitch a three-hitter while beating Montreal, 7–1.
DAILY NEWS/DANNY FARRELL

Bud Harrelson stealing home against the Phillies on September 10. The Mets took fourteen innings to win the game, 4–3. Wayne Garrett is number 11. Tim McCarver is the Phillies catcher.

DAILY NEWS/DANNY FARRELL

The Mets' weak hitting put a strain on the pitching. Agee hit a respectable .285, but with only fourteen homers and fifty RBIs. Clendenon, showing signs of age, became a part-time player; he batted .247. Worse, he only hit eleven homers and drove in a pitiful total of thirty-seven runs. Jones bounced back to hit .319, with fourteen homers. His sixty-nine RBI record was one of the lowest for any team leader in the league. Aspromonte had trouble with his legs, could not run, and did not hit. Bobby's .225 average made it clear he was not the answer to the Mets' ten-year third base problem.

Even though the pitching was disappointing by Mets standards, the staff allowed only 550 runs, fewer than any team in the league. The team batted only .249, the real reason that, when the season was over, they were tied for third place with Chicago, fourteen games behind St. Louis, the division champion.

It was the second straight season after the magic of 1969 they had left their fans disillusioned. Some of the players were also less than happy with the team's performance, particularly the pitchers. Gentry was the only one who

1971

NAME	G by POS	B	AGE	G	AB	R	H	2B	3B	HR	RBI	BB	SO	SB	BA	SA
NEW YORK 3rd (tie) 83-79 .512 14		**GIL HODGES**														
TOTALS			27	162	5477	588	1365	203	29	98	546	547	958	89	.249	.351
Ed Kranepool	1B108, OF11	L	26	122	421	61	118	20	4	14	58	38	33	0	.280	.447
Ken Boswell	2B109	L	25	116	392	46	107	20	1	5	40	36	31	5	.273	.367
Bud Harrelson	SS140	B	27	142	547	55	138	16	6	0	32	53	59	28	.252	.303
Bob Aspromonte	3B97	R	33	104	342	21	77	9	1	5	33	29	25	0	.225	.301
Ken Singleton	OF96	B	24	115	298	34	73	5	0	13	46	61	64	0	.245	.393
Tommie Agee	OF107	R	28	113	425	58	121	19	0	14	50	50	84	28	.285	.428
Cleon Jones	OF132	R	28	136	505	63	161	24	6	14	69	53	87	6	.319	.473
Jerry Grote	C122	R	28	125	403	35	109	25	0	2	35	40	47	1	.270	.347
Dave Marshall	OF64	L	28	100	214	28	51	9	1	3	21	26	54	3	.238	.332
Don Hahn	OF80	R	22	98	178	16	42	5	1	1	11	21	32	2	.236	.292
Tim Foli	2B58, 3B36, SS12, OF1	R	20	97	288	32	65	12	2	0	24	18	50	5	.226	.281
Donn Clendenon	1B72	R	35	88	263	29	65	10	0	11	37	21	78	1	.247	.411
Art Shamsky	OF38, 1B1	L	29	68	135	13	25	6	2	5	18	21	18	1	.185	.370
Duffy Dyer	C53	R	25	59	169	13	39	7	1	2	18	14	45	1	.231	.320
Wayne Garrett	3B53, 2B9	L	23	56	202	20	43	2	0	1	11	28	31	1	.213	.238
Mike Jorgensen	OF31, 1B1	L	22	45	118	16	26	1	1	5	11	11	24	1	.220	.373
Ted Martinez	SS23, 2B13, 3B3, OF1	R	23	38	125	16	36	5	2	1	10	4	22	6	.288	.384

Lee Stanton 25 R 4-21, John Milner 21 L 3-18, Al Weis 33 R 0-11, Frank Estrada 23 R 1-2

NAME	T	AGE	W	L	PCT	SV	G	GS	CG	IP	H	BB	SO	ShO	ERA
		27	83	79	.512	22	162	162	42	1466	1227	529	1157	13	2.99
Tom Seaver	R	26	20	10	.667	0	36	35	21	286	210	61	289	4	1.76
Gary Gentry	R	24	12	11	.522	0	32	31	8	203	167	82	155	3	3.24
Tug McGraw	L	26	11	4	.733	8	51	1	0	111	73	41	109	0	1.70
Nolan Ryan	R	24	10	14	.417	0	30	26	3	152	125	116	137	0	3.97
Danny Frisella	R	25	8	5	.615	12	53	0	0	91	76	30	93	1	1.98
Ray Sadecki	L	30	7	7	.500	0	34	20	5	163	139	44	120	2	2.93
Jerry Koosman	L	28	6	11	.353	0	26	24	4	166	160	51	96	0	3.04
Charlie Williams	R	23	5	6	.455	0	31	9	1	90	92	41	53	0	4.80
Ron Taylor	R	33	2	2	.500	2	45	0	0	69	71	11	32	0	3.65
Jim McAndrew	R	27	2	5	.286	0	24	10	0	90	78	32	42	0	4.40
Buzz Capra	R	23	0	1	.000	0	3	0	0	5	3	5	6	0	9.00
Jon Matlack	L	21	0	3	.000	0	7	6	0	37	31	15	24	0	4.14
Don Rose	R	24	0	0	.000	0	1	0	0	2	2	1	1	0	0.00

would come out and say what he felt, but then Gary was considered a bit of a malcontent. The fact remains, however, that every pitching assignment revolved around Seaver's working schedule, a fact resented by the other pitchers.

Pitchers are like thoroughbred horses. Starters work only every fourth or fifth day, and to some fans and players they seem coddled. When Seaver arrived in 1967, he worked every fourth day. Hodges and Walker instituted a five-day rotation when they arrived from Washington in 1968.

I keep a daily diary on every player's performance, and Walker was interested in perusing the pages I had kept for the pitching staff. When he checked into the Colonial Inn for the first time in spring 1968, he borrowed my book on pitchers and carefully studied how each had worked the year before under Westrum, especially how they fared after a certain number of days of rest. Walker and Hodges were planning to introduce the five-day rotation anyway, but Rube's check of my 1967 statistics, he later admitted, confirmed their decision.

At first Seaver opposed the four-day rest period between starts. Walker, a fatherly figure as pitching coach, convinced him that though he might miss a start or two during the year, he would be stronger and last longer in the games he did start because of the extra day of rest. So, Seaver accepted the change in his routine. Because he was the big winner on the staff, Hodges and Walker wanted him pitching as often as possible—provided he was rested and ready. Thus, when rain-outs came, as they often do early in the season, other pitchers were frequently bypassed in favor of Seaver. Gentry and others considered this to be preferential treatment, which it was. But Seaver was just too important, and the one thing no one could deny was Seaver's success. In his first five seasons in the majors he had won ninety-five and lost only fifty-four; twice he had been a twenty-game winner. He worked 200-plus innings every year and his earned run average for the five full seasons was an impressive 2.34. Any pitcher posting those statistics each year deserved preferential treatment.

Yet even Seaver, despite his fine efforts and special treatment, must have been disappointed by the meek offense provided. Once again, after the 1971 season, the search was on for an experienced hitter or two to back up the strong young pitching staff.

One such deal was completed on December 10, 1971—one of the most

M. Donald Grant explains to Ed Kranepool that because of a poor batting average they are about to send the original Met back to the minors to find his groove. He rebounded in 1971 with a .280 average, fourteen home runs, and fifty-eight RBIs in 119 starts.
LOUIS REQUENA

infamous in Mets history and one for which Grant would later blame me, at least indirectly.

The annual baseball winter meetings were held in Phoenix that December. Most of the major league officials and baseball writers were headquartered at the plush Arizona Biltmore Country Club. It developed into one of the most active winter sessions in years. Fifteen deals involving fifty players were consummated in a five-day period. Seventeen of the twenty-four major league clubs had entered into deals, but the Mets, after two disappointing finishes, made none.

When they were not wheeling and dealing, a great many of the officials played golf on the lush Biltmore course. Scheffing was an avid golfer. While he did tend to his business and attempt to make a deal, he also managed to get in his share of golf. Grant also was a fine golfer and, like Scheffing, held a low handicap. Their affinity for the game brought them that much closer together, but it wasn't getting the Mets any hitters.

Late in the afternoon of the final day of the meeting, I encountered Grant as he came off the course. I decried the lack of trading activity on the part of the Mets, pointing out the deals made by many other clubs.

"Don, you've got to make a deal," I pleaded, sounding like a fan but in reality looking for something to write about that would give Mets fans at home something to cheer about.

"I know," he replied. "We're trying."

Nothing happened that night or the next day. The New York press corps went home that weekend moaning about the Mets' lack of action. On December 10, five days after the meetings ended, we were informed that the Mets had finally completed a deal. Jim Fregosi, a longtime star shortstop for the California Angels, had been obtained in a five-player deal. The Mets got Fregosi, and the Angels received four players—including Nolan Ryan, the hardest-throwing right-hander in the National League. The Angels also received outfielder Leroy Stanton, infielder Don Rose, and catcher Francisco Estrada. Fregosi, who had a .268 lifetime average, was to be shifted to third by the Mets. He would be their eleventh starting third baseman in eleven seasons. Since he was relatively young—he would turn thirty two days prior to opening day—the Mets reasoned he would fill the job for at least four or five years.

Only a few voices of protest were raised over the deal. Fregosi was certainly a fine offensive player. In past years he had shown himself to be a capable infielder, hitting fifteen to twenty homers per season with an average close to .270. But he was coming off his poorest season; he had hit only .233 in 1971 in an injury-plagued season that included a siege of flu, a sore arm, a pulled leg muscle, and surgery for a nerve tumor on his foot.

Nolan had never won more than ten games and twice had losing seasons; for all his promise, he still had control problems. Ryan had requested the trade, primarily because he and his wife, Ruth, both from the little town of Alvin, Texas, were uncomfortable in New York—Ryan worried about his wife's safety when the Mets went on road trips.

Hodges, who knew Fregosi from his days in the American League, approved the deal. He also approved the trading of Ryan—California would not make the deal unless a starting pitcher was involved. Of all his starters, Hodges believed that Ryan was the one he would miss least.

Bob Scheffing insisted he was up against the wall with Ryan and had to trade him.

"Ryan was a country boy from Texas, and he and his wife were frightened by the big city. Ryan told me after the 1971 season that he didn't want to spend another year in New York. He hoped I would trade him. I don't think he would have walked away from baseball, but I couldn't take that chance.

"We really thought we had a chance to win the pennant if we could get a third baseman. Fregosi had been one of the outstanding offensive shortstops in the American League for years. We didn't think he would have any trouble shifting to third."

In retrospect, the Ryan deal was probably the worst in the Mets' history. At least when they traded Seaver in 1977, several years later, they got some help from Steve Henderson, Pat Zachry, and Doug Flynn. But Fregosi failed in New York, while Ryan soared to incredible heights with the California Angels. As of the end of the 1985 season he had won 241 games, only 29 of them for the Mets. He also became baseball's all-time strikeout leader in 1985 by striking out 209 batters to lift his lifetime total to 4,083. Ironically, he got his 4,000th strikeout against the Mets.

COMPLETE GAME ONE-HITTERS BY METS' PITCHERS*

June 22, 1962	Al Jackson vs. Houston (2–0) (Amalfitano single in 1st)
May 4, 1966	Jack Hamilton at St. Louis (8–0) (Sadecki single in 3d)
July 9, 1969	Tom Seaver vs. Chicago (4–0) (Qualls single in 9th)
April 18, 1970	Nolan Ryan vs. Philadelphia (7–0) (Doyle single in 1st)
May 13, 1970	Gary Gentry at Chicago (4–0) (Banks single in 1st)
May 15, 1970	Tom Seaver at Philadelphia (4–0) (Compton single in 3d)
April 18, 1971	Gary Gentry vs. Pittsburgh (5–2) (Clemente triple in 6th)
September 26, 1971	Tom Seaver vs. Pittsburgh (3–1) (Davalillo single in 7th)
July 4, 1972	Tom Seaver vs. San Diego (2–0) (Lee single in 9th)
July 10, 1973	Jon Matlack vs. Houston (1–0) (Helms double in 6th)
June 29, 1974	Jon Matlack vs. St. Louis (4–0) (Curtis single in 3d)
April 17, 1977	Tom Seaver vs. Chicago (6–0) (Ontiveros single in 5th)
October 1, 1982	Terry Leach at Philadelphia (1–0 in 10) (Aguayo triple in 5th)
September 7, 1984	Dwight Gooden vs. Chicago (10–0) (Moreland single in 5th)

*One-hitters pitched at home are indicated by pitcher's name **vs.** other team; those pitched in away games are indicated by pitcher's name **at** other team's home location.

Tom Seaver is only one out away from a no-hitter as he pitches to Leron Lee of the San Diego Padres, who broke it up. Seaver had to settle for the fourth one-hitter of his career on July 4, while striking out eleven and winning, 2–0.

or Yogi Berra, 1972 began with election to the Hall of Fame—the Baseball Writers Association of America announced his enshrinement on January 19. He would be inducted into the hallowed Hall at Cooperstown in August along with pitchers Sandy Koufax and Early Wynn.

But before that solemn ceremony took place, Berra would once again become a major league manager, an event he had no way of anticipating. He was happy and contented in his role as a coach. He had developed great respect for Hodges as a man and as a manager and was at home as one of the boys with coaches Walker, Pignatano, and Yost. Other managers envied the loyalty Hodges commanded from his aides.

When spring training opened, the Mets had high hopes for the upcoming season. Seven weeks later spring training ended in tragedy. On Easter Sunday, April 2, Hodges died of a heart attack after completing a round of golf with his coaches in West Palm Beach, Florida.

Hodges had guided the Mets through their most successful spring, even without help from the newly acquired Fregosi. When the new third baseman had arrived in camp to learn this new position, he was well over his normal weight. The conversion from shortstop to third base is fairly ordinary for most veterans, but the overweight Fregosi was slow in getting down for ground balls, which came at him much quicker than they had at shortstop. Hodges realized the problem and saw to it that his new third baseman was hit a lot of grounders. Hodges himself was hitting grounders to Fregosi on March 5 when one of them fractured Jim's right thumb. Fregosi spent most of the balance of spring with his thumb in a cast, appearing in only five games.

The Mets won fifteen exhibition games and lost only eight without Fregosi. On Friday, March 31, the Mets left by plane from Tampa airport to spend a final weekend on Florida's east coast playing the Yankees and Montreal Expos, followed by a couple of stops in Kinston, North Carolina, and Norfolk, Virginia, en route to New York.

At the airport, Hodges said good-bye to his wife, Joan, as she prepared to board another plane for New York. By now, Gil was ignoring doctor's orders and had resumed smoking. His heart attack was a thing of the past. Outwardly calm, Hodges boiled inside. Smoking eased the tension.

"Watch the cigarettes," Joan Hodges cautioned her husband as he kissed her good-bye. They were her last words to him.

There was talk at the time of an impending players strike. Hodges had that and other things on his mind, including another major deal. Only he, Scheffing, Grant, and the other club involved were privy to the details. It was to be announced just before the Mets left Florida two days hence.

But on Friday, March 30, while the rest of the Mets were flying to West Palm Beach, pitchers Tom Seaver and Ray Sadecki, the team's labor representatives, were attending a union meeting at the Ramada Inn outside the Dallas airport. There the players voted almost unanimously to strike for increased contributions to their pension and medical benefits funds.

While the Mets awaited the result of the vote, some of the players scattered to nearby restaurants and bars; others waited in their hotel rooms. Fregosi, who was certain the vote would be in favor of a strike, drove down to Fort Lauderdale some fifty miles south.

The vote finally came in and the strike was on. It was obvious the remaining exhibition games would be canceled.

Grant called a meeting of the players for about nine o'clock that night. He wanted to express his disappointment in their strike vote and to explain that the owners were not the bad guys union boss Marvin Miller made them out to be. To Lou Niss, Harold Weissman, and others fell the task of rounding up the

OPENING DAY LINEUP 1972

Harrelson, ss
Boswell, 2b
Agee, cf
Staub, rf
Jones, lf
Fregosi, 3b
Kranepool, 1b
Grote, c
Seaver, p

players for Grant's speech. Fregosi had left word where he would be and wasn't happy about being called back, especially to be told something he didn't want to hear. He growled some uncomplimentary remarks after Grant's talk, leaving the chairman of the board disturbed by this lack of allegiance from a newcomer to the team.

Because they were traveling north at the same time, the Mets and Yankees decided to share a charter flight. It would leave from Fort Lauderdale, Monday, April 3, with the Yankee squad, stopping at West Palm Beach to pick up the Mets. When the strike was called, many players headed for home. The others were told the charter flight would leave as scheduled and players could fly north with the team. Hodges and his coaches decided to relax Saturday and Sunday—play some golf and fly home on the charter Monday. All except Yogi Berra. He had friends and family in Miami and decided to spend the weekend with them.

On Easter Sunday afternoon, Hodges, Yost, Pignatano, and Walker played golf on the course behind the Ramada Inn. Late in the afternoon, close to five, as they were returning to the Inn, Hodges keeled over backward in the parking lot, hitting his head as he landed on the asphalt pavement. An ambulance was summoned immediately, and Hodges was taken to Good Samaritan Hospital, where he was pronounced dead twenty minutes after arrival. Doctors said later he was, for all intents and purposes, dead when he struck the pavement. His second heart attack was massive.

Because the final exhibition games had been canceled, the New York press corps had returned to New York on Saturday morning. Only Red Foley of the *New York Daily News* remained; he decided it would be more convenient to fly home on the chartered flight Monday morning. On Sunday afternoon, Foley walked around the golf course with Hodges and his coaches; he was in the hotel dining room in the early evening when Everett Kerr, the hotel manager, walked in and made some reference about Hodges being rushed to the hospital. Kerr told him of the heart attack, and Foley immediately alerted his paper in New York. He then met Koosman, the pitcher, who knew nothing about it. The two grabbed a taxi to the hospital and went immediately to the emergency room. Doctors there told them Hodges was dead. Foley called his office with the bulletin despite protests by Harold Weissman, who pleaded that the club had been unable to contact the widow. Foley gave priority to the interests of the *Daily News*, not to the Mets or Joan Hodges.

With his instinct for news and realizing his office would want to know, Foley asked Scheffing and Grant if any thought had been given to a successor to Hodges. His inquiry was polite and apologetic.

Scheffing and Grant seemed annoyed at Foley's question and brushed it off with a comment that they could not even think of something like that in this hour of grief. And yet, within the hour, Scheffing was on the telephone inviting Berra to meet with him and Grant that night at Grant's Hobe Sound home on the northern side of Palm Beach. It was there that Yogi was offered the job as Hodges' successor. On Monday morning, Hodges' body was flown to New York on the Mets-Yankees charter plane, his successor already selected.

In New York Sunday night, official Mets photographer Dennis Burke, who lived in midtown Manhattan, walked over to the *New York Daily News* on 42nd Street and offered them a photograph he had taken just days before of the entire Hodges family in a suite at the St. Petersburg Hilton. Once again the *New York Daily News* had exclusive Hodges photos, and the other New York papers were helpless to prevent this obvious preferential treatment.

Four days later, on April 6, most of the Mets players, all of the club officials, and many high baseball dignitaries attended Hodges' funeral in Brooklyn. Then the entire party of Mets officials informed the press corps that an important announcement would be made at Shea Stadium two hours later.

Even as Hodges was being laid to rest in a Brooklyn cemetery, the Mets, in their Shea Stadium clubhouse, were announcing that Berra had been chosen to succeed him and had signed a two-year contract. Grant made the announcement; Berra said he had taken the job only after Hodges' buddies had agreed to remain as his coaches. There were some who felt the Mets could have waited until the day after Hodges' funeral. The club was chastised in the New York papers for its callous handling of the announcement.

After Yogi had a chance to answer questions at his press conference, the Mets said they had another major announcement to make. In a four-player deal with Montreal, the Mets had obtained the veteran Rusty Staub in exchange for Tim Foli, Ken Singleton, and Mike Jorgensen.

The Expos were going for youth in their efforts to build a team. The Mets were going for another pennant with a tried and true veteran, a professional hitter. Staub had been signed in 1962 as a bonus boy out of New Orleans by the Houston Colt 45s club just as the Mets had signed Kranepool. Rusty had developed into the better hitter and a fine defensive right fielder and first baseman. He had become a folk hero in Montreal, where he was known as "Le Grand Orange," because of the color of his hair. He also was a slugger of note, hitting seventy-eight home runs during his last three seasons with the Expos and driving in an average of ninety runs a season.

A big, husky, slow-footed, left-handed hitter, Staub's main problem was keeping his weight down. Rusty loved to eat rich food and drink good wine. As his bulk would later attest, next to hitting, food was Rusty's passion.

The Staub deal had actually been consummated in Florida before Hodges' death. But with the strike and Gil's death, both clubs decided to hold off announcement.

It would be another nine days before Berra could make his debut as Mets manager and Staub as a player. The strike lasted thirteen days and forced the cancellation of eighty-six regular season games. It was the first general player strike in baseball history, and there was bitterness on both sides.

But when the Mets began winning, all was forgotten. Seaver pitched the home opener against Pittsburgh on April 15 and worked the first six innings of a shutout. McGraw pitched the final three, and the Mets won, 4–0. Staub went 1-for-3 in his New York debut. After losing the next two, the Mets went on a seven-game winning streak behind their new manager and were in first place with an 8–2 record on April 28. It was the best start in Mets history.

All was going splendidly for the Mets in early May when they visited San Francisco for the first time. Seaver was 3–0, Matlack 2–0, and the Mets were tied for first place.

On May 2, I got a tip that the Mets and Giants were about to swing a deal that would bring the great Willie Mays back to New York. I held off writing the story until I could do some further checking. On May 4, when we were back in New York on an off-day, I called Grant at his Wall Street office. He was taken aback when I brought up the subject of a possible deal for Mays. At first he denied it. Then, realizing I knew what I was on to, Grant tried to talk me out of writing anything.

"If you write it, it could kill the deal," he argued.

I argued that my loyalty was to my paper, the *Long Island Press*, and if there was indeed a deal being discussed, I had to write it. I told him I had the story exclusively, and he finally began to discuss it in a manner that convinced me the deal was beyond the talking stage. Only the final details needed to be ironed out.

On May 5, one day before Mays's forty-first birthday, the front page headline in the *Long Island Press* read: "SHEA HEY, WILLIE MAYS IS COMING HOME."

In his first game as a Met on May 14, three days after the big trade with the Giants, Willie Mays strokes his first home run to beat his former team in a dramatic 5–4 win.

DAILY NEWS/FRANK HURLEY

Mays had been known as the Say Hey Kid in his glory days with the New York Giants and after thirteen years in San Francisco was coming back to a city where fans worshipped him. Six days later, on May 11—a day prior to Berra's birthday—the deal was completed. For $50,000 and pitcher Charlie Williams, the Mets gave Berra Willie Mays as a birthday present.

In a way, it was a present, too, for Mrs. Payson, the club owner. She had idolized Mays in his days as a Giant at the Polo Grounds and had once offered Giants owner Horace Stoneham $1 million if he would let Willie come back to New York and play for the Mets. When Grant finally did make the deal in 1972, Mays was over the hill. But Stoneham also was in financial trouble.

"Let us have him before it's too late, while he still has something left," Grant urged Stoneham.

The Giants owner, who appreciated Mays as much as Mrs. Payson and Grant, agreed to the deal, providing the Mets would see that Willie was secure for life. With the millions Payson and Grant were making from the Mets, they could afford it. A ten-year deal was worked out whereby Mays would continue to draw the $150,000 salary Stoneham was paying him and then continue on the Mets payroll in some capacity at a substantial salary.

Mays made his debut at Shea Stadium on Sunday, May 14. As fate would have it, he hit a home run against his former Giants teammates to give the Mets a 5–4 victory. It was Willie's home run that decided the game.

Mays played with the vigor of a man twenty years younger. In his first half dozen games he contributed mightily in three victories as the Mets rolled off eleven straight wins.

In his second game as a Met, Willie walked and scored on a triple when he knocked the ball out of the catcher's mitt in a 2–1 victory over Montreal. In his fourth game he hit a two-run homer that decided a 4–3 victory over Philadelphia. In his sixth game, Willie's fourteenth inning single beat the Cubs, 3–2. In each of his first twenty games, Mays reached base at least once.

All went well for the first two months of the season. The Mets were winning, and Berra was being hailed as a solid successor to Hodges. At the start of June the Mets were in first place by five full games, with a 30–11 record. Staub was hitting home runs and driving in runs, as the Mets had hoped he would. Seaver, Matlack, and McAndrew were winning, and visions of a record to match 1969 were dancing in the minds of Mets fans. But this year there was to be no miracle.

The Mets were a solid team with experience. There were veterans in the lineup every day, and the pitching staff had come of age. But an incident on June 3 in Shea Stadium determined the team's destiny for the balance of the season—Staub, who was hitting .311 at the time, with seven home runs and twenty-six runs batted in, was hit on the right hand by a pitch thrown by Atlanta's George Stone. It hurt Staub, but no one took it seriously at the time. Besides, batters were often hit on the hand and shook it off. When Staub hit a home run the next day, there was even less consideration given to the incident. X rays had proven negative. There was no fracture.

Staub continued to play until June 18, when he left the lineup for the first time, complaining of a spasm in his right hand. Numerous medical examinations followed and several diagnoses were offered, none of which, it later turned out, proved to be correct. Rusty sat for a month nursing the painful right hand. Doctors were at a loss to explain the problem.

On July 18, Staub returned to the lineup against the Dodgers in Los Angeles. He got one single in four trips and again complained to Berra and the team trainer that he could not grip a bat. When the hand stiffened again, Staub was sent for more X rays. There, in Los Angeles, a Dr. Herbert Stark took another set of X rays, which revealed a fracture of the hook of the hamate bone in the meaty part of Staub's hand. Staub had gone almost seven weeks with a bone fracture in his hand, and no doctor had been able to detect it.

Staub flew back to New York for surgery on July 20 and did not play again until September 18. Ironically, on the day he returned, Rusty singled in the ninth inning and scored the only run of the game as the Mets beat Pittsburgh, 1–0. If the team didn't realize before how much they missed Staub's bat, they did then. Two days after Staub's June 3 injury, the Mets dropped to second place. They returned to the top June 9–10, but when they dropped to second on June 11, it was for good. By the middle of July they had fallen to fourth place, a dozen games out.

New Mets manager Yogi Berra gets the heave-ho from umpire Jerry Dale as he argues a strike call. Coach Ed Yost and batter John Milner aren't particularly pleased, either.
LOUIS REQUENA

Tommie Agee, usually a sure-handed center fielder for the Mets, suddenly looks inept on June 12. Injuries plagued Agee all summer, and he wound up with his worst year as a Met since his first (1968). In 1972 he batted only .227 with just forty-seven RBIs.
NEW YORK POST

Staub's injury was one of several Berra endured in his first season at the helm. Cleon Jones, playing first base, banged his right elbow in a Cincinnati collision with Joe Morgan on June 16 and was in and out of the lineup for several weeks. Cleon also incurred Berra's wrath when he played a fly ball lackadaisically in St. Louis. He was benched for three days and brooded over it. After a solid .319 season in 1971, Jones slumped to .245 for 1972 and missed one-third of the Mets' games.

Jones's buddy, Agee, also had his problems. The center fielder had a good first month, but in June he started having troubles in the field that brought quizzical looks in the press box. On June 12 Agee dropped one fly ball and made a poor throw on another. Reporters, puzzled by his suddenly poor defensive play, were berated and yelled at by Tommie when they approached him in the clubhouse. It was unlike the Agee they had come to know and respect. The following day two more fly balls popped out of Agee's glove and cost the Mets another game. No one dared go near the center fielder after that game. Tommie also was in one of his slumps at the plate. It stretched into twenty futile trips before he got another hit.

In late June, Agee pulled his left groin muscle and was out of the lineup a week, then came back and pulled a rib cage muscle on July 8. It was three weeks before he played again, but he was not the same player. At the winter meetings in Hawaii on November 27, the Mets dealt Agee to Houston for outfielder Rich Chiles and minor league pitcher Buddy Harris. Another star of the 1969 Miracle Mets was gone.

The reason behind the Agee trade was never officially given by the Mets. His dip in average from .285 in 1971 to .227 was reason enough, but the Mets also suspected that Tommie, who was looked up to by some of the younger black players, was not taking care of himself as well as he might. One player in particular the Mets wanted on "the straight and narrow" was John Milner, a hot prospect out of Georgia, signed by Julian Morgan, the same scout who had signed Cleon Jones. Milner respected Agee and Jones and followed them wherever they went. The Mets saw Milner as an up-and-coming left-handed power hitter, which he was in the minors. Milner answered to the nickname "Hammer," the same name given to another of his idols, Hank Aaron. Milner had power and great speed. In his two seasons in the minors prior to joining the Mets, he hit thirty-eight homers and stole thirty-six bases. At South Fulton High School in Georgia, Milner had been an all-state athlete in baseball, football, and basketball. Unfortunately, fine athlete though he was, Milner had the kind of taut muscles that were subject to pulls. Throughout his career with the Mets, he was frequently sidelined with pulled hamstring muscles, which greatly limited his effectiveness.

1972

NAME	G by POS	B	AGE	G	AB	R	H	2B	3B	HR	RBI	BB	SO	SB	BA	SA
NEW YORK 3rd 83-73 .532 13.5	GIL HODGES (DD) 47		YOGI BERRA 83-73 .532													
TOTALS			28	156	5135	528	1154	175	31	105	490	589	990	41	.225	.332
Ed Kranepool	1B108, OF1	L	27	122	327	28	88	15	1	8	34	34	35	1	.269	.394
Ken Boswell	2B94	L	26	100	355	35	75	9	1	9	33	32	35	2	.211	.318
Bud Harrelson	SS115	B	28	115	418	54	90	10	4	1	24	58	57	12	.215	.266
Jim Fregosi	3B85, SS6, 1B3	R	30	101	340	31	79	15	4	5	32	38	71	0	.232	.344
John Milner	OF91, 1B10	L	22	117	362	52	86	12	2	17	38	51	74	2	.238	.423
Tommie Agee	OF109	R	29	114	422	52	96	23	0	13	47	53	92	8	.227	.374
Cleon Jones	OF84, 1B20	R	29	106	375	39	92	15	1	5	52	30	83	1	.245	.331
Duffy Dyer	C91, OF1	R	26	94	325	33	75	17	3	8	36	28	71	0	.231	.375
Wayne Garrett	3B82, 2B22	L	24	111	298	41	69	13	3	2	29	70	58	3	.232	.315
Ted Martinez	2B47, SS42, OF15, 3B2	R	24	103	330	22	74	5	5	1	19	12	49	7	.224	.279
Dave Marshall	OF42	L	29	72	156	21	39	5	0	4	11	22	28	3	.250	.359
Willie Mays	OF49, 1B11	R	41	69	195	27	52	9	1	8	19	43	43	1	.267	.446
Rusty Staub	OF65	L	28	66	239	32	70	11	0	9	38	31	13	0	.293	.452
Jerry Grote	C59, 3B3, OF1	R	29	64	205	15	43	5	1	3	21	26	27	1	.210	.288
Jim Beauchamp	1B35, OF5	R	32	58	120	10	29	1	0	5	19	7	33	0	.242	.375
Dave Schneck	OF33	L	23	37	123	7	23	3	2	3	10	10	26	0	.187	.317
Lute Barnes	2B14, SS6	R	25	24	72	5	17	2	2	0	6	6	4	0	.236	.319

Bill Sudakis 26 B 7-49, Don Hahn 23 R 6-37, Joe Nolan 21 L 0-10

NAME	T	AGE	W	L	PCT	SV	G	GS	CG	IP	H	BB	SO	ShO	ERA
		27	83	73	.532	41	156	156	32	1415	1263	486	1059	12	3.26
Tom Seaver	R	27	21	12	.636	0	35	35	13	262	215	77	249	3	2.92
Jon Matlack	L	22	15	10	.600	0	34	32	8	244	215	71	169	4	2.32
Jim McAndrew	R	28	11	8	.579	1	28	23	4	161	133	38	81	0	2.80
Jerry Koosman	L	29	11	12	.478	1	34	24	4	163	155	52	147	1	4.14
Tug McGraw	L	27	8	6	.571	27	54	0	0	106	71	40	92	0	1.70
Gary Gentry	R	25	7	10	.412	0	32	26	3	164	153	75	120	0	4.01
Danny Frisella	R	26	5	8	.385	9	39	0	0	67	63	20	46	0	3.36
Buzz Capra	R	24	3	2	.600	0	14	6	0	53	50	27	45	0	4.58
Ray Sadecki	L	31	2	1	.667	0	34	2	0	76	73	31	38	0	3.08
Bob Rauch	R	23	0	1	.000	1	19	0	0	27	27	21	23	0	5.00
Brent Strom	L	23	0	3	.000	0	11	5	0	30	34	15	20	0	6.90
Chuck Taylor	R	30	0	0	.000	2	20	0	0	31	44	9	9	0	5.52
Tommy Moore	R	23	0	0	.000	0	3	1	0	12	12	1	5	0	3.00
Hank Webb	R	22	0	0	.000	0	6	2	0	18	18	9	15	0	4.50

Berra also lost the left side of his 1972 infield for a good spell. Shortstop Bud Harrelson missed three weeks in August with a back problem, and Fregosi missed fifteen games the same month with a pulled right hamstring.

Despite all these injuries and a team batting average of .225 that ranked last in the league, the Mets managed to finish third with an 83–73 record. Once again pitching was the reason they remained respectable. Seaver again finished strong, winning five of his last six decisions to turn in a 21–12 record. He also struck out ten batters in a game six different times, raising his career total in that department to forty-one. Matlack lived up to expectations with a 15–10 record and was voted National League Rookie of the Year. Gentry was a disappointment with a 7–10 record, and Koosman finished only four of twenty-four starts and was 11–12 at the season's end. Jim McAndrew gave the staff a lift with an 11–8 record.

Next to Seaver, the most popular pitcher on the staff was Tug McGraw, the eccentric left-handed reliever. Tug had his best season in 1972, saving twenty-seven games out of the bullpen and winning another eight. His earned run average for the year was a brilliant 1.70.

Mays, for all the hoopla attending his return, batted only .267 in sixty-nine games and hit eight home runs. But John Milner hit seventeen home runs in his rookie season to lead the club. Unfortunately, even with that display of power, he hit only .238 and drove in only thirty-eight runs.

RECORDS OF METS' MANAGERS

Manager	Years	W	L	Pct
Stengel, Casey	1962–65	175	404	.302
Westrum, Wes	1965–67	142	237	.375
Parker, Salty	1967	4	7	.364
Hodges, Gil	1968–71	339	309	.523
Berra, Yogi	1972–75	292	296	.497
McMillan, Roy	1975	26	27	.491
Frazier, Joe	1976–77	101	106	.488
Torre, Joe	1977–81	286	420	.405
Bamberger, George	1982–83	81	127	.389
Howard, Frank	1983	52	64	.448
Johnson, Dave	1984–86	296	190	.609
Totals		1794	2187	.451

Mets fans get pennant fever. Tug McGraw poses with a poster of the slogan that was the key battle cry he coined during the stretch run.

Berra was back for the second year of his contract in 1973, but by mid-season, with the Mets buried in last place, the wolves were calling for his scalp. Whispering that Grant was getting ready to unload Yogi started going around. Grant did nothing to silence the rumors with a remark he made in July.

In the first week of July, when the Mets were playing a four-game series in Montreal, I reported in the *Long Island Press* that a shake-up was being considered. The Mets were under .500, in the cellar, and eleven games out of first place.

One week earlier, in New York, Berra had brought in a relief pitcher and then, even before the pitcher completed pitching to the batter he was brought in to face, Yogi attempted another change. Baseball rules stipulate that a relief pitcher must complete pitching to at least one batter, either by retiring him or letting him get on base, before he can be replaced. The umpires advised Berra of this, and he retreated to the bench to allow the pitcher to complete pitching to one batter.

In Montreal, the same situation developed. Yogi again brought in a pitcher and attempted to bring in another before the first reliever had completed pitching to one batter.

In my story suggesting that a managerial change was imminent, I pointed out that while management might be able to defend a manager's won-lost record, there was no defense for a manager not knowing the rules.

Word of my story, which appeared in New Jersey papers owned by the Newhouse chain as well as in the *Long Island Press*, did not take long to reach Berra. That night in the Jarry Park clubhouse in Montreal, Berra screamed at me, "You can write anything you want about my managing, but don't say I don't know the rules!"

The next morning, walking toward the newsstand in the lobby of the Queen Elizabeth Hotel, I passed Yogi and his wife, Carmen. I said hello, not sure what kind of response I would get. Mrs. Berra handed me a quarter, the price of a newspaper, and said, "Here, that's all you're worth."

Yogi, of all people, jumped to my defense.

"Aw, Carm, don't say that," the manager admonished his wife.

That's Yogi. He cannot stay mad at anyone for long. Two years later, when he stayed mad at Cleon Jones long enough to have him suspended for insubordination, it cost Yogi his job. For what many considered to be one of the few times in his life, he took a strong stand, and he was fired three weeks later.

After the dismal offense of the 1972 season, Scheffing engineered a deal on November 2 that was certain to help not only the offense but the defense as well. Ken Boswell had proven he was not an everyday second baseman. Boswell was a fair enough hitter, but he lacked range in the field. To replace him in the lineup, the Mets sent pitchers Gary Gentry and Dan Frisella to Atlanta in exchange for Felix Millan and left-hander George Stone, the pitcher who had hit Staub in the hand the previous year. Although pulled from the regular lineup, Boswell wore the Mets uniform until 1977.

It was a blow to many New Yorkers to lose Gentry, who had been the surprise pitcher of 1969, as Seaver had been in 1967 and Koosman in 1968. Gary had moved into the Mets' starting rotation with less than a half season of minor league ball behind him. He was 4–4 at Williamsport in 1968, and even though the Mets knew he threw hard, they had no expectations he would win in the big leagues as quickly as he did. Unfortunately, after winning thirty-four games his first three seasons with the Mets, Gary was plagued by shoulder problems.

Felix Millan was a classy second baseman who had spent six years with the Braves and had a lifetime .281 average. If perhaps he lacked power, Felix did

15

◆ "YOU ◆

◆ GOTTA ◆

◆ BELIEVE!" ◆

OPENING DAY LINEUP 1973

Harrelson, ss
Millan, 2b
Mays, cf
Staub, rf
Jones, lf
Milner, 1b
Fregosi, 3b
Dyer, c
Seaver, p

Felix Millan tries to get off a throw to first after forcing out Tim McCarver on second base during a September game with the Cards. Millan led the Mets in batting during the '73 campaign and was a workhorse, starting 153 games at second base and leading the Mets in at-bats (638), runs (82), and hits (185).

bang out a bundle of singles every year, and his sure-footed fielding had earned him the nickname of "Felix the Cat." Millan formed an excellent keystone partner for Harrelson. He proved to be everything the Mets had anticipated, hitting a solid .290 as he hammered out 185 hits to lead the team in '73.

But few other things went well for the Mets. Milner was leading the club with five home runs in April when he pulled a hamstring and was lost. Two weeks later, All-Star catcher Grote was hit on the right wrist by Ramon Hernandez of Pittsburgh and suffered a fracture that kept him out of action until July. Jerry was back in the lineup only a few days when a foul off the bat of Pete Rose fractured the little finger on his right hand.

Desperate for a catcher, the Mets purchased Jerry May from Kansas City. In his first game behind the plate, May suffered a sprain of the left wrist. When he returned to the lineup, May suffered a pulled hamstring and was disabled. He caught only four games.

Jones strained his right wrist diving for a ball on April 19. After missing seventeen games, he came back and was hit in the left elbow by Ramon Hernandez. The wrist injury limited him to six games in May, and on June 1 Cleon was placed on the disabled list. He did not return to the lineup until July.

The injury list that season was incredible. George "Stork" Theodore, an outfielder, was hit in the left eye by a ball on June 3 in San Diego. At first it was feared he would lose the sight of the eye, but five days later he was back in the lineup. A month later, in an outfield collision with Don Hahn, Theodore suffered a fractured hip. Except for a few token appearances, the Stork was out for the balance of the season. Willie Mays, showing his age, missed several games with an aching right shoulder that limited his ability to throw. At the end of April, fluid was drained from both of Willie's knees.

Fregosi arrived in camp in 1973 in better shape than the previous year, but it did not help. He obviously was at the end of the line. Jim, never a speedster, was now even slower and, much as he tried, he could not fathom National League pitching. By mid-season he was hitting in the low .230s, while Ryan, the pitcher the Mets had given up to get him, had come into his own with the California Angels. Working on three days' rest instead of four as he had with the Mets, Ryan won nineteen games his first year and was en route to a twenty-one-win season his second year. There was much criticism in the New York press over the deal that had been made, and I was one of the most outspoken in panning the deal. That bothered Grant, who was oversensitive to any kind of criticism.

One night, as he strolled through the back row of the press box following a few cocktails and dinner in the Director's Room, Grant stopped and looked at me. I got out of my seat, and soon we were engaged in heavy conversation in the doorway that separated the press box from the television booth, where Nelson and Kiner were announcing the game. Our conversation quickly turned into an argument.

"You've been blaming us for the Fregosi deal, and you're the one who made us make that deal," Grant ranted.

"What are you talking about?" I demanded.

"When we were in Phoenix, you told me we had to make a deal," he shot back. "So we made a deal and now all you've done is knock it."

I defended myself. "I told you you had to make a deal, but I didn't tell you to make *that* deal!"

By this time the argument was getting so loud that anyone within a few feet could hear us shouting at each other. Lindsey Nelson finally got up and closed the door to the television booth, fearful that our argument and some of our blue language would go out over the air.

After the game, Nelson approached me in the press room.

"Say, I'm going to have to start treating you with more respect. I didn't know you had the power on this club to make deals," he said, breaking out into a laugh.

A few weeks later, on July 11, the Mets sold Fregosi to the Texas Rangers for cash. In his two years with the Mets he had hit .232 and .234. Ex-Met Nolan Ryan went on to win over 200 games for California and Houston, established himself as baseball's all-time strikeout king, and tossed a record five no-hitters.

Bud Harrelson, the crack shortstop, also was an injury victim that year. On June 4, in Cincinnati, Bill Plummer came crashing into him in an attempt to break up a double play. Plummer hit Harrelson's left hand, fracturing a bone and sending Bud to the disabled list. Harrelson did not play again until July 9. He was back only three weeks when, on July 31, in a run-down play, he crashed into Rennie Stennett of the Pirates and suffered a fracture of the sternum. After three weeks of rest, Harrelson returned to the lineup for the stretch run.

Even the pitchers did not escape injury. On May 8 at Shea Stadium, Marty Perez of Atlanta hit a line drive back to the box that hit Matlack squarely in the head, fracturing his skull. It was a frightening scene watching Matlack being carried off the field on a stretcher. Eleven days later Jon was back pitching six innings of shutout ball against Pittsburgh. It had been a mild fracture.

Berra also had trouble with his bullpen up until August, and it was this that prompted his observation, "If you ain't got a bullpen, you ain't got nothin'." He reduced to simple terms what many a manager has thought before and since.

Tug McGraw, who had been so effective in 1972, saved ten games up to July, but he blew many others he could have saved. Phil Hennigan, whom the Mets had obtained in November 1972 for two minor league pitchers, proved a disaster in the bullpen. He was 0–4 with only three saves when he was sent to the minors in mid-July.

It was about then that the *New York Post* decided to run a poll asking their readers to vote on who should be fired—Grant, Scheffing, or Berra. Berra won by getting the fewest votes. Most fans suggested Scheffing be fired, with Grant next. Of the 4,000 readers who responded, only 611 felt that Yogi was responsible.

Grant, obviously, was not happy with the poll. But his comment at the time had the ring of a man looking for reasons to dump his manager. When asked if he had any intention of letting Yogi go, Grant replied he would not—"unless the public demands it."

The *Post* poll proved the public was not demanding Yogi's scalp.

That is not to say the players thought him a great manager. The lack of respect the players had for Berra's managerial talents was typified by an incident in San Francisco in August during a game Seaver was pitching against the Giants. Seaver was winning but he was struggling, and Berra sent pitching coach Rube Walker out to talk to him. Seaver promptly informed Walker, whom he respected, that he intended to finish the game. "And tell that to Yogi," Seaver added. "I don't want him coming out here, because I'll finish this game." A second trip to the mound by Berra would have meant Seaver had to be removed. Tom wasn't taking any chances.

Berra kept his sanity through all the club's travails. He repeatedly pointed out that virtually every club in the league, the Mets excepted, had enjoyed a hot streak. "We still got ours coming," he kept saying. Late that season Berra made the observation that has since become a universal catch phrase. In August and September, whenever he had his entire team together after the Mets had lost a tough game or lost ground in the race, Yogi would say, "It ain't over 'til it's over."

George Basil ("the Stork") Theodore played in only 105 games for the Mets in 1973 and 1974 and had a .219 average for those two seasons. He was never a regular but was embraced by the fans because of his unusual physical makeup. He actually looked like a stork, with legs that occupied half his body, hunched shoulders, and a long nose. George was a particularly bright fellow who sometimes seemed out of place with other players. Wherever he played, the fans accepted him more readily than his managers.
UPI/BETTMAN NEWSPHOTO

Cleon Jones and Tom Seaver share one of those special moments in the Mets locker room during the pennant race in late August. Yogi Berra is on the far right. Jones, a key player in the stretch, was earlier hampered by an injured wrist. Nonetheless, in ninety starts he batted .260 with eleven homers and forty-eight RBIs.

DAILY NEWS/DANNY FARRELL

Jon Matlack threw seven shutouts during the 1973 season—but he was inconsistent and got bombed when he didn't have his good stuff. Still, he did strike out 205 batters and recorded a respectable 3.20 ERA. In this photo, he hurls a three-hitter against Pittsburgh on September 22, a game that the Mets won, 4–0.

AP

Grant wanted to fire Berra, but he could not get Scheffing to go along with him. In fact, insiders later revealed that when Grant asked Scheffing to drop Yogi, the general manager refused. "If you want to fire Yogi, you do it. I won't," he allegedly told Grant.

For the Mets, the year was only beginning. Even in late July, when they were in last place, the Mets were not that far back. On the morning of August 1, the day Seaver and Stone pitched a doubleheader win over Pittsburgh, the Mets were sixth, ten and a half games out of first place. One month later, on September 1, when Stone pitched a 4–1 win over St. Louis, the Mets were in fifth place but only four and a half games out of first place.

What with all their injuries, the Mets had posted losing records from May through July, combining for thirty-two victories while losing forty-nine. But they began to turn the tide in August, winning more than they lost (18–14) for the first time since April. Seaver won only three games in August while losing as many. Matlack won four games, Stone a pair, and Koosman three. McGraw suddenly regained his form in the bullpen. More important than just saving games, McGraw stopped blowing leads.

The August record was a harbinger of an even stronger September. After winning eighteen and losing fourteen in August, the Mets rolled to a 19–8 record in September, and when they added another victory on October 1—one day after the season was officially scheduled to end—they had won twenty of their last twenty-eight and captured the National League Eastern Division title by one and one-half games over the second place St. Louis Cardinals. They did it with an 82–79 record for a .509 percentage—the lowest ever to win a championship in the history of baseball.

McGraw's turnabout in the bullpen is considered by most who witnessed the 1973 season to have been the major factor in the Mets' rise from the basement to the penthouse. For two years he had been simply the best left-handed relief pitcher in the National League. The southpaw from Vallejo, California, had posted consecutive earned run averages of 1.70 the previous two seasons and had won nineteen while saving thirty-five. Then, just as suddenly as he had developed as a winner, he seemed to lose it. In mid-August, when the Mets were still in last place, McGraw had an 0–5 record and thirteen saves.

The Mets tried everything, including a couple of starts, to try to get Tug straightened out. In his first start, against Atlanta on July 17, he gave up ten hits and seven runs in six innings. Three of the hits were homers. His next start was better. McGraw allowed only three hits and one run to Montreal in five and two-thirds innings. He came back a few days later to save a game for Ray Sadecki. For a few weeks the Mets thought they had their young reliever straightened out. But on August 20, Tug gave up five runs and six hits in three innings as the Mets lost to the Reds in sixteen innings, 8–3.

That was the last time McGraw was hit hard. In his last nineteen relief appearances, the left-hander allowed only four runs and never more than one in any game. He did not blow a lead for the balance of the season.

It was about that time that Grant decided to go into the clubhouse one night for one of his inspirational speeches. Grant had a reputation among the players and press corps as a stuffed shirt, with a patrician manner that offended those outside his own clique. It seemed he was always trying to convince those he considered beneath him that "I'm really not a bad guy."

In his clubhouse oration, Grant sought to stress to the players that both he and Mrs. Payson still had the utmost confidence in the team and stressed that they believed in the Mets. As Grant was exiting through the players lounge, he heard McGraw shout in the background, "You gotta believe!"

Grant turned back into the clubhouse and approached the free-spirited, pixyish McGraw. Grant suspected Tug was making mockery of his remarks— and he probably was, according to other players later. Tug quickly explained to the chairman of the board that he was merely confirming Grant's feelings and trying to give the troops a rallying cry. Besides, said McGraw, a few Catholic nuns a few weeks earlier had told him, "You got to believe," and he did.

"You gotta believe!" became the official, or unofficial, rallying cry of the Mets down the stretch. In September, whenever they pulled one out of the fire or won a close game, McGraw could be found shouting "You gotta believe!" as the press corps trooped into the clubhouse.

And in fact the Mets did begin to believe.

They began the month of September five and one-half games out of first place, but George Stone opened the month with a 4–1 win over the Cardinals at St. Louis. Stone had turned into a valuable pitcher for the Mets. He went the distance only twice in twenty starts, but he usually gave six or seven quality innings before he left. He wound up the season with an excellent 12–3 record, including eight in a row at the end of the season. Earlier, on May 24 in a nineteen-inning marathon at Los Angeles, Stone pitched six scoreless innings in relief as the Mets beat the Dodgers, 7–3.

Eight days later, on September 9, Stone won again. This time he beat Montreal, 3–0, as McGraw saved the game. That win was the seventh in the last ten for the Mets and left them only three games out of first place. In one month they had reduced their deficit by five and a half games, and they were now playing only Eastern Division teams—teams they could clearly beat. At the time the Eastern Division was being referred to as the "Least Division" or the "Lost Division," mainly because every one of the six teams in it was fighting to stay at .500. At the end of the season, the Mets were the only team over .500.

The most encouraging sign to anyone following the race was that the Mets were gradually inching closer to the top and getting the same kind of pitching they did in 1969. Seaver won seven out of ten and pitched well even when he lost—dropping two 1–0 decisions and another by 3–2. Stone was winning his eight in a row, and Matlack five straight. Koosman, who had lost five consecutive starts in mid-season, righted himself and won six of seven. Two veterans, Harry Parker and Ray Sadecki, also were chipping in with solid performances.

Most important, McGraw was saving games again. Tug had picked up eight saves in his first fourteen appearances early in the year and only two in sixteen games the next two months. Then, turning it around, he saved a dozen games and won five others in the last six weeks of the season. Of the last twenty-five games the Mets won, McGraw had a hand in seventeen of them. His earned run average in his final nineteen appearances was an unbelievable 0.88. He began to make others believe.

On September 12, Matlack beat the Phillies at Philadelphia, 3–2, with McGraw's help as the Mets moved to within two and a half games of first place but still in fourth place. It was as close as they had been since the middle of May. Pittsburgh, Montreal, and St. Louis all were ahead of them.

Despite four wins in the next six games, the Mets were still in fourth on September 18. The next night, Stone won his twelfth game by beating first place Pittsburgh, 7–3. Again McGraw saved the game, and that victory moved the Mets up to third, now only one and one-half games out. Pennant fever was heating up Shea Stadium once again.

The Mets went from third to first in three days. They swept a series from the first place Pirates with their SSS troops—Stone, Sadecki, and Seaver. Fittingly, it was Seaver, with a 10–2 victory over Steve Blass on September 21, who pitched the team into first place with his eighteenth victory. The Mets were on top with a record symbolic of the National League's "Lost Division." Their record was 77–77. It was the first time since May 29 that they had been able to reach the .500 mark, and now they were in first place all by themselves with eight games remaining.

Stone's victory in the opener of the three-game series with Pittsburgh was followed the next day by a dramatic announcement. Willie Mays revealed that he would retire from the game as an active player at the conclusion of the season. Though he was still Willie Mays, the Giants hero of those bygone days when New York boasted the Yankees, Giants, and Dodgers, he was no longer the player he had been once. He was unable to play because of cracked ribs, and for the first time he admitted it was time for him to step down and "make room for the kids."

"But if we get into the World Series, I'll be there to help," he promised.

In a speech at the Diamond Club Grant said, "Both Mrs. Payson and I love Willie, and we feel we got *quid pro quo*—one thing for another. We felt our fans and the New York public deserved to have Willie in his final days."

That night, when Koosman started against the Pirates and Sadecki won it in relief, 4–3, in the thirteenth inning, there was further evidence another miracle was in the making. It surfaced in the final inning when, with Richie Zisk on first base, Pittsburgh rookie Dave Augustine belted a long drive to left that had home run written all over it. But instead of going out, the ball hit the top of the outfield fence and bounced back into the glove of Cleon Jones, who fired a perfect strike to third baseman Garrett, who sent another strike to the plate, where Ron Hodges put the tag on the sliding Zisk. The Mets won in the bottom of the thirteenth, and the Pirates left the ballpark shaking their heads.

Seaver won easily, 10–2, the next night before 51,381 witnesses as the Mets took over first place. It was the Mets' fourth straight win—a streak they would extend to seven before Montreal beat them, 8–5, on September 26.

The Cardinals, who were still in the thick of the race, came to town the next afternoon. Matlack was awesome in a 2–0 victory, allowing only four hits and striking out nine. Garrett hit a two-run home run for all the runs Matlack needed.

The Mets completed a sweep of the Cardinals as three pitchers—Stone, Parker, and McGraw—combined their efforts for a 5–2 win. But since Pittsburgh won a doubleheader the same day, the Mets' lead was reduced from one

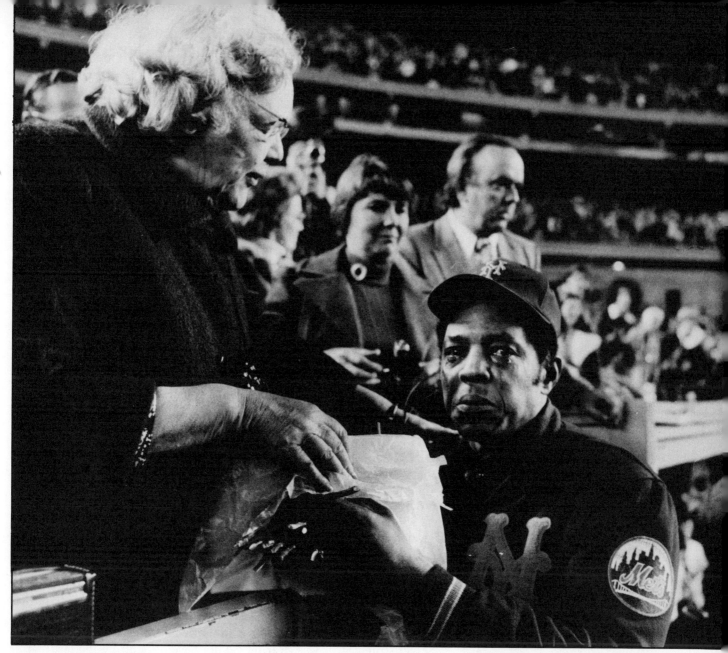

Willie Mays, overcome with emotion during his "night" at Shea, hands Mrs. Joan Payson a bouquet of flowers in gratitude for his years with the Mets.
DAILY NEWS/DANNY FARRELL

game to a half game. One week remained in the race. It could not have been tighter.

Following an off-day in which the Pirates split a doubleheader in Montreal, the Mets attracted 43,805 plus several thousand more guests for "Willie Mays Night," an emotional farewell salute to the Say Hey Kid. Mays, who hardly needed them, was showered with gifts that required more than an hour to present. Upon stepping to the microphone to express his thanks, Willie looked around at the gifts and remarked, "Seems like everybody got something but Michael." Before the night was over, a Honda motorbike was delivered to Shea for Willie's adopted son, Michael.

In his farewell speech, Willie pointed to his young Mets teammates in the dugout and said, "I see those kids over there and I see how hard they're fighting for a pennant, and to me it says one thing—Willie, say good-bye to America." Tears were streaming down his face.

The Mets then went out and presented Mays with a present of their own, a 2–1 victory over Montreal that boosted them back into a one and one-half

METS CLINCH NL EAST TITLE
(October 1, 1973)

New York

	AB	R	H	RBI
Garrett, 3b	4	1	2	0
Millan, 2b	5	1	2	0
Staub, rf	5	2	4	1
Milner, 1b	3	1	0	1
Jones, lf	3	1	1	1
Grote, c	4	0	2	2
Hahn, cf	5	0	0	0
Harrelson, ss	5	0	1	0
Seaver, p	3	0	1	0
McGraw, p	0	0	0	0
Totals	27	6	13	5

Chicago

	AB	R	H	RBI
Monday, cf	4	2	3	2
Beckert, ph	1	0	0	0
Kessinger, ss	4	0	1	1
Williams, lf	4	0	1	1
Santo, 3b	4	0	0	0
Cardenal, rf	4	0	1	0
Marquez, 1b	3	0	2	0
Fanzone, 1b	1	0	0	0
Popovich, 2b	2	0	0	0
Paul, p	0	0	0	0
LaCock, ph	1	0	0	0
Aker, p	0	0	0	0
Hickman, ph	1	0	0	0
Locker, p	0	0	0	0
Rudolph, c	4	1	3	2
Hooton, p	1	0	0	0
Rosello, 2b	3	1	1	0
Totals	37	4	12	6

Pitching	IP	H	R	ER	W	SO
Seaver (W, 19–10)	6	11	4	4	0	2
McGraw (S, 25)	3	1	0	0	0	4
Hooton (L, 14–17)	4	7	5	5	2	1
Paul	2	3	0	0	1	0
Aker	2	3	1	0	1	0
Locker	1	0	0	0	0	1

E—Santo. DP—New York 2, Chicago 2. LOB—New York 11, Chicago 6. 2B—Garrett, Harrelson. HR—Jones (11), Monday (26). S—Garrett. SF—Milner. HBP—by Aker (McGraw). Time—2:28. Attendance—1,913.

game lead with five games remaining. The Pirates and Cardinals also lost, which helped ease the tension.

Seaver lasted only two innings against Montreal the next day, giving up five runs. The Mets managed to come back and tie the score, but Parker lost in relief on a two-run home run by Bob Bailey. The loss cut the Mets' lead to one-half game, as the Pirates and Cardinals both won their contests.

The Mets' remaining four games would be played in Wrigley Field, Chicago, with single games on Friday and Saturday and a doubleheader on Sunday, the final day of the season. A Pittsburgh loss on Thursday lifted the Mets' spirits.

It rained in Chicago on Friday, so the Mets faced doubleheaders on Saturday and Sunday. Then it rained on Saturday, too, washing out the first doubleheader. Meanwhile, the Pirates lost on Friday night and again on Saturday, so now it was St. Louis the Mets had to worry about. And St. Louis was winning. The Cards beat the Phillies, 7–1, on Saturday.

On Sunday morning, it was still raining slightly but not enough to wash out the games. The Mets arrived at the park still in first place, one and one-half games ahead of second place St. Louis. Since their last game, on Wednesday night, they had actually gained a full game without playing. But they had four left to play and the Cardinals had only one remaining, which meant the Mets could not afford to lose. The Mets' record was 80–78; St. Louis' was 80–81.

The Mets lost a 1–0 heartbreaker in the first game of Sunday's doubleheader. Matlack matched Rick Reuschel for seven innings of shutout ball, but in the eighth Ron Santo singled home a run and the Cubs held on to win. In St. Louis, the Cardinals won their final game, 3–1, over Philadelphia and were at 81–81. They had to sit around and wait to see what the Mets did in their final game Sunday and the two on Monday. Officially, Sunday was the last day of the season, but as Berra kept saying, "It ain't over until it's over."

The Mets prolonged the season another day when Koosman coasted to a 9–2 win over Ferguson Jenkins and the Cubs in the second game. That left the Mets with an 81–79 record and the possibility that, unless they won or split the Monday doubleheader, a tie with the Cardinals would exist and a playoff would be necessary.

It was still raining lightly on Monday, the fourth straight day of rain in the Windy City, but the rain was not hard enough to postpone the deciding doubleheader. Seaver, wearying from the long season (he had already pitched 284 innings), was the obvious choice to pitch the first game. It was his turn, and who else would you start in such an important game?

Seaver struggled. It was clear he did not have his stuff by the fact that he gave up eleven hits in six innings. He also struck out only two batters. But the Mets picked up a run here and a run there and gave their ace a 6–2 lead, as well as some sparkling defense. When Rick Monday hit a two-run home run for Chicago in the seventh, no one told Yogi what he had to do. The call went out for McGraw one more time.

If McGraw was good the last six weeks, he was sensational in this game. The hyper little left-hander pitched the final three innings, allowing only one hit and striking out four as the Mets nailed down the Eastern Division championship with a 6–4 win.

The visiting clubhouse at Wrigley Field is the smallest in baseball. It seemed even smaller for the pennant celebration that followed. Dozens of hangers-on, newspapermen, and radio and television interviewers jammed into the tiny quarters. Grote, an inveterate prankster, delighted in dousing newspapermen with buckets of icewater; his teammates preferred to drink or squirt champagne. McGraw kept yelling "You gotta believe!" and even Grant, who was also in the clubhouse, did not mind it now.

Seaver said the victory was no comparison with 1969.

"We were so young then, we didn't understand. This is nothing like it. This time we knew what we had to do and went out and did it."

"We're mature now," said Harrelson, the shortstop who had made so many outstanding defensive plays. "We knew we had a good club and we kept fighting back through a lot of disappointment. To win when you're expected to win brings a certain satisfaction."

The Mets had won only half a title. They still had to face the heavily favored Big Red Machine from Cincinnati in the playoffs to be crowned National League champions and advance to the World Series again. They had four days to rest before the playoffs began in Cincinnati. The rest was necessary for Seaver, who was not only tired but experiencing some shoulder ailment. In a workout at Shea two days after he had started in Chicago, Seaver threw hard, and Berra announced his ace would open in Cincinnati that Saturday.

Seaver was equal to the occasion. He pitched a six-hitter and drove in a run with a double. But solo home runs by Pete Rose in the eighth and another game-ending shot by Johnny Bench in the ninth left the Mets on the short end of a 2–1 score.

Matlack was sensational in the second game, pitching a two-hitter (both singles by Andy Kosco), and when Staub homered in the fourth, that was the

Rose tries to dump Harrelson while sliding into second after a successful double play.

Rose and Harrelson exchange pleasantries.

only run Jon needed to breeze to a 5–0 win. The Mets returned home for the final three games.

It was Koosman's turn to keep things going in the third game. Just like Matlack, he was in total command. The 53,000 fans jamming Shea Stadium went wild when the Mets overcame a two-run deficit with a five-run second inning. Staub, who had been the Mets' most consistent hitter during the final weeks of the pennant race, helped Koosman to the big lead with a pair of home runs and four runs batted in.

In the fifth inning, with the Mets in front, 9–2, Rose slid hard into Harrelson at second base attempting to break up a double play just as the shortstop got off his throw. The two men began pushing each other; soon they were swinging away, and when Mets players saw Rose on top of their little infield leader and punching away, they emptied the dugout and the bullpen. The Reds did likewise and suddenly there were some sixty players and coaches at the middle of the infield. Most were trying to restore order. Others, like Cincinnati pitcher Pedro Borbon, were intent on continuing the brawl.

When play resumed and Rose took his position in left field, he was bombarded with everything the fans in left field could find to throw. Garbage, uneaten lunches, cans, a whiskey bottle, and paper cups all landed near Rose. The whiskey bottle, which came flying out of the upper deck, fell dangerously close to the left fielder. When that happened Rose headed for the dugout, and Cincinnati manager Sparky Anderson ordered his entire team off the field.

An unusual scene followed. Because they were all-time New York favorites, Berra and Mays were requested by National League President Chub Feeney to walk out to left field and plead with the fans for order. On their own, Seaver, Staub, and Jones also walked out to calm the fans down. They succeeded and the game continued with the Mets completing their easy win.

The Mets needed only one more win to become National League champions again. Stone, who had finished the regular season with eight straight wins, was Berra's choice to wrap up the playoffs.

Stone pitched well. He had a 1–0 lead for six innings, and then Tony Perez tied the game with a home run. McGraw came in to protect the tie and pitched shutout ball for four and one-third innings as the teams battled into the twelfth. Then, with Parker pitching, Rose homered and Borbon held the Mets

In the fifth inning of the third game of the playoffs, all hell broke loose on the playing field when Pete Rose slid hard into second base in an attempt to break up a double play; Harrelson objected, gave Rose a bit of a shove, and the fight was on—big burly Pete against the diminutive Bud. For many years following this memorable incident, Mets fans continued to boo Pete Rose every time he appeared back at Shea—the scene of the crime.

DAILY NEWS/DANNY FARRELL

Chaos and anarchy on the infield as Buzz Capra takes on Pedro Borbon.

scoreless in the bottom half. Two of the leading participants in Monday's brawl had gained their revenge in front of another 53,000 Metsomaniacs.

The Mets lost more than just a ballgame that day. They also lost Rusty Staub. The right fielder crashed into the outfield fence to make a game-saving catch in the eleventh and banged up his right shoulder. After that he could not swing a bat. In the final game, Jones moved to right field, Kranepool played left, and Milner took over at first base.

It was Seaver against Jack Billingham, both nineteen-game winners, in the fifth and final game. In the very first inning, Kranepool knocked in two runs with a single, and the Mets were off and running. Cincinnati nicked Seaver for a run in the third and another in the fifth to tie. If Seaver was not as effective as he had been in the playoffs opener, neither was Billingham. In the fifth the Mets broke the game open with four runs and a 6–2 lead.

Garrett opened with a double. When Billingham fielded Millan's sacrifice attempt and appeared to have a certain out at third, Cincinnati's Dan Driessen "fell asleep." Instead of tagging Garrett, as he should have, Driessen treated the play as a force—he did not bother to put a tag on the sliding runner. Garrett, of course, was safe, and now the Mets had runners on first and third.

Jones doubled in one run for a 3–2 lead. When pinch hitter Mays hit a high, slow chopper to the left side, Reds relief pitcher Clay Carroll had to wait until the ball came down. By the time he got it and threw home, it was too late. Another run was in, and Mays had an infield hit, his last regular season hit in the major leagues.

An infield out by Hahn produced another run, and Harrelson singled for the fourth run of the inning. With a 6–2 lead and Seaver pitching, the Mets fans again began to act unruly. Some of the younger ones from the upper stands began to descend to the lower stands and little by little pushed their way toward the railings on the foul lines. The box seats were now overcrowded with young fans eager to bounce out onto the field at the last out—there were still twelve to go. The aisles were jammed and there was a lot of pushing and shoving. Right in the middle of this sea of fanatics sat the Reds' officials and the players' wives.

By the ninth inning, the mob was uncontrollable. The wife of the Reds' doctor was almost trampled in the crush. Fearing for the safety of the

Jon Matlock and Yogi Berra escort a shaken Bud Harrelson back to the dugout.

Tug McGraw tries to escape the fans and media following the final out of the 1973 playoff win over the Reds on October 10. After an inconsistent first half, Tug was magnificent after mid-August, giving up only four runs in his last nineteen relief appearances.
DAILY NEWS/FRANK HURLEY

Cincinnati people, the umpires halted the game and allowed the wives and officials to leave the stands through the Reds dugout.

The fans were virtually on the field in the ninth. Seaver was tiring, and McGraw had to be summoned to get the final two outs. When he did and the Mets had completed one of the most dramatic comebacks in baseball history, players ran for their lives to escape their frenzied fans. The scene that followed on the field was a total embarrassment to the Mets and to the city of New York. The mob of young fanatics tore the entire field apart, leaving little turf. They stole all the bases, home plate, and the pitching rubber and even dismantled parts of the outfield fence. Police estimated that at least one-third of the 53,000 in attendance that day were on the field after the game.

Seaver summed up the Mets' anger and embarrassment over the actions of the "fans": "These people don't care anything about baseball or us winning. It's just an excuse for them to tear up everything in sight."

Cincinnati's Pete Rose was even more blunt: "If those are Mets fans, they must let them out of the zoo before every game and lock them up again after the game."

Fortunately for Jim Thomson and Johnny McCarthy, they would have a week in which to get Shea Stadium in shape again.

The World Series opened in Oakland on October 13. It was almost anticlimactic after all the Mets had been through the last two months. They had gone from last place, eleven and a half games out, to the World Series. Nobody expected them to be where they were after their dismal start. Now that they were in the Series, anything they did well would be that much of a bonus.

As Berra led his Mets against the colorful A's on October 13, he had already joined Joe McCarthy as the only manager to win pennants in both leagues.

Seaver had been used to win the final game of the playoffs so he could not open the Series, as the aces of staffs usually do. Instead it was Matlack, the number 3 starter, who opposed Oakland ace Ken Holtzman. Matlack pitched as well as expected, with one exception, and he allowed his mound rival to beat him at the plate. In the third inning, with two out, Holtzman doubled down the left field line. With the Designated Hitter rule in effect for the first time in the American League, pitchers did not hit except in the Series. In his first at-bat of the season Holtzman doubled, and, sure enough, it was enough to beat Matlack, 2–1. When Millan let a Bert Campaneris grounder go through his legs for an error, Holtzman scored. Then Matlack threw high to first on an attempted pickoff, and Campaneris went to second. He scored the game's winning run on a single by Joe Rudi.

The Mets played the first Series game without Staub, their leading hitter, but had him in right for the second game even though Rusty could not throw well because of his banged-up shoulder.

Game Two of the Series was the longest in history. It took four hours and thirteen minutes to complete and lasted for twelve innings. The Mets pushed across four runs in the top of the twelfth, and the A's came back with one in the bottom half as the Mets won, 10–7.

Koosman lasted only two innings. Sadecki, Parker, and McGraw followed, with Tug pitching six innings of relief before Stone took over in the twelfth and finished up. Mays, who replaced Staub in the late innings, suffered an embarrassing afternoon. The afternoon Oakland sun was brutal on outfielders, and Mays misjudged two fly balls, something he had never done before in two decades of play. It was little solace to Willie that he delivered a key hit to break the tie in the twelfth. Mays was proud of his fielding abilities and his performance that day was a humiliation.

In the twelfth inning, two errors by Oakland's reserve second baseman Mike Andrews had helped the Mets score their four runs. After the game, A's owner Charles Finley persuaded Andrews to sign a statement saying he was injured. Finley wanted to activate Manny Trillo to play second. This maneuver so irritated Oakland manager Dick Williams that he told his players he was resigning after the Series.

METS' CONSECUTIVE-GAME HITTING STREAKS

Games	Player	Year	Dates
24	Brooks, Hubie	1984	May 1–June 1
23	Jones, Cleon	1970	Aug 25–Sept 5
23	Vail, Mike	1975	Aug 22–Sept 15
20	Agee, Tommie	1970	Apr 16–May 9
19	Agee, Tommie	1970	June 22–July 8
19	Millan, Felix	1975	July 5–July 26
19	Mazzilli, Lee	1979	Aug 28–Sept 18
18	Thomas, Frank	1962	Aug 12–Aug 30
18	Millan, Felix	1973	July 13–Aug 1
18	Kranepool, Ed	1975	July 11–Aug 5
18	Mazzilli, Lee	1980	June 18–July 10
16	Torre, Joe	1975	May 24–June 9
16	Milner, John	1976	Apr 11–May 16
15	Staub, Rusty	1973	Sept 15–Oct 1
15	Stearns, John	1982	Apr 14–May 3
15	Wilson, Mookie	1984	June 8–June 23

Willie Mays pleads with umpire Augie Donatelli to change his mind about calling Bud Harrelson out while trying to score a go-ahead run in the tenth inning of the second World Series game. The Mets eventually won, 10–7, in a sloppy affair.
AP

When the Series shifted to New York, autumn had turned to winter. All three games in New York were played at night, with temperatures in the low 40s and high 30s.

Oakland won the third game, and again it went extra innings. This time the A's won it in eleven. Whereas Andrews had been the goat in the previous game, this time it was Grote, the Mets' usually dependable defensive catcher.

With Parker pitching in the eleventh and the score tied at 2–2, the A's Ted Kubiak walked on four pitches. Parker followed with a strikeout of Angel Mangual, but the third strike got away from Grote for a passed ball and Kubiak went to second. He scored the winning run on a single by Campaneris.

The Mets then won the next two, holding the A's to one run in the two games. Matlack, in a rematch with Holtzman, beat him, 6–1, this time. Staub, with a three-run home run off Holtzman in the first, gave the Mets a taste of

1973

NAME	G by POS	B	AGE	G	AB	R	H	2B	3B	HR	RBI	BB	SO	SB	BA	SA
NEW YORK 1st 82-79 .509 YOGI BERRA																
TOTALS			28	161	5457	608	1345	198	24	85	553	540	805	27	.246	.338
John Milner	1B95, OF29	L	23	129	451	69	108	12	3	23	72	62	84	1	.239	.432
Felix Millan	2B153	R	29	153	638	82	185	23	4	3	37	35	22	2	.290	.353
Bud Harrelson	SS103	B	29	106	356	35	92	12	3	0	20	48	48	5	.258	.309
Wayne Garrett	3B130, SS9, 2B6	L	25	140	504	76	129	20	3	16	58	72	74	6	.256	.403
Rusty Staub	OF152	L	29	152	585	77	163	36	1	15	76	74	52	1	.279	.421
Don Hahn	OF87	R	24	93	262	22	60	10	0	2	21	22	43	2	.229	.290
Cleon Jones	OF92	R	30	92	339	48	88	13	0	11	48	28	51	1	.260	.395
Jerry Grote	C81, 3B2	R	30	84	285	17	73	10	2	1	32	13	23	0	.256	.316
Ed Kranepool	1B51, OF32	L	28	100	284	28	68	12	2	1	35	30	28	1	.239	.306
Ted Martinez	SS44, OF21, 3B14, 2B5	R	25	92	263	34	67	11	0	1	14	13	38	3	.255	.308
Ken Boswell	3B17, 2B3	L	27	76	110	12	25	2	1	2	14	12	11	0	.227	.318
Duffy Dyer	C60	R	27	70	189	9	35	6	1	1	9	13	40	0	.185	.243
Willie Mays	OF45, 1B17	R	42	66	209	24	44	10	0	6	25	27	47	1	.211	.344
Jim Beauchamp	1B11	R	33	50	61	5	17	1	1	0	14	7	11	1	.279	.328
Ron Hodges	C40	L	24	45	127	5	33	2	0	1	18	11	19	0	.260	.299
Jim Fregosi	SS17, 3B17, 1B3, OF1	R	31	45	124	7	29	4	1	0	11	20	25	1	.234	.282
George Theodore	OF33, 1B4	R	25	45	116	14	30	4	0	1	15	10	13	1	.259	.319
Jim Gosger	OF35	L	30	38	92	9	22	2	0	0	10	9	16	0	.239	.261

Dave Schneck 24 L 7-36, Rich Chiles 23 L 3-25, 2 Jerry May 29 R 2-8, Brian Ostrosser 24 L 0-5, Lute Barnes 26 R 1-2, Greg Harts 23 L 1-2

NAME	T	AGE	W	L	PCT	SV	G	GS	CG	IP	H	BB	SO	ShO	ERA
		27	82	79	.509	40	161	161	47	1465	1345	490	1027	15	3.26
Tom Seaver	R	28	19	10	.655	0	36	36	18	290	219	64	251	3	2.08
Jerry Koosman	L	30	14	15	.483	0	35	35	12	263	234	76	156	3	2.84
Jon Matlack	L	23	14	16	.467	0	34	34	14	242	210	99	205	3	3.20
George Stone	L	26	12	3	.800	1	27	20	2	148	157	31	77	0	2.80
Harry Parker	R	25	8	4	.667	5	38	9	0	97	79	36	63	0	3.34
Ray Sadecki	L	32	5	4	.556	1	31	11	1	117	109	41	87	0	3.38
Tug McGraw	L	28	5	6	.455	25	60	2	0	119	106	55	81	0	3.86
Jim McAndrew	R	29	3	8	.273	1	23	12	0	80	109	31	38	0	5.40
Buzz Capra	R	25	2	7	.222	4	24	0	0	42	35	28	35	0	3.86
Tommy Moore	R	24	0	0	.000	0	3	1	0	3	6	3	1	0	12.00
Craig Swan	R	22	0	1	.000	0	3	1	0	8	16	2	4	0	9.00
Phil Hennigan	R	27	0	4	.000	3	30	0	0	43	50	16	22	0	6.28
John Strohmayer	R	26	0	0	.000	0	7	0	0	10	13	4	5	0	8.10
Hank Webb	R	23	0	0	.000	0	2	0	0	2	2	1	1	0	9.00
Bob Apodaca	R	23	0	0	.000	0	1	0	0	0	0	2	0	0	∞
Bob Miller	R	34	0	0	.000	0	1	0	0	1	0	0	1	0	0.00

what they were missing when he could not play. Rusty drove in five of the team's six runs and had a 4-for-4 night at the plate.

Koosman was even better the next night. He pitched the first six and one-third innings, and McGraw pitched the last two and two-thirds for a combined three-hit, 2–0 shutout. Milner and Hahn drove in the only runs the Mets needed.

Although they had to fly back across the country to Oakland, the Mets were in excellent shape to win the World Series again. They had a one-game edge with two to play, and they had Seaver and Matlack primed to start.

Seaver, who had opposed Catfish Hunter in the third game at Shea, drew the tough right-hander as an opponent again. Seaver hung tough, but Hunter was even tougher. Reggie Jackson drove in two early runs off Seaver with doubles in the first and third innings. Seaver was behind, 2–0, when he was lifted. Boswell, Garrett, and Millan singled in the eighth for one run, but then, with two runners aboard, Staub struck out on three pitches. Rollie Fingers, who got the last out for the A's in the eighth in relief, retired the Mets in order in the ninth to protect a 3–1 Oakland win, sending the Series into a seventh game.

Matlack failed to get to the third inning in the deciding game. The Athletics ripped him for four runs. Once again Holtzman surprised everyone with a double, and Campaneris followed with a home run. Rudi lined a single to center and Jackson made it 4–0 with a home run. It was 5–0 before the Mets scored a run in the sixth. They got one more in the ninth, but that was hardly enough—as Oakland won the game, 5–2, and the Series.

Ironically, the Mets out-hit the Athletics as a team .253 to .212 in the Series. They also out-homered them, four to two, and outscored them, twenty-four runs to twenty-one. But the A's won four games and the Mets only three. The pitching, which had been so great in the final two months of the season, just wasn't good enough to create another miracle.

Three months before he died of cancer, Casey returned to Shea and rode a chariot from the dugout to the bullpen during part of the Oldtimers' Day proceedings on June 28.

LOUIS REQUENA

arely four months after he almost was let go, Yogi Berra had led the Mets to an Eastern Division title, a National League championship, and the seventh game of the World Series. His reward was a two-year extension to his contract. His detractors, who had argued in July that Berra was too easygoing, now had to admit that it was his failure to press the panic button that probably had much to do with the Mets winning. Of course, a healthy team had a lot to do with the comeback, too.

Confident that with their pitching staff plus the bats of Jones, Staub, Milner, and Garrett they could win again—at least be contenders—the Mets stood pat in the off-season. Even though the other teams made moves to strengthen themselves, the Mets did not make a single major off-season deal. That subsequently appeared to have been a mistake. The Mets got off to a terrible start and fell into fifth place the second week of the 1974 season. They never got over .500 after the fourth game they played.

While they didn't realize it at the time, opening day in Philadelphia was an omen. Seaver, who had won another Cy Young Award for his great pitching in 1973, was the starting pitcher against Steve Carlton. The Mets gave Seaver leads twice in the game, and he failed to hold them. Then the Mets gained another lead and turned the ball over to McGraw, their great game saver of the previous year. McGraw served up a two-run home run to Mike Schmidt in the bottom of the ninth to give the Phillies a 5–4 victory. The Mets' two best pitchers of 1973 had failed miserably, and it was only the first game of the season. It did not get much better in the months ahead.

Seaver got off to his worst start ever. In his first eight starts, he won only once. Frustration boiled up inside him. Seaver had always been a willing interview subject. In fact, it was Seaver who first appeared at what has now become a common middle-of-the-clubhouse, center-table interview. I had suggested that to Mets publicist Harold Weissman one night years earlier, because the crush around Seaver's locker after a winning game made it impossible for all but those up front to hear his replies. I reasoned with Weissman that if Seaver sat at the table in the middle of the clubhouse where players usually sat before games and played or read the papers, almost all the reporters would have equal access to Seaver or whomever else was being interviewed. Seaver agreed, and that table soon became known to all as "the table." The hero of each win was automatically brought there.

On the night of May 7, 1974, Seaver refused to sit at the table or even talk to reporters. His record had slipped to 1–3 after a tough loss to the Giants in which Steve Ontiveros and Gary Matthews tagged him for home runs, the latter a three-run homer to win the game. Seaver was visibly upset by his start. When the season was over, his record was a mere 11–11 and his earned run average an inflated 3.20, his highest ever. It meant he was allowing one more earned run per game than he had in his first seven seasons.

By late June, when he had won only one-quarter of his sixteen starts, Seaver had to leave a game with a strained sciatic nerve in his left buttocks. He missed one turn, then came back and won two in a row to balance his record at 6–6. On July 7 he lasted only five innings, again leaving in pain. It was three weeks before Tom pitched again. In the interim the National League All-Star pitching staff was selected, and for the first time in his career Seaver was not included. He shut out St. Louis, 3–0, on July 26, and then waited a month for his next win. After winning his first three starts in September, he lost his next two. When he limped off the field on September 25th, Seaver announced he wouldn't pitch again.

At that point, Grant stepped in and made what may have been one of his finest contributions to the club. Grant had some back problems himself, and he had an osteopath, Dr. Kenneth Riland, who had treated many of the rich and famous, including Governor Nelson D. Rockefeller. After consulting with

16

♦ "IT'S OVER, ♦
♦ YOGI, ♦
♦ IT'S OVER" ♦

OPENING DAY LINEUP 1974

Garrett, 3b
Millan, 2b
Staub, rf
Jones, lf
Milner, 1b
Grote, c
Hahn, cf
Harrelson, ss
Seaver, p

team physician Dr. James C. Parkes and obtaining his permission, Grant put Seaver in touch with Dr. Riland. Seaver, who had been hobbled by the pain in his buttocks most of the season, was willing to try anything. After two treatments by Dr. Riland over a five-day period, Tom announced he was ready to try one more time.

On October 1, in the next to last home game of the season, Seaver pitched a four-hitter against the Phillies. He struck out fourteen batters but lost, 2–1. When Grant came into the clubhouse afterward, Seaver handed him the game ball. On it he had written, "I owe you one. Thanks. Tom Seaver," a sentiment Grant would remember in future contract negotiations.

Seaver's victory in his final start was encouraging for 1975's prospects, but it did little to ease the pain of the disappointing 1974 season. Not only did Seaver fail to deliver his usual twenty victories, but McGraw also went sour. The little left-hander, who had won five and saved twenty-five during the 1973 pennant campaign, won six but saved only three in 1974. In fact, the entire Mets relief corps saved only fourteen games, with Harry Parker's four leading the pack.

"Fourteen saves. A lotta guys save that many all by themselves," Berra wailed at the end of the season. "I said it before, but if you ain't got a bullpen, you ain't got nothin'."

"My two biggest disappointments this year were Seaver and McGraw," General Manager Scheffing said bluntly at the end of the campaign.

But there were other disappointments for the Mets. Once again they showed a distinct lack of power. Only one man, John Milner, hit as many as twenty home runs. Staub hit nineteen, but he batted only .258, well below his previous average. Jones and Garrett each hit thirteen. Staub's seventy-eight runs batted in was one of the lowest figures in the league for a team leader.

As Berra and Scheffing had suggested, the pitching was even worse. The only winner was Koosman, with a 15–11 record. Next to Seaver, the major disappointment as a starter was Matlack. The big left-hander won thirteen but lost fifteen. His earned run average was an attractive 2.41, but Matlack usually was either sensational or mediocre. When he was hot, he pitched shutouts. In 1974 there were seven of those, which was the most for any pitcher in the league.

"You take away those seven shutouts and Jon had a horsefeathers year," said Scheffing bluntly.

Stone, whose twelve victories were such a key in 1973, was almost a total washout in 1974. He won successive starts on May 15 and 21, then lost four in a row. In early June he was sidelined with a sore shoulder, which later was diagnosed as a torn rotator cuff. He left the club in early August, never to pitch again during the season.

Other major injuries decimated the Mets, but none of them had any effect on the club's pennant chances. Pittsburgh, St. Louis, and Philadelphia were the dominant powers in the Eastern Division. The Mets got off to a terrible start, fell to fifth place in April, and were never in contention again. Most of the summer was spent in fifth or sixth place. The team's demise was reflected at the gate. The total home attendance figure of 1,722,209 assured the club of a profit, but it also revealed the fans' discontent. The figure was the lowest in seven years.

The Mets played two months of the season without two of their established stars. On June 12, Harrelson was hit on the back of the right hand by Montreal's Carl Morton. It was the fifth time in Harrelson's career that he suffered a broken bone playing baseball. This time the Mets did not consider the injury serious enough to place Bud on the disabled list, playing an entire month with him useful only as a pinch runner. Matlack assailed the front office for making the team play with only twenty-four able bodies, but his complaints fell on deaf ears.

Two months after Harrelson was hit by Morton, Grote was hit on the right hand by a foul tip off the bat of Houston's Doug Rader. There was no fracture, but Grote's hand was so sore that he could not catch again.

Thus the Mets played an entire month without their regular shortstop and all of September without their regular catcher. In addition, Rusty Staub's hand troubled him most of the year. He also appeared to be playing grossly overweight. All of this added up to a rather dismal season, which mercifully came to an end after the Mets dropped eight of their last ten games. It was almost as if they could not wait to get the season over with—a far cry from the previous year, when they had extended the season an extra day to win the pennant.

One who certainly could not wait for the end was Scheffing. On the same day that Seaver pitched and won his final game, Scheffing announced he was stepping down as general manager. He had served the five years he had promised Grant after reluctantly accepting the post in January 1970. It was clear that Scheffing and his wife couldn't wait to get back to Arizona.

Rumors about Scheffing's imminent retirement had started early. Two men were mentioned as possible successors: Joe McDonald, the Mets' farm director, and Nelson Burbrink, director of player development. Scheffing had leaned heavily on McDonald's rule book expertise and business acumen during his reign as general manager, and had handpicked him over Burbrink, a former major league catcher, to succeed him.

It was a Horatio Alger success story come true. Born in Staten Island, New York, McDonald had been raised in Brooklyn, where his father served as usher at Ebbets Field while the son was an attendant at the Dodgers' press gate. Joe had an accounting degree from Fordham University, and he was hired in 1962 as the statistician for the Mets' radio-TV team. The following year he moved into the front office as a secretary in the farm department, where he was to gain stature during Herzog's tenure as director of player development. During that time Whitey was the baseball brains; McDonald took care of the paperwork. Now McDonald had ascended to the top position in the organization as general manager. There were those who felt the Mets needed someone with a little more baseball experience, especially more knowledge in trading. Grant made it clear that no one else had even been considered for the post.

"We believe in developing our own people," the chairman of the board stated. "We believe in Joe McDonald. He must have had something to do with producing the talent that won a world championship and two pennants in the twelve years he has been here. He has been well trained."

The last line brought smiles to the faces of veteran members of the press corps. Well trained, yes—trained to do whatever Grant ordered. If Scheffing would not oppose anything Grant suggested, how could anyone expect McDonald to do so.

McDonald went to work immediately to resolve some of the Mets' problems. Garrett had hit only .224 as the regular third baseman, so the Mets went out and bought themselves another veteran. This time it was Joe Torre, who five years earlier had been the key man in the deal they never made. Torre was thirty-four and had seen his best years with the Braves and Cardinals. Now he was coming back to New York, where he had been raised and was a schoolboy star. The Torre deal was made on October 13 in Los Angeles during the World Series. It was important that the deal be concluded as soon as possible. The Mets had a big exhibition series ahead.

As if all the trouble they had suffered during the dismal 1974 season were not enough, the Mets now had to travel halfway around the world to Japan. It

METS' ALL-STAR GAME SELECTIONS 1962-1986

Year	Player
1962	Richie Ashburn, of
1963	Duke Snider, of
1964	Ron Hunt,* 2b
1965	Ed Kranepool, 1b
1966	Ron Hunt, 2b
1967	Tom Seaver, rhp
1968	Jerry Grote,* c
	Jerry Koosman, lhp
	Tom Seaver, rhp
1969	Cleon Jones,* of
	Jerry Koosman, lhp
	Tom Seaver,* rhp
1970	Bud Harrelson,* ss
	Tom Seaver,* rhp
1971	Bud Harrelson,* ss
	Tom Seaver, rhp
1972	Willie Mays,* of
	Tug McGraw, lhp
	Tom Seaver, rhp
1973	Willie Mays, of
	Tom Seaver, rhp
1974	Jery Grote, c
	Jon Matlack, lhp
1975	Jon Matlack, lhp
	Tom Seaver, rhp
1976	Dave Kingman,* of
	Jon Matlack, lhp
	Tom Seaver, rhp
1977	John Stearns, c
1978	Pat Zachry, rhp
1979	Lee Mazzilli, of
	John Stearns, c
1980	John Stearns, c
1981	Joel Youngblood, of
1982	John Stearns, c
1983	Jesse Orosco, lhp
1984	Dwight Gooden, rhp
	Keith Hernandez, 1b
	Jesse Orosco, lhp
	Darryl Strawberry,* of
1985	Dwight Gooden, p
	Ron Darling, p
	Gary Carter, c
	Darryl Strawberry, cf
1986	Gary Carter,* c
	Sid Fernandez, p
	Dwight Gooden,* p
	Keith Hernandez,* 1b
	Darryl Strawberry,* of

*Starting player

Rusty Staub is out at the plate as Chicago's Steve Swisher applies the tag. The Mets won the double-header on April 20, anyway. Del Unser, number 25, looks on in desperation. Staub had his best season for the Mets in 1975 with a club record 105 RBIs, a .282 batting average, and nineteen home runs. Since Shea Stadium is considered a poor hitters' park (bad visibility, distant outfield fences, swirling winds, etc.), 105 RBIs is a considerable achievement.
DAILY NEWS/DANNY FARRELL

was their year to serve as major league baseball's representatives in an exhibition series against Japanese league teams. The Mets wanted to make sure Torre went with them because several of their regulars refused to make the long trip, notably Harrelson, Grote, Jones, and McGraw. Seaver also begged off. Nancy Seaver was pregnant and did not want to travel that distance in her condition; Tom would not go without her. But Seaver was the star pitcher of the Mets, and the Japanese promoters insisted on his presence. So the Seavers went, but Tom pitched in only five games before returning home with Nancy, who became ill. The Mets filled out their roster with minor league players and proceeded to extend their dismal season by winning nine games and losing seven.

Grant, showing his disdain for most members of the daily press corps, invited only Dick Young of the *New York Daily News* and Joseph Durso of the *New York Times* to accompany the Mets to Japan. Everyone else was ignored.

McDonald remained behind in New York, working to strengthen the club for 1975. Sadecki and minor leaguer Tommie Moore had been traded for Torre. Ten days later, while the team was in Japan, outfielder Gene Clines was obtained from Pittsburgh for catcher Duffy Dyer. A week later outfielder Bob Gallagher came from Houston in exchange for Ken Boswell. And on December 3, in what appeared to be a minor deal at the time, relief pitcher Skip Lockwood was obtained from California for Bill Sudakis, a catcher–third baseman of little note who had been sent back to the minors earlier. Lockwood went on to become the Mets' best relief pitcher in the late seventies.

It was at the winter meetings in New Orleans in December that the Mets pulled their biggest deal of the year. McGraw, the hero of the 1973 pennant, was sent to the Phillies on December 4 in exchange for Del Unser, a veteran center fielder, a relief pitcher named Mac Scarce, and rookie catcher John Stearns. The key man in the deal for the Mets was Stearns. Grote was nearing the end of his career, and Stearns would be groomed to replace him. He was considered one of the best young catching prospects in the minors. McDonald admitted that both he and McGraw cried over the telephone when the general manager called to advise the relief pitcher of the trade. McGraw had come up through the farm system, when McDonald was helping to run it.

McDonald made one final deal that week. On December 11 he obtained infielder Jack Heidemann and outfielder Mike Vail from St. Louis for shortstop Teddy Martinez. Vail played a big role in the Mets' 1975 season.

Even with the acquisition of Torre, the Mets still were short in the power department. And then, in mid-February, Schéffing's addiction to golf paid off for the Mets. It was while touring one of the Arizona courses with a friend that Scheffing learned of Horace Stoneham's need for some ready cash to pay off spring training expenses. Unlike the Dodgers, the Giants were not doing all that well in California. Stoneham, Scheffing learned, was willing to part with home run hitter Dave Kingman for $150,000. The Mets had coveted the long-ball hitter since he had hit one out of sight at Shea in 1971, his rookie year. The Mets were quick to accept the offer and on February 28, just a week before the first exhibition game, Kingman officially became a Met. Now the team had the power it had sorely lacked.

Kingman had a sensational first spring with the Mets. He hit .310 and clubbed eight home runs. The rest of the team hit six. But while they were gaining a power hitter, the Mets also were losing a consistent hitter. Cleon Jones had off-season knee surgery and struggled throughout spring training. On April 5 he was placed on the disabled list as the team headed north. Cleon would remain in Florida to get in shape with the minor leaguers. It was a mistake leaving Jones virtually on his own in Florida. A few weeks later, the Mets were embarrassed to learn that their star outfielder had been picked up by St. Petersburg police for indecent exposure. He and a female companion had been arrested in a van parked on one of St. Petersburg's downtown streets. According to the police blotter, Jones was nude at the time.

When Jones was eventually reinstated by the Mets at the end of May, he was fined $2,000 by the club and forced to read an apology for his conduct in front of reporters and television broadcasters in the Shea Stadium press room. Worse yet, Grant requested that Cleon's wife, Angela, be alongside him when he read it. Newspapers the next day likened the apology to a public flogging and blasted Grant for his handling of the case.

Eight weeks later, Jones was gone. On the night of July 18, Berra told Jones to go out to left field for late inning defense. Sulking because he was not starting, Jones refused. There were words and Berra told Cleon to go to the clubhouse. McDonald and Grant were advised of Jones's refusal to obey orders, but for four days they failed to back up their manager and suspend Jones. Yogi was adamant. He insisted Jones be suspended and be ordered to apologize for his insubordination in front of the entire team. It was a test of

Dave Kingman arrived on the scene in 1975 as the Mets power hitter. A major headache for management, Kingman went on to clout thirty-six home runs to break the team record set in 1962, but he also struck out an alarming number of times.
DAILY NEWS/ VINCENT RIEHL

1974

NAME	G by POS	B	AGE	G	AB	R	H	2B	3B	HR	RBI	BB	SO	SB	BA	SA
NEW YORK 5th 71-91 .438 17			YOGI BERRA													
TOTALS			28	162	5468	572	1286	183	22	96	538	597	735	43	.235	.329
John Milner	1B133	L	24	137	507	70	128	19	0	20	63	66	77	10	.252	.408
Felix Millan	2B134	R	30	136	518	50	139	15	2	1	33	31	14	5	.268	.311
Bud Harrelson	SS97	B	30	106	331	48	75	10	0	1	13	71	39	9	.227	.266
Wayne Garrett	3B144, SS9	L	26	151	522	55	117	14	3	13	53	89	96	4	.224	.337
Rusty Staub	OF147	L	30	151	561	65	145	22	2	19	78	77	39	2	.258	.406
Don Hahn	OF106	R	25	110	323	34	81	14	1	4	28	37	34	2	.251	.337
Cleon Jones	OF120	R	31	124	461	62	130	23	1	13	60	38	79	3	.282	.421
Jerry Grote	C94	R	31	97	319	25	82	8	1	5	36	33	33	0	.257	.335
Ted Martinez	SS75, 3B12, 2B11, OF10	R	26	116	334	32	73	15	7	2	43	14	40	3	.219	.323
Ken Boswell	2B28, 3B20, OF7	L	28	96	222	19	48	6	1	2	15	18	19	0	.216	.279
Ed Kranepool	OF33, 1B24	L	29	94	217	20	65	11	1	4	24	18	14	1	.300	.415
Dave Schneck	OF84	L	25	93	254	23	52	11	1	5	25	16	43	4	.205	.315
Duffy Dyer	C45	R	28	63	142	14	30	1	1	0	10	18	15	0	.211	.232
George Theodore	1B14, OF12	R	26	60	76	7	12	1	0	1	8	8	14	0	.158	.211
Ron Hodges	C44	L	25	59	136	16	30	4	0	4	14	19	11	0	.221	.338
Jim Gosger	OF24	L	31	26	33	3	3	0	0	0	0	3	2	0	.091	.091
Benny Ayala	OF20	R	23	23	68	9	16	1	0	2	8	7	17	1	.235	.338
Brock Pemberton	1B4	B	20	11	22	0	4	0	0	0	1	0	3	0	.182	.182
Bruce Boisclair	OF5	L	21	7	12	0	3	1	0	0	1	1	4	0	.250	.333
Rich Puig	2B3, 3B1	L	21	4	10	0	0	0	0	0	0	1	2	0	.000	.000
Ike Hampton	C1	B	22	4	4	0	0	0	0	0	1	0	1	0	.000	.000

NAME	T	AGE	W	L	PCT	SV	G	GS	CG	IP	H	BB	SO	ShO	ERA
		29	71	91	.438	14	162	162	46	1470	1433	504	908	15	3.42
Jerry Koosman	L	31	15	11	.577	0	35	35	13	265	258	85	188	0	3.36
Jon Matlack	L	24	13	15	.464	0	34	34	14	265	221	76	195	7	2.41
Tom Seaver	R	29	11	11	.500	0	32	32	12	236	199	75	201	5	3.20
Ray Sadecki	L	33	8	8	.500	0	34	10	3	103	107	35	46	1	3.41
Bob Apodaca	R	24	6	6	.500	3	35	8	1	103	92	42	54	0	3.50
Tug McGraw	L	29	6	11	.353	3	41	4	1	89	96	32	54	1	4.15
Harry Parker	R	26	4	12	.250	4	40	16	1	131	145	46	58	0	3.92
Jack Aker	R	33	2	1	.667	2	24	0	0	41	33	14	18	0	3.51
Bob Miller	R	35	2	2	.500	2	58	0	0	78	89	39	35	0	3.58
George Stone	L	27	2	7	.222	0	15	13	1	77	103	21	29	0	5.03
Randy Sterling	R	23	1	1	.500	0	3	2	0	9	13	3	2	0	5.00
Craig Swan	R	23	1	3	.250	0	7	5	0	30	28	21	10	0	4.50
Nino Espinosa	R	20	0	0	—	0	2	1	0	9	12	0	2	0	5.00
John Strohmayer	R	27	0	0	—	0	1	0	0	1	0	1	0	0	0.00
Jerry Cram	R	26	0	1	.000	0	10	0	0	22	22	4	8	0	1.64
Hank Webb	R	24	0	2	.000	0	3	2	0	10	15	10	8	0	7.20

Berra's strength as manager at a time when some players were laughing behind his back at his lack of discipline. On this issue Berra was firm and he was right. Unfortunately he did not get the support he deserved.

Grant called Berra and Jones into a meeting and attempted to dissuade Yogi from his desire to suspend Jones. Berra would not budge. Later Grant made telephone calls to Berra's coaches in Chicago and asked them to convince him to back off. They backed up Yogi. Berra's firm stand was to his credit, but it gave Grant one more reason for canning him.

Finally, in Chicago, Berra summoned writers to his suite in the Executive House on July 26. Jones, the club announced, was being released. "I did what I had to do," Berra defended his handling of the Jones case. No one disagreed. A little more than a week later, on August 6, Berra was gone, too.

Not even Kingman's slugging or Seaver's return to form helped that year. Seaver beat Steve Carlton, 2–1, on opening day, but the Mets did not win again for another eight days. They were 1–5 in a hurry and quickly fell into the cellar. In the losing streak, Seaver showed disdain for Berra when he was lifted after six innings in one game at Pittsburgh in which he felt he was pitching well. Speaking to reporters after the game, he openly criticized the manager's decision.

Seaver continued to pitch well, allowing one and two runs a game. But the Mets were not scoring many more than that, and his record in late May was a mediocre 5–4. Then Seaver went on a nine-game winning streak starting May 27. When Seaver beat the Dodgers, 6–3, at Shea Stadium May 26, the Mets were in second place only one and one-half games out of first. A month later they were in third place, struggling to stay above .500 but dropping well behind the streaking Pirates. By the time of the Jones incident, they were already ten and one-half games out of first place, and not even the most optimistic Mets fan saw any reason to hope for a miracle comeback. However, Matlack and Seaver were winning, and Kingman already had twenty-four homers when Grant decided to change managers.

On August 5, Berra was summoned to Grant's office following a loss to Montreal. The next night first base coach Roy McMillan, who had been a slick infielder, was named to replace Yogi. Grant introduced his handpicked candidate in the press room and likened him to "another Gil Hodges." He envisioned McMillan as the strong, silent type who would make a great leader. But McMillan was lost in his new role. He was silent all right. He rarely said anything. Reporters seeking his opinions or reflections after a game got little more than yes or no answers. McMillan clearly was uncomfortable in the spotlight. Grant had simply misread his personality.

In announcing the change, Grant said, "We are trying to salvage something from the season." The Mets were 56–52 when Berra was axed and in third place, nine games out. Under McMillan they were 26–27 and finished tied for third, ten and one-half games out.

Ten days after making the managerial change, the Mets also made an outfield change. They brought up from Tidewater a young outfielder named Mike Vail, who had been obtained in a deal with St. Louis in December 1974. Vail immediately became the darling of Shea Stadium fans. He had just finished a nineteen-game hitting streak in the minors when he was recalled. He immediately started another one in the majors. Vail hit safely in twenty-three consecutive games, the longest streak in the majors that year, tying the National League rookie record set by Joe Rapp of the Phillies in 1921 and matched by Richie Ashburn of the Phillies in 1948. In the thirty-eight games he played for the Mets, Vail batted .302 and a new hero was born.

Seaver also raised the hopes of Mets fans. After winning only eleven in 1974, Tom Terrific enjoyed a brilliant comeback. He won twenty-two, lost only nine, and once again had a 2.38 earned run average. At the end of the season

OPENING DAY LINEUP 1975

Clines, lf
Millan, 2b
Milner, 1b
Torre, 3b
Kingman, rf
Grote, c
Unser, cf
Harrelson, ss
Seaver, p

he was voted his third Cy Young Award, something only Sandy Koufax had achieved to that point. Tom also established a major league record by striking out 200 or more batters for the eighth straight season. And, of course, he was selected to the National League All-Star team for the eighth time in nine years.

The Mets did enjoy a brief spurt under McMillan and moved to within four games of first place on September 1. Their record at the time was 72–64, but in September they won only eleven while losing sixteen and dropped far out of the race.

The loss of Harrelson, their crackerjack shortstop, was an early blow to the Mets. Bud had been having fluid drained from his right knee off and on, but at the end of May it was no longer possible to drain the knee. Surgery was necessary. Harrelson did not play again until the first week in September, and for three months the Mets had to survive with Mike Phillips, a utility infielder, as their shortstop.

There was more trouble on the left side of the infield. Torre, despite his professional approach to the game, had slowed down to a walk, and his range was limited at third base. Joe hit .247 and grounded into twenty-two rally-killing double plays.

Kingman became the slugger the Mets expected he would be and took over left; with Unser, a fine fielder, in center and Staub in right, the Mets had a decent outfield. Kingman hit a club record thirty-six homers, but he averaged only .231, striking out an alarming 153 times. Staub hit .281, slammed nineteen homers, and drove in 105 runs for another club record.

Three of the starting pitchers had winning records. Besides Seaver's twenty-two wins, Matlack turned in sixteen and Koosman fourteen. But only Bob Apodaca was reliable in the bullpen—when he was available. He started the season on the disabled list and went on it again at the end of June when a hard bouncer off the bat of Philadelphia's Johnny Oates hit him squarely in the nose. Apodaca suffered a compound fracture that required fourteen stitches. He was placed on the disabled list and lost for a month. Apodaca saved thirteen to lead the bullpen corps even though he missed a month of combat.

Matlack was 1975's disappointment despite his sixteen victories. He had those sixteen packed away by August 29 and never won another game in six September starts. One problem was that Jon did not get much offensive support, and he grumbled whenever Mets bats were silent.

It was obvious that McMillan was not the man to turn the Mets around. After giving him his chance for two months, management did not waste time naming a replacement. On October 3 a press conference was called to announce that Joe Frazier would be the Mets' sixth manager.

"Joe who?" asked the fans.

1975

NAME	G by POS	B	AGE	G	AB	R	H	2B	3B	HR	RBI	BB	SO	SB	BA	SA
NEW YORK 3rd(tie) 82-80 .506 10.5			YOGI BERRA 56-53 .514		ROY McMILLAN 26-27 .491												
TOTALS			28	162	5587	646	1430	217	34	101	604	501	805	32	.256	.361
Ed Kranepool	1B82, OF4	L	30	106	325	42	105	16	0	4	43	27	21	1	.323	.409
Felix Millan	2B162	R	31	162	676	81	191	37	2	1	56	36	28	1	.283	.348
Mike Phillips	SS115, 2B1	L	24	116	383	31	98	10	7	1	28	25	47	3	.256	.326
Wayne Garrett	3B94, SS3	L	27	107	274	49	73	8	3	6	34	50	45	2	.266	.383
Rusty Staub	OF153	R	31	155	574	93	162	30	4	19	105	77	55	2	.282	.448
Del Unser	OF144	L	30	147	531	65	156	18	2	10	53	37	76	4	.294	.392
Dave Kingman	OF71, 1B58, 3B12	R	26	134	502	65	116	22	1	36	88	34	153	7	.231	.494
Jerry Grote	C111	R	32	119	386	28	114	14	5	2	39	38	23	0	.295	.373
Joe Torre	3B83, 1B24	R	34	114	361	33	89	16	3	6	35	35	55	0	.247	.357
John Milner	OF31, 1B29	L	25	91	220	24	42	11	0	7	29	33	22	1	.191	.336
Gene Clines	OF60	R	28	82	203	25	46	6	3	0	10	11	21	4	.227	.286
Jesus Alou	OF20	R	33	62	102	8	27	3	0	0	11	4	5	0	.265	.294
Jack Heidemann	SS44, 3B4, 2B1	R	25	61	145	12	31	4	2	1	16	17	28	1	.214	.290
John Stearns	C54	R	23	59	169	25	32	5	1	3	10	17	15	4	.189	.284
Mike Vail	OF36	R	23	38	162	17	49	8	1	3	17	9	37	0	.302	.420
Bud Harrelson	SS34	B	31	34	73	5	16	2	0	0	3	12	13	0	.219	.247
Cleon Jones	OF12	R	32	21	50	2	12	1	0	0	2	3	6	0	.240	.260

Ron Hodges 26 L 7-34, Roy Staiger 25 R 3-19, Bob Gallagher 26 L 2-15, Brock Pemberton 21 B 0-2

NAME	T	AGE	W	L	PCT	SV	G	GS	CG	IP	H	BB	SO	ShO	ERA
		27	82	80	.506	31	162	162	40	1466	1344	580	989	14	3.39
Tom Seaver	R	30	22	9	.710	0	36	36	15	280	217	88	243	5	2.38
Jon Matlack	L	25	16	12	.571	0	33	32	8	229	224	58	154	3	3.38
Jerry Koosman	L	32	14	13	.519	2	36	34	11	240	234	98	173	4	3.41
Hank Webb	R	25	7	6	.538	0	29	15	3	115	102	62	38	1	4.07
Randy Tate	R	22	5	13	.278	0	26	23	2	138	121	86	99	0	4.43
Tom Hall	L	27	4	3	.571	1	34	4	0	61	58	31	48	0	4.72
George Stone	L	28	3	3	.500	0	13	11	1	57	75	21	21	0	5.05
Bob Apodaca	R	25	3	4	.429	13	46	0	0	85	66	28	45	0	1.48
Rick Baldwin	R	22	3	5	.375	6	54	0	0	97	97	34	54	0	3.34
Harry Parker	R	27	2	3	.400	2	18	1	0	35	37	19	22	0	4.37
Ken Sanders	R	33	1	1	.500	5	29	0	0	43	31	14	8	0	2.30
Skip Lockwood	R	28	1	3	.250	2	24	0	0	48	28	25	61	0	1.50
Craig Swan	R	24	1	3	.250	0	6	6	0	31	38	12	19	0	6.39
Mac Scarce	L	26	0	0	—	0	1	0	0	1	0	0	0	0	—
Jerry Cram	R	27	0	0	.000	0	4	0	0	5	7	2	2	0	5.40
Nino Espinosa	R	21	0	1	.000	0	2	0	0	3	8	1	2	0	18.00

oe McDonald and Joe Frazier were an entry. As director of the farm system, McDonald had come to know Frazier as well as anyone in the organization and respected him for his success in the minors. He had won two pennants managing Mets farms at Memphis and Victoria in the Texas League and later with Tidewater.

Frazier had more success as a manager than he did as a ballplayer. Originally signed by Cleveland, he played briefly for the Indians in 1947. He drifted into the St. Louis organization, going almost unnoticed until 1954 when he appeared in eighty-one games with the Cardinals and hit .295. The next year his average dipped to .200. Frazier moved on to Cincinnati and later to Baltimore before he began his minor league managing career.

Not since Walter Alston was promoted to manage the Dodgers in 1954 had a New York major league club hired a manager so little known. New Yorkers were accustomed to "name" managers, but, McDonald argued, if Alson could do it, why not Frazier? The difference, of course, was that when Alston took over in Brooklyn he had an All-Star lineup that had just won two pennants. The Mets of 1976 were a far cry from the 1954 Dodgers.

"Joe Frazier has all the qualifications you would want in a manager. He wins," McDonald said in defense of his decision. And decision it was. If perhaps Grant was skeptical about hiring an unknown, McDonald convinced him Frazier could do the job.

Before Frazier even managed his first game for the Mets, a series of events took place that would shape the season.

Staub's contract was up at the end of the 1975 season, and he was seeking a new one with certain demands that irritated Grant. The details were supposed to be kept between Grant and Staub, but in his pique, Grant leaked to one reporter that Rusty insisted on one-half hour of "privacy" before games for his "constitutional." Staub also had a fear of flying and, according to Grant, demanded that when the team took charter flights he be assured that the runways were of a specified length.

The contract squabble was duly reported in newspapers for weeks, and it soon became apparent that the Mets would trade Rusty rather than give in to his demands. They tried for a deal all during the week-long winter meetings in Florida that year, but it wasn't until the final hour on the final day of inter-league trading that Grant, McDonald, and Scheffing were able to send Rusty and minor league pitcher Bill Laxton to Detroit for southpaw Mickey Lolich and outfielder Billy Baldwin. Scheffing, who had known Lolich from Scheffing's days as Detroit manager and broadcaster, was called in to intercede with the pitcher, who did not want to leave his family in Michigan to play in New York. By sweetening his contract, Scheffing was finally able to convince Lolich that New York was not such a bad place to live.

Having lost his right fielder in a December deal, Frazier lost his left fielder in a February basketball accident. Vail, who showed so much promise the final two months of 1975, was fooling around on a basketball court at Old Dominion College in Virginia when he dislocated his right foot and did damage to the Achilles tendon. His foot was placed in a cast and he reported to spring training on crutches. It was the end of June before Mike could play, and when he did he couldn't run. He was slow on the bases and slow in the field. Vail managed to play in fifty-three games, but his average was a disappointing .219 and he drove in only nine runs.

Spring training was late getting started in 1976 because of another players strike. This one was precipitated by the ruling of Judge Peter Seitz enabling players to become free agents one year after playing an entire season without a contract if they could not reach an agreement with the club that owned them. It was Dodgers pitcher Andy Messersmith who had brought the action with the backing of the Players Association. When Seitz, as arbitrator, ruled against

Tom Seaver shouts in anguish as he foul tips a ball off his ankle during a game against the Braves.
LOUIS REQUENA

the owners, the owners appealed to two courts, both of which upheld the Seitz decision. This resulted in the delay of a new basic agreement between the owners and the players, and when February 20 rolled around, the usual reporting date for spring training, and no agreement had been reached, the camps were closed. The players were not informed until February 23 that spring training was on hold.

Many players were already in Florida and Arizona, ready to begin their drills. In St. Petersburg several St. Louis Cardinals had already begun to limber up on the diamond at Eckerd College. Seaver and other teammates joined them and before long it became known as Seaver's Camp, in honor of Tom's informal Mets camp several years earlier and his method of organizing drills. Players from the Cardinals and Mets worked out together, joined occasionally by members of the Phillies and Pirates, who came over from nearby cities.

By March 12, when there still was no agreement between the owners and the union, the players—at the suggestion of the union—suddenly discontinued their informal workouts.

"If we continue working out at this time, we are only helping the owners while undercutting our own negotiators," Seaver said in closing the Eckerd College camp. Marvin Miller, of course, had suggested that the Players Association bargaining power would be strengthened if players abandoned their workouts. Owners now had to be concerned about the condition of their players if the season were to open on time. If the players continued informal workouts on their own, there was no doubt they would be in shape. Not all players agreed with Seaver, and more disagreed with Miller on his hard bargaining stance. Pete Rose of Cincinnati and George Scott of Milwaukee were outspoken opponents of Miller's position that all players should be eligible for free agency after one year of playing without a contract. A compromise on this issue was finally reached and accepted by a 17–5 vote of the Players Association team representatives, and on March 19, with both owners and the players making certain concessions and with final agreement near, Commissioner Bowie Kuhn ordered the camps opened.

A number of scheduled exhibitions had been canceled; instead of their usual twenty-five, the Mets played only fifteen, and in his first season at the helm, Frazier won only four spring training games.

That was not the Mets' only problem that spring. Seaver, who knew that free agency was right around the corner, made up his mind he did not want to leave New York or the Mets. What he wanted instead was a long-term contract and security. However, McDonald, who was known to be tight with a buck, wouldn't have any part of Seaver's request, and a war of words followed. It was carried on in the daily papers with salvos being fired by both sides. At one point, Seaver was so frustrated and upset at remarks attributed to McDonald that he walked into the general manager's office and shouted at him.

"I gave them a contract proposal in spring training I thought was fair, and I had to go back to them five days later. They did not even bother to respond," Seaver related later. "This was the way they were treating me after ten good years with the club. Why couldn't they have the courtesy to give me a yes or a no? They were trying to intimidate me if I didn't sign.

"One day I just decided to speak to McDonald, face to face. You know what he said to me? He said, 'No one is beyond being traded. I have one deal I can call back on right now.' I was livid. I said, 'Pick up the **** phone and make the trade!' But he never moved. Suddenly it began to dawn on me. Everything I had done, everything I had meant to the team could go out the window in one phone call."

And McDonald almost did. On March 28, when the Mets were in Vero

Beach playing the Dodgers in an afternoon game, McDonald met under a palm tree outside Dodger Stadium with Larue Harcourt, agent for Dodgers pitcher Don Sutton. Agreement on a deal had been reached between the Dodgers and Mets to swap pitchers. All McDonald had to do was satisfy Sutton's agent. Arrangements were being made to find a home for Sutton and his family in Connecticut and for Sutton to join the Mets' radio-TV crew when his playing days were over.

The deal never came off, and this time I may have had something to do with it. I knew the two clubs were talking. I had all the details of the deal from a reliable source, and when I spotted McDonald and Harcourt under the palm tree talking, I knew what they were talking about. I wrote the story that night at the home of a friend, John Ernst, in Vero Beach. When it was picked up by the wire services the next day, the story received national attention.

The reaction in New York, of course, was one of anger. Mets fans idolized Seaver. He was the one, solid All-Star and a perennial winner, and he had led the Mets out of the wilderness. To trade him was unthinkable. Such a furor was raised that the Mets backed off. In fact, Seaver flew back to St. Petersburg a day earlier than the team and met at the Tampa airport with Grant. In conciliatory talks, Seaver was assured he would not be traded.

One week later, Grant and Seaver met again, this time in the grounds keeper's office at Fort Lauderdale Stadium, spring home of the Yankees. There Seaver signed what was then the most lucrative contract in Mets history. The base pay was $225,000, with numerous bonuses attached for every game he won beyond nineteen and incentives for specific earned run averages. It was such a complex contract that Grant insisted on its approval by the league office. It wasn't until mid-season that the league office finally did give its stamp of approval.

If the Mets players did not immediately accept Frazier as a major league manager, they did win for him. Seaver beat Steve Rogers and the Montreal Expos, 3–2, on opening day, and Matlack shut out the Expos and bested Woody Fryman, 1–0, the second day. After losing the next three, the Mets righted themselves and played winning ball. They finished the first month with thirteen victories in twenty games and were in first place by two full games when Matlack beat Houston's Joe Niekro, 3–1, on April 30.

May turned into a cruel month as Seaver and Lolich stopped winning and Matlack won only twice. Koosman won all five of his decisions, but the team was in a slump. They were shut out four times and scored two runs or less in six other games. On May 20, when Lolich lost to the Phillies, 5–3, the Mets settled into third place and remained there for the rest of the season.

At first, third place was not all that bad, since the Mets, only four and one-half games out, still were in contention. By the end of May they were nine and one-half games out as the Phillies began to run away with the race. The gap between third place and first place began to widen further; at the end of June the Mets trailed by fourteen games. In late July, nineteen and a half games out, they were on a treadmill to nowhere.

Not even Dave Kingman's assault on Hack Wilson's National League home run record of fifty-six could bring the customers to the ballpark. Attendance for the season dipped to 1,468,754—the lowest ever at Shea Stadium—and a million short of the previous year. Now the front office was aroused. Mrs. Payson, whose millions backed the Mets when they were formed, had died the previous September; her daughter, Lorinda de Roulet, had replaced her on the board of directors. Mrs. de Roulet was a widow with two daughters, Whitney and Bebe, who had become baseball fans under Mrs. Payson's tutelage. However, Mrs. de Roulet did not have the financial resources her mother had enjoyed. Further, under the terms of Mrs. Payson's will, the ball club passed

OPENING DAY LINEUP 1976

Garrett, 3b
Millan, 2b
Kranepool, 1b
Kingman, rf
Milner, lf
Unser, cf
Grote, c
Harrelson, ss
Seaver, p

METS WITH 20 OR MORE HOMERS IN A SEASON

Year	Player	HR
1962	Frank Thomas	34
1964	Charley Smith	20
1969	Tommie Agee	26
1970	Tommie Agee	24
1970	Donn Clendenon	22
1973	John Milner	23
1974	John Milner	20
1975	Dave Kingman	36
1976	Dave Kingman	37
1981	Dave Kingman	22
1982	Dave Kingman	37*
1983	George Foster	28
1983	Darryl Strawberry	26
1984	Darryl Strawberry	26
1984	George Foster	24
1985	Gary Carter	32
1985	Darryl Strawberry	29
1985	George Foster	21
1986	Darryl Strawberry	27
1986	Gary Carter	24

*Led National League

to her husband, Charles Shipman Payson, a man with little interest in baseball. The change in control of the club was not noticeable at first because Payson permitted Mrs. de Roulet to take an active part in its daily operations. She, in turn, let Grant make all the decisions. Later M. Donald would discover that Payson had never been a Grant fan.

The Mets continued to struggle through the first half of the season even though Kingman was hitting home runs. On July 19, diving for a fly ball in a game against Atlanta at Shea Stadium, Kingman tore the ligaments in his left thumb. He was at that time leading the National League with thirty-two home runs and had seventy games left in which to match the record set by Hack Wilson forty-six years earlier. His pursuit of the record was certain to bring fans back to the park late in the season. With Kingman out of the lineup for six weeks, the Mets had no gate attraction. When he returned at the end of August Kingman played in pain but still managed to hammer out five more homers.

Even Seaver was having difficulty winning. He started thirty-four games, pitched 211 innings, and had an earned run average of 2.59. He won only fourteen and lost eleven. He received little of the bonus money he had anticipated.

While Seaver did not win, two other Mets pitchers did. Koosman, for the first time in his career, won twenty. His record was 21–10, his earned run average 2.70. Matlack also achieved a career high in victories, with a 17–10 record. In the bullpen, Skip Lockwood earned the nickname "Jaws" for coming in and chewing up the opposition. Lockwood won ten games and saved nineteen more, the best relieving the Mets had had since McGraw.

Torre came back and had a good if not a run-productive year. His average was .306, but Joe knocked in only thirty-one runs and hit only five home runs. Milner had a good season, with fifteen homers, a .271 average, and seventy-eight runs batted in. Millan played a fine game at second base and batted .282. Roy Staiger, who had been a third baseman for Frazier at Tidewater, replaced Torre as the third baseman while Joe moved over to first. Staiger fielded well, but major league pitching was too much for him. He hit .220.

In the final months of the season, when they were hopelessly out of the race, the Mets played their best ball. They were 14–12 in August and 20–9 in September, the true sign of an also-ran. With no pressure, they played well. They finished the season with an 83–76 record, the second best victory total in their history up to that point. They were also third, fifteen games out of first place. When they were tied for third the year before, under Berra and McMillan, they finished only ten and a half games out.

One incident during the summer of 1976 upset people everywhere. After losing a tough game, Frazier made a slighting reference to Artie Williams, a black umpire who had made a call that day that went against the Mets. "You all know the only reason he's here," said Frazier, a native of North Carolina. The remark was an obvious reference to Williams' color. The Mets manager was later forced to apologize, but in a city like New York you do not make slurs about a man's color. It was a blunder he couldn't recover from.

Meanwhile, with the Mets hopelessly out of the race and Torre batting over .300 and always ready with a quick quote or astute observation after a game, it wasn't long before Joe's name began to appear regularly in the sports pages. The more Torre spoke, the more appeal he had to the New York press corps. More than one hint was dropped that Torre, not Frazier, should be managing the club.

The Staub-Lolich deal did not pan out. Lolich won only eight games, while losing thirteen, and he was so overweight that people wondered how he was able to pitch at all. Staub, meanwhile, enjoyed a banner season in Detroit with fifteen homers, ninety-six runs batted in, and a .299 average.

In July, the Mets made another bad deal. They sent Unser and Garrett, two popular players, to Montreal in exchange for Jim Dwyer and Pepe Mangual. Unser and Garrett had not been performing well, but Dwyer and Mangual were worse. Mangual proved to be a terrible center fielder. After watching him a few days I wrote, "Pepe Mangual can drop anything he gets his hands on." As for production behind the plate, his average was .186. Dwyer, who never did much with the Mets, later became a handy cameo role player for the Baltimore Orioles.

In late September the Mets went on a six-game winning streak. Then, by way of proving how mediocre they really were, they closed the season by losing six straight. It was the kind of year everyone wanted to end as quickly as possible.

One of the few pleasant surprises of 1976 was Skip Lockwood, who established himself as the big man in the bullpen with ten victories and nineteen saves. The Mets sort of lucked into Lockwood. He had been signed originally by the Kansas City Athletics as a third baseman and given a $100,000 bonus by Charley Finley. But in four years in the minors as an infielder, he never hit above .264. He was converted to a pitcher in 1967. For the next eight years he was used as a starting pitcher with the Seattle Mariners and Milwaukee Brewers, and he had a 30–60 lifetime record when the Mets purchased him on July 28, 1975, from Tucson upon the recommendation of West Coast scout Harry Minor.

Lockwood had been converted to a relief pitcher by the California Angels in 1974; he had more success when he had to throw his fastball for only a few innings. In 1975 Skip had little success with the Mets, winning one game and saving three.

What Lockwood had going for him besides his fastball was his intelligence. He had already attended a half dozen colleges when the Mets obtained him, and he added a few more before he quit baseball following a brief stint with Boston in 1980.

In early June 1979, Lockwood began to experience a twinge in his shoulder. An examination revealed tiny tissue tears. He was given cortisone treatments

MOST PITCHING VICTORIES AGAINST THE METS

Steve Carlton	30–36
Bob Gibson	28–14
Juan Marichal	26–8
Phil Niekro	25–14
Don Drysdale	24–6
Larry Jackson	21–2
Burt Hooton	21–14
Jim Maloney	19–8
Don Sutton	18–11
Jim Bunning	18–12
Sandy Koufax	17–2
Rick Wise	17–9
Ferguson Jenkins	17–15
Claude Osteen	16–13

and told to rest. On June 20, 1979, he was placed on the disabled list and never pitched for the Mets again.

If 1976 was a disruptive spring for the Mets, 1977 was even worse. The seeds of discontent were planted months earlier, in the fall of 1976, when free agency swung into high gear. Seaver and several other members of the Mets felt they were no more than a hitter away from becoming contenders again. Since it was now possible to obtain a desired hitter through free agency rather than trade, it was the contention of the Mets players that the team should go out and buy what they lacked, especially since the Mets were one of the most financially successful franchises in the league. While dropping in recent seasons, their attendance was still up among the league leaders, and the Mets also had a more lucrative radio-television contract than most clubs.

The most attractive free agent on the market was Gary Matthews, who had hit .279 with twenty homers for the Giants. If the team could add Matthews to the lineup, the players thought, they could challenge anybody. Grant did make what he considered a bona fide offer. But being a Wall Street financier, Grant offered Matthews and his agent something that would result in sound and solid deferred payments—solid for Matthews' future, but not nearly as much money up front as maverick owner Ted Turner was offering Matthews to join his Atlanta Braves.

Matthews chose Atlanta. He signed with the Braves for five years for a total salary of $1.2 million, much more than Seaver had signed for the previous spring and a lot more than the $200,000 Grant again and again offered Kingman for the next five or six years, whichever contract he chose.

Kingman held out. He had hit thirty-six and thirty-seven homers the previous two years without playing a full season either year. He wanted something closer to the $2.7 million Reggie Jackson had received from the Yankees. All spring the Mets and Kingman negotiated, more often in the newspapers than in person. Grant insisted that Kingman was being pushed by Seaver, who was upset that he had signed for only $225,000 when players with far less talent were being offered far more. Seaver later announced that he had been coerced into signing the previous spring when Grant was trying to establish a salary standard for the team.

The Kingman squabble, Seaver's discontent, and Grant's failure to sign a single free agent resulted in a discordant spring camp.

"All this club needs is one more hitter to be a contender," Seaver and others, mostly pitchers, argued. They had grown weary of inadequate offensive support.

Grant brushed their complaints aside.

1976

NAME	G by POS	B	AGE	G	AB	R	H	2B	3B	HR	RBI	BB	SO	SB	BA	SA
NEW YORK 3rd 86-76 .531 15	JOE FRAZIER															
TOTALS			29	162	5415	615	1334	198	34	102	560	561	797	66	.246	.352
Ed Kranepool	1B86, OF31	L	31	123	415	47	121	17	1	10	49	35	38	1	.292	.410
Felix Millan	2B116	R	32	139	531	55	150	25	2	1	35	41	19	2	.282	.343
Bud Harrelson	SS117	B	32	118	359	34	84	12	4	1	26	63	56	9	.234	.298
Roy Staiger	3B93, SS1	R	26	95	304	23	67	8	1	2	26	25	35	3	.220	.273
Dave Kingman	OF111, 1B16	R	27	123	474	70	113	14	1	37	86	28	135	7	.238	.506
Del Unser	OF77	L	31	77	276	28	63	13	2	5	25	18	40	4	.228	.344
John Milner	OF112, 1B12	L	26	127	443	56	120	25	4	15	78	65	53	0	.271	.447
Jerry Grote	C95, OF2	R	33	101	323	30	88	14	2	4	28	38	19	1	.272	.365
Joe Torre	1B78, 3B4	R	35	114	310	36	95	10	3	5	31	21	35	1	.306	.406
Bruce Boisclair	OF87	L	23	110	286	42	82	13	3	2	13	28	55	9	.287	.374
Mike Phillips	SS53, 2B19, 3B10	L	25	87	262	30	67	4	6	4	29	25	29	2	.256	.363
Wayne Garrett	3B64, 2B10, SS1	L	28	80	251	36	56	8	1	4	26	52	26	7	.223	.311
Leon Brown	OF43	R	26	64	70	11	15	3	0	0	2	4	4	2	.214	.257
Ron Hodges	C52	L	27	56	155	21	35	6	0	4	24	27	16	2	.226	.342
Mike Vail	OF35	R	24	53	143	8	31	5	1	0	9	6	19	0	.217	.266
Pepe Mangual	OF38	R	24	41	102	15	19	5	2	1	9	10	32	7	.186	.304
John Stearns	C30	R	24	32	103	13	27	6	0	2	10	16	11	1	.262	.379
Lee Mazzilli	OF23	B	21	24	77	9	15	2	0	2	7	14	10	5	.195	.299
Leo Foster	3B9, SS7, 2B3	R	25	24	59	11	12	2	0	1	15	8	5	3	.203	.288

Benny Ayala 25 R 3-26, 2 Jim Dwyer 26 L 2-13, Billy Baldwin 26 L 6-22, 1 Jack Heidemann 26 R 1-12, Jay Kleven 26 R 1-5

NAME	T	AGE	W	L	PCT	SV	G	GS	CG	IP	H	BB	SO	ShO	ERA
		29	86	76	.531	25	162	162	53	1449	1248	419	1025	18	2.94
Jerry Koosman	L	33	21	10	.677	0	34	32	17	247	205	66	200	3	2.70
Jon Matlack	L	26	17	10	.630	0	35	35	16	262	236	57	153	6	2.95
Tom Seaver	R	31	14	11	.560	0	35	34	13	271	211	77	235	5	2.59
Skip Lockwood	R	29	10	7	.588	19	56	0	0	94	62	34	108	0	2.68
Mickey Lolich	L	35	8	13	.381	0	31	30	5	193	184	52	120	2	3.22
Craig Swan	R	25	6	9	.400	0	23	22	2	132	129	44	89	1	3.55
Nino Espinosa	R	22	4	4	.500	0	12	5	0	42	41	13	30	0	3.64
Bob Apodaca	R	26	3	7	.300	5	43	3	0	90	71	29	45	0	2.80
Bobby Myrick	L	23	1	1	.500	0	21	1	0	28	34	13	11	0	3.21
Tom Hall	L	28	1	1	.500	0	5	0	0	5	5	5	2	0	5.40
Ken Sanders	R	34	1	2	.333	1	31	0	0	47	39	12	16	0	2.87
Hank Webb	R	26	0	1	.000	0	8	0	0	16	17	7	7	0	4.50
Rick Baldwin	R	23	0	0	—	0	11	0	0	23	14	10	9	0	2.35

"We will be competitive," he reiterated. "We have a splendid bunch of boys."

Grant's use of the term *boys* annoyed the players. He had brought Mrs. Payson into the clubhouse to introduce her to the players one spring and began by separating the players with the line "Okay, new boys over here."

He sounded like a plantation owner or a prep school headmaster. The manner in which he addressed them made some of the players feel servile. The black players particularly disliked being called "boys." Grant was too insensitive to understand that.

The Mets' unhappiness in the spring was reflected in their 11–14 exhibition play record. The malaise carried over into the regular season.

Seaver beat Chicago, 5–3, on opening day, and Nino Espinosa won the second day. Because rain prevented them from playing more than three games in the first five days, Seaver came back and shut out St. Louis, 4–0, to win the fourth game. That lifted the Mets to a 3–1 record and put them in a tie for first place. It was the best record they would have all year.

By the end of April, the Mets had won eight and lost nine; the grumbling continued. Seaver was the unhappiest 4–0 pitcher in baseball. Kingman had announced on opening day that he was playing out his option and leaving the Mets at the end of the year.

On April 29 the Mets did make one player move from which they benefited. In spring training, Texas Rangers second baseman Lenny Randle had attacked and punched out his manager, Frank Lucchesi, because Lucchesi was giving Randle's job to someone else. Randle was immediately suspended and charged with assault. He could never again play for the Rangers as long as Lucchesi was manager.

When Texas placed Randle's name on the waiver list, the Mets claimed him. In San Diego, on April 29, the Mets signed Randle. Unable to decide where to play him, Frazier rotated Randle at several positions.

Randle had been developed in the Texas farm system and had a couple of good years. He hit .302 in 1974 and .276 in 1975. But when he dipped to .224 in 1976, Lucchesi began to consider Bump Wills—son of Maury Wills—for the second base job in 1977. It wasn't that Randle was washed up, but the Rangers

Mets management changes field managers in midstream once again. This time Joe Torre is in while Joe Frazier, who succeeded Yogi Berra, is out. The announcement is made at a Shea Stadium press conference on May 31 with M. Donald Grant, Joe McDonald, and Joe Torre present.

AP

began to have their doubts about him and were willing to trade him. He was another example of the kind of used merchandise that the Mets made a habit of dealing for. Over the years they brought in a string of fading stars or marginal players—people like Tommy Davis, Ken Boyer, Ed Charles, Willie Mays, Ralph Terry, Ray Sadecki, Ed Bressoud, and Bob Friend, to mention a few.

Then, forty-five games into the season and with the Mets in sixth place with a 15–30 record, Grant decided Frazier was not the man to manage the Mets. As I was later to learn, he had made the decision a few days earlier.

On the night of May 25, the Mets played an exhibition with their Tidewater farm. They then traveled to Philadelphia. Although the players would have an off-day there, Frazier refused to allow them to leave town. At the hotel bar that night I learned that he was going to have a bed check. I knew that both Torre and Koosman, unbeknownst to their manager, had gone back to New York. They were willing to pay the fine if caught.

Since Torre was a good friend, I immediately called his home in New Jersey to alert him of the bed check. He had not arrived home yet so I left a message. He called me late the next day. I informed him of the bed check and he thanked me.

One week later, on the afternoon of May 31, the Mets called a press conference to announce that Torre was replacing Frazier as manager. Only later did Torre reveal that the real reason he had gone to New York was to discuss with Grant the possibility of taking over the club. AWOL because the chairman of the board had invited him to break the rules, Torre never got around to paying Frazier's fine. By the end of the month, when fines are usually collected, Torre was the manager.

Seaver and Grant had continued their feud. At one point Grant called Seaver an "ingrate." I had joined the *New York Daily News* that year and was traveling with the club. I was a Seaver confidant and reported his side of the controversy, while my own sports editor, Dick Young, was writing management's side of the squabble. The *Daily News* ran both stories on the back page, which became known as "the battle page."

Seaver didn't want to leave the Mets, but he felt he was grossly underpaid. Young's column argued that Seaver had signed a contract in good faith the previous spring and now he was just jealous that other players were getting more money. If Seaver didn't think he was getting what he was worth, why did he sign in the spring of 1976? In Seaver's defense, I pointed out that this was before Nolan Ryan and others signed following the free agent revolution. I then suggested to Seaver a day or two before the trading deadline while the team was in Atlanta that he call Mrs. de Roulet and try to resolve the impasse with her. In a series of five long-distance phone calls with her on June 13, Seaver worked out a deal whereby, instead of getting a salary increase, his current contract would be extended three years.

Grant summoned McDonald, Frazier, and Torre to his Wall Street offices on the afternoon of May 31. It was there he told Frazier that he was out and Torre was in. It was a blow to McDonald. His handpicked manager had lasted one year and forty-five games, and he did not really care for Torre, who was the replacement.

Grant then sent the three men by limousine to Shea Stadium, where Torre was introduced as the new manager.

"The calmest, most relaxed man in that limousine was Frazier," Torre told me later.

Torre's ascension to the leadership of the club was not totally unexpected. Not only had the press bandied his name around, but he was also the logical successor if Frazier did not get the Mets off to a good start.

On the morning of June 15, I had breakfast with Seaver in the Marriott Hotel coffee shop in Atlanta, where the team was playing the Braves. He

OPENING DAY LINEUP 1977

Mazzilli, cf
Millan, 2b
Milner, lf
Kingman, rf
Kranepool, 1b
Stearns, c
Staiger, 3b
Harrelson, ss
Seaver, p

seemed at ease, apparently having worked out an extension of his contract with Mrs. de Roulet. It called for $300,000 in the first year of extension and $400,000 the next.

But when he sat with reporters and television men at poolside later, Seaver learned of a Dick Young *Daily News* column alleging that Nancy Seaver was jealous of Ruth Ryan because Nolan Ryan had signed a much bigger contract with the California Angels. Seaver pondered the allegations, then suddenly bolted from his chair. He strode briskly to his hotel room and called Arthur Richman, the club's public relations director.

"Get me out of here," he yelled to Richman over the phone. "Get me out of here."

Richman called Whitney de Roulet, who interrupted a board meeting where the Mets were listening to Lorinda de Roulet go over the agreement she and Seaver had worked out the previous day. Whitney de Roulet relayed Seaver's message to her mother.

"Tell Joe McDonald that everything I said last night is forgotten," was Seaver's message to Mrs. de Roulet. "I want out. The attack on my family is something I just can't take."

That night, shortly after the game with the Braves began, Seaver left the clubhouse, took a cab to the airport, and flew home. Writers in the press box were informed there would be a deal announced after the game. When we went to the clubhouse, we were told Seaver was gone. He had been traded to Cincinnati for four players. They were pitcher Pat Zachry, infielder Doug Flynn, and outfielders Steve Henderson and Dan Norman.

There had been rumors of a deal for days. The Mets had informed Torre of the possibility while the club was still in Houston the previous Sunday. Ironically, the call came in to Torre while he was attending Mass.

In those days, Father Joseph Dispenza of the New York Archdiocese frequently traveled with the team. It was customary for him to say Sunday morning Mass at a room in the team hotel, usually the manager's suite. On Sunday morning, June 12, during Mass in the Shamrock Hilton, Torre was called to the phone. He took the call in his bedroom. Joe was advised of the players being offered by the Reds. Seaver was informed but followed the rotation and pitched that afternoon. It had to be a very emotional game for the man who had become known as "the Franchise," as he figured it to be his last game in a Mets uniform.

Then it all turned around the next day in Atlanta when Seaver worked out arrangements with Mrs. de Roulet. He would remain a Met, that is, until he learned of Young's "jealousy" column in the *Daily News*. Right then and there he decided to get as far away from Grant as he could. Cincinnati was far enough.

Arthur Richman, the club's public relations director, had the duty of informing the press of the Seaver deal. Other deals would be announced on the charter plane en route home, he told us. The writers were upset that we were being informed of a deal in mid-air with no way of advising our newspapers. There was nothing Richman could do about it. It wasn't until we landed at Butler Aviation at LaGuardia Airport around 2:30 A.M. that we learned the Mets had used the two De Roulet daughters, Whitney and Bebe, to call the papers with the details of both deals while we were airborne.

The second deal was with the St. Louis Cardinals. Joel Youngblood, who formerly had been with Cincinnati, was obtained in a straight player swap for Mike Phillips. Youngblood could play both the infield and the outfield, had a good arm, and could run. He proved to be a valuable handyman for a couple of years until Torre, in frustration at Youngblood repeatedly missing signs and constantly complaining, sent him away.

The final deal announced that night, almost as shocking as the first, was the trade that sent Dave Kingman to San Diego for infielder Bobby Valentine and pitcher Paul Siebert.

In one night the Mets had unloaded both their leading pitcher and all-time Mets favorite and their all-time home run leader. In exchange they had accepted six players, most of them young and taken on at low salary. The management had unloaded two of their best and highest paid players because they had irritated Grant by asking for salaries equal to those of players of comparable talent elsewhere in the league. For that they were banished to Cincinnati and San Diego.

Grant's bloody coup became known in New York newspapers as "the Midnight Massacre."

Following the Seaver trade, the *New York Post* carried a headline reading, "DICK YOUNG DROVE SEAVER OUT OF TOWN."

In a story by Maury Allen, Seaver was quoted as saying: "Dick Young could call me an ingrate, a headache for Donald Grant, anything he wanted. But an attack on my family was something I could not take."

Young was easily the most important baseball columnist in the country with his nearly two million *New York Daily News* circulation and his weekly *Sporting News* column. In pointing out that Young had been the only writer critical of his salary debate, Seaver took a swipe at Young's connection with Grant.

"When Dick Young dragged my wife and my family into this, it was all the abuse I could take," Seaver said. "He's a mouthpiece for Don Grant. Grant has admitted he seeks Young's advice. He has been siding with Mets management ever since the club hired his son-in-law, Thornton Geary, Jr., to work in their sales department."

Young became a *cause célèbre* and was interviewed by newspapers and television stations across the nation. He defended Geary's position with the Mets while not denying that his relationship with Grant had provided the contact his son-in-law used to secure his position with the Mets.

"My son-in-law does work for the Mets. He has a master's degree. He is overqualified for the job. He is probably, if anything, being underpaid. I warned him against taking a job there. I said baseball people in the front office are the most overworked and underpaid in the world. But he was a nut for baseball and wanted to do it.

"What it comes down to with Seaver," Young continued, "is that he wanted more money. Everything else is extraneous. If he says he told them it was all off because of my mentioning his wife and Ruth Ryan—all because of one sentence—well, I find that pretty hard to believe. I was a critic of the ballplayers' stand long before Thornton Geary got the job with the Mets."

The New York press came down heavily on Grant for the trade. Pulitzer

SHEA STADIUM—INSIDE-THE-PARK HOME RUNS

Date	Player and Club	Pitcher and Club
June 5, 1966	Ron Hunt, Mets	Sandy Koufax, Dodgers
May 9, 1970	Bobby Bonds, Giants	Don Cardwell, Mets
July 7, 1973	Ralph Garr, Braves	Phil Hennigan, Mets
June 12, 1979	Doug Flynn, Mets	Dave Tomlin, Reds
July 10, 1982	Gene Richards, Padres	Peter Falcone, Mets
July 31, 1982	Wally Backman, Mets	Enrique Romo, Pirates
August 15, 1982	Leon Durham, Cubs	Jesse Orosco, Mets
August 31, 1983	Mark Bradley, Mets	Fernando Valenzuela, Dodgers
September 2, 1984	Carmelo Martinez, Cubs	Walt Terrell, Mets
June 9, 1985	Terry Pendleton, Cardinals	Joe Sambito, Mets

Prize–winning Red Smith, columnist for the *New York Times*, was one of Grant's harshest critics.

"For a decade, Tom Seaver has been one of the finest pitchers in the game, probably the best in the National League," Smith wrote. "He has exceptional physical equipment and he knows how to use it. More than that, he is his own man, thoughtful, perceptive and unafraid to speak his mind. Because of this, M. Donald Grant and his sycophants put Seaver away as a troublemaker. They mistake dignity for arrogance."

A month after the trade, Grant had his say in an article in the *Village Voice*.

Grant said Seaver never expressed unhappiness with the $225,000 he originally signed for in March 1976 until seven months later when a dozen players, many of them with less talent than he possessed, got huge contracts worth five times as much.

"Then it began to gnaw at him," Grant said.

"I have a simple way of explaining it," said the Mets' chairman, who obviously did not realize that his "simple explanation" was Greek to the average baseball fan. "In a duplicate-bridge tournament it boils down to how many tricks you will make in a hand. Seaver played his hand at four spades and just made the bid. But another player made five spades and just beat him out by a little bit and won the big prize, and he said 'Oh, my God, can I replay my hand?' It's as simple as that."

Lee Mazzilli, who established himself in center field and in the dreams of young female Mets fans, reaches back through the dust to grab second base as he successfully steals against the Cubs. Second baseman Mick Kelleher takes the throw. Mazzilli stole twenty-two bases in 1977, second only to Lenny Randle.

Seaver left Atlanta Stadium as the Mets were batting in the first inning. He did not say good-bye to anyone, but he did leave a note on Jerry Koosman's locker stool asking him to "tell every player individually" how he felt.

"I didn't think I could stand up and tell each guy myself," he said in revealing the note he left behind.

Seaver was met at LaGuardia Airport by his wife, Nancy, and together they drove to Manhattan instead of their home in Greenwich, Connecticut. They stayed at the Warwick Hotel, where the Seavers were put up by one of the morning network television shows on which he was to appear early the next day.

Following his television appearance, Tom and Nancy drove to Shea Stadium, where he would clean out his locker for the final time. He was greeted by nearly 100 newsmen and television people, who had been alerted he would be there. As Tom entered the clubhouse, Nancy sat in the players' wives' lounge outside, dabbing her eyes with a handkerchief.

Seaver was in a jocular mood at first. He freely discussed the background of the deal.

"I don't know if I really want to ride back through the history of all this," he said. "But it all goes back to my signing a contract last year. Things were said then and written in the press, mainly by Dick Young. My loyalty was attacked. Then, a couple of days ago, I was talking to the club and there was a little discussion about the possibility of a new contract. They didn't want to renegotiate, and I can understand that. But my proposal was to play the next two years under my current contract and talk to them about the three years after that—1979, 1980, and 1981.

"But the next day [June 15] Dick Young dragged my wife and family into it and I couldn't take that. That's when I called the Mets and told them to forget my proposal. I told them it was all over. This alliance or whatever it is—this alliance between Young and the chairman of the board—is stacked against me."

Seaver then spoke of the excitement of going to the Reds to play again for a pennant winner and joked about the runs he would have to work with.

It was not until he was asked how he felt about New York fans that he lost control. Abruptly, the levity in the conversation disappeared. Seaver lowered his head, contemplating an answer that would not come out. He was silent for several moments and then rose from his chair, walked through the circle of newsmen around him, and went into the washroom. There he was consoled by Herb Norman, the equipment manager. It was almost ten minutes before Tom could regain his composure.

"As far as the fans go, I've given them a great number of thrills and they've been equally returned. The ovation I got the other night—"

Seaver's voice broke off and he began to sob. He tried to continue but could not. His head bowed again, he asked for a reporter's notebook and scribbled a few words. He asked the reporter to read it and sat and listened quietly to what he had written: "And the ovation I got the other night after passing Sandy Koufax, that will be one of the most memorable and warmest moments in my life." (The week before, Shea Stadium fans had given Seaver a long standing ovation after he eclipsed Sandy Koufax's all-time strikeout total.)

His eyes red from weeping, Seaver arose, went to his locker to pick up his gear, and started out the door.

"I never demanded to be traded until yesterday. That was the last straw. But Grant is trying to put the onus on me," Seaver said as he left the clubhouse. He stopped to pick up Nancy and then drove home to Connecticut.

Kingman also arrived that morning to clean out his locker. He was anything but cordial. The big slugger refused to talk to reporters, and when photogra-

18

◆ THE LADIES ◆
◆ TRY ◆
◆ TO RUN A ◆
◆ BALL CLUB ◆

phers snapped his picture as he was leaving the park, he threatened to bowl them over.

Because of the Seaver deal, Grant received threatening phone calls at his office, at Shea Stadium, and at his home. He actually feared for his life and hired a bodyguard who never left his side at Shea Stadium. The bodyguard sat behind Grant in his box alongside the Mets dugout and between innings stood up to face the stands, scanning the seats like a Secret Service man guarding the President. To the best of anyone's knowledge, Grant's life was never in danger. The threatening phone calls were from cranks and from Seaver fans, but Grant could not be convinced otherwise.

The new players from Cincinnati, St. Louis, and San Diego arrived and were immediately installed into the lineup. In a smart move on the night he replaced Frazier, Torre shifted Randle to third base and told him the job there was his. Randle, feeling comfortable and wanted, had an outstanding season. He batted .304, was a daring baserunner—some might say reckless—leading the club with thirty-three steals. He was caught twenty-one times. Clearly Randle added some needed excitement. He also fielded his position well, the Mets' sixteenth "regular" third baseman in sixteen years.

Doug Flynn had come up in the Reds organization as a shortstop, then played three infield positions as a utility man with Cincinnati. A native Kentuckian and upset about leaving Cincinnati, which was near his home, he was soon grateful to the Mets for the chance to play more often. For the balance of the season he shared the shortstop duties with Bud Harrelson.

"He stares the ball into his glove," was Torre's favorite expression describing Flynn's fielding prowess.

Henderson was handed Kingman's left field job and soon became a favorite of the fans because of his consistent hitting and all-around hustle. If he did not have Kingman's awesome power, "Steve Wonder" did hit a dozen homers in ninety-nine games. His .297 average was a solid improvement over the low .200s the Mets were accustomed to with Kingman. Henderson drove in sixty-five runs in ninety-nine games which was excellent production. Norman, the other outfielder obtained in the deal, was sent to Tidewater for further seasoning.

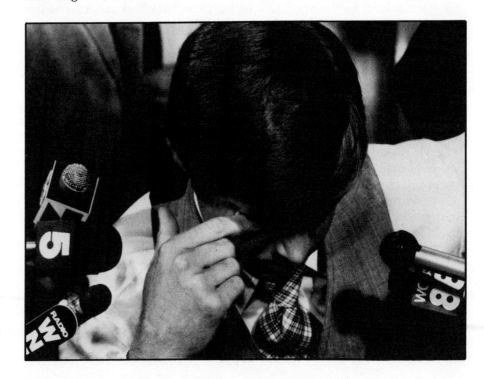

The night of June 15, 1977, dubbed "the Midnight Massacre," is a date few Mets fans will forget. It was the loss of Tom Seaver, though, that hurt the most. On the morning after the trade Seaver breaks down during a press conference called to announce his departure.

DAILY NEWS/DANNY FARRELL

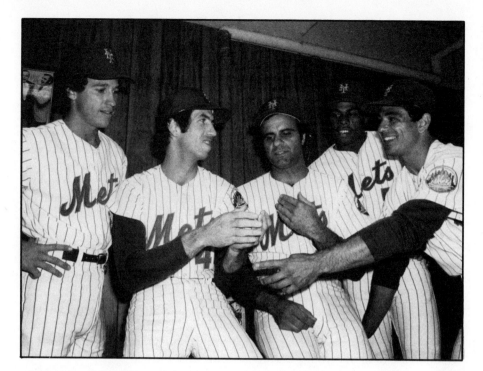

The fourth and final player in the deal, Pat Zachry, suffered from a Seaver-complex. Six-foot, five inches tall, skinny as a rail, and with a new beard, his appearance was almost Lincolnesque as he took the mound. Appearances aside, Zachry's problem was that he felt he had to be—for the fans' sake—as good as Seaver. In his mind, the trade was Seaver for Zachry; consequently he tried too hard. The previous year he had a 14–7 record with the Reds and was voted co-Rookie of the Year. He had an excellent change-up pitch, one of the best in the league, but in attempting to emulate Seaver he tried too hard and as a result wound up with a 7–6 record, with only two complete games in nineteen starts.

Valentine, who had been an outstanding high school athlete at Rippowan High School in Stamford, Connecticut, was back home. He had been drafted by the Dodgers in 1968 and had all the makings of a fine major leaguer. In 1973 he ran into a wall while playing the outfield for the California Angels, fracturing his leg so badly that he never regained his speed. The accident denied him the opportunity to become a major league regular of any consequence; with the Mets he was used only in utility roles. Siebert was strictly a relief pitcher, which is all the Mets expected him to be.

He was the son of Dick "Sonny" Siebert, the first baseman who played for Brooklyn, St. Louis, and the Philadelphia Athletics in the pre–World War II era and later coached at the University of Minnesota. Paul lasted only a season and a half with the Mets, winning two games and losing three.

Getting Valentine and Siebert for Kingman was no big deal. Getting rid of Kingman was all the Mets management had in mind when they made the trade.

Kingman was in his option year in 1977. If the Mets did not sign him to the lucrative contract he was seeking, he could walk away from them at the end of the season and they would get nothing in return. So they got the best they could for him in Valentine, a useful utility man, and Siebert, a left-hander they could use out of the bullpen.

After leaving the Mets Kingman set a record that is not likely to be equaled. After playing fifty-eight games for the Mets, he played another fifty-six for the San Diego Padres. When they, too, discovered they could not meet his contract demands, they dealt Dave to the California Angels on September 6. California played Kingman for ten games, also were unable to satisfy him financially, and in turn sent him to the New York Yankees on September 15. The Yankees wanted to keep Kingman but, again, his asking price was too high, so they let him become a free agent.

With each of the four clubs he played for that season he hit at least one home run (twenty-six in all), becoming the first man in baseball history to hit a home run with a club in each of baseball's four divisions. Kingman eventually signed a five-year contract with the Chicago Cubs. The total value of the contract was $1.375 million. He received a $250,000 signing bonus, an annual salary of $225,000, and had a clause in his contract guaranteeing him another $50,000 bonus any year in which the Cubs' attendance reached 1.6 million. All that was considerably less than the $2.7 million he had been seeking from the Mets.

Joe Torre went along with the company policy after both Seaver and Kingman were traded. He had little choice.

"I don't like to see them go," he confided, "but neither do I want unhappy ballplayers. And both Tom and Dave were unhappy."

Because they had added so many new faces in such a short time and because a few of them got off to good starts, the Mets' new promotion line, proclaimed in full-page newspaper ads, was "Come bring your kids to see our kids." A team picture of all the young players accompanied the ad.

The ad did not help in the standings, and neither did the kids. The Mets were in sixth place, fourteen games out, when Seaver and Kingman were traded. Their record stood at 26–35. They finished the season by losing sixty-three of the last 101 games. Even though Zachry beat St. Louis on the final day of the season, the Mets were thirty-seven games out of first place when it was all over. It was the first time since 1967 that the Mets finished last.

The breakup of the 1969 world champions was just about complete when Jerry Grote was traded to the Los Angeles Dodgers. The Dodgers, who were fighting for a pennant, were looking for some catching insurance. Anyone they got had to be on their roster by August 31 in order to be eligible for post-season play. On that date, while the Mets were in Houston, Grote was traded to the Dodgers for cash and a minor leaguer to be named later. The minor leaguer was infielder Randy Rogers, who never made it to the big leagues.

The thinking behind the deal was that Grote was thirty-five years of age and John Stearns was the catcher of the future. The Mets were in last place at the time, thirty-one games out. Having Grote was not going to help them, so they sought to get something in exchange for him—plus a lump of Dodgers cash.

Except for Henderson, none of the "new kids" provided much in the way of miracles—or even solid performances, for that matter. However, there was one "new face" in the crowd that year who did capture the imagination of the fans, especially the younger ones. He was Lee Mazzilli, an ambidextrous outfielder from Brooklyn who had been the club's number 1 draft pick in June 1973. He was up from the minors only because of Grant's insistence that Mazzilli was ready for the big leagues. He'd had three promising but hardly overwhelming minor league seasons. Grant's own baseball people told him Mazzilli would benefit from a full year in Triple-A ball in 1976. The chairman of the board could not be dissuaded, and Mazzilli joined the Mets in time for twenty-four games in 1976 before being installed as the full-time center fielder in 1977. Maz batted only .250 that year, but his flashy fielding, twenty-two stolen bases, and good looks soon made him the club's number 1 poster boy. Young girls, in particular, got excited whenever Mazzilli appeared in his skintight pinstriped uniform.

Mazzilli's popularity was one of the few bright spots for the Mets during 1977. Matlack, from whom so much was expected, came down with a sore shoulder and went two months without a victory. He had a couple in July and then went another two months without winning. He finished with a 7–15 record. Koosman, who had twenty-one wins in 1976, reversed his record in 1977 and was 8–20. The biggest winner on the staff was Nino Espinosa, who won ten but also lost thirteen. Things would have been worse but for Lockwood, who came out of the bullpen to save twenty games.

The fans' dissatisfaction was registered at the gate—attendance dipped to 1,066,825. In seven years the Mets had lost 1.6 million customers. No team in history had lost that many fans that fast.

◆ ◆ ◆

There was no reason to believe 1978 would be any better. Grant continued his niggardly operation of the club, refusing to indulge in the free agent market, while his crosstown rival, Yankee owner George Steinbrenner, was acquiring a stable of expensive free agents. The only free agents the Mets signed were Elliott Maddox, a former Yankee center fielder, and Tom Hausman, a minor league pitcher in the employ of the Milwaukee Brewers. Their addition made little difference.

At the time the Mets signed Elliott Maddox, he already had filed a lawsuit against the city of New York for an injury that had occurred at Shea Stadium on June 13, 1975, while playing for the New York Yankees. The Yankees were occupying Shea Stadium that season while Yankee Stadium was being renovated. While playing the outfield, Maddox caught his spikes on a drain cover and twisted his knee. He required surgery and was on the disabled list the remainder of the season. The suit, which Maddox had initiated at considerable personal expense, was dismissed in November 1985.

By now Mets fans were really fed up with the Grant approach. Whereas crowds of 50,000 were common in the good years, only once (a Jacket Night promotion on a Saturday night) did they attract that many during the 1978 season. At the end of the season, attendance had dropped to 1,007,328, the lowest since the club's first year at the Polo Grounds in 1962. Had it not been for an appearance by Pete Rose at Shea Stadium in late July, when the Cincinnati slugger was en route to tying Willie Keeler's record for hitting safely in forty-four consecutive games, the Mets might not have reached the million mark. Rose's appearance for three games drew 95,000 fans.

In addition to signing Hausman and Maddox, the Mets made a couple of other deals they thought would help. Tim Foli, who broke in with the Mets in

Mets fans were understandably upset when Tom Seaver was traded for a bunch of relatively unknown players. After all, Seaver was "the Franchise" and was admired by many as an All-American boy with the ideal wife and family. That the Mets weren't willing to satisfy his salary demands was incomprehensible. A fan backlash set in, and attendance and general enthusiasm went on a five-year tailspin.
DAILY NEWS/VINCENT RIEHL

1977

NAME	G by POS	B	AGE	G	AB	R	H	2B	3B	HR	RBI	BB	SO	SB	BA	SA
NEW YORK 6th 64-98 .395 37			JOE FRAZIER 15-29 .341			JOE TORRE 49-69 .415										
TOTALS			27	162	5410	587	1319	227	30	88	525	529	887	98	.244	.346
John Milner	1B87, OF22	L	27	131	388	43	99	20	3	12	57	61	55	6	.255	.415
Felix Millan	2B89	R	33	91	314	40	78	11	2	2	21	18	9	1	.248	.315
Bud Harrelson	SS98	B	33	107	269	25	48	6	2	1	12	27	28	5	.178	.227
Lenny Randle	3B110, 2B20, OF6, SS1	B	28	136	513	78	156	22	7	5	27	65	70	33	.304	.404
Mike Vail	OF85	R	25	108	279	29	73	12	1	8	35	19	58	0	.262	.398
Lee Mazzilli	OF156	B	22	159	537	66	134	24	3	6	46	72	72	22	.250	.339
Steve Henderson	OF97	R	24	99	350	67	104	16	6	12	65	43	79	6	.297	.480
John Stearns	C127, 1B6	R	25	139	431	52	108	25	1	12	55	77	76	9	.251	.397
Bruce Boisclair	OF91, 1B9	L	24	127	307	41	90	21	1	4	44	31	57	6	.293	.407
Ed Kranepool	OF42, 1B41	L	32	108	281	28	79	17	0	10	40	23	20	1	.281	.448
Doug Flynn	SS65, 2B29, 3B2	R	26	90	282	14	54	6	1	0	14	11	23	1	.191	.220
Joel Youngblood	2B33, OF22, 3B10	R	25	70	182	16	46	11	1	0	11	13	40	1	.253	.324
Ron Hodges	C27	L	28	66	117	6	31	4	0	1	5	9	17	0	.265	.325
Dave Kingman	OF45, 1B17	R	28	58	211	22	44	7	0	9	28	13	66	3	.209	.370
Jerry Grote	C28, 3B11	R	34	42	115	8	31	3	1	0	7	9	12	0	.270	.313
Bobby Valentine	1B15, SS14, 3B4	R	27	42	83	8	11	1	0	1	3	6	9	0	.133	.181
Roy Staiger	3B36, SS1	R	27	40	123	16	31	9	0	2	11	4	20	1	.252	.374
Mike Phillips	SS24, 3B9, 2B4	L	26	38	86	5	18	2	1	1	3	2	15	0	.209	.291
Leo Foster	2B20, SS8, 3B2	R	26	36	75	6	17	3	0	0	6	5	14	3	.227	.267
Joe Torre	1B16, 3B1	R	36	26	51	2	9	3	0	1	9	2	10	0	.176	.294
Luis Rosado	1B7, C1	R	21	9	24	1	5	1	0	0	3	1	3	0	.208	.250
Pepe Mangual	OF4	R	25	8	7	1	1	0	0	0	2	1	4	0	.143	.143
Dan Norman	OF6	R	22	7	16	2	4	1	0	0	0	4	2	0	.250	.313
Luis Alvarado	2B1	R	28	1	2	0	0	0	0	0	0	0	0	0	.000	.000

NAME	T	AGE	W	L	PCT	SV	G	GS	CG	IP	H	BB	SO	ShO	ERA
		26	64	981	.395	28	162	162	27	1434	1378	490	911	12	3.77
Nino Espinosa	R	23	10	13	.435	0	32	29	7	200	188	55	105	1	3.42
Craig Swan	R	26	9	10	.474	0	26	24	2	147	153	56	71	1	4.22
Jerry Koosman	L	34	8	20	.286	0	32	32	6	227	195	81	192	1	3.49
Tom Seaver	R	32	7	3	.700	0	13	13	5	96	79	28	72	3	3.00
Pat Zachry	R	25	7	6	.538	0	19	19	2	120	129	48	63	1	3.75
Jon Matlack	L	27	7	15	.318	0	26	26	5	169	175	43	123	3	4.21
Skip Lockwood	R	30	4	8	.333	20	63	0	0	104	87	31	84	0	3.38
Bob Apodaca	R	27	4	8	.333	5	59	0	0	84	83	30	53	0	3.43
Jackson Todd	R	25	3	6	.333	0	19	10	0	72	78	20	39	0	4.75
Paul Siebert	L	24	2	1	.667	0	25	0	0	28	27	13	20	0	3.86
Bobby Myrick	L	24	2	2	.500	2	44	4	0	87	86	33	49	0	3.62
Rick Baldwin	R	24	1	2	.333	1	40	0	0	63	62	31	23	0	4.43
Johnny Pacella	R	20	0	0	—	0	3	0	0	4	2	2	1	0	0.00
Ray Sadecki	L	36	0	1	.000	0	4	0	0	3	3	3	0	0	6.00
Doc Medich	R	28	0	1	.000	0	1	1	0	7	6	1	3	0	3.86
Roy Jackson	R	23	0	2	.000	0	4	4	0	24	25	15	13	0	6.00

Rookie John Stearns, who caught fifty-four games and batted only .214, shows his intensity on the field as he tries for a foul ball that is caught by a fan instead. Jerry Grote, the incumbent, had a particularly good year, batting .295 in 111 games. In fact, all the Mets regulars had good years, with Ed Kranepool leading the pack with a .323 batting average. The team average was .256, unusually high for a Mets club.

LOUIS REQUENA

1970, was purchased from the Giants on December 7, 1977. He was handed the shortstop job for 1978; Flynn was moved over to second base.

On December 8, the Mets unloaded two more familiar faces. Jon Matlack and John Milner were dealt to the Texas Rangers in exchange for first baseman Willie Montanez and outfielders Ken Henderson and Tom Grieve. The flurry of trading activity continued the next day when third baseman Roy Staiger was sent to the Yankees for Sergio Ferrer, a minor league shortstop. It was as close as the Mets and Yankees ever came to making a deal. (Since Ferrer was a minor leaguer and remained on a minor league roster, it was not counted as a full-fledged deal between the two rivals.)

The Mets felt longtime favorite Bud Harrelson was finished when they obtained Foli. The shortstop star of the 1969 and 1973 champions had gone steadily downhill after hitting .258 in 1973. His averages for the next four seasons were .227, .219, .234, and .178. In July 1977, Harrelson had fractured his right hand diving back to first base. In the course of his career, Harrelson had missed 320 games due to injuries. As Bud approached his thirty-fourth birthday, the Mets felt they had to get someone more durable to play shortstop.

With Foli around to play shortstop, Harrelson just sat and twiddled his thumbs in spring training. The Mets weren't going to use him, and Bud was unhappy in a bench role. Finally, on March 24, Harrelson was sold to the Phillies for cash and a minor leaguer. Now only Ed Kranepool and Jerry Koosman remained from the 1969 world champions, and Kranepool was no longer a regular.

Spring training 1978 was uneventful except for one bizarre incident that has since become known to Metsophiles as "the blueberry incident."

On Friday night, March 25, the Mets held a "sponsors' party" at the St. Petersburg Yacht Club. They brought their radio-TV sponsors to Florida for the weekend to wine and dine them. Grant, McDonald, Torre, and other Mets officials acted as hosts to the sponsors at a cocktail hour followed by dinner. The following afternoon, the Saturday edition of the *St. Petersburg Independent* had a page one story relating that McDonald had been involved in an automobile accident. Shortly after sunrise, the story read, the Mets' general manager had hit a parked city bus two blocks from the hotel.

McDonald, who had returned to his hotel room after a report was filed at police headquarters, was unavailable for comment. That night, while the Mets were beating the Yankees, Grant came up to the press box to explain that he had absolved his general manager of any improper conduct in the sunrise incident.

"Joe assured me he was not drinking and had gone right home from the sponsors' party," Grant explained.

"Where was he coming from at that hour of the morning?" reporters queried.

"He had gone out looking for some blueberries for his breakfast," Grant said in all seriousness, apparently forgetting that strawberries, not blueberries, were then in season.

After another losing spring training period in which they won ten but lost fifteen, the Mets got off to a respectable start by playing .500 ball for three weeks. Willie Montanez was a useful addition, and Flynn played second base like a Gold Glove candidate. By early April the Mets began to stumble; they fell into fifth place after dropping under .500 on April 26, and never again reached .500 that season.

Montanez was considered a "hot dog" because of his flamboyant style in playing first base. He did everything one-handed, catching throws and making a big sweep of his arm after the ball was securely in the glove. In running the bases whenever he hit a home run, he slowed down approaching second base and broke his stride to go into a little cha-cha step. The same at third base and at home plate. He delighted in following this routine while the pitcher who threw the ball fumed.

If Montanez and Flynn were dependable performers, few others were. In spring training Randle threatened to quit while attempting to renegotiate his contract. By season's end the third baseman, who had been thankful to play regularly in 1977 and had responded with a .304 average, was batting a mere .233. More and more Maddox was becoming the "regular" third baseman.

Lee Mazzilli had Grant gloating—he hit .273, slammed a surprising sixteen homers, and stole twenty bases. Stearns, who had replaced Grote as the number 1 catcher, gave promise of becoming one of the best young catchers in the league. He hit .264, hammered fifteen homers, and was number 2 man on the club with seventy-three runs batted in. In addition, Stearns stole twenty-five bases to set an all-time National League record for catchers, breaking one set by Johnny Kling of Chicago that had stood for more than seventy-five years.

Even with Montanez, Flynn, Mazzilli, and Stearns having better years than expected, the Mets remained a sad disappointment. Lockwood no longer was the big save man in the bullpen. Skip did manage to salvage fifteen games, but his 7–13 record was an embarrassment. Several others, including Dale Murray, Mardi Cornejo, Paul Siebert, and Butch Metzger, were tried in the bullpen, but the entire staff could save only twenty-six games.

The starting pitching was not any better. Koosman was settling into a losing habit with a last place club and completed the year with three victories and fifteen defeats. It was quite a comedown for the once-proud left-hander, who had been a hero of the 1969 campaign. Koosman won only three times in thirty-two starts and was in the bullpen at the end of the season. He concluded the campaign by requesting a trade and threatened to retire rather than come back to the Mets for another season. On December 8, the Mets sent him to the Minnesota Twins so he could be near his hometown of Morris, Minnesota.

Minnesota had the Mets in an unfortunate position. The Twins, Koosman said, were the only team he would report to. McDonald, in a weak bargaining position, decided to go for youth. He had done his homework and knew the Twins owned a first-year pitcher by the name of Jesse Orosco. Twins owner

OPENING DAY LINEUP 1978

Randle, 3b
Foli, ss
S. Henderson, lf
Montanez, 1b
K. Henderson, rf
Mazzilli, cf
Stearns, c
Flynn, 2b
Swan, p

Manager Joe Torre argues with umpire Eric Gregg over a double-play call in the fourth inning of a game with the Dodgers in Los Angeles on September 1.
AP

Calvin Griffin and his general manager, Howie Fox, were handling the negotiations. When McDonald asked for Orosco, Griffin looked puzzled. "Who's Orosco?" he asked. Fox and his farm director, George Brophy, had no desire to let the promising young left-hander go, but Griffin okayed the deal. Orosco went on to become one of the best relief pitchers the Mets ever owned.

Zachry was on his way to an outstanding season his second year with the Mets. He was 10–3 at the All-Star break in July. Two weeks later in New York Pete Rose stroked a hit off Pat to keep his forty-four game streak alive. Zachry was so annoyed with himself that he kicked the dugout steps in disgust and broke a bone in his foot. He did not pitch again the rest of the season. To add insult to injury, Torre fined him heavily.

Craig Swan had emerged as a big pitcher for the Mets, posting a 9–6 record that included an 8–1 second half. His earned run average of 2.43 was the best in the National League.

In 1972, when he signed with the Mets out of Arizona State, Swan was considered the number 1 prospect in the organization, but he was constantly hampered with physical problems. In 1973 a gastroenteritis attack was followed by an emergency appendectomy; on May 26, 1974, he developed tendonitis of the elbow. Two weeks later he attempted to pitch again and left after throwing only three pitches. This time it was a stress fracture of the elbow. He spent the balance of the season at Tidewater, where he pitched only nine games.

As the season progressed and the Mets headed for their second dismal sixth place finish, rumors of a front office shake-up emerged. Mrs. de Roulet, who had been recently widowed, was taking more of an active part in the operation of the club. Since her mother's death she had taken over for her father, Charles Shipman Payson, who had no desire to run the club. At first she worked with Grant. Then, in a startling announcement on November 8, 1978, Lorinda de Roulet announced that at a board of directors meeting that afternoon, she had succeeded M. Donald Grant as chairman of the board. Grant had failed to block the move.

"The time has come, more or less," said Mrs. de Roulet. "Don Grant is not happy about stepping down as chairman of the board. But it is an amicable agreement. It just seemed like the time to do it."

The seventy-four-year-old Grant would remain as board chairman until the end of the year.

"It is obvious to me Linda wants a crack at running it herself. And she will get that chance, when she wants to. I'm glad it's all over," said Grant.

1978

NAME	G by POS	B	AGE	G	AB	R	H	2B	3B	HR	RBI	BB	SO	SB	BA	SA
NEW YORK 6th 66-96 .407 24	JOE TORRE															
TOTALS			27	162	5433	607	1332	227	47	86	561	549	829	100	.245	.352
Willie Montanez	1B158	L	30	159	609	66	156	32	0	17	96	60	92	9	.256	.392
Doug Flynn	2B128, SS60	R	27	156	532	37	126	12	8	0	36	30	50	3	.237	.289
Tim Foli	SS112	R	27	113	413	37	106	21	1	1	27	14	30	2	.257	.320
Lenny Randle	3B124, 2B5	B	29	132	437	53	102	16	8	2	35	64	57	14	.233	.320
Elliott Maddox	OF79, 3B43, 1B1	R	30	119	389	43	100	18	2	2	39	71	38	2	.257	.329
Lee Mazzilli	OF144	B	23	148	542	78	148	28	5	16	61	69	82	20	.273	.432
Steve Henderson	OF155	R	25	157	587	83	156	30	9	10	65	60	109	13	.266	.399
John Stearns	C141, 3B1	R	26	143	477	65	126	24	1	15	73	70	57	25	.264	.413
Joel Youngblood	OF50, 2B39, 3B9, SS1	R	26	113	266	40	67	12	8	7	30	16	39	4	.252	.436
Bruce Boisclair	OF69, OF1	L	25	107	214	24	48	7	1	4	15	23	43	3	.224	.322
Bobby Valentine	2B45, 3B9	R	28	69	160	17	43	7	0	1	18	19	18	1	.269	.331
Ed Kranepool	OF12, 1B3	L	33	66	81	7	17	2	0	3	19	8	12	0	.210	.346
Tommy Grieve	OF26, 1B2	R	30	54	101	5	21	3	0	2	8	9	23	0	.208	.297
Ron Hodges	C30	L	29	47	102	4	26	4	1	0	7	10	11	1	.255	.314
Sergio Ferrer	SS29, 2B3, 3B2	B	27	37	33	8	7	0	1	0	1	4	7	1	.212	.273
Dan Norman	OF18	R	23	19	64	7	17	0	1	4	10	2	14	1	.266	.484
Gil Flores	OF8	R	25	11	29	8	8	0	1	0	1	3	5	1	.276	.345
Ken Henderson	OF7	B	32	7	22	2	5	2	0	1	4	4	4	0	.227	.455
Alex Trevino	C5, 3B1	R	20	6	12	3	3	0	0	0	0	1	2	0	.250	.250
Butch Benton	C1	R	20	4	4	1	2	0	0	0	2	0	0	0	.500	.500

NAME	T	AGE	W	L	PCT	SV	G	GS	CG	IP	H	BB	SO	ShO	ERA
		27	66	96	.407	26	162	162	21	1455	1447	531	775	7	3.87
Nino Espinosa	R	24	11	15	.423	0	32	32	6	204	230	75	76	1	4.72
Pat Zachry	R	26	10	6	.625	0	21	21	5	138	120	60	78	2	3.33
Craig Swan	R	27	9	6	.600	0	29	28	5	207	164	58	125	1	2.43
Dale Murray	R	28	8	5	.615	5	53	0	0	86	85	36	37	0	3.66
Skip Lockwood	R	31	7	13	.350	15	57	0	0	91	78	31	73	0	3.56
Kevin Kobel	L	24	5	6	.455	0	32	11	1	108	95	30	51	0	2.92
Mardie Cornejo	R	26	4	2	.667	3	25	0	0	37	37	14	17	0	2.43
Mike Bruhert	R	27	4	11	.267	0	27	22	1	134	171	34	56	1	4.77
Tom Hausman	R	25	3	3	.500	0	10	10	0	52	58	9	16	0	4.67
Jerry Koosman	L	35	3	15	.167	2	38	32	3	235	221	84	160	0	3.75
Butch Metzger	R	26	1	3	.250	0	25	0	0	37	48	22	21	0	6.57
Dwight Bernard	R	26	1	4	.200	0	30	1	0	48	54	27	26	0	4.31
Roy Jackson	R	24	0	0	—	0	4	2	0	13	21	6	6	0	9.00
Paul Siebert	L	25	0	2	.000	1	27	0	0	28	30	21	12	0	5.14
Juan Berenquer	R	23	0	2	.000	0	5	3	0	13	17	11	8	0	8.31
Bobby Myrick	L	25	0	3	.000	0	17	0	0	25	18	13	13	0	3.24
Bob Apodaca		28													

Ralph Kiner, Lindsey Nelson, and Bob Murphy were the longest-running trio in the history of baseball broadcasting. When the most professional and experienced of the three, Lindsey Nelson, left the Mets in 1978 to broadcast Giants games, it was a big blow to the morale of Kiner and Murphy—and fans and management. It was like deserting a sinking ship. But after a few interim failures, the broadcast team has rebounded nicely with the addition of Gary Thorne on radio and Tim McCarver and Steve Zabriski on television. McCarver, particularly, has had a huge impact as a colorful and knowledgeable broadcaster. McCarver is, in fact, treated like a superstar. He is outspoken, quick to size up a possible strategic or tactical error ("God—Mookie Wilson is playing much too deep").

In this photo the famous trio is inducted into the Mets Hall of Fame in September 1984.

IRA GOLDEN

He blamed his fall from power on the press.

"We traded Tom Seaver and the press made such a martyr of Seaver that it killed me. I did a good job for a long time. We won two pennants and one World Series. Now people say I ran the attendance down. But they forget I also ran it up to 2.7 million."

Insiders traced the change to Charles Payson. There were indications he resented the hold Grant had had over his deceased wife, especially Grant's total control of the club, in which he was a minority stockholder while Mrs. Payson owned some 85 percent. It was widely believed that Mrs. Payson left her shares of Mets stock to her husband. According to Payson, he had purchased the stock from the estate, "specifically to insure that the team she founded and loved remained in the Payson family." He also insisted that the club would never be sold. The purchase also provided tax advantages.

Payson himself attended the meeting at which Grant was deposed, pledging that henceforth there would be a change in the team's approach to the free agent market.

"While Dad was at the meeting, we had a chance to discuss the future makeup of the team, and we decided that we will try to approach Pete Rose with an offer," Mrs. de Roulet announced. "A dramatic offer and a competitive offer. If we sign him, he certainly would be a box office attraction."

Rose was a free agent and available to the highest bidder, but almost before Mrs. de Roulet could get the words out of her mouth, Rose declined. He did not want to play in New York and certainly not with a losing team.

Mrs. de Roulet took over in January, and if there was a new free-spending policy in effect, no one noticed it. In fact, there were constant reminders that every penny spent was to be carefully accounted for. Certainly there were no big player acquisitions. The Koosman trade-off for Orosco was completed in December 1978, and in late March the Mets obtained veteran third baseman–first baseman Richie Hebner from Philadelphia for Espinosa. In December Torre also had pushed for a deal that would bring left-hander Pete Falcone from St. Louis to the Mets in exchange for Grieve and a minor league pitcher.

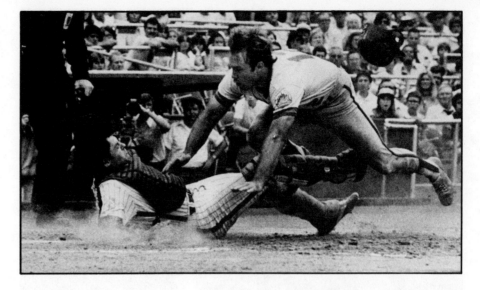

John Stearns, who took over the full-time catching responsibilities in 1978, barrels head first into the Phillies' Bob Boone and knocks the ball loose in order to score. Stearns, known affectionately as "the Dude" because of his rugged good looks, knows how to throw a good tackle—he had been an excellent defensive back in college football. He even tackled a spectator who illegally ran onto the playing field at Shea and eluded security men.

AP

Falcone was from Brooklyn and a cousin of bullpen coach Joe Pignatano. Pete, a lefty, always had good stuff, never had a sore arm, but couldn't get the ball over the plate and rarely won. Torre and Piggy thought they could turn him around.

The Mets were about to play their first exhibition game of the spring on March 10, 1979, when Mr. Payson showed up for the final workout. He rarely attended any games, much less spring training games, and now here he was at a workout. Chatting with reporters in the stands, Payson gave a first hint of things to come.

"When the season is over, we will sit down and evaluate things. There are a lot of people interested in buying this club," Payson said.

For the *New York Daily News'* March 10 editions I wrote a story quoting Payson and pointed out his hint that the Mets might be for sale.

The next day, Mrs. de Roulet, through McDonald but on stationery from her personal yacht, *Patrina II*, denied my story about a possible sale.

The statement first was read to the Mets players before they took the field against St. Louis, and copies later were distributed to the press.

"Mrs. de Roulet has asked me to say, because of somewhat conflicting recent reports by the press, that the Mets are not for sale and the family is foursquare behind you, the players.

"All that Mr. Payson actually said was that at the end of the year there would be a family conference to evaluate the team's progress. They are optimistic that we are going to have a good year.

"The Payson family has faith in the team's ability and competitive spirit and is confident you all will give 110 percent, resulting in a winning effort which will silence the rumors."

The statement did nothing to silence rumors. One story had Sonny Werblin, president of Madison Square Garden, bidding for the Mets on behalf of Gulf and Western Corporation.

"I am mystified as to the origin of the renewed rumors about the Mets," Payson said in another statement. "The team is not now, it never had been, and it never will be for sale."

When in mid-season Lindsey Nelson announced his decision to leave the Mets, it caught them by surprise. They had no inkling he was unhappy—and he was not. But Lindsey could see that the once-great operation was quickly becoming chintzy. He also felt it was time for him to be moving on.

In his book, *Hello Everybody, I'm Lindsey Nelson*, he describes his decision.

"By the time I left for spring training with the Mets in 1978, I was beginning to have some thoughts about where I might set up a permanent residence for the future. . . . [during] the four years that Nancy [his daughter] had spent at the University of Tennessee at Knoxville, I had managed to get sort of reacquainted. . . . I began to think about buying a condominium in Knoxville. I thought so much about it I stopped on the way to spring training, picked one out and made a down payment.

"I was not disenchanted with life in New York. I had not lost my feeling for that great city . . . but it seems to me that there usually comes a time in a man's life when he should say, 'There, that's enough of that,' and move on to something else."

Jim Thomson and Lorinda de Roulet both pleaded with Nelson to reconsider, but he had made his decision and would not be swayed.

With no major personnel changes and no free agents signed, the Mets went into the season in worse shape than when they had started the previous year. As the exhibition schedule neared an end, it became obvious the Mets had no pitching, at least not experienced pitching. In fact, when he broke camp, Torre was forced to take three inexperienced rookie pitchers with him just to fill out the squad. They were Mike Scott, Orosco, and Neil Allen. Scott and Orosco were back in the minors, and Allen was scheduled for return to farm play when an injury forced the Mets to keep him—you could not send an injured player to the minors. By the time he was well enough to pitch again, another pitcher was hurt, so Allen was retained. He went on to become the club's best relief pitcher, with a 6–10 record and eight saves. Lockwood won two and saved nine but came up with a sore shoulder and never pitched after June.

The only man on the staff who managed to win as many as ten games was Swan. He won fourteen and lost thirteen. Zachry won only five games after damaging the ulnar nerve in his elbow and was lost to the club after June 8. Falcone wound up the second busiest starter next to Swan, starting thirty-one games but winning only six and losing fourteen. Neither his cousin, Pignatano, nor his friend, Torre, could turn him around.

Torre knew it was a mistake opening with three inexperienced starters, but McDonald had provided him no help and he had no choice. Torre did invite Nelson Briles, a former St. Louis teammate, to try out in the spring. Torre wanted to keep him, but the austerity campaign was on and McDonald would not or could not pay Briles the money a veteran commanded. If any was needed, here was proof positive that the club was operating on a shoestring, Payson's statements notwithstanding. His support for his daughter obviously did not include access to the cash the club needed.

It did not take long for the Mets to self-destruct. In their twenty-fourth game of the season they dropped into last place. Then they became anxious enough to look for experienced pitching to replace the kids. In a matter of two months, they signed four fairly undistinguished veteran pitchers—Wayne Twitchell, Dock Ellis, Andy Hassler, and Ray Burris. These four combined to win twelve while losing seventeen.

One of the big flops of the season was Montanez. The first baseman, whom Torre had urged the Mets to go after the year before, was batting only .234 with five homers when the Mets sold him back to Texas on August 12. In that deal they got back veteran Mike Jorgensen, whom they had dealt away seven years earlier, plus a minor league pitcher named Ed Lynch. Lynch later became a dependable pitcher for the managers who succeeded Torre.

Another deal that did not pan out for the Mets was Hebner for Espinosa. Hebner played third indifferently. He did drive in fifty runs before the All-Star game and thus was in position to have a productive season, but in the

OPENING DAY LINEUP 1979

Mazzilli, cf
Chapman, 2b
Hebner, 3b
Stearns, c
Montanez, 1b
S. Henderson, lf
Maddox, rf
Flynn, ss
Swan, p

In the late 1970s the De Roulet women ran the Mets—into the ground. From left: Lorinda and daughters Bebe and Whitney.
AP

second half of the season the team slumped to a 26–50 record and Hebner knocked in only twenty-nine runs. He didn't like life with the Mets.

The Mets were a team in turmoil throughout the 1979 season. Players were coming and going as they had in the early years. In all, forty-one players played in at least one game that year, twenty-two of them pitchers. In addition, the Mets were watching every buck they spent and still sought ways to save money. For years the club had been one of the most profitable in baseball. Now they were operating at a loss.

Every so often Mrs. de Roulet called staff meetings at which she and her aides would discuss ways to cut corners and reduce expenses. By early April Mrs. de Roulet already had to ask her father to co-sign a $1 million loan to keep the club going. Later she asked for another $1 million. It was at that point that the eighty-year-old Payson decided it was time to get out.

Some of those who were privy to the staff meetings recall with laughter the suggestion made one day by Bebe de Roulet, Mrs. de Roulet's younger daughter, on a way the club could possibly save money.

"Couldn't we take the used balls and wash them?" she offered.

Veteran baseball men at the meeting had all they could do to keep from cracking up. Dozens of new balls are used in every major league game; the least little mark on a ball is enough for an umpire to throw it out of the game, never to be used again.

The De Roulets had no conception of how to run a ball club. Instead they tried cute little gimmicks to lure the fans back. One they particularly liked was adopting as mascot the mule that had been presented to "Mummy" (as they always called their mother) by a Long Island neighbor. The mule's name was Arthur, but since Arthur Richman was the public relations director, they thought it wise to give the animal another name. A contest was held and "Mettle" selected as the winning entry. The De Roulets said it combined the club name with the spirit of the team.

The mule was housed in a stall beneath the stands behind home plate. The grounds keepers, who had their quarters nearby, complained of the stench. Before every home game, Bebe de Roulet propped herself in a little sulky behind the mule and took a fast trip around the Shea Stadium warning track. She thought it was cute. What other people thought and said is better left unwritten.

Attendance at Mets games the final half of the season was a disaster. Following the All-Star break in July, the Mets only three times managed to draw as many as 20,000 customers to the ballpark. The top crowd was 27,605. The way the Mets were playing, there was no reason to embarrass them by

1979

NAME	G by POS	B	AGE	G	AB	R	H	2B	3B	HR	RBI	BB	SO	SB	BA	SA
NEW YORK 6th 63-99 .389 35	JOE TORRE															
TOTALS			28	163	5591	593	1399	255	41	74	558	498	817	135	.250	.350
Willie Montanez	1B108	L	31	109	410	36	96	19	0	5	47	25	48	0	.234	.317
Doug Flynn	2B148, SS20	R	28	157	555	35	135	19	5	4	61	17	46	0	.243	.317
Frank Taveras	SS153	R	29	153	635	89	167	26	9	1	33	33	72	42	.263	.337
Richie Hebner	3B134, 1B6	L	31	136	473	54	127	25	2	10	79	59	59	3	.268	.393
Joel Youngblood	OF147, 2B13, 3B12	R	27	158	590	90	162	37	5	16	60	60	84	18	.275	.436
Lee Mazzilli	OF143, 1B15	B	24	158	597	78	181	34	4	15	79	93	74	34	.303	.449
Steve Henderson	OF94	R	26	98	350	42	107	16	8	5	39	38	58	13	.306	.440
John Stearns	C121, 1B16, 3B11, OF6	R	27	155	538	58	131	29	2	9	66	52	57	15	.243	.355
Elliott Maddox	OF65, 3B11	R	31	86	224	21	60	13	0	1	12	20	27	3	.268	.339
Ed Kranepool	1B29, OF8	L	34	82	155	7	36	5	0	2	17	13	18	0	.232	.303
Alex Trevino	C36, 3B27, 2B8	R	21	79	207	24	56	11	1	0	20	20	27	2	.271	.333
Gil Flores	OF32	R	26	70	93	9	18	1	1	0	10	8	17	2	.194	.258
Ron Hodges	C22	L	30	59	86	4	14	4	0	0	5	19	16	0	.163	.209
Bruce Boisclair	OF24, 1B1	L	26	59	98	7	18	5	1	0	4	3	24	0	.184	.255
Dan Norman	OF33	R	24	44	110	9	27	3	1	3	11	10	26	2	.245	.373
Kelvin Chapman	2B22, 3B1	R	23	35	80	7	12	1	2	0	4	5	15	0	.150	.213
Sergio Ferrer	3B12, SS5, 2B4	B	28	32	7	7	0	0	0	0	0	2	3	0	.000	.000
Jose Cardenal	OF9, 1B2	R	35	11	37	8	11	4	0	2	4	6	3	1	.297	.568
Tim Foli	SS3	R	28	3	7	0	0	0	0	0	0	0	0	0	.000	.000

NAME	T	AGE	W	L	PCT	SV	G	GS	CG	IP	H	BB	SO	ShO	ERA
		27	63	99	.389	36	163	163	16	1483	1486	607	819	10	3.84
Craig Swan	R	28	14	13	.519	0	35	35	10	251	241	57	145	3	3.30
Kevin Kobel	L	25	6	8	.429	0	30	27	1	162	169	46	67	1	3.50
Neil Allen	R	21	6	10	.375	8	50	5	0	99	100	47	65	0	3.55
Pete Falcone	L	25	6	14	.300	0	33	31	1	184	194	76	113	1	4.16
Pat Zachry	R	27	5	1	.833	0	7	7	1	43	44	21	17	0	3.56
Wayne Twitchell	R	31	5	3	.625	0	33	2	0	64	55	55	44	0	5.20
Andy Hassler	L	27	4	5	.444	4	29	8	1	80	74	42	53	0	3.71
Dale Murray	R	29	4	8	.333	4	58	0	0	97	105	52	37	0	4.82
Dock Ellis	R	34	3	7	.300	0	17	14	1	85	110	34	41	0	6.04
Skip Lockwood	R	32	2	5	.286	9	27	0	0	42	33	14	42	0	1.50
Tom Hausman	R	26	2	6	.250	2	19	10	1	79	65	19	33	0	2.73
Roy Jackson	R	25	1	0	1:000	0	8	0	0	16	11	5	10	0	2.25
Juan Berenguer	R	24	1	1	.500	0	5	5	0	31	28	12	25	0	2.90
Jesse Orosco	L	22	1	2	.333	0	18	2	0	35	33	22	22	0	4.89
Jeff Reardon	R	23	1	2	.333	2	18	0	0	21	12	9	10	0	1.71
Mike Scott	R	24	1	3	.250	0	18	9	0	52	59	20	21	0	5.37
Ed Glynn	L	26	1	4	.200	7	46	0	0	60	57	40	32	0	3.00
Ray Burris	R	28	0	2	.000	0	4	4	0	22	21	6	10	0	3.27
Johnny Pacella	R	22	0	2	.000	0	4	3	0	16	16	4	12	0	4.50
Dwight Bernard	R	26	0	3	.000	0	32	1	0	44	59	26	20	0	4.70
Bob Apodaca		29													
Bobby Myrick		26													

watching. In the thirty-eight games the Mets played at home during the final half of the season, they won only six.

In her defense, it must be said the Mrs. de Roulet tried. She made sure the few good players would be retained. Lee Mazzilli, Frank Taveras, and John Stearns all were signed to five-year contracts.

Stearns had been a highly regarded defensive halfback at the University of Colorado, where he was All-Conference in the Big Eight and played in four successive post-season bowl games. He also was the seventeenth-round pick of the Buffalo Bills in the National Football League draft. But the Phillies picked him number 2 in the nation in the 1973 draft, and he chose baseball over football.

He was an extremely aggressive player, and Joe Torre once said of him, "He has that sack-the-quarterback mentality. At the plate, he tries to hit a three-run homer with the bases empty."

Stearns had a cocky strut and was known to his teammates by the nickname given him in his college days—"the Dude."

He could not always keep his aggressiveness under control. Once, at Shea Stadium, the game was delayed as overweight park police vainly pursued a fan who had run onto the field. Stearns watched for several minutes as the fan ran a crazy pattern, eluding the special police. Finally, in frustration, he ran out and tackled the fan himself.

One night in Atlanta Stadium, where the Braves' mascot, Chief Noc-A-Homa, does a dance on the mound prior to each game then races to a tepee in left field, Stearns, tired of watching the routine, raced out of the Mets dugout and tackled the chief in short left field.

Without her father's financial support and with attendance sinking to an all-time low of 788,905, there was no way Mrs. de Roulet could make it work. On November 8, 1979, the anniversary of her takeover as chairman of the board, the Payson family publicly announced that the Mets were for sale.

Prospective purchasers appeared at once. For the next two months, hardly a day went by without one of the New York papers chronicling a new bidder.

The final tally showed twenty-one groups mentioned as possible owners. One of the first ones was Robert Abplanalp, a close friend of former President

The cavernous Houston Astrodome, always a tough park for the Mets, was especially troublesome on June 15, when the team lost a five-hour, eighteen-inning game, 3–2. Here, Joe Torre goes at umpire Lanny Harris in the top of the eighteenth inning. Harris had called a bunt by Mets pitcher Tom Hausman foul, which kept the sacrifice from working.

AP

On January 24, 1980, the new Mets owners, Nelson Doubleday *(left)* and Fred Wilpon are introduced to the media. Lorinda de Roulet eases the transition.

NEW YORK POST/NURY HERNANDEZ

Richard Nixon and head of Precision Valve Corporation. Earl Smith, a Palm Beach neighbor of Charles Payson and a former ambassador to Cuba, was another. Herman Franks, one-time Giants coach and manager, was yet another. Sonny Werblin, representing Gulf and Western, was always considered a contender. Even Ed Kranepool got a group together.

How many of those mentioned were legitimate and how many just headline grabbers was never divulged. When the De Roulets announced that they were selling, they formed a three-person committee to screen the bids. The committee consisted of Louis A. Hoynes, Jr., a National League attorney; William A. Cameron, an attorney for the law firm representing the Mets; and Gerald F. Schanley, an executive of the Arthur Andersen accounting firm. All bids were to be directed to Robert W. Briggs of the Wall Street law firm of Carter, Ledyard and Milburn, lawyers for the club.

Ironically, despite all the names mentioned over a period of two months, the eventual purchasers did not surface until just days before the actual sale. On January 24, 1980, it was announced that Fred Wilpon of Sterling Equities, a real estate corporation; Nelson Doubleday, Jr., of the family-owned Doubleday publishing firm; and City Investing Company had purchased the club for $21.3 million. This was just eighteen years after Mrs. Payson, Grant, and Herb Walker had paid less than $2 million for the franchise. In the intervening years they had taken out countless millions in profit. Now they were taking more.

Mrs. de Roulet retained her club box on the right field side of the home dugout. The box on the side nearest home plate passed from Grant to Doubleday and Wilpon. Through the years that Grant ran the club, he attended almost every game. It was his family's entertainment center. His three grown children used the box and the director's room, where extravagant menus were prepared nightly, to entertain their friends. After Grant sold his 11 percent share—sold in a block with the Payson majority share in 1980—he was seen at Shea only once, when he turned up to accept a plaque from the National League. He did not stay for the game.

N elson Doubleday never intended to own a major league baseball club. When others bid to buy the Mets, Doubleday was not among them. In fact, the deadline for sending bids to Robert W. Briggs had come and gone by the time Doubleday was talked into joining forces with Wilpon to buy the team. The two people most responsible for bringing Doubleday into the picture were John O. Pickett, a Locust Valley, Long Island, neighbor and friend, and John Sargent, one of the operating officers of Doubleday Publishing. Pickett, a sportsman who owned the New York Islanders of the National Hockey League, had joined with Wilpon, another Long Islander with vast real estate investments, in making a $17.5 million bid for the Mets. That was not enough to satisfy the Paysons.

Wilpon, a former Lafayette High School athlete in Brooklyn whose sports claim to fame is that he was the pitcher on a school team that had Hall of Famer Sandy Koufax as first baseman, wanted desperately to buy the Mets, but until Doubleday's appearance he could not raise the necessary capital. Although Doubleday and Wilpon both lived on Long Island's Gold Coast within a few miles of each other, their only connection was as members of the board of directors of the exclusive Greenvale School in Glen Head, Long Island. They knew each other, but that was about it.

Doubleday and other executives of the publishing firm were away at a corporate Caribbean retreat when Sargent suggested they buy the Mets. The $21.1 million did not frighten Doubleday, and his firm agreed to put up 80 percent of the money.

"We had a feeling we had gone as far as we could in the book business," Doubleday explained to reporters later. "The Mets are here. The Mets obviously are down. We felt it was not that much different from selling entertainment. We are always dealing with stars, with authors and agents. It's not all that different from selling a seat at the ballpark as it is selling books to our 3 million book club members. Sure, what we paid is a great deal more than anyone has paid for a baseball team. But this is New York and New York is a bigger deal than any other city. This is a National League city just waiting to be tapped. We regard this as a long-term investment. It will eventually be profitable. It is a business and we feel we are going to do very well with it."

Although he had cemented the deal by bringing Wilpon and Doubleday together, Pickett did not remain in any official capacity with the Mets. He was too busy running the Islanders, who won four straight Stanley Cup championships. Instead, Wilpon, with about 10 percent ownership, was named president. Doubleday, with 80 percent, became chairman of the board.

The first item of business was to find someone to run the team. McDonald obviously did not fit the corporate mold of the Doubleday people. The owners began calling around for permission to talk to general managers of other clubs. The more they called, according to Doubleday, the more they kept hearing good things about J. Frank Cashen, an administrative officer in Commissioner Bowie Kuhn's office.

Cashen had been general manager of the Baltimore Orioles team shocked by the Amazing Mets of 1969. When the club changed hands Cashen went to work for a Baltimore brewery before coming to New York and the commissioner's office. He never settled in New York, living instead at the New York Athletic Club and commuting weekends to his native Baltimore.

Cashen yearned to get back with a ball club. Sources close to Kuhn say Cashen agreed to become his administrative aide with the explicit understanding that Kuhn would recommend him for the next available general manager's job. Kuhn is understood to have persuaded Doubleday and Wilpon to sign Cashen, which they did one month after taking control of the club. On February 21, 1980, Cashen was signed to a five-year contract as executive vice-president and general manager. McDonald was retained for the time being as

OPENING DAY LINEUP 1980

Taveras, ss
Maddox, 3b
Mazzilli, 1b
S. Henderson, lf
Jorgensen, rf
Stearns, c
Morales, cf
Flynn, ss
Swan, p

One of the first moves Frank Cashen made as general manager was to give Craig Swan what was then the biggest long-term contract in Mets history—$3.1 million over five years. Swan *(left)*, Cashen *(center)*, and Joe Torre *(right)* are all smiles. But there were no happy faces when Swan's shoulder stiffened and required rotator cuff surgery. He was useless for the rest of the season and for most of the term of the contract.
AP

The Mets picked a gem in the June 1980 free agent draft, Darryl Strawberry, number 1 in the country. Here, Darryl visits the Mets clubhouse and manager Joe Torre during a Mets series in Los Angeles.

UPI/BETTMAN NEWSPHOTO

vice-president, Baseball Operations. In effect he had been stripped of his powers.

Cashen was not long on the scene before he was given the nickname "Bowtie," seldom wearing any other neckwear in an era when many baseball men have abandoned ties altogether and almost certainly do not wear bowties. Just as loud sports jackets are Lindsey Nelson's trademark, bowties have become identified with Cashen.

According to Cashen, the bowtie is the result of his early days as a newspaperman in Baltimore.

"I used to have to make up the pages early in the morning in the composing room. I would lean over the type trays which had been proofed and still contained black ink. I was always soiling my long ties with black ink. So, one day I decided to try a bowtie and I never had that problem again.

"I have about forty or fifty of them, all colors—yellow, red, blue, and green. The yellow ones are my favorites. They're made of good wool and you can wear them with almost any color and they will not clash with the rest of the clothes you're wearing."

One baseball official told me shortly before Cashen was named that "he surrounds himself with good people." It did not take Cashen long to do just that in New York. Most of the "good people" had worked for him in Baltimore at one time or another. It got so that every time Cashen hired someone the event was labeled as another chapter of the Chesapeake Connection. One by one they came—Al Harazin, Lou Gorman, Joe McIlvaine. By spring of 1981, all of Cashen's top lieutenants were men who at one time had served under him in Baltimore.

Cashen inherited a ball club in 1980 that was at rock bottom. It took a driving Joe Torre to get his troops up to avoid a 100-loss season in 1979. Torre and the Mets barely accomplished that by winning the last six in a row in Chicago and St. Louis to finish at 63–99. It was enough of an accomplishment to win Torre a contract for another year, which was awarded just one month before the club was put up for sale. Mrs. de Roulet's final act with the Mets left Cashen with a manager he didn't hire.

Cashen announced from the outset that he would spend his entire first year "observing." He knew little about the club personnel except what he could read from cold statistics. He wanted to see for himself, he said, and evaluate each player's performance.

And observe is what Cashen did the first year. He made only one major player change, obtaining Claudell Washington, an outfielder, from the Chicago White Sox for a minor league player on June 7. Washington had worn out his welcome in Chicago. Perhaps he could live up to his potential in New York. It wasn't a bad deal for the Mets—they gave up nothing and in return got an everyday right fielder who hit .275 in seventy-nine games and hit ten home runs. Only Mazzilli, with sixteen, hit more. It was a powerless lineup, and the team's sixty-one homers were the lowest total in the league.

Shortly after the Doubleday people took over the Mets, they hired the Madison Avenue advertising firm of Della Femina, Travisano and Partners to hype their product. For $400,000 they got a lot of slogans, some grief, and a stiff fine from Commissioner Bowie Kuhn.

Jerry Della Femina came out swinging after getting the contract.

"Just having M. Donald Grant and those two silly sisters [Whitney and Bebe de Roulet] leave is worth 50,000 more seats," Della Femina said.

"New York is a town where we had to settle for Reggie Jackson. I would rather have a clean-cut kid who talks to kids. Let's face it, if the Mets were where they were in 1969, Reggie Jackson would have trouble getting arrested in this town."

Della Femina's campaign was to promote Lee Mazzilli, the outfielder converted to first baseman by Torre.

"He's got Bucky Dent's good looks, but he can hit."

And then the outspoken ad man took a real swipe at the Yankees with a remark that resulted in a reported $5,000 fine against Cashen and the Mets.

"I used to be a Yankee fan," said the Brooklyn-born Della Femina. "But I don't go there much anymore. I feel threatened when I go to Yankee Stadium. It's not a very positive experience."

Immediately, Yankee owner George Steinbrenner complained that the Mets' ad agency was labeling Yankee Stadium an unsafe place to attend a ballgame. Commissioner Kuhn agreed that Della Femina's remarks were indeed uncomplimentary and held the Mets responsible.

Trying to tout the team as reborn with the change in ownership, Della Femina came up with the slogan "That magic is back!" It was back in the ad

1980

NAME	G by POS	B	AGE	G	AB	R	H	2B	3B	HR	RBI	BB	SO	SB	BA	SA
NEW YORK 5th 67-95 .414 24	JOE TORRE															
TOTALS			28	162	5478	611	1407	218	41	61	554	501	840	158	.257	.345
Lee Mazzilli	1B92, OF66	B	25	152	578	82	162	31	4	16	76	82	92	41	.280	.431
Doug Flynn	2B128, SS3	R	29	128	443	46	113	9	8	0	24	22	20	2	.255	.312
Frank Taveras	SS140	R	30	141	562	65	157	27	0	0	25	23	64	32	.279	.327
Elliott Maddox	3B115, OF4, 1B2	R	32	130	411	35	101	16	1	4	34	52	44	1	.246	.319
Claudell Washington	OF70	L	25	79	284	38	78	16	4	10	42	20	63	17	.275	.465
Joel Youngblood	OF121, 3B21, 2B6	R	28	146	514	58	142	26	2	8	69	52	69	14	.276	.381
Steve Henderson	OF136	R	27	143	513	75	149	17	8	8	58	62	90	23	.290	.402
John Stearns	C54, 1B16, 3B1	R	28	91	319	42	91	25	1	0	45	33	24	7	.285	.370
Mike Jorgensen	1B72, OF31	L	31	119	321	43	82	11	0	7	43	46	55	0	.255	.355
Alex Trevino	C86, 3B14, 2B1	R	22	106	355	26	91	11	2	0	37	13	41	0	.256	.299
Jerry Morales	OF63	R	31	94	193	19	49	7	1	3	30	13	31	2	.254	.347
Dan Norman	OF19	R	25	69	92	5	17	1	1	2	9	6	14	5	.185	.283
Bill Almon	SS22, 2B18, 3B9	R	27	48	112	13	19	3	0	2	4	8	27	2	.170	.232
Jose Moreno	2B4, 3B4	B	22	37	46	6	9	2	1	2	9	3	12	1	.196	.413
Ron Hodges	C9	L	31	36	42	4	10	2	0	0	5	10	13	1	.238	.286
Mookie Wilson	OF26	B	24	27	105	16	26	5	3	0	4	12	19	7	.248	.352
Wally Backman	2B20, 3B8	B	20	27	93	12	30	1	1	0	9	11	14	2	.323	.355
Jose Cardenal	OF6, 1B5	R	36	26	42	4	7	1	0	0	4	6	4	0	.167	.190
Hubie Brooks	3B23	R	23	24	81	8	25	2	1	1	10	5	9	1	.309	.395
Mario Ramirez	SS7, 2B4, 3B3	R	22	18	24	2	5	0	0	0	0	1	7	0	.208	.208
Butch Benton	C8	R	22	12	21	0	1	0	0	0	0	2	4	0	.048	.048
Phil Mankowski	3B3	L	27	8	12	1	2	1	0	0	1	2	4	0	.167	.250
Luis Rosado	1B1	R	24	2	4	0	0	0	0	0	0	0	1	0	.000	.000

NAME	T	AGE	W	L	PCT	SV	G	GS	CG	IP	H	BB	SO	ShO	ERA
		27	67	95	.414	33	162	162	17	1451	1473	510	886	9	3.85
Mark Bomback	R	27	10	8	.556	0	36	25	2	163	191	49	68	1	4.09
Jeff Reardon	R	24	8	7	.533	6	61	0	0	110	96	47	101	0	2.62
Neil Allen	R	22	7	10	.412	22	59	0	0	97	87	40	79	0	3.71
Pete Falcone	L	26	7	10	.412	1	37	23	1	157	163	58	109	0	4.53
Ray Burris	R	29	7	13	.350	0	29	29	1	170	181	54	83	0	4.02
Tom Hausman	R	27	6	5	.545	1	55	4	0	122	125	26	53	0	3.98
Pat Zachry	R	28	6	10	.375	0	28	26	7	165	145	58	88	3	3.00
Craig Swan	R	29	5	9	.357	0	21	21	4	128	117	30	79	1	3.59
Ed Glynn	L	27	3	3	.500	1	38	0	0	52	49	23	32	0	4.15
Johnny Pacella	R	23	3	4	.429	0	32	15	0	84	89	59	68	0	5.14
Mike Scott	R	25	1	1	.500	0	6	6	1	29	40	8	13	1	4.34
Ed Lynch	R	24	1	1	.500	0	5	4	0	19	24	5	9	0	5.21
Dyar Miller	R	34	1	2	.333	1	31	0	0	42	37	11	28	0	1.93
Kevin Kobel	L	26	1	4	.200	0	14	1	0	24	36	11	8	0	7.13
Roy Jackson	R	26	1	7	.125	1	24	8	1	71	78	20	58	0	4.18
Scott Holman	R	21	0	0	—	0	4	0	0	7	6	1	3	0	1.29
Juan Berenguer	R	25	0	1	.000	0	6	0	0	9	9	10	7	0	6.00

executive's fertile imagination only. Not on the field. As the Mets continued to lose in 1980 and for the next three years, the "Magic is back" slogan became a line of ridicule in the daily reports sportswriters filed to their papers.

Della Femina subsequently switched to "Catch the rising stars." Originally, the line was "Catching a rising star," but that conflicted with the words of a popular song of bygone years, and the agency was forced to change it.

It is doubtful the advertising had any impact on the Mets' attendance. Any team, when winning, will draw customers. Losing drives them away. Mets fans only began to come back to Shea Stadium when the team started to win again under Davey Johnson.

◆ ◆ ◆

One of Cashen's first moves after taking over was to negotiate a five-year contract with pitcher Craig Swan. The right-hander was eligible for free agency at the end of the season. How would it look if the new owners allowed their best pitcher to walk away? They gave him a $3.15 million contract, and Swan became the richest pitcher in Mets history. In Cincinnati Seaver winced. If Grant had offered him half that, Tom Terrific would still be a Met.

All things considered, Torre did a tremendous job with what he had to work with in 1980. Zachry, one of his regular starters, continued to have elbow problems and was left in Florida when the team broke camp. He did not start a game until May 18 and then won only six while losing ten. Swan tore a rotator cuff in his shoulder and was sidelined from early July on. He won only five and lost nine. Burris, who had been picked up on waivers from the Yankees the year before, started more games than any other Met. But he won only seven while losing thirteen. Pete Falcone had another typical Falcone year. He won seven and lost ten.

Arms are flailing as Ellis Valentine goes into third base on a rare single by Dave Kingman in a game in St. Louis on September 11. Third baseman Ken Oberkfell is late on the tag, as indicated by umpire Randy Marsh. Valentine, acquired by the Mets during the season to add some much-needed punch to the lineup, got injured and failed miserably, batting a mere .207 for the season. Earlier in his career Valentine had gotten beaned, but the Mets hoped he would get over the trauma. He never did.
AP/WIDE WORLD PHOTOS

The surprise pitcher of the lot was Mark Bomback, a junkballer who had been obtained in a minor deal with Milwaukee in September 1979. McDonald got him in a swap for Dwight Bernard, a relief pitcher. Bomback had nine quick wins by August 10 and was the most effective pitcher on the staff, with a 9–3 record. Then he did not win another game until October 4, by which time his record was 10–8. Bomback got along famously with members of the press corps, but then I nicknamed him "Boom Boom" Bomback after he had served up some tape measure home runs. The rest of the year he gave us the chilly treatment.

When the Mets obtained Claudell Washington on June 7, 1980, from the Chicago White Sox, they should have had some idea of what they were getting. Washington was hitting .289 for the Sox, but his lackadaisical play had already prompted one Chicago fan to hang a banner from the right field stands. "Washington slept here," it read.

Washington was in his option year. Frank Cashen knew that when he obtained him. But since they gave up only minor league pitcher Jesse Anderson, it was no great risk if Washington walked.

On June 22, eleven days after playing his first game for the Mets, Washington exploded with three home runs in a game against the Dodgers at Los Angeles. He tied the club record with those three shots. Two days later he won a game with another home run. But at the end of the season, after hitting ten home runs and driving in forty runs in seventy-nine games, Claudell took his walk and signed as a free agent with Atlanta.

Torre's decision to move Allen to the bullpen in 1979 saved 1980 from becoming a complete disaster. Allen appeared in fifty-nine games; he had a 7–10 record but saved twenty-two. With Jeff Reardon, who saved another six, also on the staff, the Mets had one of the best bullpens in the league.

Considering that he did not have a pitcher who won more than ten games or a .300 hitter, Torre did an outstanding job by bringing the club home in fifth place. During the three-month period from May 14 to August 13, the Mets played as well as any team in the league. From a 9–18 start they went on to win forty-seven while losing thirty-nine to move within two and one-half games of third place.

"Joe Torre should be manager of the year for the job he has done with that club," said Pittsburgh manager Chuck Tanner.

On August 14 the Mets opened a five-game series with the Phillies that would prove devastating. Despite the fact he had his best pitchers primed for the series, Torre saw his young Mets do a complete fold. They lost all five games to the Phillies and another to the Giants to begin a dive that would see them lose twenty-three of their next twenty-six. By early September they had settled in fifth place. Despite their solid play in the middle of the season, they won only sixty-seven games—four more than the previous year.

In the absence of either consistent or power hitting, Torre emphasized speed as a major facet of his offense. As a result, the Mets stole a club record 158 bases. Mazzilli led the speed boys with 41 stolen bases, Frank Taveras had 32, and Steve Henderson 23.

As a result of their exciting mid-season play, the Mets' attendance rose by 400,000 to 1,178,659. If they were not yet contenders, the Mets were on the rise. Even Cashen had to recognize the fine job Torre turned in. He did so by rewarding Joe with a two-year contract.

Cashen began preparations for the 1981 season with four December acquisitions, two of which would prove helpful. On December 12, 1980, utility man Bob Bailor was obtained in a deal with Toronto for pitcher Roy Lee Jackson.

Bailor had been developed in the Baltimore organization and was well known to Cashen. Three days later the Mets added a Cy Young Award winner when they traded pitcher John Pacella and infielder Jose Moreno to San Diego for Randy Jones. Jones, a left-hander, had won twenty twice for the Padres but had earlier undergone surgery for a nerve problem in his arm that resurfaced in 1980. He also spent time on the disabled list with a rib cage injury, leaving him with a disappointing 1980 record of thirteen losses and five wins. Because they were giving up virtually nothing, the Mets were willing to take a chance on Jones. In the next four days, Cashen signed two free agents, something the Mets almost never did under Grant. First Cashen brought back the popular Rusty Staub as a pinch hitter, and then he signed third baseman Mike Cubbage, who had played for the Minnesota Twins. In seven days, Cashen had handed Torre two infielders, a pitcher, and a pinch hitter. The Mets were making changes and they were making news. It was a reaffirmation of the pledge Wilpon and Doubleday made the day they purchased the club: "We have the money to turn this club into a winner, and we will not be afraid to spend it."

Cashen, however, was tabbed a conservative from the start. He was secretive, cautious, and private, but he was ready to build from the bottom up. It would be a long, tedious job with little coming up through the farm system, which he was determined to make productive. It would take five years to build a winner, he said. Meanwhile, Cashen worked quietly to fill in the missing pieces with players he could buy.

On February 28, 1981, one year and one week after he had assumed control of the club, Cashen engineered his biggest deal, only this one couldn't be kept quiet. Realizing he needed a power hitter, Cashen brought Dave Kingman back to New York. Kingman had found a home for a couple of years in Wrigley Field, hitting a career high forty-eight homers in 1979. He began to show less of an interest in baseball in 1980 than the Cubs expected; after an injury-plagued season in which he hit only eighteen home runs, they were looking to unload him. The Mets got Kingman again for Steve Henderson and a reported $100,000.

Kingman showed up in St. Petersburg all smiles. He seemed as glad to get away from Chicago in 1981 as he had been to get away from New York four years earlier.

Dave's relationship with the press was always stormy. He was a total enigma. He could charm someone with his smile one moment and then turn his back on the same person a moment later. I had an experience with him in 1976 that was typical.

The Mets had played an exhibition game in West Palm Beach on March 29, 1976, and were flying back to St. Petersburg immediately after the game. Kingman had a contract to pose for some pictures for a recliner chair company, and these were taken after the game. When the picture-taking session was over, Dave discovered to his dismay that the team plane had left without him. There were no other flights to St. Petersburg that night. The pictures he had taken were shot in the Atlanta Braves' press room, and Dave must have remembered seeing me writing my story there. He came back to the press room and inquired how I was getting back to St. Petersburg. I told him I was driving in my rented car.

"Can I hitch a ride?" he asked.

I told him he could and that I would be ready in another half hour. He waited for me in the press room, and shortly after five o'clock we started the five-hour ride to St. Petersburg. Dave even offered to drive. After a stop at Yeehaw Junction, Florida, for a snack of hamburgers and milk, which he insisted on paying for, we resumed our long drive. Throughout the trip we chatted casually. Dave told me that he was a private person who did not enjoy the limelight. He lived in suburban Connecticut and rarely went into New York City. He told me his hobby was woodworking, that he especially enjoyed making furniture. It was a long, tiresome ride, but the conversation was pleasant. We talked a little about the team, mostly about things in general. When we arrived back in St. Petersburg, Dave drove to the clubhouse, picked up his car, said thank you and good night.

The next morning, as we passed each other in the clubhouse, I said good morning to Kingman. He never looked at me. He walked right past me as if I didn't exist. The day before we had spent five hours together in a car and now he didn't even know me. That was Dave Kingman.

When Kingman returned to the Mets in 1981, he came bearing gifts for the sportswriters traveling with the ball club. Whether it was suggested to him or whether he did it on his own, Kingman went out and bought silver Cross pens and had his initials engraved on each. At his welcoming press conference the next day he handed out the pens. He was as sweet as could be in answering questions and insisted he had turned over a new leaf. One year later, apparently irked by my stories, he was no longer talking to me. Kingman also went out of his way to shun female members of the press corps, who by now were admitted to the clubhouse. There were a few who attracted his fancy, and these Kingman would engage in long conversations. For the most part, however, he shouted foul remarks at any woman who entered the clubhouse. He was not alone in believing women reporters had no place there, but unlike other players who may have felt the same way, he rarely held his tongue.

Spring training 1981 produced the best young pitching prospect since Tom Seaver. His name was Tim Leary. He had attended UCLA and was the Mets' number 1 draft pick in the June 1979 draft. He was as impressive as Seaver was in his early years, and with an earned run average of 1.80 in four games, Torre and his pitching coach, Bob Gibson, thought he was ready for the big-time. Leary's progress in the spring became an issue that drove Torre and his general manager apart. Cashen felt the pitcher needed at least a half season in Triple-A ball.

In the end, Torre won. But he also lost. Leary was added to the roster, and in his first start on April 12 in Chicago, he was forced to leave the game after two innings when his elbow stiffened. Actually, the elbow had bothered him in a previous exhibition game in Jackson, Mississippi, but trainer Larry Mayol did not inform Torre. On April 21, Leary was placed on the disabled list with what Dr. James Parkes described as "muscle strain of the inner aspect of the right elbow." Leary never threw another baseball for the Mets that season.

Cashen was upset over what had happened to Leary, the prized pitching prospect in the organization, and it only served to widen the breach between him and his manager. Despite the fact that he had another year on his contract, Torre was fighting for survival and he knew it. Now Cashen was waiting for the chance to bring in his own man.

In the spring of 1981, Torre also sought to resolve the Mets' long-running third base problem by offering the job to Joel Youngblood. Youngblood had played the infield and the outfield and was proud of his arm as a right fielder. He did not like the idea of shifting to third full-time. After only a few days at that position, Youngblood went to Torre and told him he didn't want the job. For years Joel had been whining that he never got a chance to play regularly, but now, with a chance to play third every day, he declined the opportunity offered.

John Stearns, the regular catcher and always a team player, offered to play third base. A day before the season opened in Chicago, Stearns stepped on a baseball while running in the outfield, sprained his ankle, and left the park on crutches. Torre then handed the third base job to promising rookie Hubie Brooks, and Brooks responded with a .308 season and everyday improvement

OPENING DAY LINEUP 1981

Wilson, rf
Taveras, ss
Mazzilli, cf
Kingman, lf
Staub, 1b
Trevino, c
Brooks, 3b
Flynn, 2b
Zachry, p

The brightest spot of the 1981 season was the emergence of Hubie Brooks and Mookie Wilson as bona fide rookies, both products of the Mets farm system. Brooks had his best season as a rookie, batting .307. After some fielding problems, Brooks got steadier as his average declined to a low of .251 in 1983. Davey Johnson instilled confidence in Brooks, and he rebounded in 1984, having switched to shortstop, and hit .283 with sixteen home runs. Brooks was then traded in a deal that brought the Mets Gary Carter.

at his new position. Youngblood played right field for forty-one games before moving over to the disabled list with damaged ligaments in his left knee after a hard slide on June 6.

While Torre was trying to put the pieces together, Cashen was continuing his search for talent. In early April he traded Bomback to Toronto for Charlie Puleo, a right-handed pitcher. At the end of May he traded Jeff Reardon and Dan Norman to Montreal for Ellis Valentine. It wasn't one of Cashen's better deals, but at the time he was trying to put together an offense to offset the club's weak pitching. Valentine had been an outstanding prospect with the Expos who had run afoul of the Montreal club because of personal problems.

1981

NAME	G by POS	B	AGE	G	AB	R	H	2B	3B	HR	RBI	BB	SO	SB	BA	SA
NEW YORK 5th	17-34 .333 15					JOE TORRE										
4th	24-28 .462 5.5															
—	41-62 .398 —															
TOTALS			30	105	3493	348	868	136	35	57	325	304	603	103	.248	.356
Dave Kingman	1B56, OF48	R	32	100	353	40	78	11	3	22	59	55	105	6	.221	.456
Doug Flynn	2B100, SS5	R	30	105	325	24	72	12	4	1	20	11	19	1	.222	.292
Frank Taveras	SS79	R	31	84	283	30	65	11	3	0	11	12	36	16	.230	.290
Hubie Brooks	3B93, OF3, SS1	R	24	96	358	34	110	21	2	4	38	23	65	9	.307	.411
Joel Youngblood	OF41	R	29	43	143	16	50	10	2	4	25	12	2	.350	.531
Mookie Wilson	OF80	B	25	92	328	49	89	8	8	3	14	20	59	24	.271	.372
Lee Mazzilli	OF89	B	26	95	324	36	74	14	5	6	34	46	53	17	.228	.358
John Stearns	C66, 1B9, 3B4	R	29	80	273	25	74	12	1	1	24	24	17	12	.271	.333
Mike Jorgensen	1B40, OF19	L	32	86	122	8	25	5	2	3	15	12	24	4	.205	.352
Rusty Staub	1B41	L	37	70	161	9	51	9	0	5	21	22	12	1	.317	.466
Mike Cubbage	3B12	L	30	67	80	9	17	2	2	1	4	9	15	0	.213	.325
Alex Trevino	C45, 2B4, OF2, 3B1	R	23	56	149	17	39	2	0	0	10	13	19	3	.262	.275
Bob Bailor	SS22, 2B13, OF13, 3B1	R	29	51	81	11	23	3	1	0	8	8	11	2	.284	.346
Ellis Valentine	OF47	R	26	48	169	15	35	8	1	5	21	5	38	0	.207	.355
Ron Hodges	C7	L	32	35	43	5	13	2	0	1	6	5	8	1	.302	.419
Ron Gardenhire	SS18, 2B6, 3B1	R	23	27	48	2	13	1	0	0	3	5	9	2	.271	.292
Wally Backman	2B11, 3B1	B	21	26	36	5	10	2	0	0	0	4	7	1	.278	.333
Mike Howard	OF14	B	23	14	24	4	4	1	0	0	3	4	6	2	.167	.208
Brian Giles	2B2, SS2	R	21	9	7	0	0	0	0	0	0	0	3	0	.000	.000

NAME	T	AGE	W	L	PCT	SV	G	GS	CG	IP	H	BB	SO	ShO	ERA
		28	41	62	.398	24	105	105	7	926	906	336	490	3	3.55
Neil Allen	R	23	7	6	.538	18	43	0	0	67	64	26	50	0	2.96
Pat Zachry	R	29	7	14	.333	0	24	24	3	139	151	56	76	0	4.14
Pete Falcone	L	27	5	3	.625	1	35	9	3	95	84	36	56	1	2.56
Mike Scott	R	26	5	10	.333	0	23	23	1	136	130	34	54	0	3.90
Ed Lynch	R	25	4	5	.444	0	17	13	0	80	79	21	27	0	2.93
Mike Marshall	R	38	3	2	.600	0	20	0	0	0	31	26	8	0	2.61
Greg Harris	R	25	3	5	.375	1	16	14	0	69	65	28	54	0	4.43
Danny Boitano	R	28	2	1	.667	0	15	0	0	16	21	5	8	0	5.63
Ray Searage	L	26	1	0	1.000	0	26	0	0	37	34	17	16	0	3.65
Dyar Miller	R	35	1	0	1.000	0	23	0	0	38	49	15	22	0	3.32
Jeff Reardon	R	25	1	0	1.000	2	18	0	0	29	27	12	28	0	3.41
Terry Leach	R	27	1	1	.500	0	21	1	0	35	26	12	16	0	2.57
Randy Jones	L	31	1	8	.111	0	13	12	0	59	65	38	14	0	4.88
Charlie Puleo	R	26	0	0	—	0	4	1	0	13	8	8	8	0	0.00
Tim Leary	R	22	0	0	—	0	1	1	0	2	0	1	3	0	0.00
Tom Hausman	R	28	0	1	.000	0	20	0	0	33	28	7	13	0	2.18
Jesse Orosco	L	24	0	1	.000	1	8	0	0	17	13	6	18	0	1.59
Craig Swan	R	30	0	2	.000	0	5	3	0	14	10	1	9	0	3.21
Dave Roberts	L	36	0	3	.000	0	7	4	0	15	26	5	10	0	9.60

The Mets were willing to ignore them if Valentine could live up to his superstar potential. He never did.

Torre started the season with an outfield of Kingman in left, Mazzilli in center, and another promising rookie, Mookie Wilson, in right. Mazzilli developed back problems that resulted in a horrendous slump. In late May, Torre brought Kingman in to play first, shifted Mazzilli to left, and installed Wilson as the center fielder.

It did not take the Mets long to settle into fifth place. They reached the next to last spot in the division on April 26 and stayed there until the major league players went out on strike on June 12. The Mets were then fifteen games out of first place.

When play resumed two months later, a "second season" was instituted by Commissioner Kuhn. The team in first place before the strike would play the team in first place at the end of the season. Torre, sensing a chance to steal a "half pennant," stressed that point to his team when play resumed August 10.

The Mets actually were in first place or tied for the top spot for the first two weeks of the second half season. They beat Chicago two out of three upon resumption of play and won six of their first nine games before tumbling into second place. For two games they stayed above .500, and then the lack of talent started to show.

Jones, who won only one game before the players' strike, sprained his ankle on a wet pitcher's mound in Toronto in an exhibition game prior to the second season opening. Tom Hausman developed bone chips in his elbow in the same game. Hausman never pitched again that season; Jones was not used at all the final month.

Of the nineteen pitchers employed by Torre that season, no one won more than seven games. Kingman managed twenty-two homers but hit only .221. Youngblood hit .350 in the forty-one games he played but didn't play after August 14. Mazzilli slumped to .228 and Valentine to .207. Only Allen had an outstanding year. He again was the big man in the bullpen, with seven victories and eighteen saves. Of the forty-one games won by the Mets, Allen had a hand in twenty-five of them.

On the final Sunday of the season, Torre requested a meeting with Cashen to ascertain the future of his coaches. He had one year remaining on his contract. The coaches' contracts were expiring. At the meeting Torre was informed that he would be paid off and he and his coaches were being released.

It was no secret who Torre's successor would be. During the playoffs in Montreal between the Expos and Dodgers, the story broke that George Bamberger, an old friend of Cashen's from Baltimore, had been selected. Bamberger, who had pitched briefly for the New York Giants and was a native of Staten Island, New York, was a longtime pitching coach in Baltimore before becoming a successful manager in Milwaukee. A heart attack in spring training 1980 sidelined him until June; he returned for three months, then retired in September 1980.

When Cashen first contacted Bamberger, he got a flat refusal. Cashen did not give up easily, and on what could have been his last attempt, he got a "yes" from Bamberger.

"When the phone rang, I knew it was Frank. When I got up to answer the phone, I was all set to tell him no. But when I picked it up, I couldn't say no. I said yes," Bamberger explained. "What the heck, Frank is an old friend. He needed me. I couldn't let him down. I did it for Frank, no other reason."

That was the way Bamberger accepted the job as manager of the Mets at a salary he later revealed was in excess of $200,000 and included a long-term post-career salary as a consultant. He also accepted, Bamberger said, because coming back to New York, "where I grew up, was a challenge."

As a rookie in 1981, Mookie Wilson batted .271 and stole an eye-popping twenty-four bases in the shortened season. He led the club.
PETER SIMON

George Bamberger took over the team in 1982, one more member of Frank Cashen's Baltimore connection. Bamberger gave it his best but couldn't stand losing all the time and finally resigned in the middle of 1985. "Bambi" had endured a heart bypass operation and felt he could be jeopardizing his life by subjecting himself to the pressure of living in New York with a losing team.
DAILY NEWS/HARRY HAMBURG

OPENING DAY LINEUP 1982

Wilson, cf
Bailor, 2b
Foster, lf
Kingman, 1b
Youngblood, rf
Stearns, c
Brooks, 3b
Gardenhire, ss
Jones, p

Bamberger, who lived in Redington Beach, Florida, said a third reason for coming out of retirement was the proximity of the Mets' spring training base in St. Petersburg. He lived only ten minutes away.

"This way I'm home half the year, even when I'm in spring training," he explained. "And in October, when they get the kids here for the Instructional League, I can come over and watch them and work with them."

Although Bamberger was a pitcher's manager, he had developed solid hitting teams in Milwaukee. Solid hitting can overcome mediocre pitching, as Bamberger's Brewers proved. With a Mets lineup that up to that point fielded only one legitimate slugger in Kingman, Cashen, on February 10, 1982, presented his friend with another bona fide home run hitter. In a deal that sent catcher Alex Trevino and pitchers Greg Harris and Jim Kern to Cincinnati, Cashen obtained George Foster. (Kern had been obtained in a trade the previous December and never got a chance to play for the Mets.) For years, Foster had been one of the most productive sluggers in the National League. For seven consecutive seasons, he had hit twenty or more homers, with a high of fifty-two in 1977. Foster also averaged 90 RBIs per season and in three consecutive years had knocked in more than 100. He also came with a reputation pinned on him by former Cincinnati teammate Pete Rose.

"I never once saw him get his uniform dirty," said Rose. "He doesn't dive for balls and he will never go to the wall for a ball if it means crashing into the wall."

The signing of Foster was announced at a gala press conference in the Shea Stadium Diamond Club. The Mets were so proud of their newest acquisition they even, for the first time, revealed the terms of Foster's contract, one of the most lucrative in baseball history—he received $1 million just for agreeing to sign with the Mets. He also signed a guaranteed contract for five years, with salaries starting at $1.45 million and escalating to $1.8 million. There also were two option years tagged on that would cost the Mets close to another $1 million if they did not pick them up. In addition there was a bonus clause based on the Mets' attendance. Most of all, from a public relations standpoint, there was evidence in signing Foster that the new owners were willing to spend money to develop a winner.

Immediately there were predictions that with Foster and Kingman in the lineup, the pair would hit between sixty and seventy homers. Bamberger said his only concern was who to bat in the number 5 slot behind them—Ellis

Valentine or Joel Youngblood. Regardless, the Mets were going into the season with the most powerful pair of sluggers in their history.

Kingman lived up to his end of the bargain. He hit thirty-seven home runs. If Foster had hit thirty-three, they would have had their seventy. But Foster, with the pressure of having to produce, hit only thirteen. He also batted only .247. With Kingman hitting .203 and Foster .247, the Mets did not have much going for them in the middle of the lineup when one or the other did not connect for a home run. Valentine hit .288 without any power and appeared in only ninety-eight games. Twice during the year Valentine popped off, once about the way Bamberger was handling him and the second time about the way the club was treating him. At the end of the year Bamberger was glad to see Ellis leave as a free agent. He had never measured up to the standards expected of him.

Bamberger managed to keep the Mets competitive for the first two and a half months of the season. As late as June 21 they still were in third place with a 34–31 record. Playing .500 ball for as long as they did excited the fans, and attendance was on the rise again. But Bambi was doing it with mirrors, because he had no pitching staff to speak of. Cashen had gone out and gotten him hitters but left him without pitchers.

On April 1, 1982, Cashen made a deal for two pitchers, but it would be another year or two before they produced for the Mets. That deal was made close to midnight on April 1. It sent Mazzilli to the Texas Rangers for pitchers Ron Darling and Walt Terrell. It ranks as one of the best deals the Mets ever made.

Mazzilli was in a St. Petersburg Beach bar when he learned of the trade. He was stunned. The players involved bruised his ego.

"You mean they traded me for two minor leaguers?" he asked *Newark Star Ledger* writer Dan Castellano when he called the Bayfront Concourse Hotel at midnight to verify the deal. He could not believe that was all he was worth. Darling and Terrell went on to become outstanding pitchers for the Mets while Mazzilli's stock continued to drop after he left the Mets.

Bamberger was supposed to work magic with pitchers. He had earned a reputation as the brains behind the great Baltimore pitching staffs. But except for Swan, whom he coddled and brought along carefully from his rotator cuff problem, Bamberger could do nothing with the Mets' pitching staff. Swan was the biggest winner with eleven, and Puleo, the pickup from Toronto, was next with nine. Falcone had another losing season at 8–10, and Randy Jones was 7–10. As Torre had the year before, Bamberger dropped Jones from the rotation in August and rarely used him down the stretch.

The situation could have been worse. If they had not had Neil Allen, there is no telling how low the Mets might have sunk in the standings. As it was, they finished sixth with a 65–97 record and were twenty-seven games out at the end of the year. Without Allen they might have been forty-seven games out.

Allen by now had developed into one of the game's top relievers. In his last two seasons he had saved forty games while winning another fourteen. By June 14, 1982, he had already saved fifteen games and won another two. The Mets had thirty-one victories at the time, and he had a hand in winning seventeen of those. But on June 14, Allen was felled with an attack of the flu. He was confined to his hotel room and finally sent back to New York. He could keep nothing on his stomach. Upon reaching New York, he was examined by Mets doctors, who determined Allen had a colon infection. He was lost for two weeks.

For the balance of the season, Allen pitched in a weakened condition; he saved only four more games. From August 6 until September 7 he was sidelined with elbow tendonitis. He made three token appearances in September. For the Mets, this was the cruelest blow of all. The last player they could

After signing the richest contract in baseball, George Foster shows up at spring training all smiles, shaking the hand of fellow outfielder Ellis Valentine. Foster managed to post only mediocre stats in 1982 (after being awesome for the Reds) and hasn't won the hearts of Mets fans—no head-first dives or going from first to third on a single, to say nothing of not driving in the key runs to win games. On paper, his stats did improve, especially as the team improved around him, but his home runs and RBIs were generally in games already won or lost.
UPI/BETTMAN NEWSPHOTO

afford to lose was their star reliever. Shortly after Allen was sidelined in August the Mets lost fifteen in a row and dropped into the basement.

"There is no doubt in my mind that Allen would have saved thirty-five games if we had him all year," said Bamberger. "I know we would not have lost fifteen in a row if we had him. The two worst things that happened to us all year was Allen getting sick and Foster having an off-year."

In 1982, just as in the previous season, the Phillies did the Mets in. On the weekend of June 25–27, the Mets played the Phillies five games in three days and lost all five. They were down to one catcher at the time, so Stearns had to catch every inning, including doubleheaders on consecutive nights. It wore him out completely. Hubie Brooks also bit the dust in that series. Playing with a pulled hamstring—because there was no one else to take his place—Hubie aggravated it in Philadelphia. By June 21 he was placed on the disabled list, where he remained for an entire month.

Stearns, who had been the number 1 catcher, complained of a soreness in his elbow in June. He continued to play but the injury flared up in July while he was playing third base. He played until August 12 and then he, too, went on the disabled list a week later with "muscular tendonitis of the elbow." He never again was much use as a player despite his conscientious attendance in rehabilitation programs and a sincere comeback effort.

With Stearns lost for the last couple of months, Ron Hodges wound up catching seventy-four games. Hodges was a second- or third-string catcher at best, valuable coming off the bench as a left-handed pinch hitter. He was not someone who should have been a team's everyday catcher, but that is what he became in late 1982.

Right field was another disaster area. Bamberger alternated Valentine and Youngblood and neither did well. Youngblood was at .257 when he was traded to Montreal in August. Valentine batted .288 with minimal power and when at the end of the season he became a free agent, the Mets made no effort to retain him.

About the only bright spot of the season was Mookie Wilson, who established himself as the team's center fielder. A hustling player, he soon became the favorite of fans because of his daring on the bases; Wilson hit .279 and stole fifty-eight bases.

By the time the 1983 season rolled around, Cashen had pulled off one of the greatest public relations coups in the club's history. He succeeded in bringing Tom Seaver back from Cincinnati.

After a 14–2 record in the strike-interrupted 1981 season, Seaver suffered through his worst season in 1982. He was felled by the flu in the spring and did not get in his proper training routine. For a power pitcher like Seaver, the training routine in Florida is all-important. Because he was prevented from following his normal schedule in 1982, Seaver did not start a game until the season was almost two weeks old. He was not even ready then, and by July he began to experience back and shoulder problems. He started his final game on August 15, leaving after only two innings. The last six weeks of the season were spent pitching on the sidelines. Seaver's 5–13 record and 5.50 earned run average in 1982 convinced the Reds that he was finished. It was the first losing season he had experienced.

The Mets were not convinced that Tom's career was over. At the winter meetings in Honolulu Cashen inquired about Seaver's availability and was informed that he was indeed on the block. It was just a matter of working out the details of a deal. On December 16, after returning from Hawaii, the deal was completed. Seaver came back home, and the Mets sent Charlie Puleo and two minor leaguers to the Reds in exchange. It was a move roundly applauded in the New York press. Cashen and the new owners were riding a wave of popularity.

1982

NAME	G by POS	B	AGE	G	AB	R	H	2B	3B	HR	RBI	BB	SO	SB	BA	SA
NEW YORK 6th 65-97 .401 27	**GEORGE BAMBERGER**															
TOTALS			29	162	5510	609	1361	227	26	97	568	456	1005	137	.247	.350
Dave Kingman	1B143	R	33	149	535	80	109	9	1	37	99	59	156	4	.204	.432
Wally Backman	2B88, 3B6, SS1	B	22	96	261	37	71	13	2	3	22	49	47	8	.272	.372
Ron Gardenhire	SS135, 2B1, 3B1	R	24	141	384	29	92	17	1	3	33	23	55	5	.240	.313
Hubie Brooks	3B126	R	25	126	457	40	114	21	2	2	40	28	76	6	.249	.317
Ellis Valentine	OF98	R	27	111	337	33	97	14	1	8	48	5	38	1	.288	.407
Mookie Wilson	OF156	B	26	159	639	90	178	25	9	5	55	32	102	58	.279	.369
George Foster	OF138	R	33	151	550	64	136	23	2	13	70	50	123	1	.247	.367
John Stearns	C81, 3B12	R	30	98	352	46	103	25	3	4	28	30	35	17	.293	.415
Mike Jorgensen	1B56, OF16	L	33	120	114	16	29	6	0	2	14	21	24	2	.254	.360
Rusty Staub	OF27, 1B18	L	38	112	219	11	53	9	0	3	27	24	10	0	.242	.324
Bob Bailor	SS60, 2B56, 3B21, OF4	R	30	110	376	44	104	14	1	0	31	20	17	20	.277	.319
Ron Hodges	C74	L	33	80	228	26	56	12	1	5	27	41	40	4	.246	.373
Joel Youngblood	OF63, 2B8	R	30	80	202	21	52	12	0	3	21	8	37	0	.257	.361
Gary Rajsich	OF35, 1B2	L	27	80	162	17	42	8	3	2	12	17	40	1	.259	.383
Brian Giles	2B45, SS2	R	22	45	138	14	29	5	0	3	10	12	29	6	.210	.312
Tom Veryzer	2B26, SS16	R	29	40	54	6	18	2	0	0	4	3	4	1	.333	.370
Mike Howard	OF22, 2B3	B	24	33	39	5	7	0	0	1	3	6	7	2	.179	.256
Bruce Bochy	C16, 1B1	R	27	17	49	4	15	4	0	2	8	4	6	0	.306	.510
Phil Mankowski	3B13	L	29	13	35	2	8	1	0	0	4	1	6	0	.229	.257
Rusty Tilman	OF3	R	21	12	13	4	2	1	0	0	0	0	4	1	.154	.231
Rick Sweet		B	29	3	3	0	1	0	0	0	0	0	1	0	.333	.333
Ronn Reynolds	C2	R	23	2	4	0	0	0	0	0	0	1	1	0	.000	.000

NAME	T	AGE	W	L	PCT	SV	G	GS	CG	IP	H	BB	SO	ShO	ERA
		28	65	97	.401	37	162	162	15	1447	1508	582	759	5	3.88
Craig Swan	R	31	11	7	.611	1	37	21	2	166	165	37	67	0	3.35
Charlie Puleo	R	27	9	9	.500	1	36	24	1	171	179	90	98	1	4.47
Pete Falcone	L	28	8	10	.444	2	40	23	3	171	159	71	101	0	3.84
Randy Jones	L	32	7	10	.412	0	28	20	2	108	130	51	44	1	4.60
Mike Scott	R	27	7	13	.350	3	37	22	1	147	185	60	63	0	5.14
Pat Zachry	R	30	6	9	.400	1	36	16	2	138	149	57	69	0	4.05
Ed Lynch	R	26	4	8	.333	2	43	12	0	139	145	40	51	0	3.55
Jesse Orosco	L	25	4	10	.286	4	54	2	0	109	92	40	89	0	2.72
Neil Allen	R	24	3	7	.300	19	50	0	0	65	65	30	59	0	3.06
Terry Leach	R	28	2	1	.667	3	21	1	1	45	46	18	30	1	4.17
Scott Holman	R	23	2	1	.667	0	4	4	1	27	23	7	11	0	2.36
Tom Hausman	R	29	1	2	.333	0	21	0	0	37	44	6	16	0	4.42
Rick Ownbey	R	24	1	2	.333	0	8	8	2	50	44	43	28	0	3.75
Carlos Diaz	L	24	0	0	—	4	4	0	0	6	6	4	0	0	0.00
Doug Sisk	R	24	0	1	.000	1	8	0	0	9	5	4	4	0	1.04
Tom Gorman	L	24	0	1	.000	0	3	1	0	9	8	0	7	0	0.96
Brent Gaff	R	23	0	3	.000	0	7	5	0	33	41	10	14	0	4.55
Walt Terrell	R	24	0	3	.000	0	3	3	0	21	22	14	8	0	3.43

Tom Seaver had an encore with the Mets in 1983. As the banner indicates, fans were glad to have him back. He pitched on opening day, amidst great drama, and got the win, 2–0, with help from Doug Sisk. Nostalgia outweighed performance: his record, 9–14, with a 3.55 ERA for the season.

OPENING DAY LINEUP 1983

Wilson, cf
Bailor, ss
Kingman, 1b
Foster, lf
Brooks, 3b
Howard, rf
Giles, 2b
Hodges, c
Seaver, p

One month later the Mets obtained veteran pitcher Mike Torrez from Boston in exchange for a minor leaguer. It was obvious that Cashen was giving Bamberger some of the pitching strength he had missed in his first year. Seaver and Torrez would be two veteran arms to counterbalance the young pitchers the farm system was by now providing.

The Mets still were in need of a right-handed bat in spring training when Cashen sent a couple of minor leaguers to the Dodgers in exchange for outfielder Mark Bradley. That deal did not pan out, but at least Cashen was making moves, giving the fans reason to believe the team was on the rise.

Seaver returned to Shea Stadium in triumph on opening day 1983. Sensing the drama of the situation with 48,682 fans in the stands, the Mets kept Tom in the bullpen until the entire team had taken the field for the first inning. And then came the simple announcement from public address announcer Jack Franchetti, ". . . and pitching, number 41," as Seaver walked in from the right field bullpen. The crowd responded with a five-minute standing ovation.

"It was very nice, very emotional," Seaver admitted after the game. "The Mets fans have always treated me well."

Seaver did not win opening day. He pitched only six innings. But the old Seaver magic was still there. He shut out the Phillies on three hits and struck out five, then watched on television in the clubhouse as the Mets won it, 2–0. Reliever Doug Sisk picked up the victory. It was like old times at Shea, Seaver pitching and the Mets winning.

Swan won, 6–2, the next day and the new season was off to a glorious start. But then reality set in; the Mets won only four more games in April while losing eleven. While the Mets were in St. Louis in April, they made front page news—two of their players, Neil Allen and Mark Bradley, became involved in an after-hours barroom fight over a young woman. They had also broken curfew. And then the next day Bradley was late for a team meeting. Both players were fined. All this occurred before Bradley ever played a game for the Mets.

Allen had his troubles on the field as well. He'd saved nineteen games the previous year but could not get anyone out in April of 1983. He was 0–3 in a hurry, had only two saves, and also blew several leads. He admitted he was "afraid to throw the ball." At the end of the month he failed to show up at the ballpark for two days. He called in one day and said his wife was sick and he was rushing her to a Long Island hospital. But *Newsday*, the Long Island newspaper, checked all hospitals in the area and discovered there was no Mrs. Allen admitted to any of them. Late that afternoon, Marty Noble of *Newsday* drove to Allen's Syosset, Long Island, home. There, in front of his wife and Noble, Allen confessed to having a drinking problem.

When Noble's story appeared the following day, the Mets immediately had Allen checked out by the Alcohol Rehabilitation program at Roosevelt Hospital. Although it was their conclusion that Allen's drinking problem was more imagined than real, it was the beginning of the end for the once great relief star.

On May 4, with the Mets having won only six of their first twenty-one games, Cashen made a move he really did not relish. He called Darryl Strawberry up from Tidewater. Strawberry's arrival was treated in the New York press like the second coming of Willie Mays. He had many talents similar to Mays's. He could hit for power, was an outstanding fielder and thrower, and had great speed on the bases. He also was twenty-one years old, about the same age Mays was when he joined the New York Giants in 1951 on his way to becoming a legend. Strawberry's name was magic in New York even before he took his first swing.

DOUBLEDAY TO THE RESCUE

189

Veteran pitcher Mike Torrez came over from the Red Sox in 1983 to try to add some solidity to the Mets' starting rotation but wound up leading the league with seventeen losses and an unimpressive 4.37 ERA. Fans became impatient with Torrez, especially after he was bombed by Cincinnati on opening day in 1984. He was released in June with a depressing 1–5 (5.02 ERA) record.
UPI/BETTMAN NEWSPHOTO

It was ironic, in a way. In June 1980, when the Mets had first pick in the nation in the free agent draft, they debated whether to select Strawberry or Billy Beane, an outfielder from San Diego. Forces in the front office were divided over the two players even on the morning of the draft. Finally, they decided on Strawberry. How fortunate they were became evident when Beane was ignored by the other twenty-one clubs so that the Mets were able to select Billy the next time around. Six years later Strawberry was entering his fourth year of major league ball; Beane was still struggling to make the club.

At Crenshaw High School in Los Angeles—because of his build and lean, long look, his left-handed swing, and his power—Strawberry was already being referred to by local sportswriters as "the black Ted Williams." In his junior year he hit .371 with four home runs; he added five more in his senior year when he hit .400.

Strawberry had an exceptional rookie season, batting .257 but impressing everyone with his power. He hit twenty-six home runs and drove in seventy-four runs in just 122 games. He also stole nineteen bases. "Darryl is easily the best young hitter I have seen in fourteen years in the big leagues," said Coach Jim Frey, Darryl's mentor and father confessor that first season.

"Looking at him at the age of twenty-one—what he has done and what he can do—is like a horse trainer looking at Man o' War as a two-year-old. It's silly to say he will hit thirty homers, because he almost did that his first year, and he's still learning and didn't even have a full year. So you have to say he's capable of hitting forty homers, and if he does that, he's in the top two percent of his class."

Strawberry made such an impression around the league that he wound up winning the 1983 National League Rookie-of-the-Year Award. Only two other Mets, Tom Seaver (in 1967) and Jon Matlack (in 1972), received that kind of recognition.

For all of Cashen's efforts to turn the Mets around, they still played badly. After the first three games of the season they never were any higher than fifth, and when they settled into sixth place at the end of May, it was for good. It also was more than Bamberger could handle. On the morning of June 2, while the Mets were on the West Coast, Bamberger called Cashen in New York. He was going to quit, he said, and he advised Cashen to get someone to replace him right away. Twice earlier Bamberger had attempted to turn in his resignation, and both times Cashen persuaded him to remain. By June, with

1983

NAME	G by POS	B	AGE	G	AB	R	H	2B	3B	HR	RBI	BB	SO	SB	BA	SA
NEW YORK 6th 68-94 .420 22																
TOTALS			27	162	5444	575	1314	172	26	112	542	436	1031	141	.241	.344
GEORGE BAMBERGER 16-30 .348																
FRANK HOWARD 52-64 .448																
Keith Hernandez	1B90	L	29	95	320	43	98	8	3	9	37	64	42	8	.306	.434
Brian Giles	2B140, SS12	R	23	145	400	39	98	15	0	2	27	36	77	17	.245	.298
Jose Oquendo	SS116	R	19	120	328	29	70	7	0	1	17	19	60	8	.213	.244
Hubie Brooks	3B145, 2B7	R	26	150	586	53	147	18	4	5	58	24	96	6	.251	.321
Darryl Strawberry	OF117	L	21	122	420	63	108	15	7	26	74	47	128	19	.257	.512
Mookie Wilson	OF148	B	27	152	638	91	176	25	6	7	51	18	103	54	.276	.367
George Foster	OF153	R	34	157	601	74	145	19	2	28	90	38	111	1	.241	.419
Junior Ortiz	C67	R	23	68	185	10	47	5	0	0	12	3	34	1	.254	.281
Bob Bailor	SS75, 2B50, 3B11, OF3	R	31	118	340	33	85	8	0	1	30	20	23	18	.250	.282
Danny Heep	OF61, 1B14	L	25	115	253	30	64	12	0	8	21	29	40	3	.253	.395
Ron Hodges	C96	L	34	110	250	20	65	12	0	1	21	49	42	0	.260	.308
Rusty Staub	1B5, OF5	L	39	104	115	5	34	6	0	3	28	14	10	0	.296	.426
Dave Kingman	1B50, OF5	R	34	100	248	25	49	7	0	13	29	22	57	2	.198	.383
Mark Bradley	OF35	R	26	73	104	10	21	4	0	3	5	11	35	4	.202	.327
Mike Jorgensen	1B19	L	34	38	24	5	6	3	0	1	3	2	4	0	.250	.500
Tucker Ashford	3B15, 2B13, C1	R	28	35	56	3	10	0	1	0	2	7	4	0	.179	.214
Wally Backman	2B14, 3B2	B	23	26	42	6	7	0	1	0	3	2	8	0	.167	.214
Ronn Reynolds	C24	R	24	24	66	4	13	1	0	0	2	8	12	0	.197	.212
Ron Gardenhire	SS15	R	25	17	32	1	2	0	0	0	1	1	4	0	.063	.063
Clint Hurdle	3B9, OF1	L	25	13	33	3	6	2	0	0	2	2	10	0	.182	.242
Gary Rajsich	1B10	L	28	11	36	5	12	3	0	1	3	3	1	0	.333	.500
Mike Fitzgerald	C8	R	22	8	20	1	2	0	0	1	2	3	6	0	.100	.250
John Stearns		R	31	4	0	2	0	0	0	0	0	0	0	0	—	—
Mike Bishop	C3	R	24	3	8	2	1	1	0	0	0	3	4	0	.125	.250
Mike Howard	OF1	B	25	1	3	0	1	0	0	0	1	0	1	0	.333	.333

NAME	T	AGE	W	L	PCT	SV	G	GS	CG	IP	H	BB	SO	ShO	ERA
		28	68	94	.420	33	162	162	18	1451	1384	615	717	17	3.68
Jesse Orosco	L	26	13	7	.650	17	62	0	0	110	76	38	84	0	1.47
Ed Lynch	R	27	10	10	.500	0	30	27	1	175	208	41	44	0	4.28
Mike Torrez	R	36	10	17	.370	0	39	34	5	222	227	113	94	0	4.37
Tom Seaver	R	38	9	14	.391	0	34	34	5	231	201	86	135	2	3.55
Walt Terrell	R	25	8	8	.500	0	21	20	4	134	123	55	59	2	3.57
Doug Sisk	R	25	5	4	.556	11	67	0	0	104	88	59	33	0	2.24
Carlos Diaz	L	25	3	1	.750	2	54	0	0	83	62	35	64	0	2.05
Neil Allen	R	25	2	7	.222	2	21	4	0	54	57	36	32	1	4.50
Craig Swan	R	32	2	8	.200	1	27	18	0	96	112	42	43	0	5.51
Brent Gaff	R	24	1	0	1.000	0	4	0	0	10	18	1	4	0	6.10
Tim Leary	R	24	1	1	.500	0	2	2	1	11	15	4	9	0	3.38
Rick Ownbey	R	25	1	3	.250	0	10	4	0	35	31	21	19	0	4.67
Ron Darling	R	22	1	3	.250	0	5	5	1	35	31	17	23	0	2.80
Tom Gorman	L	25	1	4	.200	0	25	4	0	49	45	15	30	0	4.93
Scott Holman	R	24	1	7	.125	0	35	10	0	101	90	52	44	0	3.74

the team's record a dismal 16–30, Bamberger's stomach was churning so badly that he had to quit or possibly risk another heart attack.

"I didn't know how bad things were when I took the job," Bamberger said.

Cashen, in New York, pleaded with his friend to stay one more day until he could find a replacement. First Cashen called Earl Weaver, his former Baltimore manager. Weaver had recently retired from the Orioles. He told Cashen he wouldn't take the job. So Cashen flew to Los Angeles to join the team. After a meeting with Bamberger, Coach Frank Howard was asked to take over the club for the balance of the season.

Howard was a giant of a man with the personality of a pussycat. He was well liked by everyone. People did not dare not like this hulk of a man who stood six feet eight inches and weighed close to 300 pounds. Under Howard's quiet but driving leadership the Mets spurted to eleven wins in their next twenty-one games. Still, they were the same bad ball club they had been under Bamberger, and they soon settled down to their losing ways. Only in August, when they won sixteen and lost thirteen, did the Mets have a winning month. In that month, Orosco emerged as the new bullpen ace. He had been handed the role as number 1 reliever on June 15, after Cashen pulled off another blockbuster deal.

In the press room just prior to the June 15 game with the Cubs, Cashen announced that the Mets had obtained Gold Glove first baseman and former co-MVP Keith Hernandez in a deal with St. Louis. The Cardinals got Neil Allen and right-handed pitcher Rick Ownbey in exchange. Hernandez was one of the top quality players in the league, and the Mets were getting him in exchange for a pitcher who was not winning for them.

There was a strange background to the deal. In St. Louis, Cardinals manager Whitey Herzog was aware that several of his players were using drugs. He held a meeting and asked them to shape up and get help or he would get rid of them. He asked them to come to him privately, and he would help them. One week later, Hernandez was traded. Rumors were rampant that he was one of the users. Hernandez vehemently denied it. Two years later, at drug trials in

The mainstays of the Mets bullpen in 1983 were *(from left)* Doug Sisk, Jesse Orosco, who often credits his success to George Bamberger's support, and Carlos Diaz. Among them, the trio won twenty-one games and saved thirty. Carlos Diaz was traded (along with Bob Bailor) at the end of the season for Sid Fernandez. Sisk had the uncanny ability to walk men in key situations, then somehow managed to get out of the inning anyway. This latter talent suddenly deserted him in July 1984.
MICHAEL GERMANA

Brian Giles and Met rookie of the year Darryl Strawberry became close friends during the 1983 season. After a painfully slow start, Strawberry put together the kind of numbers the Mets were hoping for: twenty-six home runs, seventy-four RBIs, and a .257 batting average in only 117 games. Giles didn't have a bad year (.245), but he didn't improve enough to beat out Wally Backman for the second base job in 1984.
IRA GOLDEN

The sweet swing of Rusty Staub accounted for an outstanding .296 average as he led the major leagues with twenty-four pinch hits and tied the major league record with twenty-five RBIs. Rusty has proven to be one of the most popular Mets of all time.
IRA GOLDEN

Pittsburgh, Hernandez admitted he was addicted to cocaine while in St. Louis but said he had kicked the habit before leaving St. Louis.

Hernandez was virtually dumped in Cashen's lap. Earlier there had been rumors that the Mets and Yankees were about to swap Allen for catcher Rick Cerone. It was a false rumor, although the Yankees did inquire of the Mets if they were interested in Cerone. When Herzog heard that Allen might be available, he told Joe McDonald, by now the general manager of the Cardinals, to call Cashen and offer him Hernandez for Allen. Cashen jumped at the opportunity.

Even though Hernandez hit .306 in ninety-five games with the Mets and Orosco won thirteen and saved another seventeen, the Mets remained mired in last place. Seaver had the same problem he'd had in his first tour with the Mets. They couldn't score for him. Tom wound up with a 9–14 record in twenty-four starts. In one stretch he made a dozen starts in which the Mets scored only twenty-two runs for him.

RUSTY STAUB'S PINCH HITS FOR THE METS

Year	AB	H	HR	RBI	Ave.
1972	1				.000
1973	0				—
1974	4	2			.500
1975	2	1		1	.500
1981	24	9		6	.375
1982	57	12	1	13	.211
1983	81	24	3	25	.296
1984	66	18	1	18	.273
1985	42	11	1	8	.262
9	277	77	6	72	.278

Through the years at Shea, certain fans have become distinct celebrities. In the mid-sixties there was the "Mad Doctor," who always wore a yellow poncho and led cheers and chants from his seat. Actually, he was a radiologist at New York Hospital by the name of Anthony Principato. In the late seventies and early eighties, Karl Ehrhardt, pictured here, would come to Shea with a battery of different signs and would display them at critical moments. The year 1984 saw the birth of the K Korner. Mets management has generally treated these enthusiastic individuals well, giving them complementary seats. But occasionally, these eccentrics have outworn their welcomes.
LOUIS REQUENA

A dispute developed on July 26 between Rick Camp of Atlanta and Mike Torrez of the Mets. Torrez hit Camp with a pitch in the sixth inning, and Camp charged the mound. Here Keith Hernandez tackles the Braves pitcher as catcher Junior Ortiz tries to break up the fight. Umpires Doug Harvey (right) and Frank Pulli try to restore peace and tranquillity. Torrez, incidentally, went ten innings to get the win.
UPI/BETTMAN NEWSPHOTO

In what is arguably the best trade the Mets have ever made, Keith Hernandez (left) came to the Mets from St. Louis for Neil Allen (right) on June 15, 1983. Keith solidified the infield, talked sense to the pitchers by approaching the mound with good advice, and batted a solid .306 to lead the team.
IRA GOLDEN

GRAND SLAM HOME RUNS BY METS

Year	Player
1962	Kanehl, Thomas
1963	Hickman (2), Harkness, Willey
1964	Christopher, Hickman
1965	None
1966	Bressoud, B. Taylor
1967	Hamilton, T. Davis
1968	Shamsky
1969	C. Jones, Swoboda
1970	D. Marshall, Swoboda
1971	Agee, Boswell, D. Marshall
1972	Agee, Staub
1973	Milner (2), Staub (2), Grote
1974	None
1975	Staub, Kingman
1976	Milner (3)
1977	Henderson, Stearns
1978	Henderson, Mazzilli
1979	None
1980	Jorgensen
1981	Kingman (2)
1982	Hodges
1983	Foster (2)
1984	Chapman
1985	Carter (2), Strawberry (2), Foster, H. Johnson
1986	Foster, Teufel, Strawberry, Carter

Mike Torrez and Ed Lynch each won ten games to lead the staff, but the pitching for the most part was inadequate, and the team batting was a woeful .241. Foster led the club with twenty-eight homers, but Kingman, who hit twenty, sat and sulked after Hernandez arrived, rarely playing again after losing his first base job. At the end of the year he opted for free agency, and the Mets were glad to get rid of him for a second time.

Howard did the best he could under trying circumstances, but the Mets won only sixty-six and lost ninety-four and were twenty-two games out of first place at the conclusion of the season. Cashen was so distraught over the lack of progress that he took off to Ireland as soon as the season was over.

Mike Fitzgerald caught eight games for the Mets late in the 1983 season and hit a home run his first time up as a rookie against the Phillies. In 1984 he emerged (by default) as the Mets' starting catcher and had a good year defensively, but batted only .242 with two home runs, and was traded to Montreal along with Brooks for a much more productive catcher—Gary Carter.
DAILY NEWS/DANNY FARRELL

Darryl Strawberry beams after being named National League Rookie of the Year for 1983, ending four years of Dodgers dominance.

NATIONAL LEAGUE
ROOKIE OF THE YEAR

1966	Tommy Helms, Reds
1967	**TOM SEAVER, METS**
1968	Johnny Bench, Reds
1969	Ted Sizemore, Dodgers
1970	Carl Morton, Expos
1971	Earl Williams, Braves
1972	**JON MATLACK, METS**
1973	Gary Matthews, Giants
1974	Bake McBride, Cardinals
1975	John Montefusco, Giants
1976	Pat Zachry, Reds
	Butch Metzger, Padres
1977	Andre Dawson, Expos
1978	Bob Horner, Braves
1979	Rick Sutcliffe, Dodgers
1980	Steve Howe, Dodgers
1981	Fernando Valenzuela, Dod
1982	Steve Sax, Dodgers
1983	**DARRYL STRAWBERRY**

ashen's search for a new manager did not take long. Even before he told Howard he would not be retained in 1984, the general manager had contacted Davey Johnson, his Tidewater manager. They met for a preliminary discussion at the Atlanta airport in late September. Johnson had flown up from his Orlando home and Cashen was en route west to join the Mets in St. Louis. Ten days later, Johnson flew to New York on the final night of the season. There they consummated a deal that would be announced on October 13 in Philadelphia during the World Series between the Phillies and Baltimore. Johnson became the tenth manager in the club's history. His contract was for two years.

The Cashen-Johnson relationship was a strange one from the start. Their personalities are as different as day and night. Cashen is an extremely private person, almost to the point of being shy in front of people, although he can be a charmer when he is at ease. Johnson is outgoing and outspoken. Whereas Cashen weighs every word carefully when he answers a question, his manager shoots from the hip. In their Baltimore days when Cashen was the general manager and Johnson the Orioles' second baseman, Davey was annually the toughest player Cashen had to sign.

"He would come in with all these statistics he had gathered from a computer, explaining his value to the team, why he should bat higher in the lineup, etc.," Cashen said. "He wasn't easy to deal with."

But one thing Cashen did know when he hired Johnson as his manager. He knew the former Orioles player had managed well in the minors and was ready for the big leagues.

"He is a proven winner as a player and as a manager. It's exciting to have him managing the Mets. Our club is ready to make a move, and Johnson can be the catalyst."

Before he managed his first game, Johnson suffered a blow when Tom Seaver was drafted by the Chicago White Sox in what was then baseball's free agent compensation pool. Each club participating in the pool was able to protect a certain number of players while leaving others vulnerable. The Mets, never thinking that anyone would draft a forty-year-old pitcher who was an institution with his team, did not think to protect Seaver. They were more concerned with protecting young prospects they felt would be vulnerable.

The Mets' thinking was accurate in theory, according to Roland Hemond, general manager of the Chicago White Sox. But theory didn't count for much, and the Sox had a compensation pick coming from the pool after losing relief pitcher Dennis Lamp to the Toronto Blue Jays through free agency.

"As soon as I got their list, I looked to see which kids they protected. But when I saw the list and saw that Seaver was not protected, I almost jumped out of my seat," said Hemond. "Seaver, in my mind, was still a quality pitcher who could win ten or fifteen games. Where are you going to get someone who can guarantee you that. That's the reason we picked Seaver."

The Mets, of course, were devastated. Not only did they not want to lose Seaver, but from a public relations standpoint it was the worst mistake they could have made. The criticism that followed Cashen for the next few days was as harsh as that Grant received when he traded Seaver in 1977.

The Mets rode out the storm that winter and made only one other deal of any consequence. At the winter meetings in Nashville, they sent relief pitcher Carlos Diaz and utility man Bob Bailor to the Dodgers in exchange for Sid Fernandez, a left-handed minor league strikeout phenomenon, and Ross Jones, a utility infielder. The Dodgers almost immediately started a whispering campaign that Fernandez had quit playing winter ball in the Dominican Republic because of arm trouble. The Mets hastened to deny the rumors. They had taken enough criticism on the loss of Seaver. They did not now want to

January 20, 1984. The New York media is present as Tom Seaver and Frank Cashen display their emotions when Tom Seaver bids good-bye to the Mets for the second time in his career. In a major public relations faux pas, Cashen failed to protect the pitcher. Noting he was unprotected, the Chicago White Sox stole him away. Frank Cashen's name was mud for much of the spring—until the Mets started winning in earnest.

UPI/BETTMAN NEWSPHOTO

NATIONAL LEAGUE ROOKIES OF THE YEAR

Year	Player
1967	Tom Seaver, p
1972	John Matlack, p
1983	Darryl Strawberry, of
1984	Dwight Gooden, p

explain why they had traded for a sore-armed pitcher. They were vindicated when Fernandez showed up in camp ready to pitch—overweight but sound of arm. A native Hawaiian, Fernandez had left the Dominican Republic, he said, "because I was homesick."

Johnson had one advantage when he took over in February 1984. He had handled many of the Mets' young players the two years he managed the farm teams at Jackson, Mississippi, and Tidewater, and he had spent another year as a roving instructor throughout the entire system. It was at Kingsport, Tennessee, in 1982 that Johnson first came in contact with the crown jewel in the Mets organization. The Kingsport manager that year was Ed Olsen, a college coach who was a little late reporting to his club. Johnson ran the team until Olsen got there. One of the young pitchers on the Kingsport staff was a seventeen-year-old named Dwight Gooden.

After watching Gooden throw a few times, Johnson called the home office. "You better check on this guy's birth certificate," he advised. "He can't be seventeen. Not the way he throws."

Johnson recognized Gooden's potential immediately. Not only did his fastball explode, but the kid had a wicked curve that he was able to get over the plate. You rarely find this kind of talent in so young a pitcher. Of course, Gooden was a one-in-a-million find. Fresh out of Hillsborough High School in Tampa, Florida, he struck out eighty-five batters in seventy-nine innings with Kingsport and Little Falls, New York, that summer and then went on to Lynchburg, Virginia, in 1983 to startle the minors with a 19–4 record and 300 strikeouts in 191 innings.

When Gooden was called up to Tidewater late in the 1983 season, Johnson used him in two International League playoff games.

"After seeing him in those two games I made up my mind that no matter where I managed the next year, Dwight would be my opening day pitcher," Johnson said.

Whether Johnson would even have Gooden on opening day 1984 was a matter of dispute from the day he assembled the Mets pitchers and catchers in St. Petersburg that February. There was no doubt in Johnson's mind that Gooden was ready to pitch in the majors. Convincing Cashen was another matter. The general manager was dead set against it from the start, pointing out that Gooden had never pitched above Class A ball and should have at least a year in Triple-A ball before attempting to pitch in the majors. Throughout the spring there was a tug-of-war between the manager and general manager over Gooden. Cashen also remembered the Tim Leary fiasco of 1981.

Gooden did not have a sensational spring in 1984. He appeared in five varsity games, worked eighteen innings, and struck out nine. But the nineteen-year-old's poise on the mound captured everyone's imagination, sportswriters as well as veteran major leaguers. People stopped whatever they were doing and watched every time Gooden took the mound. Finally, Johnson won his case; Cashen reluctantly agreed to promote the youngster to the major league roster.

"I began working on Frank early last winter," Johnson said with a smile.

There was a general misconception around the league that Gooden made the Mets as a replacement Seaver. That was not the case. He would like to have had both Seaver and Gooden, Johnson stressed. "No matter what, I always wanted Gooden, Seaver or no Seaver," he said.

Gooden and the Mets should remain ever grateful to Johnson for the way he handled the young pitcher that season. He watched over him like a mother hen, counted the pitches the young man threw and, early in the season, picked the proper spots for him to pitch.

Johnson began his first year with a pitching staff that included three veterans—Swan, Torrez, and Dick Tidrow, who had been signed as a free

Since 1984, when Dwight Gooden joined the Mets as a nineteen-year-old rookie, he has practically rewritten the team record book for pitching feats, as well as establishing many major league firsts.
PETER SIMON

OPENING DAY LINEUP 1984

Backman, 2b
Oquendo, ss
Hernandez, 1b
Foster, lf
Strawberry, rf
Wilson, cf
Brooks, 3b
Hodges, c
Torrez, p

agent. But he had no solid catcher, with Stearns still unable to throw, and a second baseman (Wally Backman) who, as a switch hitter, could hit left-handed but not right-handed. He also was without a major league shortstop. He was not enamored of Jose Oquendo, whom the front office considered the best shortstop prospect in the organization. Johnson felt that for all Jose's talents, he didn't know how to play the position and his hitting had always been weak. In early July, Oquendo was sent back to the minors, and Rafael Santana, originally signed by the Yankees and later released by the Cardinals, was brought up to play the second half. He proved to be a dandy, dependable player at his position until he was hurt in early September.

When Santana was sidelined, Ron Gardenhire played for a while, and then Hubie Brooks was shifted from third to short. Brooks played twenty-six games at the position, and the Montreal Expos were so impressed with the way he played that they were willing to deal Gary Carter for him that December.

When Johnson surveyed what he had in spring training, he decided he wanted to establish some of the young pitchers on his staff. The two pitchers obtained in the Mazzilli deal, Terrell and Darling, were both ready for the majors. So was Gooden, Johnson felt, but he was virtually compelled to open the season with a veteran, so Mike Torrez got the starting assignment in Cincinnati on April 2. Mike failed to last two innings, giving up six runs before his departure.

Darling and Doug Sisk combined to blank the Reds, 2–0, in the second game. These two games were the start of a nine-game road trip opening the season for the Mets. Critics feared that the Mets would come back to Shea Stadium on April 17 for their home opener with only one or two wins in their first nine games. Instead, the young pitchers were surprisingly effective.

After Darling won the second game, the Mets moved to Houston, where Terrell won, 8–1. Gooden made his major league debut in the next game. The Mets flew his parents in from Tampa to witness the event. If Gooden was nervous, he didn't show it. For five innings, he held the Astros to three hits, walked two, and struck out five. The Mets won, 3–2, and Gooden had a victory in his first major league start. It was the first of seventeen that would lead him to be named National League Rookie of the Year for 1984.

Six days later in Chicago, Gooden got his first taste of how cruel major league baseball can be. The Cubs walloped him for eight hits in less than four innings and stole bases almost at will, leaving him a very embarrassed young man when he was lifted in the fourth. The Mets lost, 11–2, but Gooden learned a lesson he never forgot. The next time he faced the Cubs they saw a different pitcher.

Johnson stayed with the veteran pitchers as long as he could before making a complete turnabout. In May, Swan was released after he had made ten ineffective relief appearances. Tidrow was dropped at the same time. Torrez lasted until the middle of June and then he, too, was dropped. The three veterans combined had won two games.

By July, Johnson was going with almost an all-rookie staff of Terrell, Gooden, Darling, and Sid Fernandez, who was recalled at the All-Star break. The only veterans in the rotation were Bruce Berenyi, who had been obtained from the Reds in a June 15 deal, and Ed Lynch, a holdover who had come from Texas in the Montanez trade several years earlier.

One week prior to the end of spring training, Cashen had told the Mets writers he thought the team could win the National League Eastern Division—the same team that had finished dead last the previous year. In Cashen's opinion, there was not a standout team in the division. He was right. But then the Chicago Cubs went out and traded for pitchers Dennis Eckersly and Rick Sutcliffe and outfielders Bob Dernier and Gary Matthews, and suddenly they were a different ball club. Chicago wound up the surprise team of the Eastern

Mookie Wilson, batting here against the Expos, had another good year in 1984. He led the team with forty-six stolen bases and batted .276 and showed some power (ten home runs). The only real problem with Mookie was his tendency to strike out (ninety times), not draw walks (only twenty-six), and swing at bad pitches. Because of this, he was dropped from the lead-off spot by Davey Johnson.
PETER SIMON

RAWLINGS NATIONAL LEAGUE GOLD GLOVE WINNERS

Year	Player
1970	Tommie Agee, of
1971	Bud Harrelson, ss
1980	Doug Flynn, 2b
1983	Keith Hernandez, 1b
1984	Keith Hernandez, 1b
1985	Keith Hernandez, 1b

Division, winning their first title of any kind in forty years. If the Cubs were a surprise, so were the Mets. No one expected them to be in first place as late as July 31, and no one anticipated they would be contenders all season long and finish second.

The various series between the Cubs and the Mets in 1984 were among the highlights of the baseball season. After losing the first two meetings in Chicago in April, the Mets won the next two games in New York, 8–1 and 4–3, behind Gooden and Lynch. Gooden had fanned ten batters for the first time in his previous start against Montreal. He had not yet caught the fancy of the fans, so only 13,000 were on hand when Gooden faced Chicago for the second time May 1. But he struck out another ten in that game, and suddenly the fans realized they might have the next strikeout king in their midst. Suddenly, K card signs (K is the strikeout symbol in scoring) began appearing on the railing of the upper deck every time Gooden struck out another batter.

By the time the All-Star game rolled around in July, Gooden had captured everyone's imagination. His record was 8–6, and he had already struck out ten

1984

NAME	G by POS	B	AGE	G	AB	R	H	2B	3B	HR	RBI	BB	SO	SB	BA	SA
NEW YORK 2nd 90-72 .556 6.5		DAVEY JOHNSON														
TOTALS			26	162	5438	652	1400	235	25	107	607	500	1001	149	.257	.369
Keith Hernandez	1B153	L	30	154	550	83	171	31	0	15	94	97	89	2	.311	.449
Wally Backman	2B115, SS8	B	24	128	436	68	122	19	2	1	26	56	63	32	.280	.339
Ron Gardenhire	SS49, 2B18, 3B7	R	26	74	207	20	51	7	1	1	10	9	43	6	.246	.304
Hubie Brooks	3B129, SS26	R	27	153	561	61	159	23	2	16	73	48	79	6	.283	.417
Darryl Strawberry	OF146	L	22	147	522	75	131	27	4	26	97	75	131	27	.251	.467
Mookie Wilson	OF146	B	28	154	587	88	162	28	10	10	54	26	90	46	.276	.409
George Foster	OF141	R	35	146	553	67	149	22	1	24	86	30	122	2	.269	.443
Mike Fitzgerald	C107	R	23	112	360	20	87	15	1	2	33	24	71	1	.242	.306
Danny Heep	OF48, 1B10	L	26	99	199	36	46	9	2	1	12	27	22	3	.231	.312
Jose Oquendo	SS67	B	20	81	189	23	42	5	0	0	10	15	26	10	.222	.249
Rusty Staub	1B3	L	40	78	72	2	19	4	0	1	18	4	9	0	.264	.361
Kelvin Chapman	2B57, 3B3	R	28	75	197	27	57	13	0	3	23	19	30	8	.289	.401
Ron Hodges	C35	L	35	64	106	5	22	3	0	1	11	23	18	1	.208	.264
Rafael Santana	SS50	R	26	51	152	14	42	11	1	1	12	9	17	0	.276	.382
Jerry Martin	OF30, 1B3	R	35	51	91	6	14	1	0	3	5	6	29	1	.154	.264
Junior Ortiz	C32	R	24	40	91	6	18	3	0	0	11	5	15	1	.198	.231
Ray Knight	3B27, 1B3	R	31	27	93	13	26	4	0	1	6	7	13	0	.280	.355
Ross Jones	SS6, 3B1	R	24	17	10	2	1	1	0	0	1	3	4	0	.100	.200
Herman Winningham	OF10	L	22	14	27	5	11	1	1	0	5	1	7	2	.407	.519
John Gibbons	C9	R	22	10	31	1	2	0	0	0	1	3	11	0	.065	.065
John Stearns	C4, 1B2	R	32	8	17	6	3	1	0	0	1	4	3	1	.176	.235
Kevin Mitchell	3B5	R	22	7	14	0	3	0	0	0	1	3	1	0	.214	.214
John Christensen	OF5	R	23	5	11	2	3	2	0	0	3	1	2	0	.273	.455
Billy Beane	OF5	R	22	5	10	0	1	0	0	0	0	2	1	0	.100	.100

NAME	T	AGE	W	L	PCT	SV	G	GS	CG	IP	H	BB	SO	ShO	ERA
		25	90	72	.556	50	162	162	12	1443	1371	573	1028	15	3.60
Dwight Gooden	R	19	17	9	.654	0	31	31	7	218	161	73	276	3	2.60
Ron Darling	R	23	12	9	.571	0	33	33	2	206	179	104	136	2	3.81
Walt Terrell	R	26	11	12	.478	0	33	33	3	215	232	80	114	1	3.52
Jesse Orosco	L	27	10	6	.625	31	60	0	0	87	58	34	85	0	2.59
Bruce Berenyi	R	29	9	6	.600	0	19	19	0	115	100	53	81	0	3.76
Ed Lynch	R	28	9	8	.529	2	40	13	0	124	169	24	62	0	4.50
Tom Gorman	L	26	6	0	1.000	0	36	0	0	58	51	13	40	0	2.97
Sid Fernandez	L	21	6	6	.500	0	15	15	0	90	74	34	62	0	3.50
Brent Gaff	R	25	3	2	.600	1	47	0	0	84	77	36	42	0	3.63
Tim Leary	R	25	3	3	.500	0	20	7	0	54	61	18	29	0	4.02
Craig Swan	R	33	1	0	1.000	0	10	0	0	19	18	7	10	0	8.20
Wes Gardner	R	23	1	1	.500	1	21	0	0	25	34	8	19	0	6.39
Doug Sisk	R	26	1	3	.250	15	50	0	0	78	57	54	32	0	2.09
Mike Torrez	R	37	1	5	.167	0	9	8	0	38	55	18	16	0	5.02
Dick Tidrow	R	37	0	0	—	0	11	0	0	16	25	7	8	0	9.19
Calvin Schiraldi	R	22	0	2	.000	0	5	3	0	17	20	10	16	0	5.71

Bruce Berenyi, picked up from the Reds around the trading deadline, filled a void in the Mets rotation, pitched well, and produced a 9–6 record. In this photo, he slowed the Cubs' drive toward the pennant by allowing only two singles and two runs in a Mets win on September 3 in Chicago.

UPI/BETTMAN NEWSPHOTO

OPENING DAY LINEUP 1985

Backman, 2b
Wilson, cf
Hernandez, 1b
Carter, c
Strawberry, rf
Foster, lf
Johnson, 3b
Santana, ss
Gooden, p

or more batters in seven games. He was leading the league in strikeouts and had pitched the Mets into first place. Ron Darling was 10–3 at the All-Star game, Berenyi had won three games as a Met, and Terrell had won another six. The young Mets pitchers were the talk of baseball, but Gooden's name was the one most prominently mentioned.

Johnson kept his young team in first place until the end of July. Then the Chicago Cubs came to town, and in two days they destroyed the Mets' pennant hopes. With first place on the line, 51,000 fans showed up to watch Gooden open against Dick Ruthven. By now, Gooden was simply known to his teammates as "Doc." The nickname was given to him in Little League ball by a teammate who, whenever the team was in trouble and a strikeout was needed, urged Gooden on by yelling, "Come on, Doctor, operate on them!" Doctor soon was shortened to Doc, and today that is what all the Mets players call him.

In the July 27 game, Gooden struck out eight Cubs in eight innings and, with help from Jesse Orosco, beat Chicago, 2–1. The Mets led by four and a half games. Then, in what proved to be the turning point of the season, disaster struck the next day. Darling pitched six good innings and turned a 3–3 tie over to Sisk. But Sisk had developed a shoulder problem, which he kept hidden from Johnson. In this game he faced four batters, gave up a walk and two hits, and was hurt by an error. By the time the inning was over, the Cubs had eight runs and an 11–4 victory. The next day they swept a pair by scores of 3–0 and 5–1, and three days later the Mets fell to second place, where they remained for the balance of the season. Ten days after the series at Shea Stadium, the Mets visited Wrigley Field in Chicago to be further demolished by the Cubs. Not even Gooden could win this time. Doc lost to Ruthven, 9–3; Darling lost to Sutcliffe, 8–6; and Lynch was beaten 8–4 by Tim Stoddard; the Cubs' Lee Smith was a relief winner over Wes Gardner, 7–6, in the finale.

The Cubs' four-game sweep knocked the Mets four and one-half games out of first place; only once again in the balance of the season were they close. On August 17, when Gooden won in ten innings over Mike Krukow and the Giants, 2–0, the Mets pulled to within one and one-half games of the Cubs. But the Mets lost the next two games while the Cubs were winning theirs and soon were again three and a half back.

There were two more series between the Mets and Cubs before the end of the season. In the first one, at Shea Stadium in early September, Gooden pitched a one-hitter in which he struck out eleven batters. But the Mets could do no better than win two of the three games and were six games out when the Cubs left town. A week later when the two teams met again in Chicago, the Cubs won two out of three in a series marred by beanballs.

A few days later, in Philadelphia, some of the Mets took out their frustrations on teammate Darryl Strawberry. Keith Hernandez in particular was critical. In his second season in the big leagues, Darryl had not handled himself well. It started earlier in the year in Los Angeles, Darryl's hometown, when he tried to hit a home run every time up to impress his friends and family. Instead he went into a slump. A few days later, in San Diego, he was late getting to the park—a bad habit he had developed—and arrived to find himself benched for the first time in his career. He brooded about it and sulked on the bench, but then coming in as a pinch hitter in the ninth, he drove in the tying run in a game the Mets won one inning later.

It was not a good year for Strawberry. He missed the guidance and counseling of Jimmy Frey, who by now was managing the Cubs. Strawberry slumped throughout most of the year and his attitude was one of indifference. Veterans who watched him shook their heads. Darryl had so much talent and he was not applying himself.

For the first time in their history, the Mets sent four players to the All-Star game in 1984. They were *(from left)* Darryl Strawberry, Dwight Gooden, Jesse Orosco, and Keith Hernandez. Dwight made his first big impression on the baseball public when he struck out the side against the American League in his first inning of work.
LOUIS REQUENA

And this was the same man who had declared on the first day in camp, "If somebody has to speak up, I'll be the one. My heart was broken by what I saw last year. There were so many people who didn't care, I could not believe it. I never played on a loser before, always on winning teams. Then I got to the big leagues, and I always thought in the big leagues everyone cared. I was surprised. There were guys who didn't care. I want to be a great ballplayer with this club. I want to be a great leader."

"He quit on himself," Hernandez said. "He gave in on certain tough situations. When things got tough, he gave in. In August, I didn't think he was giving it a 100 percent effort. He was down on himself. The second year is the toughest for every player. I know how tough it was for me. There were certain situations where he gave up. He has got to toughen up. He couldn't handle things when they went bad."

Strawberry, who had gone through the entire month of August without a home run, seemed to perk up after the criticism. He hit a three-run home run to win the game in Philadelphia, and in the final series of the year in Montreal he hit three more home runs, to raise his sophomore season total to twenty-six. He also lifted his RBI total to ninety-seven. In what was considered a bad year for him, Strawberry was among the league leaders in both home runs and runs batted in when the season ended.

Gooden had a sensational year, leading the league with 276 strikeouts, the first teen-aged rookie ever to lead either major league in that department. He eclipsed the major league rookie strikeout record of 245 established by Herb Score of Cleveland in 1945 and shattered the National League rookie mark of 227, which Hall of Famer Grover Cleveland Alexander set in 1911. In addition he established a major league record with 11.39 strikeouts per nine innings, breaking the old mark of 10.71 set by Cleveland's Sam McDowell. He also broke the record of another Hall of Famer, Sandy Koufax, when he struck out thirty-two in two consecutive games. Koufax's record was thirty-one. He also set a major league record by striking out forty-three batters in three consecutive nine-inning games. As a final distinction, he struck out ten or more fifteen times in his thirty-one starts, for a Mets record. Seaver's club record was thirteen.

In Gooden and Strawberry, the Mets had two of the brightest stars on the

THE NEW YORK METS

horizon. They also had an All-Star Gold Glove first baseman in Hernandez. But they had to platoon at second with Wally Backman and Kelvin Chapman when Backman failed to hit from the right side. In August, veteran Ray Knight was obtained from Houston to play third, but he had various physical problems and required more shoulder surgery in the off-season.

The Mets' young pitching staff continued to be the talk of the league. Besides Gooden's seventeen wins, the Mets also got a dozen wins out of Darling, and eleven more from Terrell. Orosco in the bullpen established himself as the top southpaw in that category by winning ten and saving thirty-one. Sisk saved fifteen before his shoulder gave out.

Hubie Brooks became one of the offensive leaders with the Mets, hitting sixteen home runs and batting .283, which included a club record twenty-four-game hitting streak. Foster had a mediocre year with twenty-four homers and a .269 average, and Wilson, whose shoulder was acting up, was having trouble throwing from center field.

Johnson led the Mets to ninety victories in his first year—twenty-two more than the previous year—and brought the team home in second place. But Davey was disappointed. Once the Mets got into the race, he thought they had a chance to win.

"Nobody on my team had a better year than we might have expected. The Cubs had several players who had career years—years better than they had ever had before."

Johnson felt he had accomplished one goal in the establishment of his young arms as proven major leaguers. Gooden, Darling, Terrell, Sisk, Orosco, and Fernandez all were under thirty years of age. The old man of the staff was Berenyi. Lynch was twenty-nine and had earned a spot in the rotation by winning nineteen in his last two seasons. The bullpen was in good shape, with Orosco coming off his best year and Sisk likely to recover from the shoulder ailment that plagued him the second half of the 1984 season. Coming up from the minors for possible promotion were Calvin Schiraldi, Wes Gardner, and Roger McDowell. Not a lot was expected of McDowell. He had undergone surgery for removal of bone chips in his elbow in January and sat out most of the season. But Johnson saw him in the October Instructional League in Florida, was impressed with his sinker, and looked forward to giving him at least a trial.

The Mets stayed in the race until September 24, when Chicago clinched the pennant. For Darryl Strawberry and Hubie Brooks, it was a season that almost was.
LOUIS REQUENA

The one thing the Mets lacked at the end of the 1984 season was a solid major league catcher. Mike Fitzgerald had done yeoman work in replacing the all-but-retired Stearns. He shared the duties with Ron Hodges and Junior Ortiz, but none of them hit, and Johnson knew he could not possibly win without a first-string catcher. John Gibbons, a scrapper Johnson was impressed with the previous spring, had developed elbow problems and his progress was delayed. But good catchers are hard to come by, and the Mets didn't know what to do to resolve the situation. Then, almost overnight, Cashen made two dramatic trades that would dramatically reshape the Mets for 1985.

To this day the Mets will not admit there was any connection to an August 29 move and subsequent roster changes. After almost twenty-three years of searching for someone who could play third base regularly and finding a dependable performer at last in Hubie Brooks, they suddenly shifted him to shortstop after obtaining the veteran but injury-plagued Ray Knight from Houston. Then, three months later, they went out and traded Terrell, one of their top pitchers, for Howard Johnson, another third baseman. Three days after that, they completed one of the biggest deals in Mets history, when catcher Gary Carter was obtained from Montreal for Brooks, Fitzgerald, and two minor leaguers, pitcher Floyd Youmans and outfielder Herm Winningham.

The acquisition of Carter, a solid All-Star, Gold Glove catcher with the Expos for a decade, was a coup that became front page news in all New York newspapers. No club in its right mind would trade a performer as dependable and durable as Carter—especially a catcher. But in Montreal, after years of disappointment with runner-up finishes and with a new general manager in Murray Cook, the Expos were breaking up the old gang. Carter, an outgoing personality whose gung-ho style of play and ready availability to the media prompted suspicion and jealousy among his teammates, became the fall guy. Montreal owner Charles Bronfman had negotiated a long-term contract with Carter after the 1982 season to assure the club that Gary would not be lost through free agency. It was a multi-million dollar contract that Carter had earned after hitting .293 with twenty-nine home runs. But when he slipped to .270 and seventeen home runs the following year (playing with injuries a great deal of the time), the owners complained that the big money and long-term

Dwight Gooden gets a big hug from Mike Fitzgerald after striking out his 246th batter to break the all-time rookie record, September 24, 1984.

Rookie manager Davey Johnson helped turn the Mets into contenders in 1984 with his incisive personnel moves (using Backman instead of Giles, Santana instead of Oquendo, getting rid of old-timers Swan and Tidrow, and bringing up Kelvin Chapman to platoon with Wally Backman), a good sense of rapport with his players, and instilling a winning attitude, to say nothing of his computerized strategy. As the pennant race heated up, Johnson found himself constantly surrounded by the media.

Sid Fernandez, a temperamental left-hander from Hawaii, warms up before an exhibition game against the Yankees in Fort Lauderdale. Fernandez was wild in that game and was later sent back to the minors. Once he did join the Mets rotation, he was overpowering. Despite a hard-luck 9–9 record, he led the major leagues in strikeouts (180) per innings pitched (170).

PETER SIMON

contract had spoiled him. Even when Carter bounced back and hit .294 in 1984, the Expos were still determined to get rid of him.

Cashen was fortunate in that he had a strong friendship with John McHale, the president of the Expos, and in that the Mets had the kind of young players the Expos were seeking for Cook's rebuilding program. Cashen and McHale had both worked in Commissioner Kuhn's office and lived at the New York Athletic Club when they were in town.

"I once told John," Cashen revealed later, "that if he were ever going to dismantle his club, I'd be interested in Carter."

The Mets also happened to have what the Expos were looking for—a shortstop who could hit home runs. That Brooks had only recently gone back to shortstop (he played shortstop at Arizona State) after establishing himself as a solid third baseman was of little consequence. Montreal wanted Brooks to play shortstop because he would give them more production there with his bat. But they replaced Carter with Fitzgerald, who had hit only two home runs in 1984. They filled one void but created another.

The fact that Brooks had been shifted to shortstop only one month before the end of the season, that the Mets may have had some inkling the Expos would trade Carter and get Hubie as shortstop, did cross the minds of the more suspicious writers. There also was the remark Joe McIlvaine, Cashen's right-hand man, made the day after the Terrell-for-Johnson deal. Why another third baseman and why give up a winner like Terrell? newsmen asked.

"There may be some other moves coming," McIlvaine replied.

That was at the end of the winter meetings. Within forty-eight hours, Cashen was on his way to West Palm Beach to discuss with Carter his feelings regarding a trade to New York—the catcher had to approve the deal. He quickly agreed.

"After the season when I heard some of the things that were said about me, I had a meeting with John McHale," Carter later related. "I told him if the Expos felt that I was the reason they had never won, then maybe he better trade me. He told me they would try and accommodate me."

On December 12, the big deal was announced. Carter flew up from Florida to attend a gala press conference in the Shea Stadium Diamond Club. Not since Foster's acquisition in 1982 and Seaver's return later the same year was there so much optimism surrounding the Mets. With an All-Star catcher like Carter

Gary Carter shows the Mets his stuff when he wins the game on a dramatic tenth inning home run on opening day. The crowd of 46,781 went wild on this cold day as the Mets beat the Cards, 6–5.

DAILY NEWS/HARRY HAMBURG

handling the young pitching staff and hitting home runs, with Gooden an almost certain twenty-game winner, and with Darryl Strawberry over his sophomore jinx, surely the Mets would be favorites to beat out the Cubs.

Foster perhaps summed up best what Carter's presence in the lineup meant.

"He's one of those guys who, when he comes up, he can hurt you. Often you have to get a new ball," said the left fielder.

One thing was certain: With Carter the Mets would have the most powerful lineup in their history—Hernandez, Carter, Strawberry, and Foster—one solid .300 hitter followed by three home run threats.

The Mets fans could not wait for the 1985 season to get started. Season ticket sales rose to an all-time high. Carter's arrival had generated an enthusiasm the Mets had not seen since the Miracle of 1969.

Carter immediately fit in with his new club. If there was resentment over his gregarious personality or Joe College enthusiasm, there was no outward display of that among the players. Like the fans, the players believed that Carter was the one bat they needed to put them over the top.

In the season's opener at Shea Stadium April 9, Carter substantiated all the optimism by smashing a tenth inning home run off the Cardinals' Neil Allen for a 6–5 victory. The 46,781 fans who turned out to greet their new hero were ecstatic.

The Mets beat the Cardinals again, 2–1, in extra innings the next day, and Carter played a big part in that victory, too. With the score tied in the eleventh and Hernandez on first base, Carter singled past third to send Keith to third base. A bases-loaded walk finally forced in the winning run.

The year 1985 was a gutsy one for Gary Carter. All season long he played with a large assortment of injuries yet remained steady throughout and had one of the finest years in Mets history (.281 batting average, thirty-two home runs, and 100 RBIs). On April 28, Carter is involved in a collision at home plate in an eighteen-inning game against the Pirates, which the Mets won, 5–4. Carter broke a few ribs but kept right on playing.
LOUIS REQUENA

Hubie Brooks *(left)*, traded to the Expos for Gary Carter, was always a popular player with his Mets teammates and is here seen horsing around with them on a visit to Shea in late July. Rafael Santana *(center)*, who took over for Hubie as shortstop and had a very steady year, and Darryl Strawberry join in the welcoming party.

PETER SIMON

Carter's heroics were not to be believed. In the third game of the season against Cincinnati, the catcher's home run in the fourth inning was the only run of the game, as Berenyi bested Mario Soto, 1–0.

In the fifth game, with both teams scoreless in the sixth, Carter led off with a home run off Jay Tibbs. The Mets won, 4–0, behind Gooden's four-hit, ten-strikeout pitching. In his first five games as a Met, Carter had hit three home runs and had personally won two of the games.

There seemed to be no stopping the Mets. They won the first five in a row and then, after losing one to Pittsburgh, Ron Darling and Jesse Orosco came back to combine on a one-hitter that stopped the Pirates, 2–1. Three days later, Gooden and Orosco combined on a three-hitter as the Mets beat Philadelphia, 1–0, on a ninth inning single by Hernandez.

The first sign that there might be trouble ahead came in a three-game series at St. Louis on April 22–24. The Cardinals won two of the three games to begin a domination over the Mets that would last most of the season and eventually result in another second place finish for Johnson's young team. Gooden, who won his first two decisions, lost to Joaquin Andujar, 5–1, in the rubber game of the St. Louis series. In the same series, the Mets also lost Bruce Berenyi, their number 3 starter, who was disabled with a sore shoulder on April 23 and did not work again in the season.

The Mets returned home to blank the Pirates, 6–0, behind Darling; Wally Backman stroked five hits to tie a club record. Two days later, Clint Hurdle's eighteenth inning ground ball scored Wilson with the winning run to end a five-hour, twenty-one-minute marathon that also included a grand slam home run by Strawberry.

The Mets ended the month of April with a 12–6 record and a new hero virtually every day. But there was one disturbing factor. In spite of their good record, the Mets as a team were not hitting all that well. The team average continued to hover around the .230 mark. The only club in the league with a lower average was San Francisco.

By May, Wilson was beginning to have difficulty throwing and had to sit out a week. In his place, the Mets called up Len Dykstra from Tidewater. In his second major league at bat, Dykstra, who was known as a spray hitter with little power, belted a two-run home run off Soto to highlight a 9–4 victory over Cincinnati. If Dykstra could hit home runs, could the Mets be denied a pennant?

Carter continued to belt home runs. On May 7 his grand slammer off Bruce Sutter, the highest-priced relief pitcher in the game, broke a 1–1 tie and gave the Mets a 5–3 victory. Seemingly there was nothing that could stop the Mets.

1985

NAME	G by POS	B	AGE	G	AB	R	H	2B	3B	HR	RBI	BB	SO	SB	BA	SA
NEW YORK 2nd 98-64 .605 3			**DAVEY JOHNSON**													
TOTALS			27	162	5549	695	1125	239	35	134	651	546	872	117	.257	.385
Keith Hernandez	1B152	L	31	158	593	87	183	34	4	10	91	77	59	3	.309	.430
Wally Backman	2B122	B	25	145	520	77	142	24	5	1	38	36	72	30	.273	.344
Raphael Santana	SS145	R	27	154	529	41	136	19	1	1	29	29	54	1	.257	.302
Howard Johnson	3B93, SS5	B	24	126	389	38	94	18	4	11	46	34	78	6	.242	.393
George Foster	OF119	R	36	129	452	57	119	24	1	21	77	46	87	0	.263	.460
Mookie Wilson	OF77	B	29	93	337	56	93	16	8	6	26	28	52	24	.276	.424
Darryl Strawberry	OF98	L	23	93	393	78	109	15	4	29	79	73	96	26	.277	.557
Gary Carter	C139, 1B6, RF1	R	31	149	555	93	156	17	1	32	100	69	46	1	.281	.488
Kelvin Chapman	2B34	R	29	62	144	16	25	3	0	0	7	9	15	5	.174	.194
Lenny Dykstra	OF53	L	22	83	236	40	60	9	3	1	19	30	24	15	.254	.331
John Christenson	OF28	R	24	51	113	10	21	4	1	3	13	19	23	1	.186	.319
Danny Heep	OF68	L	27	95	271	26	76	17	0	7	42	27	27	2	.280	.421
Ronn Reynolds	C11	R	26	28	43	4	9	2	0	1	1	0	18	0	.209	.256
Clint Hurdle	C12, 70F	L	28	43	82	7	16	1	0	3	7	13	20	0	.195	.354
Rusty Staub		L	41	51	45	2	12	3	0	1	8	10	4	0	.267	.400
Ray Knight	3B67, 2B12	R	31	90	271	22	59	12	0	6	36	13	32	1	.218	.328
Tom Paciorek	OF21, 1B1	R	39	46	116	14	33	3	1	1	11	6	14	1	.284	.353
Larry Bowa	SS3, 2B3	B	39	11	19	2	2	1	0	0	2	2	2	0	.105	.304
Ron Gardenhire	SS9, 2B2, 3B3	R	27	26	39	5	7	2	1	0	2	8	11	0	.179	.282
Billy Beane	OF1	B	23	9	8	0	2	1	0	1	0	3	0	.250	.375
Terry Blocker	OF4	L	21	18	15	1	1	0	0	0	0	1	2	0	.067	.067

NAME	T	AGE	W	L	PCT	SV	G	GS	CG	IP	H	BB	SO	ShO	ERA
		25	98	64	.605	37	162	162	32	1188	1306	515	1039	19	3.11
Dwight Gooden	R	20	24	4	.857	0	35	35	16	276	198	69	268	8	1.53
Ron Darling	R	24	16	6	.727	0	36	35	4	248	214	114	167	2	2.90
Rick Aguilera	R	23	10	7	.588	0	21	19	2	122	118	37	74	0	3.24
Sid Fernandez	L	21	9	9	.500	0	26	26	3	170	108	80	180	0	2.80
Ed Lynch	R	28	10	8	.556	0	31	29	1	191	188	27	65	1	3.44
Jessie Orosco	L	27	8	6	.571	17	54	0	0	79	66	34	68	0	2.73
Roger McDowel	R	24	6	5	.545	17	62	2	0	127	108	37	70	0	2.93
Bruce Berenyi	R	29	1	0	1.000	0	3	3	0	13	8	10	10	0	2.63
Wes Gardner	R	24	0	2	.000	0	9	0	0	12	18	8	11	0	5.25
Tom Gorman	L	27	4	4	.500	0	34	2	0	52	56	18	32	0	5.13
Terry Leach	R	29	3	4	.429	1	22	4	1	55	48	14	30	1	2.91
Doug Sisk	R	27	4	5	.444	2	42	0	0	73	86	40	68	0	5.30
Calvin Schiraldi	R	22	2	1	.667	0	10	4	0	26	13	11	21	0	8.89
Joe Sambito	R	31	0	0	.000	0	8	0	0	10	21	8	3	0	12.66
Randy Myers	L	22	0	0	.000	0	1	0	0	2	0	1	2	0	0.00
Randy Nieman	L	23	0	0	.000	0	4	0	0	4	5	0	2	0	0.00

And then it happened. On the afternoon of May 11, while Fernandez was shutting out the Phillies, Strawberry dove for a sinking line drive off the bat of Juan Samuel and tore the ligaments in his right thumb.

"That is the one moment of the season I will never forget," Johnson said later. "It turned the whole season around for us. It was our darkest hour, as far as I was concerned."

The Mets, who were 18–8 up to that point and in first place, played the next seven weeks without their leading slugger. In his first sixteen games Strawberry had hit six home runs and driven in a dozen runs. Of all the things that happened to the Mets during the season, nothing was more damaging than the loss of Strawberry. From a team that was playing ten games above .500 with Strawberry, they slipped to 20–23 in his absence. They also fell to second place.

The Mets felt the loss of Strawberry almost immediately. In the next dozen games they lost seven times and suffered three shutouts. Even the incomparable Doc Gooden was having difficulty. Doc lost back-to-back decisions to a couple of Cy Young winners—2–0 to Lamar Hoyt and the San Diego Padres on May 20 and 6–2 to Fernando Valenzuela and the Dodgers on May 25.

Then on May 30 in San Francisco, Gooden pitched a six-hitter, striking out fourteen batters and winning, 2–1, to start a fourteen-game winning streak. As might be expected, the Mets began thinking the worst was behind them. But humiliation was just around the corner.

Next to their final game in St. Louis in October, the game the Mets would like most to forget from the 1985 season is the one that took place in Philadelphia on June 11. That night the Phillies plastered the Mets with a twenty-seven-hit attack that resulted in a 26–7 drubbing. It was the worst defeat in Mets history.

Tom Gorman, an emergency starter, retired only one batter in the first inning as the Phillies sent twelve men to the plate and scored nine runs. Von Hayes hit two home runs in the first inning, including a lead-off homer and a grand slam. It was the most runs scored in a National League game since the Giants beat the Dodgers, 26–8, on April 30, 1944.

"It was an embarrassment," said Davey Johnson.

It had been expected that the Mets and defending champion Cubs would be fighting it out for the Eastern Division title, but when a rash of injuries hit the Cubs, the Mets were able to handle them without any problem—even without Strawberry.

What was hailed as the first "crucial" series of the season drew crowds totaling 172,000 to Shea Stadium for four games with Chicago on June 17–20. And when the Mets swept the four games behind Darling, Lynch, Gooden, and Fernandez, there was little doubt in any fan's mind that this year the Mets had outdistanced the Cubs.

That optimism was dimmed a week later when the Mets visited Chicago and won only one of three games. Then they went down to St. Louis, and with a still-hurting Strawberry back in the lineup, they were swept away in three games. They had a chance to salvage the final game when Gooden pitched one-run ball for eight innings and left with the score tied, 1–1, but Orosco lost in the eleventh inning and new storm clouds were on the horizon. Not only were the Cardinals suddenly becoming the team the Mets would have to beat but Orosco, their star reliever, was unable to do the job. The left-hander insisted there was nothing wrong with him, but later it was confirmed that he had a tender elbow. There were times his appearance was called for when Johnson did not even have him up in the bullpen.

"I have to be careful how I use him," the manager admitted.

The Mets suddenly went into a tailspin, losing six in a row. One week after being tied for first they dropped to fourth after losing the finale in St. Louis.

Ron Darling proved he was a winner in 1985. After pitching well before the All-Star game in 1984, he seemed to fizzle out with a number of no-decisions and losses. In 1985, despite a few no-decisions, he kept coming on strong and wound up the year with a sterling 16–6 record and a 2.90 ERA.

PETER SIMON

The Cardinals, with speedster Vince Coleman introduced to their lineup, had become the new force in the division.

On the night of July 2, the Mets snapped their six-game losing streak when Darling beat the Pirates. That started a nine-game winning streak in which the Mets batters finally started producing the kinds of numbers that had been expected since spring training. The streak included one of the most incredible games of the season. In Atlanta on the night of July 4, in a game delayed by rain, the Mets and the Braves played a nineteen-inning marathon that consumed six hours and ten minutes playing time and did not end until 3:55 A.M. It was the latest any National League game had ever been played. The final score was 16–13; the Mets slammed twenty-eight hits, five of them by Carter. Hernandez became the first Met to hit for the cycle (homer, triple, double, single) since Mike Phillips in 1976. Twice in extra innings the Mets were but one out from victory only to have the game tied by home runs, once by outfielder Terry Harper in the thirteenth, and again by pitcher Rick Camp in the eighteenth. Ron Darling pitched the nineteenth inning, the first time since attending Yale that he pitched in relief.

The team bus that had left the Atlanta Hilton for the ballpark at 5 P.M. on July 4 returned at 5 A.M. on July 5.

"It's the first time I ever came back from a game when the sun was coming up," Darling said.

Leading up to the All-Star game on July 16, the Mets won twelve out of thirteen and by now were in second place. Gooden again was selected to the All-Star team, but he never got to pitch. He had blanked Houston, 1–0, the Sunday before the game and was not available. The previous year, in San Francisco, Doc had startled the baseball world by striking out the first three American Leaguers he faced in a two-inning scoreless appearance.

That shutout victory by Gooden in Houston prior to the All-Star game was number 7 in a string of fourteen consecutive victories. The fourteenth came on August 25 against San Diego when Gooden became the youngest pitcher in baseball history to win twenty games in a single season. Gooden was twenty years, nine months, and five days old when he won his twentieth. In 1939, when Bob Feller won twenty games, he was twenty years, ten months, and five days old.

The game that Gooden remembered most in his winning streak was the second one in Los Angeles on the night of June 4. He was paired with Dodgers star Fernando Valenzuela. For seven innings they battled along in a 1–1 tie. One of the two hits Doc allowed was a sixth inning home run by Pedro Guerrero. In the eighth inning, when the first two Dodgers reached base on singles and first base was open, Gooden walked Guerrero intentionally and then proceeded to retire the next three batters—on nine pitches! He struck out Greg Brock, got Mike Scioscia to foul out on the first pitch, and then fanned Terry Whitfield. In the next inning, one of Gooden's own three hits off Valenzuela drove in a run.

"That was about as good as I can pitch, getting out of that situation," Gooden said after the game.

The early July streak enabled the Mets to enjoy their best month of the season and the best road trip in club history. The July 4th marathon in Atlanta was the start of a three-city tour that saw the Mets win ten out of eleven. It was the most victories any Mets team ever scored on a road trip.

The Mets lost Wilson because of his sore shoulder, but Dykstra was doing well as a replacement. Strawberry came back and was hitting home runs again. In the game of July 20 against the Atlanta Braves, Darryl smashed two homers—one with the bases full and the other with two aboard—to drive in seven runs as the Mets romped, 16–4, behind Gooden. The very next day, Sid Fernandez had dizzy spells before the game and could not start. Terry Leach

Danny Heep, waiting on the on-deck circle, enjoyed a good year in 1985, batting .280 with forty-two RBIs. He filled in well for the injured Strawberry, but the Mets' record of 20–23 during the period was the major reason for their second place finish.

PETER SIMON

started in El Sid's place and responded with six strong innings as the Mets rolled to a 15–10 win. The thirty-one runs in consecutive games was another Mets record. George Foster drove in five runs in the 15–10 win, slamming his fifteenth homer with two mates aboard.

One week later, the Mets thrashed Houston in a twin bill, 16–4 and 7–3. The twenty-three runs in a doubleheader was another club record.

The only problems were behind the plate and in the bullpen. In the Houston series in July, Carter's right knee gave way on him and he had to be flown home, thus missing a chance to start another All-Star game to which he had been elected. For the next few days the Mets did not know if Carter would play again the rest of the year. Besides his knee, Gary's ankle also bothered him. Hours of therapy by trainer Steve Garland had Carter ready to go again six days later. If Gary was not 100 percent, he was gutsy enough to tough out the rest of the year. Immediately after the season ended. Carter underwent arthroscopic surgery on his right knee for the second time in two years.

The trouble in the bullpen stemmed from Orosco's ineffectiveness and Doug Sisk's control problems. Sisk had to be sent to the minors to try and resolve his difficulty. He came back but was never the same and eventually underwent elbow surgery on September 27. Only Roger McDowell prevented the bullpen from deteriorating completely. Just one year away from elbow surgery himself, he turned in a 6–5 record and seventeen saves and was a legitimate candidate for rookie of the year.

Sisk had arrived on the major league scene almost unannounced late in the 1982 season. He had been pitching at Jackson in the Texas League, where that year they converted him to a reliever. He had a natural sinker and he was a tireless workhorse, ideal qualities for a reliever. During the course of a season a ball club usually keeps writers informed of outstanding prospects in the organization, the better to look forward to the future, especially after losing games. Sisk was never mentioned by Mets officials in 1982, perhaps because he was not overly fast, had control problems, and had been picked up rather cheaply.

"It cost them $342.50 to sign me," Sisk said. "That was the cost of a one-way plane ticket from Seattle, Washington, to Kingsport, Tennessee. I was passed over in the draft, and they thought so little of me they didn't even give me a round-trip ticket when I signed."

A big day for Darryl Strawberry against Atlanta on July 20. Here he gets high fives from Carter, Dykstra (number 4), and Backman for hitting a grand slam home run in the first inning. He followed that up with another round tripper and a double, which led to a seven-RBI day in a big 16–4 pounding. The Mets hit five home runs (Heep, Hurdle, and H. Johnson in addition to the Straw Man) for the first time since 1970.
DAILY NEWS/DANNY FARRELL

On September 12, Keith Hernandez is the hero of the day with a single in the ninth. The win put the Mets temporarily in first for the last time in 1985.
PETER SIMON

METS' NO. 1 PICK IN JUNE FREE AGENT DRAFT

Year	Player
1965	Rohr, Les, lhp
1966	Chilcott, Steve, c
1967	Matlack, Jon, lhp
1968	Foli, Tim, if
1969	Sterling, Randy, rhp
1970	Ambrow, George, if
1971	Pugi, Rich, if
1972	Bengston, Richard, c
1973	Mazzilli, Lee, of
1974	Speck, Bob, rhp
1975	Benton, Butch, c
1976	Thurberg, Tom, of
1977	Backman, Wally, if
1978	Brooks, Hubie, if
1979	Leary, Tim, rhp
1980	Strawberry, Darryl, of
1981	Blocker, Terry, of
1982	Gooden, Dwight, rhp
1983	Williams, Eddie, if
1984	Abner, Shawn, of
1985	Jeffries, Gregg, if
1986	May, Lee Jr., of

In eight games with the Mets in 1982, Doug saved one. But the next year he was one of the heroes of Tom Seaver's homecoming by pitching the final three innings of the opening day game won by the Mets.

Reflecting on his sudden moment in the spotlight, Sisk remarked, "If it wasn't for ground balls, I'd be selling apples in Yakima right now. Five years ago I was sitting on a beach throwing rocks at seagulls. Now I'm throwing baseballs past major league batters. Sometimes it doesn't seem real."

Sisk went on to save eleven games in 1983 and fifteen in 1984. He was a tremendous right-handed partner to the left-handed Jesse Orosco. Together, they saved forty-six games in '84.

But the season ended abruptly for Sisk—and for the Mets as well—when on July 28 he blew a tie against the Cubs in a game that Chicago eventually won. Davey Johnson called that loss the turning point in the race with the Cubs.

In 1985, Sisk could not locate home plate and the Shea Stadium fans grew restless. Doug was booed unmercifully every time he emerged from the bullpen.

Despite problems in the Mets bullpen, there was a never-say-die attitude to this young club, much of it the result of Johnson's leadership. He was not one to panic in spite of all the setbacks. The worst of those were losing Strawberry for seven weeks, Wilson for almost two months, and his number 3 starter Berenyi for most of the season. Fortunately, rookie Rick Aguilera, who came along to take Berenyi's place, won ten games. At the end of the year, Johnson cited the loss of Berenyi, Strawberry, and Wilson as the reasons his team did not win.

The first week in August, the Mets lost the first of a four-game series to the Cubs in Chicago, then followed with three wins and took over first place on August 5 when Strawberry hit three home runs in a 6–4 victory. While the team was mid-air en route to Montreal, Howard Johnson, listening to his portable radio, picked up a sports broadcast that mentioned the St. Louis loss. The Mets were flying high and they were in first place.

After learning they had moved into first place, the Mets hung around the Sheraton Centre hotel in Montreal the morning of August 6 to learn if they were going on strike. Negotiations were in progress in New York, and player representative Keith Hernandez waited in his room for the call from the union representatives.

Finally, around one o'clock, Hernandez came down to the lobby and informed the players that the strike was on; he advised them to go home. There would be no game with the Expos that night. In fact some players had already departed for the airport; others, expecting a strike to be called, had left the club in Chicago the previous evening. Ray Knight and Tom Paciorek, two veterans, flew home to Atlanta. By late afternoon all but a few of the players had departed.

Davey Johnson went back to New York and was on board a plane about to depart for Florida the next afternoon when Jean Coen, executive assistant to Frank Cashen, learned that the strike was settled. She managed to get word to an Eastern Airlines passenger agent, and Johnson got off the plane and flew to Montreal instead.

After a two-day hiatus, play resumed on August 8, and the Mets took up right where they'd left off, with a 14–7 win over Montreal. It was win number 4 in a streak that would extend to nine before the Mets lost again.

From Montreal, the Mets returned home to sweep a series from the Cubs. They extended their winning streak to seven games before losing and closed out the month of August with a 17–11 record in second place, two games behind the Cardinals. They had six games left with St. Louis and making up two games would not be all that difficult. Or so they thought.

The Mets came home from California to take on St. Louis in a three-game series starting September 10. The West Coast trip included heroics by Gary Carter, Doc Gooden, and Keith Hernandez, sparking the team to seven victories in ten games.

The trip began with Hernandez fighting a slump that had seen him deliver only one single in twenty-three trips to the plate. When he went 0-for-4 on August 31 in San Francisco, he was benched the next day—in his own hometown. Keith was not happy with Johnson's decision, but with left-hander Dave LaPoint on the mound for the Giants, he could not argue the manager's strategy. But revenge was sweet for Hernandez before the sun set that day.

The Giants had a 3–1 lead going into the top of the ninth inning. Howard Johnson started the Mets' comeback with an opposite-field double off Scott Garrelts. Then Rusty Staub scored Johnson with another double, the ninety-eighth pinch hit of his illustrious career. The rally almost died when Larry Bowa, running for Staub, was tagged out after overrunning third base on Mookie Wilson's single. When the Giants went to their bullpen again and brought in right-hander Mark Davis, Johnson went to his bench and gave Hernandez a chance to redeem himself, which he promptly did. He drove a pitch over the right field fence for a two-run home run that gave the Mets a 4–3 victory.

In the four games in San Francisco, Carter also went on a home run binge, hitting a home run in each of the three games he started.

From San Francisco, the Mets flew down to San Diego, where they continued their hot roll with three consecutive victories over the Padres. With his grandparents in attendance in the opening game, Hawaiian southpaw Sid Fernandez pitched his first complete game victory in the majors by holding the Padres to five hits in a 12–4 romp. Carter continued hot in the San Diego series. After delivering three singles in Fernandez's victory, the catcher hit home runs his first three times up the next night as Rick Aguilera coasted to an 8–3 victory. In the third and final San Diego game, Carter hit two more home runs to raise his season total to twenty-five. He had played six games on the West Coast trip to that point and hit eight home runs.

The September 6–8 series in Los Angeles was a memorable one. Tickets for the opening game, which paired Gooden against Valenzuela, were impossible to obtain. Scalpers had a field day; tickets on the street were going for as much as $500 a pair.

Gooden and Valenzuela did not let the fans down. They fired blanks for nine innings before 51,868 Dodger Stadium fans, the largest Los Angeles crowd of the season. At the end of nine, after he had permitted only five hits and struck out ten, Gooden was lifted for a pinch hitter. Both teams threatened in extra innings before the Mets finally pushed across two runs when Darryl Strawberry tagged Valenzuela for an opposite-field double in the thirteenth that scored two runs. Jesse Orosco pitched out of a bases-loaded jam in the bottom of the thirteenth to pick up his fifteenth save.

Even though the Mets lost the pennant on the second to last day of the season, the Mets fans' love affair with their heroes continued all winter long. After years of poor attendance in the late seventies and early eighties, fans started coming out of the woodwork during the second half of 1984 and showed their numbers in 1985 by setting an all-time New York City baseball record with 2,751,437 paid admissions.
PETER SIMON

METS VS. NATIONAL LEAGUE, 1962–1986

		Eastern Division		
Cubs	Expos	Phillies	Pirates	Cardinals
224–220	157–161	191–255	198–239	190–251

		Western Division			
Braves	Astros	Dodgers	Reds	Padres	Giants
155–181	145–192	136–200	136–203	113–98	146–160

Fred Wilpon *(left)*, president of the Mets, visits with his "rival," Yankee owner George Steinbrenner, during a spring game in Florida. Although each man professes to wish nothing but success for the other's team, an interesting battle for the spotlight has emerged in recent years. Steinbrenner particularly hates to see the Mets get better TV ratings and higher attendance figures. After years of Yankee dominance in the New York market, the balance of power shifted in 1985.

PETER SIMON

The following afternoon, on national television, a free-for-all developed when Mariano Duncan, the rookie Dodgers shortstop, complained about the "junk" that Ed Lynch was throwing. After Gooden's fastball the previous night, Lynch's slow pitches were baffling the Dodgers. The Dodgers bench, led by Duncan and his Dominican idol, Pedro Guerrero, were on Lynch from the start, complaining about his off-speed pitches.

In his first two trips to the plate, Duncan tried bunting for base hits but was thrown out. When Lynch struck him out in the sixth inning, he shouted to the rookie, "Go back to the bench and shut up!" The short-tempered Duncan flared up, made a retaliatory comment, and was motioned to the mound by Lynch. Within moments, there was a brawl at the center of the diamond, with Guerrero acting like a wild man. The entire Dodgers bench had rushed out on the field, but Guerrero was almost uncontrollable.

Order was finally restored. Lynch gave up a home run to Mike Marshall and left at the end of the inning. He had injured his right hip in the fight and was of little help to the club the rest of the season.

The Mets eventually lost the "brawl-game," 7–6, but ended their road trip with another thirteen-inning marathon that was not decided until Mookie Wilson hit a home run off ex-Met Carlos Diaz in the fourteenth inning to give the Mets a 4–3 victory. The win went to the much-maligned Doug Sisk, who pitched two perfect innings in relief. Sisk, who had not won a game since June, picked up two victories on the West Coast trip.

At home to face the Cardinals on September 10, the Mets were greeted by 50,195 fanatics for the opening game. The fans were not denied their thrills. In the very first inning, Howard Johnson hit a grand slam home run off Danny Cox to climax a five-run outburst. Ron Darling almost blew the 5–0 lead, giving up four runs in seven innings. But Roger McDowell closed the door for the last two and two-thirds innings and the Mets held on for a 5–4 win. It was

METS' ANNUAL BATTING LEADERS

Year	Games	At-Bats	Runs	Hits	Doubles
1962	Thomas, 156	Thomas, 571	Thomas, 69	Thomas, 152	Thomas, 23
1963	Hickman, 146	Hunt, 533	Hunt, 64	Hunt, 145	Hunt, 28
1964	Christopher, 154	Christopher, 543	Christopher, 78	Christopher, 163	Christopher, 26
1965	McMillan, 157	Kranepool, 525	Lewis, 64	Kranepool, 133	Kranepool, 24
1966	Kranepool, 146	Boyer, 496	Jones, 74	Hunt, 138	Boyer, 28
1967	Davis, 154	Davis, 577	Davis, 72	Davis, 174	Davis, 32
1968	Jones, 147	Jones, 509	Jones, 63	Jones, 151	Jones, 29
1969	Agee, 149	Agee, 565	Agee, 97	Jones, 164	Jones, 25
1970	Harrelson, 157	Agee, 636	Agee, 107	Agee, 182	Agee, 30
1971	Harrelson, 142	Harrelson, 547	Jones, 63	Jones, 161	Grote, 25
1972	Kranepool, 122	Agee, 422	Harrelson, 54	Agee, 96	Agee, 23
1973	Millan, 153	Millan, 638	Millan, 82	Millan, 185	Staub, 36
1974	Garrett/Staub, 151	Staub, 561	Milner, 70	Staub, 145	Jones, 23
1975	Millan, 162	Millan, 676	Staub, 93	Millan, 191	Millan, 37
1976	Millan, 139	Millan, 531	Kingman, 70	Millan, 150	Millan/Milner, 25
1977	Mazzilli, 159	Mazzilli, 537	Randle, 78	Randle, 156	Stearns, 25
1978	Montanez, 159	Montanez, 609	Henderson, 83	Henderson/Montanez, 156	Montanez, 32
1979	Mazzilli/Youngblood, 158	Taveras, 635	Youngblood, 90	Mazzilli, 181	Youngblood, 37
1980	Mazzilli, 152	Mazzilli, 578	Mazzilli, 82	Mazzilli, 162	Mazzilli, 31
1981	Flynn, 105	Brooks, 358	Wilson, 49	Brooks, 110	Brooks, 21
1982	Wilson, 159	Wilson, 639	Wilson, 90	Wilson, 178	Stearns/Wilson, 25
1983	Foster, 157	Wilson, 638	Wilson, 91	Wilson, 176	Wilson, 25
1984	Hernandez/Wilson, 154	Wilson, 587	Wilson, 88	Hernandez, 171	Hernandez, 31
1985	Hernandez, 158	Hernandez, 593	Hernandez, 87	Hernandez, 183	Hernandez, 34
1986	Hernandez, 158	Hernandez, 551	Hernandez, 94	Hernandez, 171	Hernandez, 34

*Based on 502 plate appearances, except 1981 computed on 326 appearances.

the first time that Hernandez appeared before the home fans since his confession in a Pittsburgh drug trial that he had regularly used cocaine while with the St. Louis Cardinals. His first time at bat he got a standing ovation from the fans.

"It gave me goosebumps," he later admitted. "I never expected it. I haven't experienced anything like that since I returned to St. Louis after the trade and got a standing ovation."

Three weeks later, when he returned to St. Louis, 46,026 Cardinals fans stood and booed their former idol.

The match-up of the two best pitchers in the National League—Gooden and John Tudor—the next night lured another 52,616 fans to Shea Stadium. For the second consecutive start, Gooden pitched nine innings of shutout ball. But in the tenth inning he was replaced by Jesse Orosco, who again served up a home run ball to pinch hitter Cesar Cedeño, and the Mets lost, 1–0.

The rubber game on September 12 brought out another 46,295 to see Ed Lynch and Joaquin Andujar square off. Neither starter lasted very long. Andujar was rocked for six runs in the first two innings, but Lynch gave five runs back and was out after five. The Cardinals tied the score in the top of the ninth. After Wilson beat out an infield hit and took second on Backman's sacrifice, Hernandez again came through with another big hit—a single that delivered Wilson with the winning run for the Mets.

The Cardinals refused to die after losing two out of three to the Mets. Instead, they went off on a winning streak while the Mets struggled. Following the big St. Louis series, the Mets won nine and lost six of the next fifteen games before moving into Pittsburgh to take on the last place Pirates. It should have been a weekend for the Mets to wipe up the cellar dwellers and get their act together before taking on the Cardinals again in St. Louis. Instead, the Mets were lucky to win two out of three from the Pirates.

Ron Darling pitched his most impressive and courageous game on October 1 in St. Louis. He pitched nine innings of four-hit shutout ball against the Cards in a game many thought Dwight Gooden should have pitched. But Dave Johnson showed he had confidence in Darling, who certainly rose to the occasion. Here, between innings, Darling tries to cool off.

DAILY NEWS/DANNY FARRELL

Triples	Home Runs	RBIs	Stolen Bases	Batting Average*
Neal, 9	Thomas, 34	Thomas, 94	Ashburn/Chacon, 12	Mantilla .275
Hickman, 6	Hickman, 17	Thomas, 60	Kanehl, 6	Hunt .272
Christopher, 8	Smith, 20	Christopher, 76	Christopher/Hunt/D. Smith, 6	Hunt .303
Kranepool, 4	Swoboda, 19	C. Smith, 62	Christopher/Lewis, 4	Kranepool .253
Bressoud, 5	Kranepool, 16	Boyer, 61	Jones, 16	Hunt .288
Jones, 5	Davis, 16	Davis, 73	Harrelson/Jones, 12	Davis .302
Swoboda, 6	Charles, 15	Swoboda, 59	Jones, 23	Jones .297
Boswell, 7	Agee, 26	Agee, 76	Jones, 16	Jones .340
Harrelson/Jones, 8	Agee, 24	Clendenon, 97	Agee, 31	Agee .286
Harrelson/Jones, 6	Agee/Jones/Kranepool, 14	Jones, 69	Agee/Harrelson, 28	Jones .319
Martinez, 5	Milner, 17	Jones, 52	Harrelson, 12	Staub .293
Millan, 4	Milner, 23	Staub, 76	Garrett, 6	Millan .290
Martinez, 7	Milner, 20	Staub, 78	Milner, 10	Jones .282
Phillips, 7	Kingman, 36	Staub, 105	Kingman, 7	Unser .294
Phillips, 6	Kingman, 37	Kingman, 86	Boisclair/Harrelson, 9	Millan .282
Randle, 7	Henderson/Milner/Stearns, 12	Henderson, 65	Randle, 33	Randle .304
Henderson, 9	Montanez, 17	Montanez, 96	Stearns, 25	Mazzilli .273
Taveras, 9	Youngblood, 16	Hebner/Mazzilli, 79	Taveras, 42	Mazzilli .303
Flynn/Henderson, 8	Mazzilli, 16	Mazzilli, 76	Mazzilli, 41	Henderson .290
Wilson, 8	Kingman, 22	Kingman, 59	Wilson, 24	Brooks .307
Wilson, 9	Kingman, 37	Kingman, 99	Wilson, 58	Wilson .279
Strawberry, 7	Foster, 28	Foster, 90	Wilson, 54	Wilson .276
Wilson, 10	Strawberry, 26	Strawberry, 97	Wilson, 46	Hernandez .311
Wilson, 8	Carter, 32	Carter, 100	Backman, 30	Hernandez .309
Dykstra, 7	Strawberry, 27	Carter, 105	Dykstra, 31	Hernandez .310

Keith Hernandez looks wistful on the second to last day of the season, the day in which the Mets officially lost the pennant to the Cards. Despite another great year for Keith (he led the team with a .309 average, had two 5-hit games, had the most hits with 183, led the major leagues with 24 game-winning RBIs, and won another Gold Glove Award), 1985 was tough for him off the field. Not only was he involved in an unpleasant divorce, but he testified during the Pittsburgh drug trials and admitted to being addicted to cocaine during part of his years with St. Louis. On his first night back to Shea Stadium, following repentant testimony, he was given an emotional standing ovation.

PETER SIMON

In a game many veteran members of the team later claimed was their undoing, the Mets dropped the Pittsburgh opener on September 27. The Mets took a 2–0 first inning lead, which Ed Lynch lost in a hurry. Suffering back spasms and an aching hip, he had to leave after two innings. It was Lynch's last appearance of the season.

A two-run homer by Strawberry gave the Mets a 5–2 lead in the third, but they could not hold it. First Tom Gorman and then, in rapid succession, Wes Gardner and Terry Leach paraded to the mound in a vain effort to stop the Pirates, who went on a rampage and scored six runs. The Pirates wound up winning, 8–7, and there were whispers in the clubhouse later that Johnson had erred in bringing in the inexperienced Gardner in such a key game. No one would say it for publication, but that was what they felt.

Aguilera pitched the Mets to a 3–1 victory the next day, but in the third and final game on Sunday afternoon prior to their final incursion into St. Louis, the Pirates almost made that an academic exercise. After the Mets scored four runs in the fourth inning of the September 29 matinee, the Pirates came right back with one run in the seventh and three more in the eighth to take a 7–6 lead into the ninth. A loss would have left the Mets four games behind the Cardinals with only six to play, an almost insurmountable deficit to overcome.

But the Mets roared back in dramatic fashion. Howard Johnson homered to tie the score in the ninth inning, and Carter won the game, 9–7, with a two-run homer in the tenth. So the entire season boiled down to the three games scheduled in St. Louis on October 1–3, which took on a World Series-type atmosphere.

In the opener, Darling pitched one of his finest games of the season. He matched shutout innings with Tudor for nine innings. Then Orosco took over for the Mets, and in the eleventh, Ken Dayley, a left-hander, replaced Tudor. It was still a 0–0 game. Dayley struck out both Hernandez and Carter to open the eleventh, and then Strawberry hit one of his longest home runs of the season—a tremendous drive that ricocheted off the big scoreboard in right center. The Mets won, 1–0, and now the Cardinals led by only two games.

In the second game, Gooden was a 5–2 winner over Andujar. The Doctor was not up to snuff, allowing nine hits, but he still managed to strike out ten and pitched the Mets to within one game of first place. A victory in the third game would send the Mets home tied for the lead.

Gooden was awesome in 1985, so much so that he was expected to win every game he started. Late in the season, when the Mets were battling the Cardinals for the pennant, John Rufino, one of the clubhouse attendants, chided Gooden, whose record at the time was 22–4.

"You know, Doc, if you hadn't blown those four games, this team would be in first place," Rufino told him.

The task of pitching the Mets into first place in the third and final game of the St. Louis showdown series fell heavily on the shoulders of rookie Rick Aguilera. He had faced the Cardinals only once before, on June 29, when errors did him in—he lasted only two innings in a 6–0 loss. But Aguilera had won three in a row when he went to the mound against Danny Cox on the night of October 3, and, with Bruce Berenyi and Ed Lynch both sidelined, he was the Mets' best bet.

The Mets had a chance to blow the game wide open in the first inning and move into first place. Instead, they blew it and settled for one run. In the first, against Cox, Mookie Wilson singled, Wally Backman grounded out, and Keith Hernandez singled for a 1–0 lead. Gary Carter and Darryl Strawberry followed with singles to load the bases. Sacks full and only one out! But what should have been a big inning fizzled when George Foster grounded to Terry Pendleton and Hernandez was forced at the plate. That brought up Howard

Johnson, who two weeks earlier in New York had faced the very same Cox and walloped a grand slam home run. This time Cox got Johnson also to hit to Pendleton and the third baseman stepped on the bag for the inning-ending out.

By the sixth inning, Aguilera had given up four runs and Cox had settled down. He and the Cardinals were coasting with a 4–2 lead. When Len Dykstra walked as a pinch hitter to open the seventh for the Mets, Whitey Herzog went to work. With a two-run lead and the luxury of a four-man bullpen that included two right-handers and two left-handers, Herzog was able to manipulate his pitchers so that no matter who Davey Johnson brought off the bench, Herzog could trump him with a pitcher throwing from the same side. If Johnson sent up a right-hander, Herzog brought in a right-hander. If Johnson sent up a left-handed batter, the Cards manager countered with a left-handed pitcher. It was a classic bit of strategy and if some fans blamed Johnson for being outmaneuvered, they forget that Herzog had the advantage. When you have two runs to work with you can afford a mistake and not get burned.

Ken Dayley, a left-hander, came in to strike out two batters, but Hernandez crossed him up with an opposite-field double past the shortstop. With the dangerous Carter coming up, Herzog immediately went to hard-throwing right-hander Todd Worrell. Worrell got Carter on a pop to the second baseman.

In the eighth, when Worrell gave up a run and the tying run was on, Johnson sent left-hander Danny Heep up to bat for Rafael Santana. So Herzog reached into his bullpen again and brought in left-hander Ricky Horton. Horton retired Heep on a short pop to the center fielder. Ron Gardenhire, who had gone in to play second base after the seventh inning player switches, was duck soup for Horton, even batting right-handed. Horton got him looking at a third strike.

The cat-and-mouse game continued right down to the final inning as the Mets scratched in vain for the tying run. Horton retired the first two batters before Hernandez, who had five hits, beat out a hit to short. With Carter coming up again, Herzog went to his pen for the last time and brought in the right-handed Jeff Lahti. Lahti ended the game and the Mets' pennant hopes by retiring Carter on a fly ball to right field. For all intents and purposes, the Mets' season was over.

Back in New York the following night, the Mets beat Montreal while St. Louis was whipping Chicago to guarantee themselves nothing worse than a first place tie. The next afternoon, while the Expos were beating the Mets, 8–3, the Cardinals clinched the division with another victory over Chicago. Even before the Mets' final out had been recorded, they knew their fate was sealed. The big scoreboard in Shea Stadium flashed the final score from St. Louis.

"That was the worst moment of the year for me," said Carter. "I sat on the bench and looked at the scoreboard. It was all over. Everything we had accomplished was for nothing. There was no tomorrow."

On the final day of the season, October 6, the Mets and their fans staged an unscheduled love-in. Most of the regulars watched as a team composed mainly of farmhands lost to Montreal, 2–1. Despite the fact the race was over, 31,890 fans showed up for the final day. Immediately after the game, the huge DiamondVision scoreboard in left field showed a series of highlights of the season. Mets players stood in the dugout watching the films. The moment it was over, they emerged from the dugout and began waving their caps to the fans, a display of appreciation for the support they had received over the year.

Suddenly, in a spontaneous gesture, Wally Backman threw his cap to a fan in the stands. There was a roar of approval and with that, the entire team flung their caps into the stands as souvenirs.

"I never saw anything like it," said Keith Hernandez. "We didn't plan it.

The "K Korner" sprang up on the third home game of the 1984 season. Dennis Scalzitti *(right)* originated the idea as he noticed how special Dwight Gooden was. He and his cohorts Bob Belle *(center)* and Neil Kenny *(left)* show up at each home game replete with "K" signs and colorful outfits, ready to post another "K" each time Dwight comes through. With such an emphasis on the "K Korner," manager Davey Johnson became worried that Dwight would deliberately go after the much anticipated strikeout and stop concentrating on getting the batter out. As it turned out, "Dr. K" posted fewer strikeouts in 1985 than in 1984 but had a far superior overall record.

The "K Korner" has become a popular feature not only at Shea but also at various away games, manned by other Mets followers. Dennis and Bob have parlayed their idea into a small merchandising business.
PETER SIMON

Rejoice!
DAILY NEWS/DANNY FARRELL

Wally started it and we just followed. The fans loved it and we were glad we did it. After the support they gave us all year, it was the least we could do. Good for Wally. I'm glad he started it."

The general attitude of all the Mets after the season ended was a unanimous "we owe you one." The fans had turned out in record numbers. No New York team ever attracted more fans in a single season. And even after they were out of it, 77,294 showed up the final two days to show their appreciation for a super effort.

By 1985, the first steps had already been taken toward winning the 1986 flag for those loyal Mets fans. Two months after the season ended, Frank Cashen completed a deal for the left-handed pitcher the Mets staff needed. In exchange for rookies Calvin Schiraldi and Wes Gardner plus two minor leaguers, the Mets obtained southpaw Bob Ojeda from the Boston Red Sox. Ojeda comes over to the Mets with a lifetime record of 44–39; he could be the quality starter or reliever that Davey Johnson has been looking for.

Reflecting on the near-miss 1985 season and the prospects for 1986, Cashen made a bold mid-winter prediction: "I think we should be the favorite next season."

In baseball, no matter how bitter the disappointments, there is always a next year.

By the time spring training rolled around in February 1986, the Mets machine had been fine tuned by General Manager Frank Cashen. His prime objective over the winter had been twofold: to obtain a right-hand-hitting second baseman (a replacement for Kelvin Chapman) to alternate with Wally Backman, and—even more important—to sign a left-handed pitcher who could work effectively against speed clubs like St. Louis. During the disappointing 1985 season, Johnson lamented the fact that he did not have a single left-hander who could start against the National League champion Cardinals. He did have Sid Fernandez, but El Sid's big windup and slow delivery to the plate left second base easy pickin's for the base thiefs from St. Louis.

Cashen engineered two major deals that put all the pieces in place for manager Davey Johnson. On November 13, 1985—the day Doc Gooden was in town for the press conference announcing his unanimous victory in the Cy Young Award voting—the Mets also announced the acquisition of Bob Ojeda, a twenty-eight-year-old left-hander from the Boston Red Sox. Four Mets farmhands, pitchers Calvin Schiraldi and Wes Gardner and outfielders John Christensen and LaSchelle Tarver went to Boston in exchange for Ojeda and minor leaguers Tom McCarthy, John Mitchell, and Chris Bayer—all pitchers. Ojeda had compiled a 44–39 record in four-plus seasons in Boston. The moment the deal was announced, Cardinals manager Whitey Herzog proclaimed it a tremendous acquisition for the Mets.

"Any left-hander who can win in Fenway Park is going to do all right in the National League," Herzog said. Whitey knew what he was talking about. His own John Tudor, a twenty-one-game winner in 1985, had spent his early years pitching for the Red Sox.

Two months later, on January 16, 1986, the Mets pulled off their second major deal, obtaining Tim Teufel from the Minnesota Twins to platoon with Backman at second. Cashen gave up three more minor leaguers—outfielder Billy Beane and pitchers Bill Latham and Joe Klink.

Now Johnson had everything he could ask for to make a successful run at the pennant. Always a take-charge manager, Davey was supremely self-confident when he greeted his troops in St. Petersburg in late February. A remark he made to reporters covering the club the day camp opened was misinterpreted and frequently misquoted, paving the way for charges of arrogance that soon escalated into a hate campaign that dogged the Mets throughout the season.

"We don't want to just win; we want to dominate," Johnson said of the upcoming pennant race. After two near misses, the manager was convinced his team was ready to win and win big. Besides, as a master at instilling confidence in his players, he wanted the Mets to think like winners.

Unfortunately, Johnson's opening day comment was twisted in some newspapers. Instead of it coming out "we want to dominate," Davey was misquoted as saying "we will dominate."

Even some of his own players misinterpreted his remark. Later in the season when Keith Hernandez appeared on the "Today Show," he said, "Davey blew my mind back in the spring when he said we would waltz in."

Johnson never said that, but his purported prediction aroused teams around the league. Everywhere the Mets went they were despised. Granted, they had a swagger about them, but that was really nothing more than the confidence their manager successfully instilled in them. Just the same, when they began to outdistance the rest of the National League's Eastern Division, the Mets quickly became the team people loved to hate—at least, outside New York.

An otherwise peaceful spring training was marred by two incidents. First, Commissioner Peter Ueberroth announced penalties against a number of

21

◆ DAVEY IS ◆
◆ DETERMINED ◆
◆TO DOMINATE◆

OPENING DAY LINEUP 1986

Dykstra, cf
Backman, 2b
Hernandez, 1b
Carter, c
Strawberry, rf
Foster, lf
Johnson, 3b
Santana, ss
Gooden, p

The "Big Boys" in the middle of the Mets batting order pose before a 1986 spring training game in Florida. As it turned out, Foster, Hernandez, Carter, and Strawberry failed to achieve "career" years, but, except for George Foster, each contributed heavily to the Mets' success. After an inconsistent first half, Foster was benched in favor of Kevin Mitchell, Danny Heep, and Mookie Wilson, then released after an ill-timed and ill-advised statement to the press.
PETER SIMON

Bob Ojeda arrived from Boston over the winter in trade for John Christensen, LaSchelle Tarver, Wes Gardner, and Calvin Schiraldi. Pitching with crafty style and consistency all season, Ojeda led the Mets in total victories (eighteen) and was second in the National League in ERA (2.57).
PETER SIMON

confessed cocaine users; Hernandez was one of them. Commissioner Ueberroth ordered the users either to pay stiff fines and perform community service work for several hundred hours or accept a one-year suspension. Hernandez responded that he would fight the ruling and file a grievance with the Players' Association. The Mets were uneasy while Hernandez wrestled with the issue. Where could they hope to go without their premier first baseman? Their anxiety was short-lived. A week later, Hernandez reluctantly submitted to the penalties.

On March 5, the Mets suffered a staggering blow when Mookie Wilson was struck in the right eye by a ball thrown by shortstop Rafael Santana during a routine spring training rundown exercise. Wilson had been making slow but certain recovery from two shoulder operations and was almost certain to open the season in center field. The eye injury, though not as serious as first believed, nevertheless kept Mookie out of action for six weeks. Suddenly the popular Len Dykstra had no competition for the center field job. Despite Dykstra's hustle, attractive to both fans and management, he had hit only .254 in his rookie year, not a number to thrill the tough-minded Johnson.

The third base situation was also causing some concern. After three injury-riddled seasons with the Houston Astros and the Mets and a disappointing .218 average in 1985, Ray Knight, at thirty-three, was on his way to oblivion. He did not hit well in the early spring and with youngsters like switch-hitting Howard Johnson and right-handed-hitting Kevin Mitchell behind him, Knight's position on the club was tenuous at best.

The front office offered Knight around the league but found no immediate takers for a slow thirty-three-year-old third baseman who had a history of physical disabilities. Then they considered giving Ray his outright release and just paying him off. However, two men retained confidence in Knight. One was the manager, who argued against the release. The other was batting instructor Bill Robinson, who worked with Ray on changing his stance.

Robinson persuaded Knight to come out of his backward leaning crouch—got him to stand up straighter and to move his hands higher and nearer his shoulder. Knight was sold on the new stance when he hit a monstrous home run into the teeth of a howling wind at Orlando on March 23; the Mets withdrew his name from trade talks with other clubs, a move that would have significant effect once the regular season got under way, especially in postseason play.

In the preseason polls, the Mets were the unanimous choice to win their division, but once the season got under way and they lost three of their first five games, the headlines of the New York tabloids began asking, "What's wrong with the Mets?" They had been expected to romp into the lead, but after winning their first two games and losing the next three, the critics were all over them.

Doc Gooden beat the Pirates on opening day, but his third pitch of the season was tagged for a home run by R. J. Reynolds. It was, perhaps, the first indication that Dr. K would not be the dominant pitcher he had been in 1985.

Although he would later move into the starting rotation, Ojeda opened the season in the bullpen. In his very first appearance, Bob was a winner, with three and one-third innings of good relief. It was the first of eighteen games the left-hander would win during the season as he became the Mets' most successful pitcher.

The Mets opened at home on April 14. The 47,752 paying customers who greeted them went home disappointed when Howard Johnson's error in the thirteenth inning paved the way for four runs and a 6–2 St. Louis victory. Losing their first meeting of the season to the Cardinals was demoralizing, a blow to the Mets dream of dominating the team that had tormented them the year before.

An off-day followed by two postponements gave the Mets a chance to regroup. When they did swing back into action on April 18, it was the start of what Johnson had hoped for. Suddenly the Mets *were* dominating.

Ron Darling beat the Phillies, 5–2, for the first of eleven consecutive victories the Mets reeled off before they lost again, in Atlanta on May 1. Beating the Phillies and Pirates five straight did not have as much meaning as the four-game sweep the Mets engineered in St. Louis April 24–27. In the first of those victories, the Mets won in the tenth inning on a walk to Wally Backman, who stole second and was driven home by George Foster's single. With that win they moved into sole possession of first place, where they stayed for the rest of the season.

The sweep in St. Louis seemed to convince the Mets 1986 would be their year. Following the tenth inning victory in the opener, Gooden shut the Cardinals out, 9–0, in the second game. In the third game, with Sid Fernandez starting for the first time against St. Louis, the Mets jumped on Danny Cox

1986

NAME	G by POS	B	AGE	G	AB	R	H	2B	3B	HR	RBI	BB	SO	SB	BA	SA
NEW YORK 1st 108-54 .667	DAVEY JOHNSON															
TOTALS			27	162	5558	783	1462	261	31	148	730	631	968	118	.263	.385
Keith Hernandez	1B146	L	32	149	551	91	171	34	1	13	83	91	69	2	.310	.392
Wally Backman	2B92	B	28	124	387	67	124	18	2	1	27	36	32	13	.320	.307
Rafael Santana	SS111	R	28	139	394	38	86	11	0	1	28	36	13	0	.218	.253
Ray Knight	3B130	R	33	137	486	51	145	24	2	11	76	10	63	2	.298	.423
Darryl Strawberry	RF127	L	24	136	475	76	123	27	5	27	93	72	141	28	.259	.502
Lenny Dykstra	CF98	L	23	147	431	77	127	27	7	8	45	58	55	31	.295	.445
George Foster	LF62	R	37	72	233	28	53	6	1	13	38	21	53	1	.227	.429
Gary Carter	C121, 1B7, LF1, RF2	R	33	132	490	81	125	14	2	24	105	62	63	1	.255	.438
Mookie Wilson	CF53, LF27	B	30	123	381	61	110	17	5	9	45	32	72	25	.289	.430
Danny Heep	LF39, RF11	L	28	86	195	24	55	8	2	5	33	30	31	1	.282	.420
Howard Johnson	3B29, SS22, LF1	B	25	88	220	30	51	14	0	10	39	31	64	8	.245	.445
Tim Teufel	2B70	R	27	93	279	35	69	20	1	4	31	32	42	1	.247	.369
Kevin Mitchell	LF26, RF21, SS20, CF6, 3B3, 1B1	R	24	108	328	51	91	22	2	12	43	33	61	3	.277	.466
Lee Mazzilli	LF6, 1B3, RF1	B	31	39	58	10	16	3	0	2	7	12	11	1	.276	.431
Ed Hearn	C34	R	26	49	136	16	36	5	0	4	10	12	19	0	.265	.389
Kevin Elster	SS9	R	22	19	30	3	5	1	0	0	0	3	8	0	.167	.006
Barry Lyons	C2	R	25	6	9	1	0	0	0	0	2	1	2	0	.000	.000
Stanley Jefferson	C5	B	23	14	24	6	5	1	0	1	3	2	8	0	.208	.375
John Gibbons	C5	R	23	8	19	1	9	2	0	1	1	3	5	0	.474	.842
Dave Magadan	1B4	L	23	10	18	3	8	0	0	0	3	3	1	0	.444	.444

NAME	T	AGE	W	L	PCT	SV	G	GS	CG	IP	H	BB	SO	ShO	ERA
			108	54	.666	16	162	162	27	1484	1304	509	1083	11	3.11
Rick Aguilera	R	24	10	7	.588	0	28	20	2	141	145	36	104	0	3.88
Rick Anderson	R	29	2	1	.666	1	15	5	0	49	45	11	21	0	2.72
Bruce Berenyi	R	31	2	2	.500	0	14	7	0	39	47	5	30	0	6.35
Ron Darling	R	25	15	6	.714	0	34	34	4	237	203	81	184	2	2.81
Sid Fernandez	L	23	16	6	.727	1	32	31	2	204	161	91	200	1	3.52
Dwight Gooden	R	21	17	6	.739	0	33	33	12	250	197	80	200	2	2.84
Terry Leach	R	30	0	0	.000	0	6	0	0	6	6	3	4	0	2.70
Ed Lynch	R	29	0	0	.000	0	1	0	0	1	2	0	1	0	0.00
Roger McDowell	R	25	14	9	.608	22	75	0	0	128	107	42	65	0	3.02
John Mitchell	R	20	0	1	.000	0	4	1	0	10	10	4	2	0	3.60
Randy Myers	L	23	0	0	.000	0	10	0	0	10	11	9	13	0	4.22
Randy Nieman	L	31	2	3	.400	0	31	1	0	35	44	12	18	0	3.79
Bob Ojeda	L	28	18	5	.782	0	32	30	7	217	185	52	148	2	2.57
Jesse Orosco	L	28	8	6	.571	21	58	0	0	81	64	35	62	0	2.33
Doug Sisk	R	28	4	2	.666	1	41	0	0	70	77	31	31	0	3.06

for four runs in the first inning and held on to win, 4–3, when Backman went behind second base to initiate a dazzling, game-ending double play. In the fourth and final game, Bob Ojeda started for the first time against the Cardinals and out-duelled former Boston teammate John Tudor to give the Mets a 5–3 victory.

The triumphant Mets left St. Louis with the Cardinals in a state of shock. The New York team was in first place by four and a half games. Backman sounded an ominous warning: "They better not let us get too far in front."

The rest of the Eastern Division soon realized what a prophetic observation that was. The Mets, it seemed, could do no wrong. No matter how well any other team played, the Mets played better. On May 10, the Mets were five games in front of the rest of the pack. Following their eleven-game winning streak, they lost only one game, then won another seven in a row. Their record after the first twenty-four games of the season was a daunting 20–4. They were, as Johnson had hoped—or expected—in spring training, dominating the division.

It was during the four-game sweep in St. Louis that Johnson made one of his boldest moves of the season. After having won the first three games with Rafael Santana and Howard Johnson at shortstop, the manager suddenly started Kevin Mitchell at short for the first time in the major leagues. Mitchell, a third baseman in the minors with some outfield experience, had played only one other game at shortstop for the Mets, in the final exhibition of the spring at Jackson, Mississippi. But with the left-handed Tudor going for the Cardinals on April 27, Johnson wanted the right-handed rookie in the batting lineup and decided the only place for him to play was at shortstop.

It turned out to be a stroke of genius on the manager's part. In Mitchell's second at-bat against Tudor in the fourth inning, he enhanced Johnson's reputation by leading off with his first major league home run. That triggered a three-run outburst by the Mets. In the fifth inning, with Ojeda holding a slim one-run lead in his duel with Tudor, Mitchell stroked a two-out single; Teufel followed with a home run that gave the Mets a 5–2 lead. They eventually won, 5–3.

Johnson later explained his insertion of Mitchell at shortstop with the kind of logic that stamps him an outstanding manager. "I always felt that, if it wasn't a total liability, you should go with the best offense you can put out there and go with defense later. It never made much sense to me to start with a defensive team, get behind, and then have to pinch hit for it. I had to do that my first year here, but not now.

"Anybody who plays the left side of the infield, if he can run, should not find playing shortstop a major adjustment."

Mitchell was not the smoothest shortstop the Mets had, but he did offer a solid right-handed bat in the lineup, and that was the offense Johnson was looking for. With Santana, his best defensive shortstop, hitting a mere .170, the move made sense. Once Ojeda had a comfortable lead, Santana replaced Mitchell.

"I like middle infielders with pop in their bats," Johnson said. "They will hit for the extra base for you, and that's more important—early in the game—than defense. I like that better than, say, a Luis Aparicio, who will hit .260, play great defense, and steal a base."

During the early season spurt the Mets also received unexpected help from Knight. The manager's faith in the veteran third baseman was amply rewarded when Ray hit .306 for the month of April, slammed six home runs in his first nine games, and drove in a dozen runs in those same nine games. Knight was clearly a candidate for Comeback Player of the Year if he could keep it up.

For the first two months of the season, Knight did just that. His average for the month of May jumped to an impressive .348, and though he stopped hitting home runs, he was still knocking in runs. While the Mets were posting an 18–9 record for the month and increasing their lead to six games, Knight drove in fourteen runs.

It was also in May that Knight became embroiled in the first of four brawls the Mets were involved in during the season.

In a game at Shea Stadium between the Mets and the Dodgers on May 27, a tight pitching duel between Bob Welch and Ron Darling was broken up when the Mets suddenly erupted for six runs in the sixth inning. Welch was KO'd and Tom Niedenfuer, in relief, served up a grand slam home run to George Foster. Knight was the next batter. When Niedenfuer hit him with his first pitch, Knight charged the mound. The two wrestled each other to the ground as players from both benches stormed onto the field.

"I felt sure he was throwing at me," Knight said later. "I felt he did it on purpose. He did what he had to do; I did what I had to do."

Around the league, the Mets were increasingly considered an arrogant bunch. Players from other teams resented the wild demonstrations after Mets home runs and game-winning hits and the curtain calls that Shea Stadium fans demanded after every home run. Rivals were particularly irked at the clenched fist response by Gary Carter each time he stepped out of the dugout to

Ray Knight gets an autograph from his long-time idol Gary Carter in the Mets locker room. Carter and Knight were the closest of friends all season long.
PETER SIMON

Suffering a prolonged batting slump in June, Carter gets some hitting tips from coach Bill Robinson. Despite a low season average (.255), he managed to make his hits count and was third in the league, tying a Mets club record (with Rusty Staub) of 105 RBIs.
PETER SIMON

celebrate a home run. By late May, the Mets, comfortably leading their division, were despised by teams wherever they went.

"We'd hate the Mets even if they weren't in first place," said one member of the St. Louis Cardinals. "No one can stand Carter."

It wasn't just the players who became involved in the on-field battles. On June 6 in Pittsburgh, during the opening game of a twi-night doubleheader, first base coach Bill Robinson precipitated the second bench-clearing brawl of the season when he objected to the illegal pitches he alleged Rick Rhoden to be throwing. Robinson, who had been a teammate of Rhoden several years earlier, was aware that the Pirates pitcher sometimes "doctored up" the ball.

After Rhoden retired the Mets in one inning, Robinson made a crack that infuriated Rhoden as the two of them crossed paths.

"Why do you have to cheat? You're such a good pitcher, you don't have to," the Mets coach said accusingly.

Rhoden turned and pushed Robinson in the chest. Robinson pushed him back, and within seconds there were fifty players and coaches on the field ready to do battle.

"If it was me, I would have decked Rhoden," Davey Johnson said after the game.

Two fights in the space of two weeks did little to lessen the growing conviction that the Mets were a bunch of arrogant louts who enjoyed bullying other teams.

The Mets saw it the other way around. "They can't beat us on the field, so they try to beat us up," charged Wally Backman, self-appointed team spokesman on some matters.

The third brawl of the season occurred on the night of July 11 in New York, in the first inning of a game with the Atlanta Braves. Carter had just walloped a three-run home run off David Palmer; the Atlanta pitcher followed by hitting Darryl Strawberry with a pitch. Like other Mets, annoyed at being thrown at almost every time a teammate hit a home run, Strawberry started toward the mound to take it out on Palmer. The Braves pitcher threw his glove at Strawberry. Before the Mets outfielder could get to the mound, he was tackled by Ozzie Virgil, the Atlanta catcher, but Keith Hernandez got to Palmer and took care of him for Strawberry.

Roger McDowell *(left)*, Jesse Orosco *(center)*, and Doug Sisk once again formed the heart of the Mets bullpen in 1986. McDowell and Orosco became the first pair of relievers to get twenty or more saves during a season since the 1983 Giants, and only the second in National League history. Of the forty-six saves the bullpen registered, Orosco had twenty-one and McDowell had twenty-two. Orosco was particularly effective in postseason and was on the mound in dramatic fashion for both final playoff and World Series victories.
PETER SIMON

Keith Hernandez bails out at a high inside fastball. Hernandez, always a selective hitter, led the league in walks (with ninety-four).
PETER SIMON

The Mets went on to win the game, 11–0, as Sid Fernandez pitched his first major league shutout. That lifted El Sid's record to 12–3; people began speculating that the Hawaiian left-hander was on his way to a twenty-wins season. In addition, Carter hit a grand slam home run in the 11–0 game and drove in seven runs.

At the end of June the Mets had a nine and one-half–game lead. The only team with even a remote chance of catching them was the Montreal Expos. The Mets had lost two out of three to the Expos the first time they played them in Montreal, June 16–18, and when the Expos came to New York a week later, the Canadians took the first two games of the series. The Mets came back to win the third game, 5–2, behind Fernandez.

Ex-Met Hubie Brooks, now the star shortstop of the Montreal club, lamented his team's failure to sweep. "Nine games out is so close to ten," Brooks sighed. "Seven would have been so close to five."

While Knight tailed off in June, Carter became the big bat in the lineup. He had his best month of the season, with a .279 average, hit five home runs, and drove in twenty-two runs.

As first-half play ended on July 11, the Mets led the National League's Eastern Division by thirteen games. It was the biggest lead at the break for any National League team since the inception of divisional play in 1969. So dominating were the Mets that they sent a five-man delegation to the All-Star game in Houston. The quintet was made up of Carter, Strawberry, Hernandez, Gooden, and Fernandez.

With the best attack in the league to support them, the Mets pitchers were all enjoying great seasons. Ron Darling had an 8–2 record; Gooden was at 10–4; Fernandez was 12–3; and Ojeda was 10–2. Sportswriters conjectured that the Mets could wind up with four 20-game winners. The only sour note to the first half season was the three-game sweep the Cincinnati Reds pulled off at

Ray Knight contributed to two bench-clearing brawls over the season, including this one with the Dodgers in May, prompted by a knockdown pitch from Tom Niedenfuer. Bill Robinson, Bud Harrelson, and Gary Carter come to Knight's rescue—Knight is on the ground.
DAILY NEWS

Boxer Mike Tyson came to Shea Stadium specifically to meet Ray Knight, to get some punching tips after hearing about Knight's going after opponents on the Dodgers and Reds.

PETER SIMON

Kevin "World" Mitchell had the whole world in his hands for the first half of the 1986 season and looked like a candidate for Rookie of the Year honors. He was hitting .324 as late as August 14. In an effort to get his bat in the lineup at all costs, Davey Johnson inserted him into six different positions in the field and eight spots in the batting order.

PETER SIMON

Shea Stadium July 7–9. It was the last time until September, when the Phillies also did it, that the Mets were swept in a three-game series. In July they responded by sweeping the Braves in four to post a 59–25 first-half record.

The Mets opened the second half season in Houston with a blow-out win in the first game, 13–2, behind Ojeda, but then they lost the next three. It was during this visit, on July 19, that four Mets players were arrested following an altercation outside Cooters Executive Games and Burgers, a local night spot favored by a young crowd. Tim Teufel, accompanied by Ron Darling, Rick Aguilera, and Bob Ojeda, was celebrating the arrival of his first child earlier in the week. When the time came to leave, Teufel started to take his unfinished beer bottle with him. Houston city policemen, working as authorized off-duty security guards, advised him it was against the law to leave the premises with an open bottle. A scuffle ensued, which resulted in Teufel and Darling being charged with aggravated assault, a felony. Aguilera and Ojeda were charged with hindering an arrest, a misdemeanor. All four spent the night in jail.

Happy to get away from Houston, the Mets moved on to Cincinnati, where on July 22 they played one of their wackiest games of the season. In a five-hour, fourteen-inning marathon, the Mets outlasted the Reds to win, 6–3, on a three-run home run by Howard Johnson.

It was in this game that brawl four took place. Going into the ninth inning, the Mets trailed by a 3–1 score, apparently beaten, and then the Reds' usually reliable Dave Parker dropped a two-out, routine fly ball in right that enabled two runs to score, sending the game into extra innings.

In the tenth inning, Reds pinch runner Eric Davis slid hard into third base; coming out of his slide, he elbowed Ray Knight under the jaw. The two exchanged words, and suddenly Knight led off with a right cross to Davis's jaw. Again the benches cleared and a free-for-all ensued.

It was also in this game that Davey Johnson, strapped for reserve players under the twenty-four-man rule, wound up flip-flopping relief pitchers Jesse Orosco and Roger McDowell between the mound and the outfield in the late innings. It was also in this game that Gary Carter played third base for the first time, becoming number 80 in the long list of Mets who played third base during the team's first quarter century.

The Mets concluded their series in Cincinnati on July 23. It was just as well they would not meet the Reds again during the 1986 season.

"I wish we had another series against [the Mets]," said Dave Parker. "Maybe we could have another fight. There are a few things I would like to resolve. There are too many tough guys over there. I think it's time to show them there are tough guys everywhere. I'm sorry our season series is over with them."

"You know, now people and other clubs are looking for us to fight," Wally Backman responded. "They're more aware of us, and we're more aware of the fighting, too. No one is planning to have another one, but it wouldn't surprise me if there was one."

There were no more fights, but there were plenty more victories for the Mets as their lead continued to grow. By the end of July, after winning sixteen out of twenty-seven, the Mets held a commanding fifteen and a half–game lead. Lenny Dykstra, like Knight a doubtful starter in the spring, was the leading hitter of the month, with a .357 average, and Bob Ojeda was 3–0, to raise his record to 12–2. However, all was not well with the Mets.

For one thing, Dwight Gooden was not winning the way everyone had expected he would. Nor was he firing his famed fastball and striking batters out as he had during his first two years. By the end of July, Dr. K could boast only two games in which he struck out ten or more batters. His record was 10–4, respectable for anyone else but Gooden. He had made ten starts in which he did not win or was not involved in the decision. People asked where his fastball had gone; Gooden responded that he wasn't trying to strike people out.

"Last year, if I was throwing ninety [miles per hour] and got two strikes, I'd go up to ninety-two and go after the batter," Gooden explained. "Now, I just stay at ninety. If he hits a ground ball, that's okay. It would be better if he hit a grounder on the first pitch, but I can still throw hard. If I can get the job done without getting tired, why shouldn't I?"

After leading the league two consecutive seasons in strikeouts, the Doctor had to settle for a tie for fourth at the season's end. Still, with 200 strikeouts, Gooden became the first pitcher in major league history to strike out 200 batters in each of his first three years in the big leagues.

It was in the second half of the season that Davey Johnson made an especially tough decision, though some would say his lead was secure enough to try anything. During the series in Cincinnati, after the All-Star break, Johnson announced he was benching left fielder George Foster, who was earning $2 million a season, replacing him with a platoon of Mookie Wilson and Kevin Mitchell. Santana, the fine defensive shortstop who had shared the job with Howard Johnson and Mitchell through the first half, would finish the season at shortstop.

Benching Foster was a brave move on Johnson's part, who was beginning to feel his oats. He knew no one was going to catch the Mets, and this was his way of telling the front office that he really didn't want Foster around. He had been telling that to Frank Cashen for months in one way or another, but the general manager was not about to turn loose a player making $2 million a year and whose contract called for a $1 million buyout.

It all came to a head in Chicago the first week in August. Unhappy with his lot as a benchwarmer–pinch hitter, Foster sounded off in an August 5 interview in Chicago with Jim Corbett of the Gannett newspapers, operating out of Westchester County, New York.

One week earlier, the Mets had signed free agent Lee Mazzilli, and sent him to their Tidewater farm to get in shape. Foster saw this as a possible threat to his retention past the September 1 deadline for postseason play. Mazzilli was signed to a minor league contract but with some assurance that he would eventually be brought back by the Mets. As the club's number 1 draft pick in 1973, he had suffered through the lean years with the Mets and then was dealt to Texas during Cashen's rebuilding years. Now Lee was back in the organization and Foster was concerned.

When Corbett approached Foster on the subject of his role on the team, the left fielder made no bones about his discontent.

"I'm not saying it's a racial thing, but that seems to be the case in sports these days," Foster reportedly told Corbett. "When a club can, they replace a George Foster or a Mookie Wilson with a more popular white player."

Foster insisted he never used the word *white*. Corbett said he did. Regardless, the mere suggestion that there was anything racial behind Johnson's decision to bench Foster infuriated the manager.

When the team bus arrived back at the Sheraton Plaza Hotel after the game, Johnson confronted Foster. He asked the outfielder if he really felt any of his moves were "racially motivated."

"He did not give me a satisfactory answer. He walked away from me," Johnson reported later.

The Mets manager immediately sought out Cashen. When the two met, Johnson insisted he could not remain as manager if Foster or anyone else on his team maintained that his moves were racially motivated. Cashen concurred. The next morning, Cashen summoned Foster to his suite and advised him the club was giving him his unconditional release. On August 7, the club announced Foster's release. The same day, Mazzilli's contract was purchased from Tidewater.

Four days later, Foster called a press conference at Shea Stadium. He insisted his remarks had not been racially motivated. He insisted he did not use the

In 1986, Darryl Strawberry had another year below his potential. At one point in August, he went 0 for 47 at Shea and was booed mercilessly by fans who expected more. Darryl, a sensitive twenty-four-year-old from California, thought his treatment unnecessarily harsh and threatened at one point to ask for a trade. (He also didn't take kindly to being switched out of the lineup during the sixth game of the World Series.) Despite a high number of strikeouts (141) and poor hitting against lefties, Darryl still had a respectable year—batting .255, with a career high of twenty-seven home runs and ninety-three RBIs.

PETER SIMON

Gary Carter *(left)* and Ed Hearn *(right)* shared catching duties in 1986. Hearn proved surprisingly capable as Carter's substitute, hitting .265, with four home runs in thirty-four starts. In August, when Carter injured his hand, Hearn batted .275 and the Mets were 8–3.
PETER SIMON

word *white* in his comments to Corbett. He said that he did not feel his benching was racially motivated, since he was replaced by Wilson and Mitchell, both black.

"I only wanted to make one small point when I spoke to that Westchester reporter," he said. "It wasn't that important until it got misinterpreted."

Nonetheless Foster did not deny saying "I'm not saying it's a racial thing, but. . . ."

The implication finished him with Johnson.

"Good riddance," said Backman, one player who felt that Foster did not give 100 percent every time.

Ray Knight, who had been a teammate of Foster in Cincinnati, defended George.

"He is a solid man who is very sensitive," Knight said. "A lot of guys thought for a long time that George should be gone. But I understand it completely. I know a lot of guys here thought he was not really part of this team. They thought he quit. He never quit. I know in his heart he didn't quit. George was a loner. But knowing him as well as I do, it is unlike George to make any racial references.

"I think his remarks were misinterpreted or misrepresented."

Foster left the Mets with a .227 average, thirteen homers, and thirty-eight runs batted in. His friends on the Mets were few. Knight, Strawberry, and Wilson were closest to him. The majority of Mets felt George could have hustled more than he did.

With their new lineup featuring the defense of Santana at shortstop and the hitting platoon of Wilson and Mitchell in left, the Mets continued to make a mockery of the pennant race. By the end of August, their lead was up to nineteen games. Keith Hernandez, who had slumped badly at times during the season, came alive and batted .368 in the month, driving in twenty-six runs in thirty-two games. The Mets won twenty-one and lost eleven in August and completed their most successful West Coast tour ever by winning eight out of nine in Los Angeles, San Francisco, and San Diego.

Roger McDowell was simply sensational in relief during the month of August. Despite giving up a three-run homer to Jerry Mumphrey in Chicago that cost the Mets a game August 5, the right-handed sinkerball specialist compiled a 4–2 record for the month and also saved eight other games.

When the Mets finally clinched the National League East on September 17 against the Cubs with Gooden on the mound, Shea went wild. After the crazed Mets fans finally left the field (in shambles), several of the players held a private celebration on the mound. Included in the affair are *(clockwise)* Kevin Elster, Rick Aguilera, Ed Hearn, Howard Johnson, Darryl Strawberry, and Bob Ojeda.
DAILY NEWS

Throughout the season, the Mets bullpen proved to be one of its strongest departments. McDowell and Jesse Orosco were superb. Together they accounted for forty-three saves while also gaining credit for 22 victories. The pair had a hand in 65 of the team's 108 victories. No other relief corps could make that claim. None even came close.

With the race a runaway, the Mets' marketing department began to bill the final month as "a September to remember." They were not content merely to promote victories, which was all the players had on their minds.

The big question was *when* the Mets would clinch the Eastern Division title. On September 10, after Darling beat the Expos, 2–1, the Mets' lead stood at twenty-two games. It was the biggest lead any National League team had achieved in eighteen years of divisional play. The magic number for clinching the division title was down to two. Pete Flynn, the head grounds keeper at Shea Stadium, and the rest of his crew breathed easier. It seemed certain the Mets would clinch the title on the road, which meant that Shea Stadium would not be torn up by exuberant Mets fans—the cavemen, as some of their detractors called them.

An estimated 10,000 Mets fans traveled to Philadelphia's Veterans Stadium for the clincher on September 12. The Phillies ruined the anticipated party by sweeping the weekend series, sending the Mets on to St. Louis, where a 1–0, thirteen-inning loss in the first game of a two-game series further delayed the celebration. When the Mets beat St. Louis, 4–2, on September 16, at least a tie for the title was assured, but Pete Flynn's worst fears were soon to be realized. The Mets were coming home to wrap it up.

On the night of September 17, with 47,823 fanatics squeezed into a sold-out ballpark—the twelfth sellout of the season—the Mets became the Eastern Division champions with a 4–2 win over the Cubs as Gooden pitched a six-hitter. Hernandez, who was sidelined with a case of the flu, was unable to start. His replacement at first base, rookie Dave Magadan, singled his first three times up and drove it two runs. In the seventh inning, flu and all, Hernandez took over at first.

"I wanted to be on the field when we won it," he said later. As the unofficial captain of the team, no one deserved to be there more than Hernandez.

Hernandez barely escaped with his life as he caught Wally Backman's throw from second base for the final out of the game. Thousands of fans poured onto the field as Backman was fielding Chico Walker's grounder, and the Mets had to fight their way off as best they could. Some escaped through the bullpen gates; others crawled out from under the wild mob on the field.

The fans grabbed everything that wasn't nailed down, from the bases to home plate, and every patch of grass they could pull up. Police were unable to control the mob, and mob it was.

Pete Flynn, surveying the pockmarked field at midnight, muttered, "These fans don't deserve a winner." Flynn's crew worked around the clock to get the field back in shape for a day game the next afternoon. They even had to resod to fill the holes left by the crazed fans.

On the night they clinched the title, the Mets had a nineteen-game lead. They finished the season twenty-one and a half games ahead of the Phillies, the widest margin ever for a winning team since divisional play was inaugurated in 1969.

Although the Mets did not have a twenty-game winner, they did have six pitchers with ten or more victories. Ojeda was the biggest winner, with an 18–5 record. His earned run average of 2.57 was second best in the league.

As a team, the Mets led the league in hitting, with a .263 average. They also scored more runs (783) than any other team and were third in the home run category, with 148. Their pitching staff, which won a club record 108 games, also led the league in earned run average, with 3.11, and allowed fewer home runs (103) than any other staff in the league.

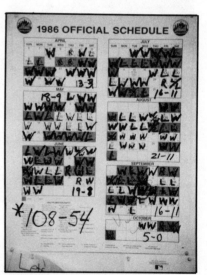

A daily record of Mets game activity, kept on a large schedule hung up on the locker room wall.
PETER SIMON

After the Mets had clinched and were in their final days of the season, Davey Johnson had only one goal in mind.

"I want to win one hundred and five games," Davey said. "If we do that, it means we will be one hundred games over .500 in my three years here."

The Mets won 108 games. In three years, Johnson had taken a team that won 68 games the year before he arrived and improved their record by 40 games. But his 90, 98, and 108 victories (296 wins out of a total 486 games played) in three seasons went unrecognized by the baseball writers voting for manager of the year. In twenty-five years the Mets had gone from a record 120 losses in a 162-game schedule to an out-front record of 108 wins and only 54 losses.

Anticipating a probable snub again, Johnson said, "I felt I should have won it the last two years, so it won't bother me if I don't win it this year." (When the votes were cast in early November, Houston's Hal Lanier emerged the 1986 winner.)

Johnson's only concern in the final week of the 1986 season was getting his team ready for the playoffs against Houston. The regular season had been easy. Now the hard work would begin. Little did Davey realize how hard the postseason would be.

Ray Knight caps off a remarkable comeback year with a home run (his eleventh) on the last day of the year and is high-fived by Darryl Strawberry. Then Strawberry himself connects for a grand slam to end the season on a high note, a 9–0 trouncing of the Pirates.

PETER SIMON

The regular season was a piece of cake for the Mets compared to what they encountered in postseason play. After dominating all they surveyed during the 162-game regular season schedule, the Mets suffered a rude awakening in October. Suddenly their dominance was brought into question, first by the Houston Astros and then by the Boston Red Sox. In the National League Championship Series—popularly known as "the playoffs"—the Mets were almost forced into a seventh-game showdown with Mike Scott, a one-time Met who had already defeated them twice. In the World Series, they were but one strike away from elimination in the tenth inning of the sixth game when they were saved by a Boston error that produced another Mets miracle.

The offbeat aphorism Yogi Berra came out with in 1973 never seemed more apropos: "It ain't over until it's over." Berra's Mets of 1973 survived—at least to the World Series—and Davey Johnson's Mets of 1986 went all the way. But, as they will be the first to admit, it wasn't easy.

The Mets clinched the Eastern Division title on September 17 in their 145th game. That left them seventeen games in which to prepare for the playoffs. By August, it was fairly obvious the Houston Astros would be their playoff opponents, as the Astros successfully fought off a stubborn San Francisco Giants team. On September 25, eight days after the Mets clinched, the Astros nailed down the Western Division title when Scott pitched a 2–0 no-hitter, out-duelling Juan Berenguer, another of the many pitchers reared in the Mets' organization.

The Astros were the dominant team in their division the way the Mets were in theirs, and Scott was their leading pitcher. In winning his eighteenth game in the no-hitter, Scott moved his team ten full games ahead of the second-place team in the Western Division, and that was where the Astros finished the year: ten games ahead of the Cincinnati Reds, who made a late spurt to nose out the Giants for second place. Houston, who won twenty-two games and lost only nine from September 1 on, were clearly ready to take on the Mets.

During the regular season, the Mets had beaten the Astros seven times in their dozen meetings. The Mets won five out of the six games at Shea Stadium; the Astros won four out of the six in the Astrodome. The Astrodome had always been a house of horrors for the Mets. Their all-time record in the Dome was a frustrating 54–90 and now, in the showdown series of the season, they were scheduled to play four of the seven playoff games there.

The scheduling upset the Mets even before the playoffs began. Under normal circumstances, the National League playoffs would have opened in the home of the Eastern Division champion. But the National Football League's Houston Oilers had prior rights to the Dome for the weekend of October 11–13, so the playoffs opened on Wednesday, October 8, in Houston. The Mets and the City of New York were miffed at the switch, but there was little they could do about it.

The Mets were the established favorites long before the first pitch was thrown. They had announced their intention of going with a four-man pitching rotation of Dwight Gooden, Ron Darling, Bob Ojeda, and Sid Fernandez. Hal Lanier, the Houston manager, decided he would operate with three starters in the scheduled seven-game series—Mike Scott, Bob Knepper, and Nolan Ryan.

The Mets were delighted to learn they'd be facing two right-handers. They had feasted on right-handed pitching all year, winning sixty-two games while losing only thirty-two. They were more vulnerable against left-handers. Their record against southpaws was 46–22, and the only left-hander in the league who had given them any real trouble was Knepper. He had defeated them three times in four starts. Scott had failed to win his only regular season start against the Mets, and Ryan had lost three of the four games he started and was not involved in the decision in the fourth.

The starting lineup for the first game of the playoffs assembles on the foul line at the Astrodome in Houston. This particular lineup (*left to right:* Santana SS, Knight 3B, Wilson LF, Strawberry RF, Carter C, Hernandez 1B, Backman 2B, Dykstra CF) is generally considered the regular one, but Davey Johnson employed a platoon at second base and center field all season long and gave the regulars constant rest in order to give the subs (Heep, Johnson, Mitchell, Hearn, Mazzilli, et al.) playing time. As a result, the championship was truly a complete team effort.
DAILY NEWS

The Mets, meanwhile, had Gooden and Fernandez scheduled to start, and they held identical 2–0 records against Houston. Darling and Ojeda were both 1–1. The Mets definitely appeared to have the pitching edge, especially when Lanier announced that Scott and Ryan would pitch the first two games and Knepper would not appear until the third game.

While Scott had been no problem for the Mets the one time they'd faced him during the regular season, he was a force they could not write off in the playoffs. In the October 8 opener in the Dome, the right-hander was clearly superior to Gooden, hurling the Astros to a 1–0 victory. Scott allowed only five hits, walked only one, and struck out fourteen. Glenn Davis won the game for the Astros with a second inning home run.

As expected, there were wails from the Mets that Scott was doctoring the ball. Wally Backman, who had played with Mike in the minors, said he knew what the Houston pitcher was doing to the baseball. Already before the playoffs Ray Knight had told a New York television reporter that both Scott and Ryan were applying a foreign substance to the baseball. The most vociferous Met on the subject was catcher Gary Carter. In his first trip to the plate during the game, Carter asked home plate umpire Doug Harvey to inspect the ball. The Mets were sure Scott was scuffing the ball with sandpaper to create the tremendous drop to his fastball. Scott called it his "split-fingered fastball." The Mets called it a lot of other things. So did other clubs beaten by Scott during the regular season.

Scott remained calm through all the allegations.

"If they think I'm throwing it, fine," he said. "If it has them thinking I have another pitch, fine. It's to my advantage to have them think I've got another pitch."

Umpire Harvey looked at several balls thrown by Scott and said he did not detect anything illegal. The balls were not scuffed.

"I guess then that it's just hearsay," Carter said after Scott was given a clean bill of health. "But I caught Mike in the All-Star game, and he threw some pitches that I know no human being can throw. I caught baseballs that were scuffed."

Even Davey Johnson chimed in, showing up with a collection of baseballs used in the game that had been returned to him on the bench.

"No question it's sandpaper," Johnson said, exhibiting several baseballs with scuff marks. "Even Scott's hands aren't strong enough to make these marks. And the marks are all in the same place."

When Backman was asked why the Mets waited until after the game to register their loudest complaints, the second baseman had a ready answer: "You can't win. This is too big a series. You think they're going to throw Mike Scott out of a playoff game? They [the umpires] look the other way."

Scott's scuffed baseballs were the major topic of discussion after the first playoff game. The fact that he had shut the Mets out on five hits was overlooked. Even if he was doctoring up the ball at times, not every ball he threw could have been scuffed. The Mets simply could not hit him.

Game 2 in the playoffs was a different story. Nolan Ryan was unhittable in the first three innings. He retired the first ten Mets in order and struck out five of the first nine batters he faced. But with one out in the fourth, Backman singled up the middle to break up the no-hitter; Keith Hernandez followed with a solid hit to center. When Carter doubled off the right center field wall, the Mets had the lead for the first time in the playoff. Backman scored, then Hernandez made it 2–0 when he scored on a Darryl Strawberry sacrifice fly.

One inning later, the Mets hammered Ryan for three runs and a 5–0 lead as Backman singled in one run and Hernandez tripled to right center for two

Houston pitching kept Mets batters off-stride during the playoffs. They struck out a record total of fifty-seven times and hit a collective .189.

more. As they had anticipated, the Mets did well against Ryan. And Bob Ojeda, their reliable left-hander, held the Astros in check. Despite being in trouble in seven of the nine innings, Ojeda pitched a complete game and wound up with a 5–1 victory that sent the series back to New York all tied up.

Knepper was the one pitcher the Mets feared in the playoffs, and they had trouble with him through the first five innings of the third playoff game. Ron Darling had been roughed up for four runs in the first two innings, and a Shea Stadium crowd of 55,052 sat in virtual silence until Kevin Mitchell and Hernandez opened the sixth inning with singles and Houston shortstop Craig Reynolds missed a Carter grounder for a run-scoring error. That brought Strawberry to the plate, a left-handed batter who had trouble hitting left-handed pitching. Darryl ripped into Knepper's first pitch for a home run that tied the score.

The Mets fans erupted with Strawberry's home run, then fell silent again in the very next inning when relief pitcher Rick Aguilera walked Bill Doran and third baseman Ray Knight threw Billy Hatcher's sacrifice bunt into right field for a two-base error. Dennis Walling's infield force at second enabled Houston to reclaim the lead when Doran scored from third.

His club down to its last three outs, Davey Johnson sent Wally Backman up to pinch hit for Tim Teufel in the ninth. Backman, an excellent bunter, pushed a perfect bunt between the mound and first base and beat it out for a hit.

Backman's bunt caused a furor much like that created by J. C. Martin's controversial bunt in the 1969 World Series with Baltimore. In seeking to elude the tag as he raced down the first base line, Backman appeared—at least to the eyes of the Astros—to go outside the base path. However, umpire Dutch Rennert ruled that since the fielder did not actually have the ball in his possession when Backman went by him, the runner was able to "establish his own base path."

Houston manager Hal Lanier argued loud and long but to no avail. His contention that Backman should be out for running outside the base path was disregarded. A few moments later, following a passed ball and a fly out by pinch hitter Danny Heep, little Len Dykstra drove a Dave Smith pitch into the right field seats for a two-run homerun that gave the Mets a crowd-stunning 6–5 victory. It was New Year's Eve and V-J Day all wrapped up into one at Shea that afternoon. You would have thought the Mets had won the title. All it did was give them a 2–1 edge in the playoffs—and create a storm of controversy, plus considerable second guessing of Lanier.

When the Astros took the lead in the seventh, Lanier brought in his number 2 reliever, Charlie Kerfeld, who promptly retired all three batters he faced in the eighth. But when the Astros took the field in the ninth, Dave Smith had replaced Kerfeld on the mound. During the season, Smith was Houston's ace reliever, with thirty-three games saved. Replacing Kerfeld with Smith was the way Lanier operated all season, but in a playoff series, every move by a manager is scrutinized. When Smith gave up the home run to Dykstra, a little man not known for his power, Lanier was criticized for not having stuck with Kerfeld in the ninth.

The Mets fans were sent into a state of frenzy by Dykstra's homer, and so, too, were the Mets. Keith Hernandez, a man who had already been through a thousand baseball thrills and not one to show his emotion easily, was unable to control himself in the clubhouse later.

"It's the greatest thing I've seen," the veteran first baseman said of Dykstra's homer.

"It was the greatest home run of my career, and I didn't even hit it," burbled reserve catcher Ed Hearn.

All the joy of Saturday's victory was tempered by the next day's loss—again to Mike Scott, who was again suspected of scuffing the ball. The Mets were

A leaping Bob Ojeda tags out the Astros' Kevin Bass as he tries to score from third on a grounder back to the pitcher in the end inning of game 2 of the playoffs. Umpire Lee Weyer makes the call. The Mets won the game, 5–1, behind Ojeda to pull even.

In one of the many dramatic come-backs by the Mets in postseason, little Lenny Dykstra smashes a two-run homer off Dave Smith in the bottom of the ninth to power the Mets to a 6–5 victory in the third game of the championship series. At the plate, Dykstra is mobbed by his teammates.

UPI/BETTMAN NEWSPHOTO

Len Dykstra is once again the center of attention after the Mets win the pennant over the Astros in six games. It was Dykstra's pinch hit triple off lefty Bob Knepper, opening the ninth inning, that sparked the Mets to a three-run rally to tie the game and force it into extra innings. The Mets finally won it in sixteen innings, 7–6, in one of the most memorable games in post-season history.
UPI/BETTMAN NEWSPHOTO

Davey Johnson, known for his sensitive stomach, takes to his fingernails during the sixteen-inning nail-biter in Houston.
UPI/BETTMAN NEWSPHOTO

mesmerized by Scott. They managed only one single off the right-hander in the first seven innings and had to settle for three singles in the entire game as Soctt again went the distance. The lone run they scored in a 3–1 defeat was the result of an infield hit, an infield out, and a sacrifice fly.

Meanwhile, the winning Houston runs were flukes that ruined an otherwise fine performance by Sid Fernandez, the Mets' number 4 starter. In the second inning, with a man on first and two out, Alan Ashby lifted a foul fly back of third base near the stands. Normally, it would have been a routine catch for either the third baseman or the shortstop, but temporary stands had been erected in front of the regular box seats to accommodate league and club officials. Ray Knight and Rafael Santana went back for the catch; Santana called Knight off the ball and then failed to catch it when the temporary seats confused him. Knight could have caught the ball but deferred to Santana.

Given that reprieve, Ashby followed with a home run into the left field bleachers; 55,038 fans groaned. Two innings later, Dickie Thon also homered for Houston, giving Scott a comfortable 3–0 lead, which he protected to the end. In two complete game performances against the Mets, the Great Scott had limited the best hitting team in the National League to one run and eight singles.

The rain that followed on Monday, October 13, offered baseball writers covering the playoffs time to dwell in depth on the Mets' accusations that Scott was scuffing up baseballs. Press conferences were held that included the managers of both teams and veteran umpire Doug Harvey, who swore that he had detected no marks on baseballs thrown by Scott while Harvey was working behind the plate. The Mets offered eleven balls in evidence.

"They're all scuffed in the same place," Davey Johnson maintained.

When Hal Lanier suggested that the Mets, who had had the baseballs in their possession for twenty-four hours, might have scuffed them themselves, Johnson responded, "I'll take a lie detector test if they want me to."

The Mets made their protest official by delivering the baseballs to National League President Charles S. Feeney. Feeney held a hearing and reported no evidence of Scott's scuffing the baseballs.

"A man is innocent until proven guilty," Feeney said. "But we will be watching Mike Scott closely when he pitches again."

If the rain-out gave the nation's sportswriters plenty of controversy, it also gave the Astros an extra day to rest their pitching staff. Lanier had been toying with the idea of starting rookie left-hander Jim DeShaies, but the off-day enabled him to come back with Ryan for a second time.

Ryan had been good, albeit a loser, in game 2 of the playoffs. In game 5, he was virtually unhittable. For the first six innings, the only run he allowed was a fifth inning home run by Darryl Strawberry, which matched the run the Astros had scored off Dwight Gooden in the top half of the same inning.

Ryan allowed one other hit in the nine innings he worked and struck out twelve in an overpowering performance. Seventeen years earlier, Ryan had performed brilliantly in the playoffs and World Series as a Mets relief pitcher. Now he was pitching as well as a man can, but after nine innings he was forced to leave the game with the score tied, 1–1. Later, it came out that Ryan had pitched the final five innings with a slight fracture in his ankle, the result of a slide into second base in an effort to break up a double play.

While Ryan was methodically mowing down the Mets, Gooden was struggling. For the first time in his career, Dr. K was allowed to pitch more than the regulation nine innings. This time Gooden went ten innings, but he was in trouble in virtually every one; the Astros combed him for nine hits. Superb defense enabled Gooden and the Mets to survive as long as they did. In the eighth inning, the Astros had the potential winning run on second base with one out when Walling lined to Mookie Wilson. The left fielder made a fine catch and then doubled up Doran off second base.

Jesse Orosco replaced Gooden in the eleventh inning and was perfect in relief, retiring all six batters he faced. In the Mets' half of the eleventh, Backman again initiated the rally that won the game when he beat out a hit to the Astros' third baseman. When Kerfeld tried to pick Backman off at first base, his throw overshot the first baseman; Backman scooted to second with the potential winning run. Strategy dictated an intentional walk to the left-handed-hitting Hernandez and the Astros adhered to logic. That brought Gary Carter to the plate, the most frustrated of the Mets. The catcher had been virtually helpless at the plate and was 1 for 17 when he faced Kerfeld.

With the game on the line, Carter finally came through. He worked the count to 3–2 on Kerfeld and then drove a single up the middle that brought Backman home with the run that made the Mets 2–1 winners and sent them back to Houston with a 3–2 edge in the playoffs.

"It wasn't getting me down," Carter said of his slump, "but it did have me thinking a lot."

The Astros were doing a lot of thinking, too.

"I felt we should have won in nine," said a dejected Ryan, an obvious reference to a call made at first base by umpire Fred Brocklander in the second inning. On that inning-ending double play, the Astros argued that Craig Reynolds had beat the throw to first base. Several television replays indicated that Reynolds had beaten the throw, but Brocklander ruled Reynolds out, which negated the run Kevin Bass scored from third base. If Brocklander had ruled Reynolds safe, the run would have scored and the Astros would have won, 2–1, in nine innings. Instead, they lost by that score in eleven innings.

For the second time in the three games at Shea Stadium, the Astros had lost to an umpire's decision at first base. They were glad to be out of New York.

Despite holding a one-game edge and needing only one more win to be crowned National League champions, the Mets were not thrilled to be going back to Houston. They knew that if they did not win game 6, they would have to face Mike Scott again in game 7, not a happy prospect, considering what Scott had already done to them.

That prospect loomed very large through most of game 6. The Astros scored

Mets shortstop Rafael Santana leaps over sliding Red Sox Marty Barrett to complete a double play in the first inning of the World Series opener. The Mets lost the game, 1–0, on an error by Tim Teufel at second base. The normally slick-fielding Mets looked like the early 60s vintage Mets on several occasions during the series, with a Hernandez error in game 2, lackadaisical outfield play by Strawberry in game 5, and an error by Santana, also in game 5.
DAILY NEWS

After all the hoopla surrounding Mike Scott's scuffing during the playoffs, it seemed only fitting that Umpire Jim Evans came out to the mound to check some tape on Dwight Gooden's hand at the request of Bosox manager John McNamara. The tape was ordered removed, which seemed to undo Gooden, who was hammered for six runs in five innings in game 2, which the Red Sox won, 9–3, while collecting eighteen hits.

UPI/BETTMAN NEWSPHOTO

three runs in the first inning off Ojeda; the Mets were unable to score against Knepper. Two singles off the left-hander were all the Mets had to show for the first eight innings. Then suddenly the Mets came alive. Game 6 became the most exciting of what had already been a spectacular playoff series.

Again it was the pesky Len Dykstra who ignited the Mets and frustrated the Astros, leading off the ninth inning with a long drive to right center that he raced into a triple. Many of the Houston players believed center fielder Billy Hatcher should have caught the ball, that he was playing Dykstra too far toward his right and not deep enough. Kevin Bass, the Astros' right fielder, later claimed that Dykstra had to have been using a corked bat to hit the ball that far.

Dykstra's triple immediately became a run when Mookie Wilson swung at an 0–2 pitch and singled to right. After an infield out moved Wilson to second, Hernandez doubled to right center, making the score 3–2, with the potential tying run on second base.

Knepper was relieved by Dave Smith. Smith needed only two outs to nail down the victory for the Astros, but, although he had routinely been getting two quick outs all season, he walked the first two batters he faced. Then he gave up a game-tying sacrifice fly to Knight, and the game went into extra innings. Many in the Astrodome crowd of 45,718 had departed in the ninth inning, thinking the Astros' 3–0 lead was safe. What they missed was a spine-tingling finish to one of the most exciting baseball games ever played.

"I didn't think we had a chance to come back," Darryl Strawberry admitted later.

It was now a sudden death game for the Mets, and for the Astros as well. With both starting pitchers gone from the game, it was a battle of bullpens. After Smith held the Mets scoreless in the tenth, Larry Anderson took over; he turned in three more hitless innings. Roger McDowell, who was pitching to keep the Mets alive, was spectacular, with five shutout innings in which he allowed only one harmless single.

In the fourteenth, with Aurelio Lopez pitching for Houston, Gary Carter opened with a single, and Strawberry followed by drawing a walk. Knight's sacrifice attempt resulted in Carter being forced at third base, but Backman singled to right, allowing Strawberry to race home with the run that gave the Mets a 4–3 lead. The Mets mobbed Strawberry even before he reached the dugout, but their joy subsided in the bottom of the fourteenth when Billy Hatcher ripped a Jesse Orosco pitch off the foul pole in left to tie the game once again.

"That put a lump in a lot of people's throats," Backman admitted.

The tension continued to mount in both dugouts. Then, in the sixteenth inning, the Mets apparently wrapped it all up with a three-run outburst against Lopez and Jeff Calhoun.

It started with a pop fly to right field by Strawberry that Lanier felt should have been caught. The pop dropped in for a double. When Knight, heeding a plea from Davey Johnson to "go to right field," drilled a single to right, Strawberry scored the go-ahead run. Knight took second on the play at the plate. Calhoun relieved and helped the Mets to another run with a walk and two wild pitches before Dykstra drove in the third and final run of the inning.

With a three-run lead and Orosco on the mound, the Mets were ready to pop the champagne corks at their celebration party. But the Astros were not ready to give up yet. With one out in the bottom half of the sixteenth inning, Davey Lopes walked, and singles by Bill Doran and Hatcher followed for one run.

After an infield force for the second out and another single by Glenn Davis, the Astros had the tying run on second base and the dangerous Kevin Bass at the plate. Bass was particularly formidable against left-handed pitchers, and he was also known as an outstanding fastball hitter.

As Bass approached the plate Hernandez called Carter aside on the first base line. "You call for any fastballs," he is alleged to have warned the catcher, "and I'll come to the plate and we'll fight."

Carter knew enough not to signal for an Orosco fastball. Instead, with a 3–2 count on the dangerous Bass, Carter called for a slider. It was a wicked pitch and might have been called a ball, but Bass couldn't take that chance. He chased it, missed, and struck out. The longest and most exciting game in National League playoff history was over. The Mets were National League champs!

The scene on the mound was unforgettable. As Bass swung and missed to end the game, Orosco threw his glove in the air, leaping as high as he could and throwing his arms in the air in exultation. He was immediately surrounded and pounded and mauled by the entire Mets team. Players, coaches, trainers, and batboys were just one mound of hysterical men in the center of the diamond.

Lee Weyer, who had been umpiring at second base, started toward home plate. As he passed the mound, the man in blue stooped down, picked up a loose cap thrown in the air by one of the Mets, and stuffed it in his pocket. Even someone as impartial as an umpire wanted a souvenir from this fantastic game.

"It was unbelievable," said Dykstra, who batted .304 in the playoffs, with a home run and triple that proved to be two of the most decisive hits. "It was like a dream game."

Ron Swoboda, one of the heroes of the 1969 Mets and now a television announcer, approached Hernandez in the raucous Mets clubhouse. "Man, you just erased the tapes on my Series," Swoboda told the first baseman.

"I think it's the best series people have seen in a long time," Backman claimed. "I can't think of one that was better, even when I was a kid."

But Hernandez made the strongest point of all when the clubhouse scene quieted down a bit.

"I didn't say it yesterday," the veteran first baseman said, "but I didn't want

Len Dykstra was the hitting star of game 3 of the World Series, with four hits, including a lead-off home run off Oil Can Boyd. Here he slides home safely on Carter's single in the seventh inning as the Mets romp to a 7–1 win behind Ojeda. The umpire is Harry Wendelstedt.

UPI/BETTMAN NEWSPHOTO

It looked like a sad ending to a big Mets inning when Hernandez got trapped off third and Carter, thinking Hernandez would score, went to third on the throw. However, the pitcher Al Nipper (right) threw too late to Spike Owen (near the bag), allowing Hernandez to get back. Owen then chased Carter back to second, got distracted when he thought Hernandez was going to try to score, and finally flipped too late to second to get Carter.

to have to go to a seventh game against Mike Scott. We would have battled him, but it wasn't a pleasant prospect."

In the losers' clubhouse, Hal Lanier offered the most sobering observation: "Any time you go into the ninth inning with a three-run lead, you should win and we didn't win," said the Houston manager. "It's a big disappointment to me."

The plane ride back to New York on the United Airlines charter was a wild one, but most of the noise was made by the Mets' wives. They had been invited to the first two playoff games in Houston but not on the return trip for the sixth game. Many of them flew down on their own. When the Mets won, the club generously invited them to fly back free on the team charter. It was a costly mistake. The wives were intent on whooping it up and when the stewardesses passed around pieces of a huge cake congratulating the Mets, more of it was thrown than was eaten. Two days after the flight, the Mets were presented with an extra bill for $7,500 by United Airlines, to cover the costs of cleaning and repairing the plane, which had to be taken out of service until the work was completed.

Despite their exhilarating win in Houston, there was one factor throughout the playoffs that was disturbing. The Mets, who had led the National League in hitting all season and had outscored every other team, batted a mere .189 in the six games. They had picked a bad time to have their first real batting slump of the season. If it carried over into the World Series, the Mets would be in trouble.

"We had a slump in July, too," pitching coach Mel Stottlemyre recalled, "but the pitching carried us then."

On the eve of the World Series against Boston, the Mets were established as heavy favorites by the Las Vegas bookmakers. In fact, the gamblers were reluctant to take bets on the Mets, asking instead that bettors place their bets on how many games it would take the Mets to wipe out the Red Sox.

The Mets' front office was confident, throwing a lavish pre–World Series party on a gaily decorated ferry moored at a pier off 18th Street on the Hudson River. Bands played on every deck, and food and drink were freely available. The ferry sailed guests out to and around the brightly lit Statue of Liberty. The party cost the Mets $200,000 and was the most memorable in Series history.

The stands were packed to capacity when the Series opened on Saturday, October 18. A crowd of 55,076 fans jammed into the huge horseshoe-shaped stadium on the shores of Flushing Bay; the mood was festive . . . at first. Once the game was under way, the fans mostly sat in silence, watching left-hander Bruce Hurst stifle the Mets bats. Pitching the first eight innings, Bruce Hurst allowed only four singles and twice in the early going—in the second and third innings—easily pitched out of trouble.

Ron Darling, the Mets' hard-luck pitcher all season, was dealt the cruelest blow in the opener. The former Yale right-hander, who grew up rooting for the Red Sox, allowed only three hits in six innings and matched Hurst zero for zero as the tension mounted.

In the seventh inning, Darling issued a lead-off walk to Jim Rice, then allowed him to reach second on a wild pitch. But he retired the next batter as Rice held second. And then it happened. Rich Gedman sent a routine bouncer to second base. Tim Teufel bent down to field it—and let the ball go right through his legs for an error. Rice, racing home, beat Darryl Strawberry's throw from right field, giving Boston a 1–0 lead. It was the only run they would need. Ex-Met Calvin Schiraldi relieved in the ninth and completed the shutout.

"It went right through the wickets," Teufel said as he faced reporters crowded around his locker. "I should have had it."

Teufel had put his glove down for the ball but not down far enough, and the ball skipped under his glove. It was the Mets' most costly error of the season.

There was an unusual incident behind home plate as Rice was scoring. Darling, who was backing up his catcher in the event of an overthrow, collided with on-deck batter Dave Henderson; both went sprawling. Fortunately, neither player was hurt.

The Mets were upset over being shut out and losing the first game, but they were embarrassed and in a state of shock after also losing the second game, 9–3. What was most devastating was the way the Red Sox hammered their ace, Doc Gooden, for eight hits and six runs in the five innings he lasted. It was Gooden's third postseason start, and he was still looking for his first victory. So, too, were the Mets. On a night when they KO'd Boston ace Roger Clemens in four and one-third innings, their own number 1 man was unable to win.

Hernandez, the peerless first baseman with a collection of eight Gold Gloves for his fielding, contributed to Gooden's downfall with a rare throwing error during a three-run third inning. After Gooden issued a lead-off walk to Spike Owen, Hernandez pounced on a Clemens bunt and fired in the dirt on a bounce that Rafael Santana was unable to handle. The error opened the door to three base hits that resulted in three Boston runs.

Ray Knight falls into the Mets dug-out during game 4, in pursuit of a foul pop. His teammates help soften the blow, but the ball falls beneath his legs.

DAILY NEWS

"I threw a palm ball to second that Bob Stanley would have been proud of," Hernandez said, referring to the specialty pitch of one of Boston's relief pitchers. "There was no excuse for it. I just didn't have a grip on the ball when I threw it."

But even after giving Boston a 3–0 lead, the Mets bounced back with two runs in their half of the inning, with Hernandez driving in the second run.

"We had the feeling on the bench we were going to win," said Wally Backman. "Clemens was having an off-night, and we knew eventually we would get to him if Doc could hold them."

But in the very next inning, Henderson led off with a home run against Gooden, and in the fifth inning, after Rice opened with a single, Dwight Evans also homered. In five innings, the Sox earned six runs to deflate the Mets. The National League champions were down, 0–2, in the seven-game series, which was moving up to Boston.

The Mets looked around for anything resembling hope, an unfamiliar position for them, considering how they had dominated their opposition during the regular season.

"Kansas City lost the first two games last year and look what they did," Hernandez reminded his teammates. "It won't be easy, but we can do it."

"We've had the [bleep] beaten out of us, but we can come back," said Backman. "We've been coming back all year. But we are frustrated by what has happened."

"I know in my heart we are going to come back," said Ray Knight, who in the end would lead the comeback. "We are too good to have come this far to continue like this. Don't ask me why I feel the way I do, but I do. I'm sure we'll win."

Following an off-day, the World Series resumed in Boston's friendly little Fenway Park on October 21. If the Mets needed any extra incentive, Boston starter Oil Can Boyd provided it with statements made during an off-day press conference. Boyd, known for his braggadocio, told reporters he intended to "master" the Mets. The Mets did not work out on the off-day, much to the chagrin of the hundreds of reporters seeking material for stories. Davey Johnson, sensing the mood of his team after two straight shellackings and a draining playoff series, felt it would be more beneficial to his players if they just got away from the ballpark for twenty-four hours—and from the probing press as well.

Johnson's psychology worked. Boyd's remarks also spurred the Mets. Len Dykstra came out swinging as the lead-off batter and drove Boyd's third pitch of the game into the right field seats. It was the first time in the World Series the Mets had the lead.

"I definitely read what Oil Can said, and I didn't take kindly to it," said Dykstra, who added three singles to his record before the night was over.

Dykstra's home run was the infusion of heart the Mets needed. The Mets had three more runs before the inning was over, as Backman, Hernandez, Carter, and Danny Heep also delivered base hits. Carter knocked in two runs with a double; Heep singled Carter home.

Boyd was almost unhittable for the next five innings, but the damage had been done. Bob Ojeda, who had been traded to the Mets by the Red Sox in the off-season, was magnificent for seven innings. Left-handers are supposed to have difficulty winning in Fenway Park, with its famed "Green Monster" wall in short left field, but Ojeda, who had learned how to pitch there, held his former teammates to one run for seven innings. Roger McDowell relieved in the eighth. The sinker-ball specialist never pitched better, retiring all six batters he faced—five on ground balls—to protect Ojeda's 7–1 victory.

With their first victory and thirteen hits to bolster them, the Mets came roaring back to square the World Series at two victories each in the fourth game. Once again, Ron Darling was effective. This time the Mets gave him support both in the field and at the plate. The Red Sox, taking a gamble with a

Gary Carter tags out Jim Rice, who is trying to score on a double by Dwight Evans in the second inning of the seventh game of the Series, but nevertheless Boston hit Darling hard and got off to a 3–0 lead.

UPI/BETTMAN NEWSPHOTO

2–1 edge in the Series and desirous of giving their regular starters as much rest as possible, started Al Nipper in game 4. Nipper was the number 4 or number 5 starter on the Boston staff and had a sub-par 10–12 record during the season.

The gamble failed to pay off. After holding the Mets to one hit for three innings, Nipper was rocked for three runs in the fourth: Backman singled. Carter poked a two-run homer into the Green Monster screen. Then Strawberry doubled and Knight singled, and the Mets were in front, 3–0.

In the seventh inning, after Wilson singled, Dykstra hit his second Series home run off Steve Crawford. Boston's Dwight Evans went back to the wall for Dykstra's long drive. He got a glove on the ball but could not hold it; it dropped into the bullpen for a two-run homer.

After the game the Red Sox raised the same question Kevin Bass had raised in Houston. Was Len Dykstra using a corked bat?

Nobody questioned the validity of Gary Carter's bat when he drove his second home run of the game over the Green Monster screen in the eighth inning. The catcher had come alive in the two games in Fenway Park, with two homers, two doubles, and a single in his first two games. The Mets were back to their usual confident selves again; they had tied the Series.

"It was the game of my life," said Darling, the winning pitcher.

Sid Fernandez, in an unusual relief appearance in game 7, held the Bosox hitless over two and a third innings and struck out four. This excited the crowd and paved the way for a Mets comeback.
DAILY NEWS

In game 5 the Mets gave the ball to Gooden once again, hoping the Doctor would take them back to New York one game up in the Series. Once again Bruce Hurst proved to be a pitcher the Mets could not handle. In the four innings Gooden lasted, the Red Sox whacked him for nine hits and four quick runs.

"They hit his fastball like they knew it was coming," Backman said of Gooden.

As ineffective as he was, Gooden did not get much help in the field. Sloppy defensive play resulted in a couple of tainted Boston runs. Darryl Strawberry misplayed a double into a triple in the second inning, and Rafael Santana booted a grounder that led to another run in the third. The Mets did not score off Hurst until Teufel hit a meaningless homer in the eighth. Hurst had blanked the Mets for sixteen and two-thirds innings up to that point. Another run in the ninth left the Mets on the short end of a 4–2 score and down by a 3–2 score in Series, but at least they were going home. They knew they had to win both games there if they were to reign as world champions.

In the history of the World Series, there have been few games to match the excitement of game 6 at Shea Stadium. Game 6 of the 1975 World Series between the Cincinnati Reds and Boston Red Sox is regarded by baseball purists as perhaps the greatest Series game ever played. It was won by Boston, 7–6, on a twelfth inning home run by Carlton Fisk.

The sixth game of the 1986 World Series certainly matched the 1975 game, at least for sheer excitement, if not for purity. For one thing, no team had ever come within one strike of winning the World Series and then failed to win it. The Boston Red Sox did just that on the night of October 25, 1986. The Red Sox came that close not once but twice in the same inning, before losing in the tenth, 6–5, on a wild pitch and an error by first baseman Bill Buckner.

Ojeda was not as sharp as he had been in Boston in game 3, and the Red Sox quickly reached him for runs in the first and second innings for a 2–0 lead. The Mets, meanwhile, were helpless against Roger Clemens, the twenty-four-game winner, until he ran out of gas in the fifth. In that inning, a walk to Strawberry, a stolen base, singles by Knight and Wilson, and an error in right field by Evans enabled the Mets to tie the score. But a throwing error by Knight after a walk and infield force enabled the Red Sox to go ahead again as the Mets failed on a double play attempt on an Evans grounder. The Sox were able to take a 3–2 lead without benefit of a base hit.

The Mets were down to their last six outs when Lee Mazzilli came off the bench to pinch hit a single off Schiraldi, who had replaced Clemens. Mazzilli eventually scored the tying run when Carter, getting an unusual green light from Johnson to swing away at a 3–0 pitch, came through with a sacrifice fly.

The game went into extra innings. The Mets, with what appeared to be a superior bullpen going into the Series, had already used McDowell and Orosco, their two best relievers, and were now down to Rick Aguilera, a starter not used to late relief work. Johnson had brought in Orosco to get just one out in the eighth and angered Strawberry by removing him from the game so that Mazzilli could remain in as the right fielder. The flip-flop of positions is a strategy followed by many managers, but Strawberry considered it an insult to be removed from a World Series game. The next day he refused to shake hands with his manager in the pregame ceremonies. (It wasn't until the day after the final game of the Series, when Knight told Strawberry to "grow up and act like a man," that Strawberry shook hands with his manager and the incident was forgotten.)

Aguilera, in his unaccustomed relief role, appeared to blow the entire season when he served up a lead-off home run to Henderson in the tenth. Two outs later, Wade Boggs doubled and Marty Barrett singled; the Sox had a 5–3 lead and were only three outs away from winning the World Series.

Seconds after the final pitch, a strikeout to Marty Barrett, Gary Carter and Jesse Orosco show unbridled emotion at capping off a storybook year for the world champion New York Mets—116 victories!

Then it happened. Reaching back for miracles that might have been left over from the 1969 season, the Mets rallied.

"Don't ask me how we did it," said a beaming Wilson. "We did it . . . mirrors, magic wands, whatever . . . what does it matter? We did it!"

The Red Sox did it to themselves almost as much as the Mets did it to them. Schiraldi retired the first two batters he faced in the tenth and had a 2–1 count on Carter when the catcher singled to left. Kevin Mitchell had an 0–1 count on him when he singled to center; Carter stopped at second. Mitchell was hitting for Aguilera, who had taken Strawberry's spot in the lineup in the flip-flop strategy Johnson devised in the ninth inning.

With runners on first and second, two out, and Knight up, the third baseman let the count go to 0–2 before looping a single to center that delivered Carter.

"I didn't want that to be my last at-bat of the season," Knight said. "I didn't want to spend the whole winter thinking that I made the last out and we lost the World Series."

Mitchell made it all the way to third on Knight's single. At this juncture, Johnny McNamara decided to switch to Bob Stanley to relieve Schiraldi. It was a move that would eventually cause the Boston manager sleepless nights.

Wilson was at bat. The big right-hander worked the count on Mookie to 2–2. The Red Sox again were one strike away from victory. Then suddenly a low inside pitch got away from Gedman. It was ruled a wild pitch, enabling Mitchell to come racing home with the tying run. Shea Stadium rocked with the noise from the 55,078 fans. The Red Sox, who had been on the top step of their dugout in anticipation of a victory celebration on the field, retreated to their seats on the bench.

The score was tied, Knight was on second base, and the count on Wilson was 3–2. Mookie kept the Mets alive by fouling off several pitches. Finally he bounced what appeared to be a routine grounder to first base. The game looked to be over, but Bill Buckner, who was all set to field the ball, let it trickle through his legs for an error that brought an awkwardly leaping Knight home from second base with the winning run. (A foot injury earlier in the season had compromised Knight's running speed.)

Pandemonium erupted at home plate as thirty or so Mets swarmed over Knight the moment he reached the plate. They had been spared execution by a tricky bouncing ball.

"The ball bounced and bounced and then it didn't bounce," said Buckner, trying to explain his error.

The game was a second guesser's delight. Both McNamara and Johnson made moves that were subject to question. In the end, the biggest second guess was why, with a two-run lead, the Boston manager had not inserted Dave Stapleton at first for defense in the tenth inning. It was a move he had made throughout the Series whenever the Sox had the lead. The one time he didn't make it, it cost him the game.

The 6–5 victory left the city of New York in a tizzy. Fans danced in the streets of Manhattan. It was the night to go off Daylight Savings Time and back to Standard Time, and bars in the Big Apple used that confusion as an excuse to stay open all night. Horns honked and sirens blared, and the dazed Mets counted their blessings.

The Mets' joy over their miraculous comeback on Saturday night was dampened considerably the next day when a heavy rain prevented game 7 from being played on Sunday night, October 26, as scheduled.

"We had the momentum going," said Hernandez. "It is to their advantage to have an extra day. It gives them a chance to regroup."

It also gave Hurst an extra day of rest and enabled the Red Sox to come back with the tough left-hander instead of Boyd, who had been roughed up in game 3. The edge definitely was with the Sox this time, even though the Mets had

Players stream out from the dug-out and the field to swarm Jesse Orosco, knocking him to the ground and nearly smothering him.

Darling going for them. The Mets felt the same way about Hurst as they had about Scott in the playoffs. They were not keen to face him in the seventh game, but having struggled into the seventh game against all the odds on Saturday night, the Mets were ready for anything. So were the Shea Stadium fans, who after a season of thrilling baseball, were expecting one more heart-stopper. Surely they would not be disappointed.

Unfortunately, Darling was not as sharp as he had been in his first two starts. That was obvious when Evans and Gedman tagged him for back-to-back homers in the second. A walk plus two more singles by Boggs and Barrett made it 3–0 for Boston in a hurry. Hurst, meanwhile, was untouchable for the first five innings. One single was all the Mets bats could contribute.

Darling was replaced by Sid Fernandez in the fourth, and the left-hander immediately injected some electricity and new hope into the game for Mets fans. The huge crowd came alive as El Sid shut the Sox down, striking out four of the eight batters he faced in a near-perfect relief performance. With his inspiring performance, Fernandez seemed to be telling the Mets they were not dead yet.

And they weren't. Echoing his performance in game 6, Lee Mazzilli got the Mets started with a pinch hit single with one down in the sixth. It was only the second hit off Hurst. Wilson followed with another single and Teufel walked, and the Mets found themselves with bases loaded and only one out. Then, as he had all year, Keith Hernandez came through in the clutch. His single to left center scored two runs and put pinch runner Backman in position at third base to score the tying run when Carter looped a ball into right field. However, that also resulted in Hernandez being forced at second base. Hernandez, angered by the right field umpire's indecisive call, was calmed by the fact that the Mets had at least tied the score.

One inning later, the Mets scored three more runs to take a 6–3 lead. Knight, who had almost lost his job at third in spring training, greeted reliever Schiraldi with a home run that put the Mets ahead for good. After that, Schiraldi came apart at the seams. He gave up two more hits, was charged with a wild pitch, walked two batters, and gave up a sacrifice fly to Hernandez. It was 6–3 in the Mets' favor when the Red Sox came to bat in the eighth.

To the Boston team's credit, they did not lie down and die. Buckner and Rice singled and Evans doubled for two runs, driving McDowell from the box. That left it up to Orosco to get the final six outs that would make the Mets world champions.

Jesse was more than equal to the occasion. Not only did he contribute a single during a two-run eighth inning insurance rally, but he retired all six Sox he faced in the final two innings and struck out Marty Barrett to end the game.

As he had in the playoffs, Orosco got the final out of the Series. If, during the regular season, Orosco was not the dominant reliever he'd once been, he certainly distinguished himself well in postseason play. He pitched in four games in the World Series for a total of five and two-thirds innings and did not allow a run.

On October 30, 1986, Mets fans, 2 million strong, showed their love and support for their heroes during a ticker tape parade up lower Broadway. Here Keith Hernandez and Gary Carter proudly display the World Series trophy handed to the team in front of City Hall.
DAILY NEWS

The scene in the Mets' clubhouse after the game was one of the wildest in World Series history. The Mets didn't drink their champagne; they sprayed it all over Mayor Ed Koch and anyone else who showed up. Hernandez, who had been on a world championship team before, couldn't control himself.

"This is the greatest team, the greatest bunch of guys I ever played with," he shouted.

If there was one thing the Mets did that was typical in winning the playoffs and the World Series, it was to score late in the game. Of the fifty-two runs they scored against Houston and Boston in thirteen postseason games, twenty-eight—more than half—came after the sixth inning. That was their trademark during the season, and it held up in the postseason games.

The day after they were crowned world champions, the Mets were treated to one of the wildest tickertape parades up Broadway that any heroes have ever known. Two and a quarter million fans turned out. Open-air cars carrying the players had difficulty driving through the cheering throngs. On the steps of City Hall, Mayor Koch gave them keys to the city as well as "I Love New York" scarves.

Davey Johnson's wish came true during regular season play. The Mets didn't just win, they dominated. But postseason play was another story. When it came to Houston and Boston, the Mets relied on something else. *Heart* is the only word that comes to mind.

Numbers in italics refer to statistical tables.

A

Aaron, Hank, 95–96, 97, 122
Abplanalp, Robert, 173
Adler, Julius, 28
Agee, Tommie, 62, 67, 69, 70, 76, 80, 84, 87, 89,
    91, 121, 122
Aguilera, Rick, 211, 214, 215, 224, 232, 241, 245
Alexander, Grover Cleveland, 73, 201
Allen, Maury, 158
Allen, Neil, 171, 183, 185–186, 189, 191, 192, 193,
    205
Allen, Richie, 57
Alou, Jesus, 71, 82
Alston, Walter, 149
Altman, George, 41
Anderson, Craig, 19, 22, 28, 39
Anderson, Jesse, 179
Anderson, Larry, 236
Anderson, Sparky, 134
Andrews, Mike, 137, 138
Andujar, Joaquin, 206, 213, 214
Antonelli, Johnny, 20
Aparicio, Luis, 221
Apodaca, Bob, 147
Apple, Ray, 22
Ashby, Alan, 234
Ashburn, Richie, 20, 23, 27, 33, 146
Aspromonte, Bob, 72, 110
Augustine, Dave, 130

B

Backman, Wally, 191, 198, 202, 203, 206, 209, 213,
    214, 215, 217, 219, 222, 224, 226, 227, 230,
    231, 232, 235, 236, 237, 240, 241, 242, 243,
    246
Bailey, Bob, 132
Bailor, Bob, 179–180, 191, 195
Baldwin, Billy, 149
Bamberger, George, 183, 184, 185, 186, 187, 188,
    191
Banks, Ernie, 82
Banner Day, 32–33, 36
Barrett, Marty, 241, 246, 247
Baseball Hall of Fame, 52, 117
Bass, Kevin, 235, 236–37, 240
Bateman, John, 72
Batting, Mets' annual leaders in, 212–213
Bautal, Ed, 42
Bayer, Chris, 217
Beane, Billy, 176, 217
Bearnarth, Larry, 35
Beauchamp, Jim, 67
Beckert, Glenn, 89
Belanger, Mark, 97, 100, 101
Belle, Bob, 215
Bell, Gus, 19, 20, 27
Bench, Johnny, 78, 133
Berenguer, Juan, 229
Berenyi, Bruce, 199, 200, 202, 206, 210, 214
Bernard, Dwight, 179
Berra, Yogi, 49, 52, 53, 54, 64–66, 117, 118,
    119–123, 125, 127–128, 132, 134, 135, 137,
    141–147, 152, 155, 229
Bethke, Jim, 49–50
Billingham, Jack, 82, 135
Blair, Paul, 97, 98, 99, 100
Blass, Steve, 91
Blueberry incident, 166–167
Blume, Bernard, 13
Blume, Clint, 13
Boggs, Wade, 241, 246

Bolin, Bobby, 45
Bomback, Mark, 179, 182
Booker, Pedro, 134–135
Bosch, Don, 61
Boswell, Ken, 70, 80, 82–83, 84, 89, 90, 96, 125,
    139, 144
Botz, Bob "Butterball," 20
Bouchee, Ed, 19
Bowa, Larry
Boyd, "Oil Can," 242–43, 245
Boyer, Clete
Boyer, Ken, 56, 58, 59, 66, 156
Bradley, Mark, 188, 189
Branca, Ralph, 47
Bressoud, Ed, 19, 58, 156
Briggs, Robert W., 174, 175
Briles, Nelson, 171
Brock, Greg, 208
Brock, Lou, 91
Brocklander, Fred, 235
Broglio, Ernie, 35
Bronfman, Charles, 203
Brooks, Hubie, 181–182, 186, 194, 198, 202, 203,
    204, 206, 223
Brophy, George, 168
Brown, Gates, 43
Buckner, Bill, 241, 245, 247
Buford, Dan, 97, 99, 100, 101
Bunning, Jim, 45, 46, 47
Burbrink, Nelson, 60, 143
Burke, Dennis, 118
Burnette, Jim, 22
Burright, Larry, 35
Burris, Ray, 171, 178
Burros, 16

C

Calhoun, Jeff, 236
Callison, Johnny, 45
Campaneris, Bert, 137, 138, 139
Campbell, Dave, 108
Camp, Rick, 193, 208
Canizzaro, Chris, 19, 21, 48
Carden, Jay, 82
Cardwell, Don, 61, 75, 77, 84, 87, 88, 90, 92, 93
Carlton, Steve, 43–44, 76, 91, 92, 108, 141, 146
Carroll, Clay, 135
Carter, Gary, 182, 194, 198, 203, 204, 205, 206,
    208, 209, 211, 221–22, 223, 224, 230, 231,
    235, 236, 237, 240, 241, 243, 245, 246
Carty, Rico, 96
Cashen, J. Frank, 104, 175, 176, 177, 179–180, 181,
    182, 183, 184, 185, 187, 188, 191, 192, 194,
    195, 196, 203, 204, 216, 217, 225
Castellano, Dan, 185
Cepeda, Orlando, 31, 95, 96
Cerone, Rick, 192
Chacon, Elio, 19, 32
Champion, Bill, 88
Chapman, Kelvin, 202, 203, 217
Charles, Ed, 63, 70, 71, 74, 76, 80, 82–83, 98, 99,
    104, 105, 156
Chesapeake Connection, 176
Chilcott, Steve, 69, 70
Chiles, Rich, 122
Chiti, Harry, 31
Chrisley, Neil, 20
Christensen, John, 217
Christopher, Joe, 19, 23, 48, 51, 55
Cisco, Galen, 46
Clemens, Roger, 239, 241, 242
Clemente, Roberto, 93

Clendenon, Donn, 82–83, 89, 91, 92, 97, 98, 99, 101, 102, 104, 108, 109, 112
Clines, Gene, 144
Coaching staff, 13. *See also under specific name*
Coen, Jean, 210
Coleman, Clarence "Choo Choo," 19, 37
Coleman, Vince, 208
Collins, Kevin, 82
Conigliaro, Tony, 58
Conley, Gene, 35
Continental League, 14–15
Continentals, 16
Cook, Cliff, 31, 43
Cook, Murray, 203
Corbett, Jim, 225, 226
Cornejo, Mardi, 167
Cosell, Howard, 47
Cowan, Billy, 48
Cox, Danny, 212, 214, 215, 219
Craig, Roger, 19, 20, 22, 23, 25, 27, 28, 31, 36, 38–39, 40, 41, 64
Crandell, Del, 46
Crawford, Shag, 101
Crawford, Steve, 240
Cubbage, Mike, 180
Cuellar, Mike, 97, 101
Cy Young Award winners, *78*, 141, 146–147, 180, 207

D

Dale, Jerry, 121
Dalrymple, Clay, 100
Daniel, Dan, 17
Dark, Alvin, 47
Darling, Ron, 185, 198, 200, 202, 206, 207, 208, 212, 213, 214, 219, 221, 223, 224, 227, 229, 230, 232, 239, 240, 243, 246
Daviault, Ray, 19
Davis, Dwight F. "Pete," 15, 16
Davis, Eric, 224
Davis, Glen, 230, 236
Davis, Mark, 211
Davis, Tommy, 60, 62, 63, 69, 156
Davis, Willie, 82, 88
Dayley, Ken, 214, 215
DeGregorio, Joseph, 53
DeMerit, John, 19
Denehy, Bill, 65
Deringer, Paul, 39
Dernier, Bob, 198
De Roulet, Bebe, 151, 157, 172, 177
De Roulet, Lorinda, 151–152, 156, 157, 168, 170, 171, 172, 173, 174, 177
De Roulet, Whitney, 151, 157, 172, 177
DeShaies, Jim, 235
Designated Hitter rule, 137
Devine, Vaughan "Bing," 49, 57, 61, 62–63, 65, 66
DeWitt, Bill, 31
Diaz, Carlos, 191, 195, 212
Didier, Bob, 95, 96
DiLauro, Jack, 82, 88
Dillon, Steve, 43
Dispenza, Joseph, 157
Donatelli, Augie, 138
Donnelly, Ed, 22
Doran, Bill, 232, 235, 236
Doubleday, Nelson, Jr., 174, 175, 180
Doubleheader, longest in major league history, 45
Doyle, Paul, 95
Drake, Sammy, 19
Driessen, Dan, 135
Drysdale, Don, 49, 54
Duncan, Mariano, 212
Dunston, Shawon, 176
Durocher, Leo, 47, 82, 84
Durso, Joseph, 144
Dwyer, Jim, 153

Dyer, Duffy, 87, 144
Dykstra, Len, 206, 208, 209, 215, 218, 224, 232, 236, 237, 240, 243

E

Eckersly, Dennis, 199
Eckert, William D., 60, 71, 79
Ehrhardt, Karl, 192
Eilers, Dave, 58–59
Elias Sports Bureau, 28
Ellis, Dock, 110, 171
Ellsworth, Dick, 45
Ernst, John, 151
Espinosa, Nino, 155, 165, 169, 171
Estrada, Francisco, 114
Evans, Dwight, 240, 241, 242, 246, 247

F

Falcone, Peter, 169–170, 171, 178
Farley, James A., 13
Feeney, Charles S., 234
Feeney, Chub, 134
Feller, Bob, 75, 208
Femina, Jerry Della, 177–178
Fernandez, Chico, 35
Fernandez, Sid, 191, 195, 196, 199, 204, 207, 208, 211, 217, 219, 223, 229, 230, 234, 246
Ferrara, Al, 108
Ferrer, Sergio, 166
Fingers, Rollie, 139
Finley, Charley, 137, 153
Fisher, Jack, 41, 42, 55, 59, 60, 62, 64
Fisk, Carlton, 241
Fitzgerald, Mike, 194, 203
Fitzpatrick, Bruce, 22
Flood, Curt, 36, 61
Flynn, Doug, 115, 157, 162, 163, 166, 167
Flynn, Pete, 227
Foley, Red, 118
Foli, Tim, 110, 119, 166
Foster, George, 184, 185, 186, 202, 204, 205, 209, 214, 219, 225–26
Foster, Phil, 97
Fox, Howie, 168
Foy, Joe, 105
Franchetti, Jack, 188
Franks, Herman, 174
Franzier, Joe, 147, 149, 151, 152, 155, 156, 162
Free agent draft, Met's picks in, *210*
Fregosi, Jim, 114–115, 117, 118, 123, 126, 127
Frey, Jimmy, 200
Frick, Ford, 14
Friend, Bob, 42, 54, 156
Frisella, Dan, 69, 71, 125
Fryman, Woody, 151

G

Gagliano, Phil, 52, 54
Gallery, Tom, 21
Gardenhire, Ron, 198, 215
Gardner, Wes, 200, 202, 214, 216, 217
Garland, Steve, 209
Garrelts, Scott, 211
Garrett, Adrian, 41
Garrett, Wayne, 63, 80–81, 82, 89, 95, 96, 109, 112, 130, 135, 139, 141, 142, 143, 153
Gaspar, Rod, 80, 90, 97, 100
Gatewood, Aubrey, 20
Geary, Thornton, Jr., 158
Gedman, Rich, 239, 245, 246
Gentry, Gary, 81, 84, 85, 88, 90, 92, 93, 95, 99, 103, 105, 110, 111, 112–113, 123, 125
Gibbons, John, 203
Gibson, Bob, 31, 47, 70, 75, 76, 91, 92, 181
Giles, Brian, 191, 203

Giles, Warren, 14
Gilliam, Junior, 32
Gimbel, Bernard, 13
Ginsberg, Myron "Joe," 21, 22
Gold Glove Award winners, *199*, 214
Gonder, Jesse, 51
Gonzalez, Tony, 95, 96
Gooden, Dwight, 196, 197, 198, 199, 200, 201–202, 203, 205, 207, 208, 211, 213, 214, 215, 217, 219, 223, 224–25, 227, 229, 230, 235, 239, 241, 242
Goossen, Greg, 51
Gorman, Lou, 176
Gorman, Tom, 207
Graham, Wayne, 63
Grand slam home runs, *193*
Grant, M. Donald, 13, 14, 15, 64, 65, 79, 96, 105, 106, 107, 108, 112–113, 117–118, 119, 125, 127, 128, 129, 130, 132, 142, 143, 144, 145, 146, 149, 151, 154, 155, 156, 158, 159, 162, 164, 165, 166–167, 168, 174, 177
Greenberg, Hank, 13, 21
Green, Pumpsie, 35
Gregg, Eric, 168
Grieve, Tom, 166
Griffin, Calvin, 168
Griffin, Tom, 85
Grote, Jerry, 57, 58, 71, 76, 80, 82–83, 98, 99, 100, 102, 104, 126, 138, 143, 144, 164, 166, 167
Guerrero, Pedro, 212
Guinn, Skip, 82

H

Haddix, Harvey, 58
Hahn, Don, 42, 110, 126, 135, 139
Hall, Bob, 101
Hamilt, Dawes, 22, 25
Hamilton, Jack, 58, 63
Hands, Bill, 82, 84, 89
Harazin, Al, 176
Harcourt, Larue, 151
Harder, Mel, 44
Harkness, Tim, 35
Harper, Terry, 208
Harrelson, Bud, 60, 67, 70, 80, 82–83, 91, 95, 98, 99, 111, 112, 123, 126, 127, 133, 134, 135, 138, 142–143, 144, 147, 162, 166
Harris, Buddy, 122
Harris, Greg, 184
Harris, Lanny, 173
Harris, Luman, 97
Hart, Jim Ray, 71
Harvey, Doug, *193*, 230, 231, 234
Hassler, Andy, 171
Hatcher, Billy, 236
Hausman, Tom, 165, 173, 183
Hayes, Von, 207
Hearn, Ed, 232
Hebner, Richie, 169, 171–172
Heep, Danny, 208, 209, 215, 232, 243
Heffner, Don, 44
Heidemann, Jack, 145
Hemond, Roland, 195
Hemus, Solly, 28, 44
Henderson, Dave, 239, 242
Henderson, Jim, 28
Henderson, Ken, 166
Henderson, Steve, 115, 157, 163, 164, 179, 180
Hendricks, Elrod, 97, 99, 101
Hennigan, Phil, 127
Herman, Babe, 17
Hernandez, Keith, 191, 192, 193, 194, 200, 201, 202, 205, 208, 209, 210, 211, 213, 214, 215–216, 217, 218, 222, 223, 226, 227, 231, 232, 235, 236, 237, 239, 242, 243, 245, 246, 247, 248
Hernandez, Ramon, 126

Herzog, Whitey, 64, 66, 105, 143, 191, 192, 215, 217
Hickman, Jim, 19, 29, 31, 39, 61, 62, 82
Hiller, Chuck, 50, 52–53
Hitting, Mets' consecutive game streaks, *137*
Hodges, Gil, 11, 19, 20, 25, 27, 29, 32, 36, 37, 65–72, 77–78, 80, 82, 84–85, 89, 90, 92, 93, 94, 95, 96, 98, 99, 100, 102, 105–115, 120, 146
Hodges, Ron, 130, 187, 203
Holtzman, Ken, 91, 137, 138, 139
Home attendance, 14
"Homer" (mascot), 38
Home runs
    best career against Mets, *61*
    grand slam, *193*
    inside Shea Stadium, *158*
    by player, *15*
    players with 20 or more, in season, *152*
Hook, Jay, 19, 21, 22, 27, 28, 30, 31, 37
Hornsby, Rogers, 17, 44
Horton, Ricky, 215
Houk, Ralph, 22, 37, 49
Howard, Frank, 191, 194, 195
Hoy, Marc, 22
Hoynes, Louis A., Jr., 174
Hoyt, Lamar, 207
Hunter, Billy, 101
Hunter, Catfish, 139
Hunt, Ron, 35, 36, 45, 50, 52, 54, 60, 61
Hurdle, Clint, 206, 209
Hurst, Bruce, 239, 241, 245, 246
Hurth, Charles, 15

J

Jackson, Al, 19, 22, 23, 28, 31, 33, 39, 42, 47, 48, 49, 52, 53, 75
Jackson, Larry, 27, 54, 55, 76
Jackson, Reggie, 139, 154, 177
Jackson, Roy Lee, 179
Jarvis, Pat, 96
Jenkins, Ferguson, 83, 84, 89, 132
Jets, 16
Johnson, Bob, 105
Johnson, Bob W., 66
Johnson, Davey, 97, 98, 102–103, 104, 178, 182, 195, 196, 198, 199, 200, 202, 203, 207, 210, 211, 213, 215, 216, 217, 219, 222, 228, 229, 234, 241, 243, 248
Johnson, Howard, 203, 209, 210, 211, 212, 214, 218, 219, 224, 225, 231, 232, 236, 245
Jones, Cleon, 82–83, 84–85, 89, 90, 93, 95, 102, 103, 104, 109, 112, 122, 125, 126, 128, 130, 134, 135, 141, 142, 144, 145, 146, 183, 185
Jones, Randy, 180, 185
Jones, Sherman "Roadblock," 19, 25, 27
Jorgensen, Mike, 110, 119, 171

K

Kanehl, Roderick "Hot Rod," 22, 26, 29
Keane, Johnny, 49
Keeler, Willie, 165
Kellerher, Mick, 160
Kenny, Neil, 215
Kerfeld, Charlie, 232, 235
Kern, Jim, 184
Kerr, Everett, 118
Kessinger, Don, 84, 89
Killeen, Evans, 22, 25
Killiam, Mrs. Dorothy J., 15
Kiner, Ralph, 21, 37, 107, 126, 169
Kingman, Dave, 145, 146, 147, 151, 152, 154, 155, 156, 158, 161–162, 163, 164, 178, 180–181, 183, 184, 185, 194
K Korner, 192, 215
Klaus, Bobby, 48, 50

Kling, Johnny, 167
Klink, Joe, 217
Knepper, Bob, 229, 230, 232, 236
Knight, Ray, 202, 203, 210, 218, 221, 223, 224, 226, 230, 232, 234, 236, 240, 241, 242, 245, 247
Koch, Ed, 248
Kolb, Gary, 61
Koonce, Cal, 75, 84, 93
Koosman, Jerry, 60, 69, 70, 71, 73, 75, 76, 77, 78, 81, 82, 84, 85, 87, 88, 89, 90, 91, 92, 95, 96, 97, 98, 99, 101, 102, 105, 108, 109, 110, 111, 118, 123, 125, 128, 129, 132, 134, 137, 139, 142, 147, 151, 152, 161, 165, 166, 167, 169
Kosco, Andy, 133
Koufax, Sandy, 32, 45, 54, 75, 117, 147, 161, 201
Kranepool, Ed, 11, 35, 36, 37, 38, 46, 48, 59, 60, 70, 77, 80, 83, 93, 95, 100, 109, 114, 119, 135, 161, 174
Kress, Red, 28, 44
Kroll, Gary, 57
Krukow, Mike, 200
Kubiak, Ted, 138
Kuhn, Bowie, 79, 82, 150, 175, 177, 183, 204

L

Labine, Clem, 22
Lahti, Jeff, 215
LaMotte, Dr. Peter, 81
Lamp, Dennis, 195
Landrith, Hobie, 19, 21
Lanier, Hal, 228, 229, 232, 234, 235, 236, 238
LaPoint, Dave, 211
Lary, Frank, 49
Latham, Bill, 217
Lavagetto, Harry "Cookie," 17, 28, 31, 32, 44, 45
Laxton, Bill, 149
Leach, Terry, 208–209, 214
Leary, Tim, 181, 196
Lee, Leron, 116
Lepcio, Ted, 19
Lewis, Johnny, 48, 49, 53
Lockwood, Skip, 144, 152, 153, 165, 171
Loes, Billy, 20
Lolich, Mickey, 149, 151, 152
Lopes, Davey, 236
Lopez, Aurelio, 236
Lucchesi, Frank, 155
Luchese, John, 70
Lynch, Ed, 171, 194, 199, 200, 207, 212, 213, 214

M

MacDonald, Joe, 70
MacKenzie, Ken, 20, 28, 31, 35
Maddox, Elliott, 165
Magadan, Dave, 227
Maloney, Jim, 42, 53
Managers, 123. See also under specific name
Mangual, Angel, 138
Mangual, Pepe, 153
Mantilla, Felix, 19, 27, 31, 35
Mantle, Mickey, 17, 50
Marichal, Juan, 54, 88
Maris, Roger, 17, 35, 50
Marshall, Jim, 20
Marshall, Mike, 212
Marsh, Randy, 178
Martin, J. C., 232
Martinez, Teddy, 145
Martin, J. C., 66, 71, 95, 97, 98, 101
Matlack, Jon, 111, 119, 121, 123, 127, 128, 129, 132, 133–134, 135, 137, 138, 142, 146, 147, 151, 152
Matthews, Gary, 141, 154, 199
Matthews, Hurth, 17
Matthews, Wid, 17

Mauch, Gus, 21, 75, 77, 84
May, Dave, 99
May, Jerry, 126
Mays, Willie, 31, 46, 61, 71, 119–120, 126, 130, 131, 134, 135, 137, 156, 189
Mazeroski, Bill, 42
Mazzilli, Lee, 160, 164, 167, 173, 177, 179, 183, 185, 198, 225, 241, 246
McAndrew, Jim, 69, 75, 76, 77, 81, 84, 85, 87, 88, 91, 93, 109, 121
McCarthy, Joe, 137
McCarthy, John, 93, 136
McCarthy, Tom, 217
McCarver, Tim, 91, 112, 126, 169
McCovey, Willie, 71, 87
McCullough, Clyde, 44
McDonald, Joe, 143, 144, 145, 149, 150–151, 155, 156, 157, 166–167, 170, 171, 192
McDougald, Gil, 17
McDowell, Roger, 202, 209, 212, 224, 226, 227, 241, 243, 247
McDowell, Sam, 201
McGraw, Frank "Tug," 49, 54–55, 60, 81, 87, 88, 93, 96, 109, 110, 119, 123, 124, 127, 128–129, 130, 132, 133, 134, 136, 137, 139, 142, 144, 152
McGraw, Hank, 55
McHale, John, 204
McIlvaine, Joe, 176, 204
McIntyre, Harry, 39
McKenna, Tom, 106
McMillan, Roy, 45, 48, 50, 59, 146, 147, 152
McNamara, Johnny, 245
McNally, Dave, 97, 101, 102
Meadowlarks, 16, 17
Meany, Tom, 17, 28
Menke, Denis, 84
Messersmith, Andy, 149
Mets
    All-Star game selections, 143
    annual leaders in batting, 212–213
    career home runs against, 61
    coaching staff, 13
    complete game one-hitters, 115
    consecutive game hitting streaks, 137
    free agent draft picks, 210
    home attendance, 14
    home run statistics, 15, 152, 158, 193
    managers, 123
    one-run games, 68
    pitching leaders, 44
    pitching victories against, 153
    rotating schedule, 112–113
    third basemen, 31
    triple plays, 70
    victories against, 153
    year-by-year records, 50
    youngest, 16
"Mettle" (mascot), 172
Metzger, Butch, 167
Midnight massacre, 149–159, 162
Millan, Felix, 125, 135, 137, 139, 152
Miller, L. B., 31
Miller, Marvin, 79, 117–118, 150
Miller, Norm, 71–72
Miller, R. B., 31
Milner, John, 121, 122, 123, 126, 133, 135, 139, 141, 152, 166
Minor, Harry, 153
Mitchell, John, 217
Mitchell, Kevin, 218, 221, 225, 226, 232, 245
Mizell, Wilmer "Vinegar Bend," 32
Moford, Herb, 27
Monday, Rick, 132
Montanez, Willie, 167, 171
Moore, Al, 38
Moore, Tommie, 144
Moose, Bob, 92

Moran, Al, 35
Moreno, Jose, 122
Morgan, Joe, 122
Morgan, Julian, 122
Morton, Carl, 142–143
Moses, Robert, 12, 16
Mumphrey, Jerry, 226
Murff, Red, 70
Murphy, Bob, 21, 107, 169
"Murphy Drag," 72
Murphy, Johnny, 17–18, 19, 22, 65, 66, 72, 77, 80,
    82, 105, 108
Murray, Dale, 167
Musial, Stan, 50

N

Napoleon, Danny, 51
Napoli, Lou, 75
National League Eastern Division championship
    games
    in 1969, *89*, 91–92
    in 1973, 132–136
National League statistics, *211*
Neal, Charlie, 20, 27, 29
Nelson, Lindsey, 21, 107, 126–127, 169, 170–171,
    176
Niedenfuer, Tom, 221
Niekro, Joe, 151
Niekro, Phil, 84, 94, 95
Nipper, Al, 240
Niss, Lou, 17, 21, 27–28, 36, 110, 117–118
Noble, Marty, 189
Norman, Dan, 157, 182
Norman, Herb, 31, 161
Nunn, Howie, 20, 23
NYBs, 16

O

Oates, Johnny, 147
Oberkfell, Ken, 178
Ojeda, Bob, 216, 217, 219, 220, 221, 223, 224, 227,
    229, 230, 232, 236, 241, 243
Oliver, Nate, 71
Olsen, Ed, 196
O'Malley, Walter, 12–13, 14, 41
Ontiveros, Steve, 141
Opening day lineup
    in 1962, *27*
    in 1963, *35*
    in 1964, *41*
    in 1965, *49*
    in 1966, *57*
    in 1967, *65*
    in 1968, *73*
    in 1969, 79, *80*
    in 1970, *105*
    in 1971, *110*
    in 1972, *117*
    in 1973, *125*
    in 1974, *141*
    in 1975, *146*
    in 1976, *151*
    in 1977, *156*
    in 1978, *167*
    in 1979, *171*
    in 1980, *175*
    in 1981, *181*
    in 1982, *184*
    in 1983, *188*
    in 1984, *198*
    in 1985, *200*
    in 1986, *217*
Oquendo, Jose, 198, 203
Orosco, Jesse, 167–168, 191, 201, 206, 210, 211,
    213, 224, 227, 235, 236, 237, 241, 247
Ortiz, Junior, 193, 203

Otis, Amos, 80, 105
Owen, Spike, 239
Ownbey, Rick, 191

P

Pacella, John, 180
Paciorek, Tom, 210
Palmer, David, 222
Palmer, Jim, 97, 99
Pappas, John, 21–22
Pappas, Milt, 95
Paratee, Roy, 55
Parker, Dave, 224
Parker, Harry, 67, 129, 130, 132, 134, 137, 138,
    142
Parker, Salty, 64
Parkes, Dr. James, 142, 181
Parsons, Tom, 47, 57
Patterson, Arthur E., 13
Payson, Charles Shipman, 12, 152, 168, 169, 170,
    172, 174
Payson, Joan Whitney, 15, 17, 18, 20, 35, 37, 65,
    108, 109, 120, 129, 130, 151, 169
Pendleton, Terry, 214, 215
Perez, Marty, 127
Perez, Tony, 134
Perry, Gaylord, 46, 50
Pfeil, Bobby, 63, 87, 96
Phillips, Mike, 147, 157, 208
Pickett, John O., 175
Piersall, Jimmy, 37, 38, 39
Pignatano Joe, 31, 66, 68, 77, 117, 118, 170, 171
Pitching
    complete game one-hitters, *115*
    leaders by year, *44*
    victories against the Mets, *153*
Player statistics
    from 1962, *32*
    from 1963, *39*
    from 1964, *44*
    from 1965, *53*
    from 1966, *60*
    from 1967, *62*
    from 1968, *75*
    from 1969, *103*
    from 1970, *108*
    from 1971, *112*
    from 1972, *122*
    from 1973, *138*
    from 1974, *145*
    from 1975, *147*
    from 1976, *154*
    from 1977, *165*
    from 1978, *168*
    from 1979, *172*
    from 1980, *177*
    from 1981, *182*
    from 1982, *187*
    from 1983, *190*
    from 1984, *199*
    from 1985, *206*
    from 1986, 219
Player strikes, 117–118, 149–150
Plummer, Bill, 127
Powell, Boog, 97, 99, 101, 102
Principato, Anthony, 192
Puleo, Charlie, 182, 185, 187
Pulli, Frank, 193

Q

Qualls, Jimmy, 84

R

Radatz, Dick, 45
Rader, Doug, 143

Randle, Lenny, 153, 155, 160, 162
Rapp, Joe, 146
Reardon, Jeff, 179, 182
Rebels, 16
Reed, Ron, 95
Reichler, Joe, 60
Renko, Steve, 69, 70, 82, 110
Rennert, Dutch, 232
Reuschel, Rick, 132
Reynolds, Craig, 232, 235
Reynolds, R. J., 219
Rheingold Brewery, 12, 38
Rhoden, Rick, 222
Ribant, Dennis, 49, 59, 61
Rice, Jim, 239, 242
Richards, Paul, 12, 20, 80, 97
Richert, Pete, 101
Richman, Arthur, 53, 157, 172
Rickey, Branch, 14, 15, 67
Riland, Dr. Kenneth, 141–142
Robinson, Bill, 22, 218, 222
Robinson, Brooks, 97, 98, 99, 100, 102
Robinson, Frank, 36, 97, 98–99, 100, 101, 102
Robinson, Jackie, 14
Robinson, Sheriff, 44
Rockefeller, Nelson, 97
Rogers, Sandy, 164
Rogers, Steve, 151
Rohr, Les, 63, 71
Rookie-of-the-Year Award winners, 35, 60, 78, 123, 196
Roseboro, John, 59
Rose, Don, 114
Rose, Pete, 35, 93, 126, 133, 134, 135, 136, 150, 165, 168, 169, 184
Rudi, Joe, 137, 139
Ruffing, Red, 28, 44
Rufino, John, 214
Ruthven, Dick, 200
Ryan, Nolan, 69, 70, 71, 73–74, 75, 76, 80, 81, 88, 90, 91, 93, 95, 96, 99, 100, 108, 109, 110, 114, 115, 126, 127, 156, 229, 230, 231, 232, 235
Ryan, Ruth, 158

S

Sadecki, Ray, 62, 117–118, 129, 130, 137, 144, 156
Samuel, Amado, 41
Samuel, Juan, 207
Santana, Rafael, 198, 203, 206, 215, 218, 219, 221, 225, 226, 234, 239, 241
Santo, Ron, 89, 90, 132
Sargent, John, 175
Scalzitti, Dennis, 215
Scarce, Mac, 144
Schanley, Gerald F., 174
Scheffing, Bob, 105–106, 110, 114, 115, 117–118, 127, 128, 142, 143, 145, 149
Schiraldi, Calvin, 202, 216, 217, 239, 241, 247
Schmelz, Al, 63
Schmidt, Bob, 43
Schmidt, Mike, 141
Schreiber, Ted, 35
Scioscia, Mike, 208
Scott, George, 150
Scott, Mike, 171, 229, 230, 231, 232, 234, 235, 237
Seaver (George Thomas) Tom, 57, 58, 59–61, 69, 70, 71, 73, 79, 81, 82, 84, 85, 88, 89, 91, 93, 97, 100, 101, 103, 105, 106–107, 108, 109, 110, 111, 113, 115, 116, 117–118, 119, 123, 125, 127, 128, 129, 130, 132, 133, 134, 135, 136, 137, 139, 141–142, 146, 147, 148, 150, 151, 154–159, 161, 162, 163, 164, 169, 178, 187, 188, 195, 196, 201, 204, 210
Seitz, Peter, 149–151
Selkirk, George, 65
Selma, Dick, 43, 69, 75, 76, 84, 90

Shamsky, Art, 66–67, 70, 84, 89, 93, 95, 97
Shaw, Bob, 59
Shaw, Don, 81
Shea Stadium, 41, 42, 43
Shea, William A., 13, 14, 15, 16, 42
Short, Chris, 26
Shor, Tools, 23
Siebert, Dick "Sonny," 163
Siebert, Paul, 158, 167
Simmons, Curt, 47
Simpson, William, 15
Singer, Bill, 71
Singleton, Ken, 110, 119
Sisk, Doug, 188, 191, 198, 200, 209, 210, 212
Siwoff, Seymour, 28
Skyliners, 16, 17
Skyscrapers, 16
Smith, Bobby Gene, 19
Smith, Charley, 48, 51
Smith, Dave, 232, 236
Smith, Earl, 174
Smith, Lee, 200
Smith, Red, 159
Snider, Duke, 35, 36–37
Soto, Mario, 206
Spahn, Warren, 28, 43, 49, 50, 51
Sportsman of the Year Award, 108
Staiger, Roy, 152
Stallard, Tracy, 35, 45, 49
Stanky, Eddie, 49
Stanley, Bob, 242, 245
Stanton, Leroy, 114
Stapleton, Dave, 245
Stargell, Willie, 53, 88, 110
Stark, Dr. Herbert, 121
Staub, Rusty, 11, 71–72, 82, 119, 121, 122, 125, 133–134, 135, 137, 139, 141, 143, 144, 147, 149, 152, 180, 192, 211
Stearns, John, 144, 166, 167, 170, 173, 181–182, 186–187, 198, 203
Steinbrenner, George, 165, 177, 212
Stengel, Casey, 11, 15–16, 17, 18, 21, 22–23, 27, 28–29, 31, 35–39, 40, 42, 43, 44–45, 46, 47, 48, 49–55, 57, 62, 66, 70, 86, 91, 104, 140
Stennett, Rennie, 127
Stephenson, John, 46, 47
Stock, Wes, 69
Stoddard, Tim, 200
Stone, George, 84, 121, 125, 128, 129, 130, 134, 137, 142
Stoneham, Horace, 13, 45, 120
Stottlemyre, Mel, 239
Straiger, Roy, 166
Strawberry, Darryl, 176, 189, 191, 194, 200, 201, 205, 206, 207, 208, 209, 211, 214, 222, 223, 226, 231, 235, 236, 239, 240, 241, 245
Sudakis, Bill, 144
Sutcliffe, Rick, 198, 200
Sutter, Bruce, 206
Sutton, Don, 73, 151
Swan, Craig, 168, 171, 176, 178, 185, 189, 196, 199
Swisher, Steve, 144
Swoboda, Ron, 42, 49, 50, 51, 55, 70, 76, 77, 86, 89, 90–91, 93, 97, 100, 102, 104, 110, 237

T

Tanner, Chuck, 179
Tarver, LaShelle, 217
Taveras, Frank, 173, 179
Taylor, Bob, 41
Taylor, Ron, 87, 93, 96, 99, 109
Taylor, Sammy, 26
Terrell, Walt, 185, 198, 200, 202, 203
Terry, Ralph, 156
Teufel, Tim, 176, 217, 221, 224, 232, 239, 241, 246
Theodore, George Basil "the Stork," 126, 127
Third basemen, 31

Thomas, Frank, 20, 25, 27, 29
Thomson, James K. "Big Jim," 17
Thomson, Jim, 93, 136, 171
Thon, Dickie, 234
Thorne, Gary, 169
Throneberry, Marv, 19, 29, 31, 32, 64
Tibbs, Jay, 206
Tidrow, Dick, 196, 199
Topping, Dan, 21, 49
Torre, Joe, 80, 92, 143, 144, 147, 152, 155, 156,
    157, 162, 163, 164, 166–167, 168, 169–170,
    171, 176, 179, 181, 182, 183, 185
Torrez, Mike, 188, 189, 193, 194, 196, 198, 199
Trevino, Alex, 184
Trillo, Manny, 137
Triple plays, 70
Tudor, John, 213, 214, 217, 219, 221
Turner, Ted, 154
Twitchell, Wayne, 171

U

Ueberroth, Peter, 217–18
Unser, Del, 144, 147, 153

V

Vail, Mike, 145, 146, 149
Valentine, Bobby, 158, 163
Valentine, Ellis, 178, 182–183, 184–185, 186, 187
Valenzuela, Fernando, 207, 208, 211
Veale, Bob, 61
Virgil, Ozzie, 222

W

Wagner, Robert, 12, 13, 15, 16, 27, 41
Wakefield, Bill, 41
Walker, Chico, 227
Walker, Herb, 15, 174
Walker, Luke, 174
Walker, Rube, 66, 69, 70, 77, 113, 117, 118, 127
Walls, Lee, 19–20
Washington, Claudell, 177, 179
Watt, Ed, 102
Weaver, Earl, 101, 102, 104, 191
Wegener, Mike, 89
Weis, Al, 62, 67, 70, 72, 84, 102
Weiss, George, 14, 16, 17, 18, 20–21, 28, 35, 44,
    47, 49, 52–53, 57, 65
Weissman, Harold, 53, 59, 77, 106–107, 117–118,
    141

Welch, Bob, 221
Werblin, Sonny, 170, 174
Westrum, Wes, 44, 45, 49, 54, 57, 58, 61, 62,
    63–64, 66
Weyer, Lee, 77, 98, 237
Whalen, Bill, 22
White, Ernie, 44
Whitfield, Terry, 208
Whitney, John Hay, 12
Willey, Carlton, 35, 37, 43–44
Willhite, Nick, 63
Williams, Artie, 152
Williams, Billy, 84, 89
Williams, Charlie, 120
Williams, Dick, 137
Wills, Bump, 155
Wills, Maury, 155
Wilpon, Fred, 174, 175, 180, 212
Wilson, Don, 71
Wilson, Hack, 151, 152
Wilson, Mookie, 182, 183, 187, 199, 202, 206, 208,
    211, 212, 214, 218, 225, 226, 235, 236, 240,
    245, 246
Winningham, Herm, 203
Wise, Rick, 77
World Series
    Mets in 1969, 11, 95–104
    Mets in 1973, 137–139
    Mets in 1986, 239–248
Worrell, Todd, 215
Wynne, Billy, 62, 63
Wynn, Jimmy, 71, 84

Y

Yastrzemski, Carl, 77
Year-by-year records, 50
Yost, Ed, 66, 69, 117, 118, 121
Youmans, Floyd, 203
Youngblood, Joel, 157, 181, 182, 183, 185, 187
Young, Dick, 11, 114, 156, 158, 161
Young, Don, 82, 83, 84
Young, Irving M., 73

Z

Zabriski, Steve, 169
Zachry, Pat, 115, 157, 163, 164, 168, 171, 178
Zimmer, Don, 19, 20, 25, 27, 30, 31, 76
Zisk, Richie, 130

JACK LANG has been writing major league baseball for over forty years. His first assignment for the *Long Island Press* in 1946 was covering the Brooklyn Dodgers, with whom he remained until the club moved to Los Angeles after the 1957 season. From 1958 to 1961, Lang covered the New York Yankees. In 1962, he began covering the New York Mets and is the only daily beat writer who has been with the club since their inception. Born in Brooklyn, Lang attended New York University. A former past chairman of the New York Chapter of the Baseball Writers Association of America, he has served as that organization's national secretary-treasurer since 1966 and in that office conducts the Most Valuable Player, Cy Young, and Hall of Fame elections. He lives in Fort Salonga, New York.

PETER SIMON is a freelance photographer and author. Among the nine books he has published are *Decent Exposures* (Wingbow Press, 1974); *Carly Simon Complete* (Knopf, 1975); *Reggae Bloodlines* (with Stephen Davis, Doubleday, 1977); *On the Vineyard* (Doubleday, 1980); *Reggae International* (with Stephen Davis, Knopf, 1983); and *Playing in the Band* (with David Gans, St. Martin's Press, 1985). Specializing in photojournalism, alternative life-styles, and music, his photographs have appeared in *Rolling Stone, Musician, Life, Time, Newsweek,* the *Village Voice, Atlantic Monthly, Islands Magazine, Popular Photography,* and *New Age*. He became a Mets fan in 1962 and has been addicted to the team ever since. He lives in New York City and on Martha's Vineyard.